Returning to Shakespeare

As author

Francis Bacon and Renaissance Prose (Cambridge, 1968)

The Artistry of Shakespeare's Prose (London, 1968, 1976)

Classical Rhetoric in English Poetry (London, 1970; Carbondale, Ill., 1989)

Towards Greek Tragedy (London, 1973)

In Defence of Rhetoric (Oxford, 1988, 1989)

As editor and contributor

The World of Jonathan Swift (Oxford, 1968)

Rhetoric Revalued (Binghamton, NY, 1982)

Occult and Scientific Mentalities in the Renaissance (Cambridge, 1984)

Arbeit, Musse, Meditation: Betrachtungen zur 'Vita activa' und 'Vita contemplativa' (Zürich, 1985)

As editor

Henry Mackenzie, 'The Man of Feeling' (Oxford, 1967, 1987)

Shakespeare: the Critical Heritage, 1623–1801, 6 vols (London and Boston, 1974–81)

Public and Private Life in the Seventeenth Century: the Mackenzie-Evelyn Debate (Delmar, NY, 1986)

English Science, Bacon to Newton (Cambridge, 1987)

Returning to Shakespeare

Brian Vickers

Routledge
London and New York

First published 1989
by Routledge
11 New Fetter Lane, London EC4P 4EE
29 West 35th Street, New York, NY 10001

Printed in Great Britain by
Butler & Tanner Ltd, Frome and London

British Library Cataloguing in Publication Data
Vickers, Brian
    Returning to Shakespeare
    1. Drama in English. Shakespeare, William,
    1564–1616 – Critical Studies
    I. Title
    822.3′3

    ISBN 0 415 03389 6

Library of Congress Cataloging in Publication Data
Vickers, Brian.
    Returning to Shakespeare.

    Bibliography: p.
    Includes index.
    1. Shakespeare, William, 1564–1616 – Criticism and
interpretation. 2. Shakespeare, William, 1564–1616 –
Criticism and interpretation – History. I. Title.
PR2976.V48 1989   822.3′3   88–35728
ISBN 0 415 03389 6

Contents

For my teachers

Acknowledgements

Chapter 2 appears for the first time. For the other essays, all of which have been revised and in some cases up-dated, I record the first publication, thanking the journals and publishers involved for permission to reprint, and also thanking those persons whose invitations gave rise to my writing the essays. Chapter 1 was an invited paper at the Shakespeare Association of America 1984 meeting (Ellen Caldwell) and appeared in *Jahrbuch der Deutschen Shakespeare-Gesellschaft West* 1986 (Werner Habicht); Chapter 3 was first printed in *Daedalus* 108 (1979), a special issue on hypocrisy (Stephen Graubard and the American Academy of Arts and Sciences); Chapter 4 appeared as *Coriolanus* in the Edward Arnold 'Studies in English Literature' series in 1976 (David Daiches); Chapter 5 was given as a short paper at the 19th International Stratford Shakespeare conference, 1980 (Philip Brockbank), and appeared in *Shakespeare Survey* 34 (1981) (Stanley Wells and Cambridge University Press); Chapter 6 was an invited lecture at the Universität München in 1983 and has just appeared in *Das Shakespeare-Bild in Europa zwischen Aufklärung und Romantik* (Bern, 1988) (Roger Bauer, Ulrich Broich); Chapter 7 was the lead review in the *Times Literary Supplement* for 14 December 1973 (Arthur Crook); and Chapter 8 appeared as preface to Muriel Bradbrook, *Artist and Society in Shakespeare's England* (Brighton, 1982) (Sue Roe and Harvester Press). For assistance with the manuscripts, proofs, and index I thank Dr Margrit Soland.

Returning to Shakespeare:
an autobiographical preface

At various points in my life I have put down whatever I was doing and gone back to Shakespeare. Earlier this might have been in preparation for an examination; later, for a lecture-course, a theatre review, or a book review. I use the word 'returning' partly to record the fact that Shakespeare is always there, in my consciousness, as an enrichment and a challenge, partly because I find it necessary periodically to move away to other literary forms and other periods. However great the writer, or composer, to limit oneself wholly to one *oeuvre* is unhealthy, as specialism cramps and confines the imagination. How little they know of Shakespeare who only Shakespeare know! I respond warmly to Dame Peggy Ashcroft's recent remark: 'I often think how wonderful it would be if we could ban Shakespeare for five years. It would do him and all of us so much good.'[1] To return, then, after a self-imposed absence, is to experience afresh the sensation of reading or seeing something well known but new, not yet fully explored, still challenging us to develop all the skills and draw on all the experience of life needed to understand and respond to it.

Choosing and assembling the essays that make up this volume has made me think about the ways in which I have come to know Shakespeare. It seems worth recording how I acquired this knowledge, such as it is, not because it was in any way unusual, rather because it was so ordinary – and for just that reason seldom recorded. I owe a great deal to schools and teachers. It would be nice to say that my primary school in the Rhondda valley had given the first impulse, but the teachers at Cwmclydach Junior, Clydach Vale (Tonypandy), had more urgent tasks. It was when we moved to London in 1948, and I entered St Marylebone Grammar School, that my education really began. This was a small, traditional grammar school (some 500 boys), founded in 1792 by 'The Philological Society' and long known as the Philological School, situated on Marylebone Road. As a result of the 1902 Education Act the London County Council took it over as 'a public secondary school for boys', renaming it St Marylebone Grammar School. The 1944 Education Act widened the social background of the boys entering it, who had to pass the 'eleven-plus' exam, and survive an interview with the head-master. (I recall with pain being asked, 'What do you read?' and proudly answering, 'Books, sir' – I was distinguishing them from comics – only to be met by the withering reply, 'I didn't think you read paving-stones!')

The headmaster, from 1924 to 1954, was Philip Wayne, who could be both frightening and genial. He is best known today for his translation of *Faust* in Penguin Classics; he also produced the useful three-volume edition of Wordsworth's poems (one of the few arranged chronologically) in the Every-man Library, a collection of English letters, and some Shakespeare plays for a school edition. As well as being a fine cellist, to whom I owe my first experience of chamber music, he was an enterprising actor and producer, who had taken school plays on tour to Germany before the war. His contacts with the literary world were such that he was able to attract for a time, as teachers, men who later became distinguished as scholars and writers. Among my teachers were Neville Rogers, the Shelley critic and editor (with whom I also read *I promessi sposi*); Thomas Blackburn, poet, memorable reader of Browning, and author of a remarkable autobiography (*A Clip of Steel*, 1969); and gifted younger men, such as Guy Back and James Smyth. The school play was an important annual event, and we were lucky to have two dedicated producers: Rory Hands, with unforgettable productions of Sheridan and Goldsmith, and G. H. Bailey, who in my time put on *Richard II* and *Hamlet*. The experiences of learning a part, rehearsing, and performing, with all the excitement and unexpected transformations of personality on stage, are ones that I am glad to have had. To see a school audience fully absorbed by a Shakespeare play, a common enough sight in England still, whatever the gap between hopes and fulfilment, is oddly reassuring.

The classroom teaching that we received was traditional, exposing us directly to the plays. Again I cite Peggy Ashcroft, since, like her,

> I was very fortunate in that I went to a school where we started reading Shakespeare at about the age of ten. We didn't go in for glossaries and footnotes; we stood up in class and read out the texts; so the characters then started to come alive to us, as they had been alive in my mind. And then I became absolutely addicted to language.[2]

For me, too, 'Shakespeare was the most exciting part of my school life, by far'. Reading around the class, which we did frequently (two to three lessons a week, and two or three plays a year), was a challenge to one's acting abilities and to one's understanding of the language, failures in which were instantly obvious to the teacher and, more important, to the other members of the class. The degree to which we absorbed some of the set plays for the General Certificate examinations, Ordinary and Advanced Levels – *Julius Caesar, Henry IV, Parts 1* and *2, Antony and Cleopatra* – was astonishing. We virtually knew them by heart, and were constantly quoting them for – especially for! – the most bizarre applications in everyday life. The teacher's role in all this was more that of actor-manager. I can still vividly recall Philip Wayne doing *Julius Caesar* with us, and realizing, thanks to his performance of the roles, the soliloquies of Brutus and Cassius with extraordinary immediacy. These were not words on the page but minds and souls in motion, coolly manipulative, confused, and self-deceived, set graphically before us. The atmosphere of these lessons, indeed the ethos of the school as a whole, encouraged a degree of closeness between teacher and pupil, an intellectual openness, where difficult questions could be put without any self-consciousness, such as I have seldom experienced since. All good teachers are actors, one might say, but in sharing with us their performances of Shakespeare (and other dramatists: to Rory Hands I owe a rare introduction to the greatness of Racine) our teachers were involving us in the experience of the plays at an elementary but also fundamental level.[3]

When I went up to Cambridge in 1959, after two years of languishing in the Royal Artillery, I found an educational system which still – happily – gave special place Shakespeare. One of the seven examinations in the first part of the English tripos was devoted to his work, with three or four plays singled out for special study, and the Tragedy paper in part two gave the chance of comparing him with dramatists from the Greeks to the present day. The Cambridge English faculty at that time was very distinguished: Basil Willey, F. R. Leavis, Joan and Stanley Bennett, George Rylands, F. L. Lucas, T. R. Henn, Hugh Sykes Davies, and Muriel Bradbrook were among those who had studied at Cambridge in the 1920s and 1930s and had taught there ever since. More recent arrivals included C. S. Lewis, Graham Hough, Raymond Williams, David Daiches, Matthew Hodgart, Donald Davie, John Holloway, John Northam, Elizabeth Salter, John Stevens, Derek Brewer, L. C. Knights, Leo Salingar, Anne Barton, and Denis Donoghue. Younger Cambridge graduates included A. C. Spearing, Tony Tanner, and J. H. Prynne. Few English departments of this century could match that list. Yet the pressures of keeping up with a weekly supervision essay, and also a practical criticism and/or a translation class, coupled with the impossibility of co-ordinating the teaching offered by more than twenty colleges, meant that one couldn't always follow the lecture-courses one wanted. It is hard to study ten different topics simultaneously.

At the faculty level the lectures of Muriel Bradbrook and T. R. Henn provided the most valuable Shakespeare teaching for me. I pay tribute below (Chapter 8) to the former, who combined a phenomenal historical knowledge of Elizabethan drama with most acute analytical powers. Tom Henn was very different: an elderly, impressive-looking figure with a military bearing who walked with a stick (even his limp was soldier-like), an expert on Yeats and fly-fishing, it seemed, who carried a small leather suitcase that contained, as well as a mass of papers and books, a bottle of sherry and two glasses. He was not an original researcher but had a wide knowledge of Shakespeare scholarship and criticism, and lectured in a booming voice with some histrionic effect. (It was said that his account of Gloucester's blinding in *King Lear* was so powerful that people had fainted in the lecture-room.) Above all, Tom Henn was very helpful to students who stopped to ask questions after the lecture, and he encouraged me to sit for the Charles Oldham Shakespeare scholarship, an open examination held in October each year. The attraction of this competition was its challenge to get to know 'the whole of Shakespeare', to read all the plays one had never read, the historical background, modern criticism – here was an enormous field of knowledge to be mastered.

Deciding to sit for the Oldham at the beginning of my second year, I spent most of the long vacation preceding it studying Shakespeare. I already had a ticket for the London University library, gained one for the British Museum reading room, and even went up to Stratford-on-Avon to use the Shakespeare Institute library and go to the theatre. I read all the plays in chronological order, using the New Arden editions (where available) and the New Cambridge. I learned to view Dover Wilson's 'reconstructions' of the stage-action and supposed historical meaning of Shakespeare – especially the notorious *Hamlet* – with suspicion, but was grateful for Alice Walker's editions in that series, which seemed to me outstanding. The New Ardens, if less elegant typographically, were more helpful, with the notes on the page, fully documented, and to some of them – Kenneth Muir's *Macbeth* and *King Lear*, G. K. Hunter's *All's Well that Ends Well* – I owe a lasting debt. I couldn't afford to buy hardback editions of single plays (there were few paperbacks then), so I had to transfer notes of all kinds to the handy one-volume edition by C. J. Sisson,[4] which has been annotated in so many different coloured inks that it seems as if an army of scribblers has been at it.

Looking back, I am amused and touched at the enthusiasm I must have had to spend several months of my summer holiday voluntarily studying Shakespeare – something must have really stung me. But I did not win the scholarship; nobody was good enough that year. So the following summer I did it all over again, this time doing more work on the history of Shakespeare criticism, the make-up of the Elizabethan theatre, acting conditions and conventions, the nature of the texts and printing practices. I used to carry the *Sonnets* around, reading them in the intervals of the Proms, or again while queuing up at Stratford (Dorothy Tutin a memorable Cressida in Peter Hall's 1960 production, set in a sand-pit). The study of Shakespeare had become an absorbing interest, filling most hours of the day. I won the prize at the second attempt, but more important, obviously, I had learned how many sources of knowledge need to be brought to bear to understand a writer, in particular one working in such a fluid medium as Elizabethan drama, intended for performance not for posterity, for a public both popular and learned. It takes a lot of historical knowledge to realize the degree to which the texts we so unthinkingly use are not only imperfect records of staged events but are themselves the product of 300 years of editorial practice, embodying conventions of typography, layout, the prescription or description of theatrical business in terms that reflect, all too clearly, the conventions of the age in which the editor is working. The most important thing I learned in these studies was a critical attitude to Shakespeare scholarship, itself the product of changing taste and fashion.

Apart from the lectures organized by the English faculty I also benefited from teaching provided by my college, Trinity. My director of studies, who admitted me to Cambridge, as the official letter put it, on the basis of 'traces of alpha in your Shakespeare paper' (it now sounds like a medical diagnosis), was Dr R. T. H. Redpath; my first supervisor W. G. Ingram – names instantly recognizable to Shakespearians as editors of Shakespeare's *Sonnets*.[5] Theirs is widely acknowledged to be the best-balanced modern edition, neither pushing idiosyncratic theories of composition or biographical allusion, nor getting lost in endless discoveries of ambiguity. It was a new experience to be close to a work of scholarship in the making, and I was excited to be asked to do some research for them, into the dating of the *Sonnets*. This might have been my first venture into print, but my conclusions were so inconclusive (that is, every possible date between the 1580s and Shakespeare's death had been proposed by one writer or another) that they were not printed. I was lucky to be assigned to Will Ingram, who had studied with R. W. Chambers and had been a schoolmaster for many years before becoming a lecturer in the university's Department of Education. He had a profound love of literature, wide knowledge, and an infectious good humour, all qualities much valued by someone emerging from the mindlessness of military service. Later on I worked with another experienced teacher, Leo Salingar, who – like Raymond Williams – had learned his craft in a university extramural department (at Cambridge and Oxford, respectively). Leo's approach to drama was based on a detailed knowledge of literary and social history, acting conditions – including provincial tours by companies when their London theatres were closed – and an unusual (for that time) interest in genre. His study of the classical traditions informing Shakespeare's comedy is a model of its kind,[6] and as a teacher he was searching and thought-provoking. Being at Trinity had another great advantage, access to the college library at a period before a series of disastrous thefts brought security consciousness to the level where the use of rare book rooms is fraught with tension and suspicion. I was able to use freely, almost without supervision, the collection of Shakespeare Quartos and Folios bequeathed to Trinity by that great and under-appreciated editor, Edward Capell.[7]

After graduating I stayed on at Cambridge to do research on Francis Bacon as a prose writer, trying to place him in the relevant classical and

Renaissance contexts. I had immersed myself in rhetoric and poetics, theories of metaphor, the aphorism, and related topics, when the examiners for the Harness Shakespeare Essay competition (held every three years) announced the topic for 1965: 'The structure and imagery of Shakespeare's prose'. This seemed too great a challenge to pass over, so I set to work in the evenings and weekends to discover how the plays use the contrasting media. The first problem was to isolate prose, so to speak, in order to get a clear idea of its presence within each play and its place within Shakespeare's development as a whole. This was a critical problem, but also a bibliographical one – simply finding an edition with margins wide enough to annotate. So I got hold of two copies of the old Globe edition (I blush to admit), cut them up, and mounted them on double-folio size paper, which a local printer prepared and bound for me. I could then scribble away to my heart's content, the only difficulty being to condense my findings to the essay's word-limit (20,000 words). Contributions had to be submitted anonymously, so I chose a pseudonym associated with Raleigh, 'Ignoto', and was fortunate enough to be awarded the prize. (I thereby achieved the unusual feat of publishing books on the prose of Bacon and of Shakespeare in the same year, which aroused suspicion in some quarters.)

What the experience of working on Shakespeare's language had taught me was that here, too, just as with dramatic form and acting styles, Elizabethan dramatists were working with a series of conventions that were widely understood and carried with them a set of signals conveying information about, and judgements on, character and motive. Surviving play-manuscripts show that it was a common practice to fold the paper twice, giving four vertical columns: the characters' speech-headings would fill the first column, verse would take up the next two, while prose would extend across the page. There are explicit references in the text of several Elizabethan dramatists to characters changing their speech and gesture as they shift from verse to prose, or back, and these changes of medium mark off behaviour changes. To go 'down' to prose is the mark of losing reason or mental control (in drunkenness or madness), or dissimulating; to go 'up' to verse is to signal a new dignity, whether real or imaginary (see Chapter 1). It was fascinating to observe Shakespeare deploying these conventions to gain another register of meaning, and then creating prose characters and prose worlds. In the modern theatre, unfortunately, it is rarely possible to hear the difference, verse being so lightly stressed; and in recent criticism and editions the reader looks in vain for guidance as to the why and wherefore of the prose/verse distinction.

In Cambridge, in the 1960s, it was unquestioned that a writer's language was of major importance: that awareness is becoming increasingly rare. In recent years critics have brought an ever-smaller range of approaches to bear on Shakespeare. In this age of fragmentation and specialism, it seems to be enough to use just feminism, or ideology, or psychoanalysis, in none of which does Shakespeare's language – seen in appropriate historical and analytical

6

terms – play any particular role. Many critics today wish to acquire status and identity by belonging to a clearly defined and separate school, with its own methodology and values;[8] few of them seem to ask themselves, 'What else ought I to know?' The range of questions asked – and hence of answers – gets progressively narrower, critical writing more repetitive, easily identifiable in terms of a group style, while our understanding of Shakespeare is diminished in the process.

The very concepts of acquiring knowledge and deepening one's ability to understand and respond to a text may be dismissed in some quarters as outmoded individualism, in the same way that formal examinations are damned as repressive agents of an exploitative technocratic-capitalist system linked, in the special case of Great Britain, to imperial pretensions now shown to be hollow. Having become a university lecturer and Fellow of a Cambridge college in the 1960s I came to see teaching and examining from the other side; and having subsequently moved around and taught in other university systems I can now see the British system from a distance and with added experience. The result, in both cases, has aroused in me great respect for the way that this system can develop, in both teachers and students, a first-hand knowledge of literature, and can evaluate students' abilities to argue their own interpretations in formal written examinations. When I began to serve on examination committees in Cambridge I was amazed at the care taken over marking both college entrance and university examinations: two independent readings of each script, separately marked, with additional scrutiny by external examiners of many sample and all border-line cases; constant discussion by a committee of up to a dozen examiners in setting and evaluating the papers; lengthy examiners' meetings to produce an agreed list – all of this taking four to six whole weeks for each examiner involved. ... The fairness and care for detail shown in these meetings was impressive, and even the disagreements about the relative merits of candidates were encouraging, in that the whole procedure remained human, not mechanical. The Cambridge English faculty also reacted positively to the major defects of a formal examination taken at the same time by all undergraduates – namely, that not everyone responds well to such a period of concentrated activity, and that one week's examinations are not a fair guide to the quality of work done throughout the year – by instituting a series of options for the submission of long essays or other projects in lieu of certain papers, so further complicating the examiners' work and extending it throughout the year.

While obviously not perfect, and subject to increasing debilitation by a short-sighted government policy of reducing university expenditure by making experienced teachers retire early, the British public examination system seems to me outstanding in its integrity, and for producing something like a collective judgement by the teaching staff as a whole. In America, as in continental Europe, examinations are more closely linked to specific lecture-courses or seminars, given by individual teachers, and marked by them or by their assistants. The student has to accumulate a certain number of these grades (in many cases just the signature of the person concerned), and is very obviously at the mercy of the teachers involved, who can overvalue favourites and downgrade critics. These are perhaps rare events (although I have known too many of them), but they are deficiencies inherent in a system of grading which is individualistic rather than collaborative. The enormous emphasis placed on student composition in the British system, with frequent essays in the course of a term (in Cambridge one at least for each weekly supervision), encourages a fluency of expression which students in Europe have great difficulty in attaining, having neither the context nor the individual attention of a teacher who marks their essays regularly and often in great detail. The teaching conditions, too, are disadvantageous in many European universities, with eighty or even 200 people attending a seminar (meant, surely, for not more than twenty), an overcrowding from which only the most vocal, or those sitting nearest the front, are likely to benefit. The strict limitations, in British universities, on the number of terms that a student may take to reach each stage of his degree, and the precise structuring of a course or syllabus – both factors unknown in many European faculties – encourage an intense and well-planned acquisition of knowledge. In my experience, too, British students are expected to be considerably more critical than their European counterparts about the knowledge acquired, and the process of acquiring it. They are far less respectful of authority as such.

All these factors encourage British university students to become more closely involved with the text they read, and sometimes act. I can't speak from a wide knowledge of American universities, but a degree in English literature at a British university demands, by European standards, acquaint-ance with a great many texts from a wide historical spread. In America, one writer has recently observed, it would be possible to score the maximum 800 points on the Scholastic Aptitude Test without knowing any Shakespeare.[9] The main advantages – to return to Shakespeare – of an educational system based on the intensive knowledge of specific texts are, first, that a student learns to read with great attention to detail, even down to grammatical and philological issues; and, second, that a teacher can rely on the whole group of students having a common knowledge of these books. The teacher can talk with them, as they can talk with each other, about a shared experience. This may seem commonplace to British eyes, but it is rare enough in Europe. At Cambridge, both as student and teacher, I was used to being able to cite specific passages more or less from memory, or to argue out an interpretation by giving chapter and verse. We were all 'inward' with the books we were reading. The third advantage of knowing texts in such detail is that it reduces the likelihood of bizarre interpretations based on a partial aspect of a play, or even on one or two word-groups taken out of context. I say reduces, since nothing will deter critics determined to force through a partial interpretation, but at least a lecture audience or reading public familiar with the whole work is less likely to be convinced by the eccentric. At some stage they will protest, 'But what about this scene? or this passage?' Such healthy reactions can only be counted on from people who have long been exposed to a play, if possible in the theatre as well as on the page.

My point in writing these 'home thoughts, from abroad' is not to claim the superiority of British universities or of their products – far from it! – but to argue that its text-based system has distinct advantages for the study of literature, and that Shakespeare studies have benefited especially from it. Schools, universities, examination boards, are all institutions, of course, and in some eyes they are by definition deeply suspect. Yet institutions are only groups of men and women engaged in a common pursuit, and my teachers and colleagues at Cambridge impressed me with their great dedication to and love for literature. The dialogue that they had with each other and with their students was not without disagreements, of course, sometimes acrimonious: but it was in itself a liberating experience to realize that there could be no one right way to read or evaluate a book. The range of opinions, literary and political, was so wide among both teachers and students that it becomes meaningless to claim that the Cambridge, or any other English department, politicized knowledge in any limiting sense. Some shades of opinion (anarchist, Maoist) were rare, but otherwise knowledge was political only in the sense that all knowledge is political, or social – or any other term for shared human experience. For the institutions, and individual teachers from and with whom I learned to read Shakespeare, I feel nothing but gratitude. To those who pour scorn on them I would reply, with Hans Sachs, 'Verehre ihre . . . Meister!'

Yet there were and are weaknesses which could be remedied. The disadvantage of a separate Shakespeare paper is that it cuts him off from his historical context – unless teaching and examining emphasize a historical approach. All too often the Shakespeare paper is regarded as a soft option, a continuation of Advanced Level study without any fresh perspectives. Neither teachers nor students are called on to show any knowledge of Renaissance politics, religious beliefs and practices, social attitudes, ethics, attitudes to nature, literary theory, that whole complex within which a writer works, and both draws from and criticizes. The plays are studied as isolated literary works, some historical knowledge being involved – changes in the language, an awareness of dramatic conventions derived from direct experience of Elizabethan drama – but often latent, never coherently formulated to the point where it can be inspected and improved. My last official task before leaving Cambridge in 1972 was to mark the Shakespeare paper in part one of the Tripos, some 286 scripts, as I recall. The best ten were remarkable: essays on the last plays, in particular, of a freshness and sensitivity that I would have been glad to have emulated. But the majority of the candidates thought it enough to present a series of character-studies, with moralizing commentary, and occasional remarks on the language. I felt a sense of frustration that such a high concentration of scholarly and critical ability in

Cambridge produced such stale and mediocre work.

Raymond Williams, writing an autobiographical account of his first experiences of studying Shakespeare at Cambridge (in 1939), noted that the common practice of 'close readings of the texts without much attention to history' could, by a *deformation professionnelle*, produce 'Shakespeareans of a specific kind: people who lived, at least while at work, in an internal exile from their own time, saturated and in some cases dazzled by that distant but technically recoverable world'. That fact is directly related, I think, to his observation that Cambridge examiners repeatedly claim that the quality of work on Shakespeare is much lower than on other topics.[10] It seems to me that the emphasis on the text, admirable principle to start with, has led to the plays being put into an ahistorical context (of course, there are still lots of topics to keep one busy), which effectively mutes their reality and immediacy. To take a comedy which touches importantly on marriage – *The Taming of the Shrew*, say, or *All's Well that Ends Well* – and read it in the light of Renaissance attitudes to the family; or to confront *King Lear* or *Coriolanus* with its sources, and all the complexity of Shakespeare's treatment of them – such exercises in historical criticism, paradoxically enough, bring Shakespeare's reliance on, yet independence of, his social and intellectual context into much sharper focus. The increased clarity of vision makes the plays seem that much more individual, and immediate. We neglect history at our peril.

From a student of Shakespeare in a Renaissance context I next became a historian of his reception in English criticism, textual editions, acting and producing, between 1600 and 1800. This came about fortuitously, like so much else in life, thanks to the late Geoffrey Bullough (who had been, together with L. C. Knights, the kindest and most helpful examiner of my Cambridge dissertation on Bacon's prose). He had been approached by Brian Southam, then of Routledge and Kegan Paul, who had recently launched the 'Critical Heritage' series, and was looking for someone to edit the volumes on Shakespeare. I must have mentioned to Geoffrey my interest in the history of Shakespeare criticism, which went back to the days of the Charles Oldham scholarship, and he recommended me to Routledge. I had originally wanted to write a critical study of Shakespeare's reception from Ben Jonson to Coleridge, but since no adequate collection of texts existed I agreed to attempt one as a preliminary step.

My original plan was to produce two volumes covering the period 1601 to 1800, but the amount of significant material turned out to be far greater than anyone had expected. One of the main obstacles to planning the series was the inadequacy of the reference books. Given the profusion of scholarship and criticism of Shakespeare in our time one might imagine that adequate reference tools exist. But, as Francis Bacon once said, 'the opinion of plenty is the cause of want'. In fact, amazingly enough, there is no reliable bibliography of Shakespeare criticism for the period up to the 1950s. The *New Cambridge Bibliography*, I regret to say, is inaccurate and woefully incomplete. The sections in other cumulative bibliographies do not reveal any first-hand knowledge of the literature, and to find a reliable chronological listing of the major critical works one has to go back to S. A. Allibone in 1870 and R. W. Babcock in 1931 – although these, too, are not without error.[11] Lacking any reliable bibliographical tool, I resigned myself to reading through the catalogues of the British Museum, the Bodleian, Cambridge University Library, and the Folger Shakespeare Library, Washington, DC. The publication of the catalogue of the Birmingham Shakespeare Library was of some help, even though it misleadingly describes itself as a 'Shakespeare Bibliography' (see Chapter 7). Not convinced that these sources were sufficient, I then read through the monthly book review sections in the *Critical Review* and the *Monthly Review* for the period 1749 to 1801. The lengthy and tedious process of working on the journals, together with the work I did on unpublished manuscripts in various libraries, enabled me at least to identify some anonymous contributions as the work of such critics as William Guthrie and George Steevens. Further study of this area will certainly uncover much more information about the authorship of essays in eighteenth-century journals; indeed this part of our literary heritage has been sadly neglected. There is nothing like an adequate bibliography of the journals, to begin with, let alone an index to their contents (although rumour has it that such an index is being prepared). The most useful basic tool I found is Milford and Sutherland's 1936 catalogue of the Bodleian's holdings, the interleaved and annotated copy of which in that library's catalogue room represents the fullest listing known to me.[12] But of course it is not complete. ... Some of these gaps in our knowledge of the past will soon be filled: the *Short Title Catalogue of Eighteenth Century Books*, now under way, will be of inestimable value, and will certainly cause the picture that I assembled to be modified.

As far as Shakespeare criticism is concerned – essays or books on the plays – the aim of the series was not to present only 'the best' criticism (however that might be established), but to show how critical traditions formed and evolved over a period of time, and to enquire what these traditions tell us about the conditions governing the writing, and reading, of literature. When I first began work on the project, in 1968, I conceived of it as an up-dating of D. Nichol Smith's well-known and pioneering (for 1903) anthology, *Eighteenth Century Essays on Shakespeare*.[13] That is, I planned to limit it to 'pure' literary criticism, as seen in the formal essay tradition (Addison, Steele, Johnson, Morgann, Richardson), or in such exceptional documents as Dr Johnson's *Preface to Shakespeare*. Yet as I worked on it I came to realize that although an up-dating of Nichol Smith was desirable, that kind of limitation to straight literary criticism gave only a partial and restricted account of Shakespeare's true heritage. In it he would be the preserve of professional essayists and academics, the reading of him would be of a non-problematical text (since critics of this kind did not usually concern themselves with the technicalities of editing), a procedure performed in leisure, in the privacy of a study or a library.

In opposition to this restriction of scope I chose to represent all the areas in which Shakespeare provoked discussion, starting with the critics – who, after all, did most to form literary taste. What had always fascinated me about the history of Shakespeare criticism was the diversity of judgements he had provoked. Juxtaposing two writers from the same generation will show the extremes of celebration, and censure:

> When the hand of time shall have brushed off his present Editors and Commentators ... the *Apalachian* mountains, the banks of the *Ohio*, and the plains of *Scioto* shall resound with the accents of this Barbarian.
>
> (Maurice Morgann, 1777)

> His characters are in fact all monsters, his heroes madmen, his wits buffoons, and his women strumpets, viragos, or idiots. ... His creations are as preposterous as they are numerous, and whenever he would declaim, his thoughts are vulgar and his expressions quaint, or turgid, or obscure. There is not a rule in dramatic composition which he does not habitually violate.
>
> (William Shaw, 1785)[14]

On the one hand reverence, admiration, resulting in excesses of bardolatry long before the Romantic and Victorian critics chimed in; on the other, severe, often violent denigration. The original ground for offence was that Shakespeare had broken all the rules of propriety and correctness enunciated by the theorists of the first coherent system in modern literary criticism, Neo-classicism. This version of Aristotle, two or three times removed (via sixteenth-century Italy, seventeenth-century France), held that works of literature ought to conform to rules governing genres (no mixture of comedy and tragedy), or social types (no clowns in tragedies), or verbal composition (no word-play in serious literature). To the modern reader, the Neo-classics' folly of judging a writer by a critical system evolved after he wrote, is obvious; yet today we still judge all past writers by critical systems that blend modern and ancient ideas, often indiscriminately. The history of Shakespeare criticism, as I understand it, can be a valuable guide or caution, reminding us that we too work within a historical framework, with its assumptions and expectations of which we may be as unaware as Dr Johnson, or as aware but unrepentant as Thomas Rymer.

Shakespeare, I soon discovered, was the most praised and the most blamed of English writers. In that, as in so many ways, he was unique, and the history of the changes of taste in Shakespeare criticism offers a major guide to the development of English literary history. It is not the whole story, of course, since he was a lyric poet and a dramatist and thus discussions of epic poetry exclude him (although he is often compared with Spenser and Milton), and he does not figure much in criticism of the novel. Yet, these exceptions apart, the history of his reception raises all the important issues concerning the twin processes of scholarship and criticism. Indeed, in the period from 1600 to 1800 we move from a first stage of naïve commentary and analysis to a succeeding stage of critical self-awareness, in discussions of the act of criticism itself (see Chapter 5).

In addition to straight literary criticism I included substantial excerpts from the prefaces and notes to the series of editions that mark the greatest contribution of the eighteenth century to the study of Shakespeare: Nicholas Rowe (1709), Pope (1725, 1728), Lewis Theobald (1733), Hanmer (1744), Warburton (1747), Dr Johnson (1765, 1773, 1778), Edward Capell (1768, 1774, 1783), George Steevens (1773, 1778, 1785, 1793, 1803), and Edmond Malone (1780, 1790, 1793, 1821). Pope's edition had many virtues, and some notorious faults, but it was soon outclassed by Theobald's, the first serious edition of an English writer. The notes to Theobald represent, despite their occasional prolixity, the first attempt to grapple with the many problems of interpretation at first hand, critical, historical, philological, inaugurating a debate which never looks like ending. The amount of learning accumulated by these editors and other commentators, such as Thomas Edwards, Heath, and Tyrwhitt was formidable, covering virtually every aspect of Elizabethan life and literature. Since each edition absorbed almost all the notes of its predecessors, and devoted further scrutiny to them, the resulting volumes may have been unwieldy, but they were an invaluable mine of information then, and to us are essential evidence of the workings of critical taste in the supposedly objective area of scholarship.

In making my own first-hand comparison of each of these editions with its predecessors – a process involving the movement of trolley-fulls of dilapidating brown calf around rare-book rooms – I acquired a great respect for two editors in particular who had been much maligned in their day, Lewis Theobald – ridiculed by Pope[15] – and Edward Capell, unfairly treated by Steevens and Malone.[16] As for Dr Johnson, a man and writer whom I value enormously, closer acquaintance with the prolonged genesis of his Shakespeare edition, with the bibliographic evidence of all its irregularities, last-minute cancels and corrections, left me regretting that he had not begun it earlier in life. His *Proposals* for an edition, drafted in 1756, remain a model of almost everything that we would expect from an editor, but work on the *Dictionary*, ill-health, and other distractions meant that he was seldom able to give his full energies for long to the editing of Shakespeare.[17] Thus his edition remains an odd mixture of genuinely penetrating commentary, especially on human behaviour and moral problems, and the desultory and perfunctory. It seems necessary to state this divided impression in the face of some persistently uncritical admiration of him, especially in America.

Another Shakespearian who came to seem over-praised the more I studied him was David Garrick. He has been given almost all the credit for the boom of Shakespeare performances in the 1740s and onward: yet, as several scholars have shown, that boom was in existence before he made his début and continued independently of him.[18] He was undoubtedly a great actor, with a remarkably expressive face and gestures, although prone to certain affectations in delivery.[19] His main services to Shakespeare were the rather ambivalent ones of adapting the plays to make star vehicles, adding death-scenes, pruning large amounts of plot in order to yield an 'opera' or successful double-bill, or else to placate Neo-classic taste (in his notorious version of *Hamlet*). As the leading actor-manager of his day he might have been able to halt the mania for adaptation which meant that many of Shakespeare's greatest plays were seen, for over a hundred years, in mangled versions (see Chapter 6). But the conservatism that affected both audiences and managers, together with a keen sense of what would be commercially unprofitable, kept Garrick from any reckless experiments. Yet, on the other hand, he was a great collector of old editions of plays (used and abused by Johnson), which he bequeathed to the British Museum Library. Like Johnson, Garrick could have done so much to forward a true understanding of Shakespeare (strikingly evident in contemporary editions), but a combination of vanity and caution held him to the familiar routines.

Having brought together a wide range of literary and textual criticism, reviews of performances of original plays and adaptations, not to mention poems to Shakespeare, 'centos' of his work and other trivia, the lasting impression that this work left on me was of a remarkable homogeneity of taste over a long period of time. The fact that adaptations made on Neo-classical principles in the 1680s and 1690s still held the London stage in the 1830s – the fact that no theatre-goer had ever seen King Lear or Cordelia die – means that taste remained fixed within relatively narrow bounds across a period that literary historians would divide into several different epochs. The fact that, with very few exceptions, everyone disapproved of Shakespeare's word-play or bawdy, and many (not least Dr Johnson) had difficulty with his bolder metaphors, means that large areas of Shakespeare's language were censored out or abandoned as incomprehensible. At the risk of seeming to endorse a Whig interpretation of history as a continual progress towards the better, one must concede that modern scholarship and criticism have brought increased understanding on many levels. Yet we, too, are the victims, often unconscious, of contemporary assumptions and attitudes, which a later age will describe as representative of the time in which we worked. Our goal should be to fuse both historical and modern methods of interpretation, while realizing that the modern is itself just as much a part of history.

My own involvement with history, at any rate that of Shakespeare's reception, turned out to be protracted. Instead of the two volumes I planned, there were six; and instead of the three years I'd projected, it took ten. And whereas I had hoped to reach 1830 as a stopping-point (to take in that remarkable generation of poets and critics, Keats, Coleridge, Hazlitt, Lamb, and lesser-known writers), by the time I suspended work in 1980, to get back to other projects, I had only reached 1801. As for the analytical study of Shakespeare and his critics, to which this collection was just preparative, that remains a plan, or at least a hope.

Those, in brief, are some of the influences that have formed me as a Shakespearian, and may help to explain the direction my work has taken.

In the first part of this book I bring together four essays concerned with the relationship between form and meaning. Since it has become obligatory in some current 'political' approaches to Shakespeare (in the terms, that is, of modern 'cultural politics') to dismiss all other approaches as 'empty formalism', I wish to insist on the integral relationships between form and meaning, the structure of literary works and our experience/interpretation of them. I begin with a short essay on those crucial shifts of medium in drama from prose to verse and back, and what they tell us about Shakespeare's control of tone, tempo, and character. Then I turn to grammar as a key to reading the *Sonnets*, the ways in which personal pronouns literally represent personal relationships. Third, I look at some of Shakespeare's representations of hypocrisy, focusing in particular on two formal properties, the aside and the soliloquy, and some implications of the audience becoming more closely involved with the hypocrite than with his dupes. Hypocrisy is also an important element in the play I single out for special attention, *Coriolanus*, where politics is shown as a process of manipulation, and where Coriolanus himself becomes an agent in some actions, a puppet in others. My analysis of the later stages of the play in terms of goals and agents owes a general debt to the morphological analyses of Vladimir Propp, one of the first writers to show how formal structures embody meanings and values.[20] In the second part I treat the history of Shakespeare criticism from various aspects: one short period (the last quarter of the eighteenth century) in which, by a process of internal debate, objection, and restatement, a decisive shift in critical method took place; and one long, the century of adaptations, in which nothing shifted. The last two essays pay tribute to a library, and a scholar, and trace some of the metamorphoses of Shakespeare studies between the Romantics and the present day.

B.W.V.
Zürich, June 1988

Notes

1 Quoted in *The Times*, 9 December 1987.
2 'Playing Shakespeare', *Shakespeare Survey* 40 (1988): 11–19, at p. 11.
3 My experience of St Marylebone Grammar School was very different from that of Benny Green, the jazz critic, as recorded in the Colour Magazine of the *Mail on Sunday* for 22 November 1987, in a punningly titled article, 'Benny's school breaks up' (pp. 24–6). The school's governors refused an ill-conceived plan to form a comprehensive school by 'amalgamating' it with another school several blocks away, without adding new buildings (which would have meant permanent processions of children from one site to the other through some of the busiest traffic in London), and in retaliation the Inner London Education Authority (as the London County Council had become) closed it down in the 1970s. Mr Green is photographed in a largely derelict building, and in his text relieves himself of a lot of resentment dating back some fifty years (what did they do to him, one wonders, or he to them?). Philip Wayne is described as 'a dangerous academic lunatic', with a 'crazed fantasy of being a proficient cellist' (those who heard him play, and those who played with him – including Kenneth Sillito, who joined the school as a prodigiously gifted violinist in 1954 – will know how false that remark is). Further, he had a despicable 'moral cruelty, by which I mean his relentless pursuit of certain ideals' which were presented as 'vital to our spiritual survival'. Mr Green does not mention what those ideals were, nor what was 'cruel' about them, preferring snide remarks about 'the insanity which afflicts so many of his profession', and offensive comments on former teachers who are still alive. But he does give details for his claim that the school

> alienat[ed] everyone from English Literature by pressing Shakespeare on us when we were too young to understand anything [come, come, Mr Green, were you ever that young?] ... Even the most venerable classics were bowdlerized into respectability, and we were given to understand that Cleopatra had died a virgin, that Dido and Aeneas were just good friends, and that those lines in *Venus and Adonis* where the goddess instructs, 'Graze on my lips, and if those hills dry [*sic*: 'be' omitted], stray lower, where the pleasant fountains lie', were connected in some vague way with landscape architecture.

Here, even making allowances for Mr Green's *ressentiment*, disbelief sets in: if the texts were 'bowdlerized', would those lines have been left in? Was there ever, in fact, a bowdlerized *Venus and Adonis*? And if so, was it read in schools? Otherwise it seems just a cheap joke.
4 London, 1954.
5 *Shakespeare's Sonnets*, ed. W. G. Ingram and Theodore Redpath (London, 1964; second edn, 1978).
6 Leo Salingar, *Shakespeare and the Traditions of Comedy* (Cambridge, 1974). See also his study, with G. Harrison and B. Cochrane, 'Les Comédiens et leur public en Angleterre de 1520 à 1640', in *Dramaturgie et Société*, ed. J. Jacquot (Paris, 1968), pp. 525–76, and an important volume of essays, *Dramatic Form in Shakespeare and the Jacobeans* (Cambridge, 1986).
7 See H. M. Adams, 'The Shakespeare collection in the library of Trinity College, Cambridge', *Shakespeare Survey* 5 (1952): 50–4.
8 See my review of recent Shakespeariana: 'Bard-watching', *Times Literary Supplement*, 26 August–1 September 1988, pp. 933–5.
9 J. E. Howard and M. F. O'Connor (eds), *Shakespeare Reproduced. The Text in History and Ideology* (London, 1987), Editors' Introduction, p. 10.

10 'Afterword', in J. Dollimore and A. Sinfield (eds), *Political Shakespeare. New Essays in Cultural Materialism* (Manchester, 1985), pp. 234–5.

11 See *The New Cambridge Bibliography of English Literature*, ed. George Watson, *Vol. 1: 600–1660* (Cambridge, 1974); *Vol. 2: 1660–1800* (1971); S. A. Allibone, *A Critical Dictionary of English Literature ... Vol. II* (London, 1870), pp. 2006–54; R. W. Babcock, *The Genesis of Shakespeare Idolatry 1766–1799* (Chapel Hill, NC, 1931; New York, 1978).

12 R. T. Milford and D. M. Sutherland, *A Catalogue of English Newspapers and Periodicals in the Bodleian Library, 1622–1800* (Oxford, 1936), with typescript chronological arrangement and interleaved up-dating. A very welcome new publication is Carolyn Nelson and Matthew Seccombe (eds), *British Newspapers and Periodicals, 1641–1700. A Short-Title Catalogue of Serials Printed in England, Scotland, Ireland, and British America* (New York, 1988). As for individual journals and contributors, J. M. Kuist recently located, and edited, the invaluable file kept by the Nichols family of contributors to the *Gentleman's Magazine*: see his book *The Nichols File of the Gentleman's Magazine* (Madison, Wisc., 1982), and my review in the *Times Literary Supplement*, 7 January 1983. See also J. G. Basker, *Tobias Smollett, Critic and Journalist* (Newark, Del., 1987) for a study of Smollett's journalism.

13 (Glasgow, 1903), revised edn H. Davis and F. P. Wilson (Oxford, 1963).

14 For convenience sake I list titles and dates of the individual volumes: *Shakespeare: the Critical Heritage, Vol. 1: 1623–1692* (London and Boston, 1974); *Vol. 2: 1693–1733* (1974); *Vol. 3: 1733–1752* (1975); *Vol. 4: 1753–1765* (1976); *Vol. 5: 1765–1774* (1979); *Vol. 6: 1774–1801* (1981). These quotations are from vol. 6, pp. 170 and 394 respectively.

15 See ibid., vol. 2, pp. 16–19, 426–42, 458–63, 471–529.

16 See ibid., vol. 5, pp. 32–7, 42–3, 51–2, 303–27, 363–4, 555–9; vol. 6, pp. 32–3, 37–8, 44, 218–72, and index, p. 644.

17 See ibid., vol. 4, pp. 268–73; vol. 5, pp. 17–32, 48–51, 55–243, 510–51; vol. 6, pp. 313–15, 393–5, 567–72, and index, p. 647.

18 See ibid., vol. 3, pp. 11–14; vol. 4, pp. 16–29; vol. 5, pp. 10–17; and vol. 6, pp. 58–62.

19 See ibid., vol. 4, pp. 28–9, 253–5, 323–4, 424–34, 455–8.

20 See Vladimir Propp, *Morphology of the Folk-Tale* [1928], trans. L. Scott, 2nd edn, rev. L. A. Wagner, intro. A. Dundes (Austin, Texas, 1968); and Brian Vickers, *Towards Greek Tragedy* (London, 1973), pp. 172–3, 183–91, and Chapter 5, 'Structure and ethics in Greek myth' (pp. 210–67).

Part I
Forms and meanings

1

Rites of passage
in Shakespeare's prose

In every Shakespeare play where prose appears (as it does in all but four: *Henry VI, Parts 1* and *3*; *King John*; *Richard II*), characters constantly move from prose to verse, or from verse to prose, and back again. In all but five plays verse is the statistically dominant form and prose has the role of the essential but inferior complement. If we establish a hierarchy of social ranks, with kings at the top, servingmen, citizens, sailors, pirates at the bottom, then prose as the normal medium extends upwards to a given point but no further. If we establish a hierarchy of psychological normality, those characters who predominantly speak verse can fall down into prose when they lose their reason: Ophelia, Othello, Lear, Lady Macbeth. (Characters from the prose domain never go mad – their dramatic status would not warrant it.) If we think of expressiveness, or emotional seriousness, or danger to the state, these again are higher realms from which prose is largely absent. If prose is the lower medium, then the movement up to verse is a movement to a higher rank, and can be described in terms of the rituals known in anthropology as rites of passage. When boys reach puberty, in primitive societies today as in ancient Greece, a group of them will go away into the mountains, jungle, or other hostile environment to undergo hardship and trials which, if successfully endured, allow them to return to society at a higher level, as adults. In his pioneer study *Les Rites de passage* (1908), Arnold van Gennep defined three stages within such rituals: *séparation*, separation from society; *marge*, the transitional period of testing, outside society; and *agrégation*, the rein-corporation of the individual into society in his new status.[1] No such event occurs in Shakespeare, of course, and my use of this model is meant to stimulate thought about how we might classify the many shifts between verse and prose that take place in Shakespeare, most frequently in the middle-period plays.

One preliminary point that may still need to be made is that the switches between the two media are not arbitrary, but motivated according to a series of conventions practised by other Elizabethan dramatists.[2] The motivation, however, can come from a number of sources. The ones I have so far mentioned might be called mimetic, that is, the distinctions king/servant, sane man/madman, are distinctions that exist in real life, outside the theatre, and are rendered within a Shakespeare play by the distinction between verse and prose. To speak English verse is the sign of a minimum control over reason and grammar, so that, for similarly mimetic reasons, in Shakespeare drunks do not speak verse (the barge-scene in *Antony and Cleopatra* shows some famous men teetering on the verge of prose, and indeed relapsing into it), nor do foreigners, nor those with strong British regional accents.[3] But in addition to such external mimetic motivation, where the dramatist renders distinctions from life in the appropriate stylistic medium, we must differentiate various internal motivations, internal to the play as an aesthetic unit and to the characters as autonomous individuals. As an example of the first, changes dependent on effects of atmosphere or mood within a play, I would instance the way in which, in *Measure for Measure*, the Duke, in his disguise as a Friar, intervenes at the point where Isabella, realizing that Claudio is not wholly willing to die so that she should retain her chastity, collapses into hysterical abuse. At this point (III.i.151) the Duke-Friar steps forward with his composed and rational prose outlining a complex plot by which Angelo can be brought to book, and the play recovers its balance. Here prose has the effect that Leo Spitzer attributed – in my view, wrongly – to verse as a whole in Racine's drama, that of 'Dämpfung', muting or damping down emotions.[4]

As for character-inspired motivations for the change of media, to which the rest of this essay will be devoted, some of these can be described as socially induced, reflecting the social hierarchy within the play. Nobles and gentry speak verse among themselves, but when a servant enters speaking prose it is presumably a sign of good breeding, or adaptation, to descend to prose with them. It constitutes a gesture of respect not to make social inferiors conscious of their inferiority. Examples of this category of adaptation would be the entry of Constable Dull and Costard (*Love's Labour's Lost*, I.i.181), which reduces the assembled company to prose, or the more serious cross-examination performed by Angelo and Escalus (*Measure for Measure*, II.i.45). When the judges speak to their fellows on the bench, they do so in verse (*Love's Labour's Lost*, I.i.304ff.; *Measure for Measure*, II.i.134ff.). The fact that Olivia speaks prose to Malvolio underlines his status as a domestic servant (*Twelfth Night*, I.v.etc.), and that she does so when he appears cross-gartered may be an instance of humouring a madman by descending to his level (III.iv.16ff.). Yet when Malvolio, much abused, enters in the final scene (V.i.328ff.) Shakespeare permits him the dignity of verse, showing that the gulled and cured vain man nevertheless deserves some sympathy. Two prose characters for whom sympathy has wholly evaporated by the final scene are Parolles (*All's Well*) and Lucio (*Measure for Measure*). Parolles, who has had his moments of verse during the play, enters the final scene wholly discredited, and speaking prose. The King addresses him in verse to start with, but then comes down to Parolles' level in prose, the medium in which Lafeu and Diana also address him, recognizing his inferior ethos (*All's Well that Ends Well*, V.iii.238ff.). The parallel pretender and deceiver, Lucio, who has occasionally aspired to verse, begins the last scene, indeed, speaking verse, his more respectable front still intact (*Measure for Measure*, V.i.134ff.). But as the Duke cross-examines Mariana, Lucio's natural licentiousness comes out in bawdy jokes (179ff.), for which he is silenced. When Escalus cross-examines him, this is done in prose, as befits his true status (260ff.), and when Angelo invites Lucio to state what he can witness against the Friar-Duke, the medium drops to prose for all four speakers (327–33), to be catapulted back to verse as Lucio pulls off the hood and reveals the Duke's identity. Yet when the Duke addresses Lucio and sentences him, he replies in suitably chastened prose (500ff.), relegated to the medium where he belongs.

A special class of prose-speakers for whom verse-speakers descend to the lower level are clowns, who may sing lyrics or speak verse for satiric purposes, but who are almost invariably addressed in prose the moment they appear. Clowns seem to have a lower centre of gravity, or a magnetic field that converts everything to prose. This convention, so standard in the comedies that it escapes notice (especially in modern theatre-productions, where it is very rare to be able to *hear* any difference between prose and verse), stands out in the tragedies, where the clown's reduction of the medium imposes an often uneasy mood of relaxation or verbal indulgence, outside the time of the tragic action, frustrating its rhythm. In the comedies prose appears with Speed and Launce in *Two Gentlemen*, Biondello in *The Taming of the Shrew*, Launcelot Gobbo in *The Merchant of Venice*, not to mention Lavatch (*All's Well*), Feste, Touchstone, Thersites, Falstaff, and Autolycus.

Internal social considerations can govern the converse shift, from prose to verse. When the servant or clown for whom the medium had descended leaves the stage, discourse can revert to its normal level. This phenomenon can be seen in the rather similar clown-scenes in *Titus Andronicus* and *Antony and Cleopatra*, on which Jonas Barish has commented,[5] as in the comedies in general. On the exit of a servant, Malvolio, Viola reverts to verse, ending the scene with a soliloquy (*Twelfth Night*, II.ii.), as she does again after the exit of a clown, Feste (III.i.). In both cases the soliloquy conveys important self-reflection, a move from light-hearted banter to serious self-revelation that is made with even more significance by Cressida, after the exit of Pandarus – the spirit of prose at its most banal (*Troilus and Cressida*, I.ii.281) – and by Hal, after the exit of Falstaff (*1 Henry IV*, I.ii.195).

In these cases verse takes on another dimension of seriousness by its juxtaposition with the prose of jest and the evasion of responsibilities. The problem that Hal faces with Falstaff is in part a problem of media. When he and Poins scatter Falstaff and his robber band they speak verse to each other at the end of the scene (II.ii.104ff.), and as soon as Falstaff has gone into hiding Hal addresses the Sheriff searching for him in verse (II.iv.506). Yet as the responsibilities of public life invade Hal's apprenticeship to pleasure, the distinction – prose with Falstaff/verse without him – breaks down, as we see when he addresses his fat friend in verse to urge him to the wars (III.iii.199ff.), a change of tone so marked that Shakespeare makes Falstaff reply in a couplet – as Milton Crane noted, Falstaff is only given verse for mockery.[6] In the scenes before battle Hal and Westmoreland address Falstaff in affectionate prose (IV.ii.49ff.), and on the eve of battle Hal still shares that medium with his old crony (V.i.121ff.). But once the fighting begins, with Falstaff in shameless prose (the soliloquy describing how he has led his 'ragamuffins where they are pepper'd'), Hal enters in the heroic medium and rebukes him for his idleness (the cowardice he can't see, as we can): 'What, standst thou idle here? Lend me thy sword' (V.ii.40.). Brought down to prose by Falstaff for a few lines of word-play, Hal leaves him with another line of verse, marking the difference of ethos between them. When Hal discovers Falstaff's 'corpse', feigning death to escape Douglas, he speaks a verse epitaph over him – the wrong medium, but that doesn't matter since the death isn't real, either, and when Falstaff receives his true epitaph it will be in prose (*Henry V*, II.iii.9ff.). As far as Falstaff is concerned, leaving prose for verse is a true *rite de passage* for Hal, so that when we see him together with Poins in the sequel speaking prose without Falstaff present (*2 Henry IV*, II.ii.) we realize that his metamorphosis is not yet complete.

The move up to verse can be made for the exit of a person from a lower but also for the entrance of one from a higher rank. If characters who have the ability to speak either prose or verse have been talking prose among themselves, or if the medium is prose for some other reason, the entry of a person of rank or status can be the signal for the move to the higher level. Petruchio's servants, speaking prose among themselves, go up to verse for the entry of their master returning with his bride (*Taming of the Shrew*, IV.i.120), as do Valentine and Viola on the entry of their master, Orsino (*Twelfth Night*, I.iv.9). The two murderers sent to dispatch Clarence speak prose to each other for their semi-comic, semi-serious dialogue on conscience (*Richard III*, I.iv.86–160), but when Clarence awakes they quite properly address him in verse. (In any case, hardly any serious murder in Shakespeare is plotted or executed in prose, and no serious or admirable character is denied the resonance of verse at his death.)

Here the convention of changing media out of respect for the person merges into another category, that of changing to the higher medium for a more serious subject-matter. In two cases involving admirable heroines and dubious companions it is hard to separate the two categories. When Lucio goes to prompt Isabella on how to persuade Angelo – a scene in which persuasion has much of the ambivalence that Shakespeare commonly associated with rhetoric[7] – he moves up to verse (*Measure for Measure*, I.iv.16ff.; II.ii.43ff.);

and when Cloten, one of the most ruthlessly mocked prose-characters in the late plays, woos Imogen he, too, is allowed to ascend to her medium (*Cymbeline*, II.iii.86ff.). She is indeed a princess 'out of his star': all the more reason not to drag her down to his level.

The move up to verse can be ineffective, deservedly so. In *All's Well that Ends Well* Parolles' use of verse seems to have connotations of falseness, as when he relays to Helena the news that Bertram is leaving Rossillion without consummating their marriage:

> The great prerogative and rite of love,
> Which, as your due, time claims, he does acknowledge,
> But puts if off to a compell'd restraint;
> Whose want, and whose delay, is strew'd with sweets ...

and so on through a honeyed and insincere figure (II.iv.41ff.). Prose is Parolles' natural medium, and when he is captured and blindfolded, apparently by the enemy, moving up to verse reveals his desperation: 'O, let me live,/And all the secrets of our camp I'll show' (IV.i.69ff., 83ff.).

But when he has been exposed as a liar and a traitor, left alone on stage, Shakespeare allows him to end the scene with a soliloquy in verse:

> Yet am I thankful. If my heart were great,
> 'Twould burst at this. . . . Simply the thing I am
> Shall make me live.
>
> (IV.iii.330ff.)

While noting that Parolles is given some kind of dignity in verse, we should also observe that Shakespeare seldom ends a scene with a soliloquy in prose – Thersites and Falstaff are the only characters who do so more than once. Yet Falstaff finally aspires to verse, not for mockery this time, but for ingratiation:

> God save thy Grace, King Hal! my royal Hal! ...
> God save thee, my sweet boy! ...
> My King, my Jove! I speak to thee, my heart!
>
> (*2 Henry IV*, V.v.41ff.)

Where Falstaff has spent his life deceiving others, here he deceives himself, and is thrust out of this medium so far above his resources, social or moral: 'I know thee not, old man, fall to thy prayers'. Falstaff is forcibly returned to prose, 'knapp'd o'th'coxcomb' by verse, and subsides to his own level: 'Master Shallow, I owe you a thousand pound'.

If the move from prose to verse for a person of a higher rank represents – when honestly carried out – a gesture of respect, the failure to do so can signify deliberate disrespect. An amusing instance of this comes when Orlando, romantic lover whose normal level is verse, enters unknowingly on to a prose-scene with one blank-verse line: 'Good day and happiness, dear Rosalind!' at which Jaques instantly observes with disgust, 'Nay then God buy you, an' you talk in blank verse', marching off the stage in a huff (*As You Like It*, IV.i.30f.: his exit is unaccountably not marked in the Riverside edition). Far more insulting is the behaviour of Achilles in *Troilus and Cressida*. The alternation of scenes in that play establishes verse as the appropriate medium for the Greek leaders engaged in the *vita activa* in their council-scene (I.iii.), while for those hanging out in the *vita inactiva* in Achilles' tent – Thersites, Ajax, Patroclus, Achilles – all too often the medium is a scabrous unheroic prose. We first see Ajax and Thersites trading metaphors of boils and scabs; Achilles enters in verse (II.i.55f.), but soon comes down to their level. They revert to verse when Thersites leaves, but in the next scene Achilles is discovered indulging himself in a prose catechism with Thersites, when Agamemnon, Ulysses, Nestor, Diomed, and Calchas appear. Faced by the Greek leaders come to manipulate him back to the war Achilles stalks off before they can reach him, pointedly speaking prose: 'Come, Patroclus, I'll speak with nobody. Come in with me, Thersites' (II.iii.69f.). Unlike Achilles, Patroclus answers Agamemnon respectfully, in verse: only Achilles is powerful enough to ignore the Greek generals.

Another instance of disrespect involving the refusal of verse concerns Hotspur, reading the letter from a fellow rebel who has had cold feet – the letter is in prose, and Hotspur interrupts it with angry comments in prose, an unusual effect in Shakespeare – and then being confronted with his wife. Where we might have expected him to grant her the respect of verse, he goes on in the same business-like prose: 'How now, Kate? I must leave you within these two hours'. The casualness, and implicit disvaluation of her contained in that form, are exposed by her reply in verse:

> O my good lord, why are you thus alone?
> For what offence have I this fortnight been
> A banish'd woman from my Harry's bed?
>
> (*1 Henry IV*, II.iii.36ff.)

Even after her thirty-line speech of pathos and wifely love, describing his disturbed dreams, when Hotspur answers it is in the verse of public business, ignoring all that she has said: 'What ho! Is Gilliams with the packet gone?' (II.iii.65.). Hotspur's refusal of verse is less a deliberate snub, as with Jaques and Achilles, than a sign of how the illegality of rebellion can destroy family and loving relationships, as the sequel demonstrates all too clearly.

As these last few examples show, gestures of respect or disrespect, moving from verse to prose or back again, are often caused by the entry of one or more characters, with the result that those characters on stage have to re-adjust themselves, choose which medium they are going to use. Changes of media are most often precipitated by entrances and exits. But the switch can also be motivated by changes of mood. The move from verse to prose can often signify a drop in seriousness, to mockery or ridicule; from tension to relaxation; or from public to private discourse. As instances of mockery we can cite the reaction of the court of Navarre to the Pageant of the Nine Worthies (*Love's Labour's Lost*, V.ii.484ff.), or that of Athens to 'Pyramus and Thisbe' (*Midsummer Night's Dream*, V.i.106ff.). In both cases prose underlines the distance between the conversational style of the courtiers and the variously absurd verse-styles of the inset play. In *The Merchant of Venice*, in a verse-scene, when Gratiano tries to cheer up Antonio with an 'exhortation' that misfires, as soon as he has left Bassanio drops into prose suddenly, for five lines of mocking comment: 'Gratiano speaks an infinite deal of nothing, more than any man in all Venice. His reasons are as two grains of wheat hid in two bushels of chaff' ... (I.i.114ff.). The scene then continues in verse. A more consistent use of prose for mockery in this play is Portia's satirical review of her suitors (I.ii.), a scene echoed in *Troilus and Cressida* with the heroine's mockery of the Trojan warriors (I.ii.177ff.), which includes even Troilus. One of the striking features of that play, indeed, is that no one is spared mockery, and hardly any one fails to mock others. Thus in the scene where the Greek leaders visit Achilles in his tent, the oafish Ajax remains in prose, to which even Agamemnon descends. Having duped Ajax into thinking that he is their chosen man against Hector, the Greek leaders, who had earlier made such a fuss about being mocked by Thersites and Patroclus, now mock Ajax in asides (also, naturally enough, in prose):

AJAX. I'll let his humours blood.
AGAMEMNON. [*Aside*]. He will be the physician that should be the patient.
AJAX. An' all men were of my mind –
ULYSSES. [*Aside*]. Wit should be out of fashion.

(II.iii.212ff.)

The use of prose for mockery in *Much Ado about Nothing* is so widespread as to make illustration superfluous. After the emotional upset of the church scene, with Claudio's mistaken denunciation of Hero, and her apparent death, it does not surprise us that when Beatrice and Benedick are alone they revert to their natural medium of prose. Yet, as they finally declare their love for each other – having been tricked into so doing – Beatrice asks one favour:

BENEDICK. Come, bid me do any thing for thee.
BEATRICE. Kill Claudio.

(IV.i.288f.)

It seems to me that the fact that this request comes in prose is a sign that it is not to be taken seriously, since it, too, like so much else in the play, is based on false appearances. (It is hard to recall any seriously intended murders in Shakespeare being plotted or executed in prose.) For the same reason, perhaps, although Leontes' jealousy in *The Winter's Tale* reaches painful extremes, the fact that he never speaks prose means that he is not really mad, just temporarily disturbed.

The reverse move, from prose to verse, is usually the sign of increased seriousness. Sometimes this is within a light-hearted context, a move from jesting about love to declaring a more serious passion. So in the opening scene of *The Taming of the Shrew*, after the business-like prose conversation of Gremio and Hortensio about Katherine as an obstacle to their wooing Bianca (I.i.105–45), when Lucentio is left alone with his servant Tranio he moves up to verse to declare his true and romantic love: 'Tranio, I burn, I pine, I perish, Tranio' (148ff.).

Similarly, in *Much Ado*, Claudio waits until Benedick, the mocker of love, has gone before he moves up to verse to reveal to Don Pedro his love for Hero (I.i.290ff.). The convention is sustained, but subtly mocked, in *Twelfth Night*, where Viola, bearing the suit of Orsino, waits until Maria leaves before launching into the higher style appropriate to romance (I.v.167ff.). At first Olivia answers mockingly, in prose, but as Viola warms to the task Olivia comes up to verse, the stronger emotion lifting the medium with it. Indeed, at the end of the scene it is Olivia who is left alone on stage – in that key situation of the end-of-scene soliloquy that tells all – to declare her new-found, misbegotten love in verse. In *All's Well* Helena goes up to verse whenever she talks of her love for Bertram, moving in and out of prose several times within a scene (I.i.; I.iii.; II.v.; III.ii.; III.v.), in the flexibility that marks the mid-period plays.

The move up to verse can herald a darker mood, though. In *The Merchant of Venice* Shylock and Bassanio have been discussing Antonio's desired bond of three thousand ducats in prose, with some bitter mockery from Shylock on being invited to dinner: 'Yes, to smell pork, to eat of the habitation which your prophet the Nazarite conjur'd the devil into. I will buy with you', he goes on, but not eat, drink, 'nor pray with you. What news on the Rialto? Who is he comes here?' At this point Antonio enters, and Shylock instantly switches to verse in an aside to us:

> How like a fawning publican he looks!
> I hate him for he is a Christian

(I.iii.41ff.)

This is a crucial moment, revealing to us alone at this point his real hatred, so strong that only verse can express it. Another angry man is Duke Frederick. He first appears speaking prose (*As You Like It*, I.ii.149), but when Orlando not only defeats his wrestler but reveals his identity as the youngest son of Sir Rowland de Boys, the Duke moves up to verse to give his displeasure more force (224ff.). In the scene following, Celia and Rosalind are conversing in prose about Orlando when Duke Frederick enters in verse, 'his eyes full of anger', to banish Rosalind (I.iii.41): as the girls discuss their plight the scene remains serious in verse.

In *Much Ado* the shift to verse expresses the bitterness and sense of betrayal felt by Claudio at Hero's supposed infidelity. In the masque scene, with its dancing and witticisms in prose, Don John delivers his slander under pretence of addressing Benedick. Left alone to digest the news Claudio moves up to verse (II.i.172–82), dissimulating his upset by reverting to prose on Benedick's return. A similar but more dramatic shift occurs in the wedding scene, which begins in a relaxed prose until Claudio takes over, with his mistaken hurt dignity: 'Give not this rotten orange to your friend,/She's but the sign and semblance of her honour' (IV.i.23ff.). Since the infidelity is illusory, an evil plot, Claudio in verse is in the wrong medium, as it were, but unknowingly. Leonato, Hero's father, knowingly compounds confusion by being party to the plot announcing Hero's death. He and Antonio whip Claudio's emotions up in verse with their threatened challenge, a level of seriousness from which Claudio gratefully subsides into prose for the scene in which he and Don Pedro mock Benedick 'the married man', gulled by them into loving Beatrice. Conscious of being the trapper here, and unaware of being the gull of Don John's plot, Claudio moves uneasily between verse and prose, comedy and seriousness, not fully at home in either. His ambiguity contrasts with the certitude of Ford, once he has been made to confront his mad jealousy, putting aside his suspicions to beg forgiveness in the most eloquent and sincere form that he knows:

> Pardon me, wife, henceforth do what thou wilt.
> I rather will suspect the sun with [cold]
> Than thee with wantonness.
>
> (*Merry Wives of Windsor*, IV.iv.6ff.)

Ford's embracing of verse and forgiveness are both authentic, learned from corrective experience. The move upwards can be a sign of insincerity, as with Parolles and Falstaff, or one of honest self-revelation, as with Cressida and Hal with their end-of-scene soliloquies. The choice of prose can accompany a deliberate disguise, as with Julia in *Two Gentlemen*, who adopts it to support her new role as a boy in her search for Proteus (IV.ii.26ff.). The Duke turned Friar in *Measure for Measure* cultivates at least two different prose-styles, a plain and business-like one for his benevolent deceptions, and that of a moralist disappointed with the world – a persona within which he can also rise to more serious denunciatory verse as the occasion warrants (for verse within this prose role see III.ii.19–39; 261–82; IV.ii.108–13). The Duke's shifts between the media are too flexible to admit of any tidy categorization. More deliberate (as one would expect) is the oscillation of another ruler disguised to enquire into the behaviour of his subjects, King Henry V. On the eve of Agincourt, dressed as a commoner, the King moves among his soldiers speaking prose. He first meets Pistol, that illegitimate verse-speaker, in a bizarre confrontation (*Henry V*, IV.i.35–63), but then becomes involved in a long discussion with soldiers Williams and Bates on the rights and wrongs of war, and the responsibility of the ruler for the death of his people. Although in prose – as one says, perhaps too much influenced by the conventions of the comedies – this is one of the most serious scenes in the play (91–229), and when the soldiers have left the King ascends to verse for what is to me the most deeply felt speech of all:

> Upon the King! let us our lives, our souls,
> Our debts, our careful wives,
> Our children, and our sins lay on the King!
> We must bear all. O hard condition,
> Twin-born with greatness.

(230–84)

In his own persona the King speaks verse, entering on to a prose-scene between Fluellen and Gower to express his anger at the French murder of the luggage-minders, and continuing in verse to Fluellen (IV.vii.55–118). Yet when he reverts to the business of his night-watch, which included his challenge to Williams, and Pistol's to Fluellen, he descends to their level in prose (120–67). His public status is reasserted in the final confrontation with Williams, where he speaks verse to the common soldier's prose, yet rewards his honesty (IV.viii.24–72). Who would not have been deceived by a king disguised, and in prose?

In Shakespeare's plays people receive, by and large, the medium they deserve. It would be as inconceivable to find Richard II speaking prose as it would be to meet Thersites in verse. As with Elizabethan concepts of society, where each man was supposed to labour in his vocation and place, each character usually belongs to one medium and only moves out of it for special and clearly defined purposes, love, hate, respect, mockery, dissimulation, self-revelation. Usually, too, people adjust to the governing medium out of politeness or indulgence, or with an ear for over-all harmony. These being the conventions whose occurrence is so regular that we barely notice them, the exceptions to them are the more striking. I want to consider, finally, two anomalies: characters using a medium that doesn't belong to them; and two or more characters inhabiting different media simultaneously.

For the first category, people outside their true medium, let us return to Pistol. This camp-follower, rogue turned soldier about to become beggar, has no right to speak in verse. Elizabethan audiences would presumably have spotted at once that he was 'putting on the style' with his phrases cobbled together out of distant memories of Kyd, Marlowe, and Greene. Whatever Shakespeare's source or inspiration, Pistol is a brilliant invention, locked as he is in a verse-form and range of reference derived from the heroical plays in the London theatres of the 1580s and 1590s, as far removed as could be from his debased reality. One never knows with the half-lines in Pistol's verse whether they represent Vergilian hemistichs, portentous silences, or lacunae in his memory. The sense of his living in a closed world, stylistically speaking, is beautifully conveyed when Falstaff, frustrated in his attempts to get a simple answer to a simple question, wanting to know his 'happy news', is forced to move up to Pistol's manner:

> FALSTAFF. I pray thee now deliver them like a man of the world.
> PISTOL. A foutre for the world and wordlings base!
>   I speak of Africa and golden joys.
> FALSTAFF. O base Assyrian knight, what is thy news?
>   Let King Cophetua know the truth thereof.
>
> (2 Henry IV, V.iii.96ff.)

– an effect not unlike that if W. C. Fields had turned up in a performance of *Mourning Becomes Electra*!

Yet Shakespeare has prepared a come-uppance for Pistol by confronting him with Fluellen, honest soldier and proud Welshman. In their first scene together, where Fluellen begins with a feeling of respect for Pistol's bravery at the bridge (how obtained we know not), they dispute about the iconography of the goddess Fortune, Pistol in verse, Fluellen in prose, more coherently (III.vi.20–60). Gower has seen through Pistol, and Fluellen vows revenge should he be abused. That opportunity arrives with Pistol's reckless threat to 'knock his leek about his pate/Upon Saint Davy's day' (IV.i.54f.), dutifully relayed to Fluellen by the King. When Pistol appears, 'swelling like a turkey-cock', perhaps like the old tragic actors who 'strutted and bellowed', Fluellen beats his pate and forces him to eat the leek raw (V.ii.). Honest prose defeats dissembling verse, and the braggart goes off to be a thief.

A more violent end meets an earlier pretender to verse, suitably violent as befits the rebel Jack Cade. He harangues his followers in prose, yet is deflated by mocking asides from them, Shakespeare leaving us in no doubt what to think of his pretensions (*2 Henry VI*, IV.ii.31ff.). When confronted by Sir Humphrey Stafford and other representatives of law and order, in order to challenge legitimacy at its own level Cade 'knights' himself, and ascends to verse:

>   It is to you, good people, that I speak,
>   Over whom, in time to come, I hope to reign,
>   For I am rightful heir unto the crown.
>
> (129ff.)

But he cannot sustain his usurped style for very long, soon relapsing to prose, in which he conducts his grotesque inquisition of Lord Say:

> Thou hast most traitorously corrupted the youth of the realm in erecting a grammar school.... It will be prov'd to thy face that thou hast men about thee that usually talk of a noun and a verb, and such abominable words as no Christian ear can endure to hear.
>
> (IV.vii.32ff.)

Say responds in verse, as a true humanist: 'Kent, in the Commentaries Caesar writ,/Is term'd the civill'st place of all this isle' (60ff.). Say is so eloquent that even Cade feels remorse (104f.), but still has him killed. Having shown Cade's pointless destructiveness Shakespeare reins him in by confronting him with more speakers who exemplify the old definition of the orator as a *vir bonus peritus dicendi*. First Lord Clifford harangues the mob in verse, appealing to their patriotic instincts to fight France. After his energetic verse Cade's prose shows that medium at its most laboured and puffy: 'Has my sword therefore broke through London gates, that you should leave me at the white Hart in Southwark?' (IV.viii.20ff.). Cade is left in the baser medium, running for his life (55ff.), only to meet his nemesis in Alexander Iden, an esquire of Kent, who has inherited his land legitimately and envies no other man's possessions. It is no accident that Iden speaks verse, Cade prose, and that the verse-man should kill the prose-man: the hierarchy of order matches the hierarchy of styles.

The pretensions of Cade and Pistol are exposed by representatives of legitimacy. Less thoroughgoing and less dangerous aspirations to verse can be allowed to subside of themselves. Thus, in the Induction to *The Taming of the Shrew* – a unique example of a play outside the play, not to be taken as a measure by which the rest of the play must be dismissed for lacking seriousness[8] – the tinker Christopher Sly, brought back in a drunken stupor to the house of a mischievous lord, is deceived into thinking that he is really a gentleman. As the delusion begins to work (Ind. ii.1–67), Sly gradually levitates up to verse, as if hypnotized, or like someone in an early painting by Chagall, just taking off:

> Am I a lord, and have I such a lady?
> Or do I dream? Or have I dream'd till now?
> I do not sleep: I see, I hear, I speak;
> I smell sweet savours, and I feel soft things.

(68ff.)

Yet, when confronted with his supposed wife, desires of the flesh begin to reassert themselves, and he relapses into prose and bawdy (125ff.). If deception and disguise bring Sly up to verse, Ajax is metamorphosed by flattery. He has been established as a prose-character in the first scene at Achilles' tent (*Troilus and Cressida*, II.i.), where even Agamemnon addressed him in prose, by the law of adaptation to the lower centre of gravity. However, when the Greek leaders, intent on humiliating Achilles, flatter Ajax with the prestigious combat with Hector, Ajax sees a heroic future beginning to form for himself, and slowly, ponderously, after several moments of silent thought, moves up to verse: 'If I go to him, with my armed fist/I'll pash him o'er the face' (II.iii.202f.). Yet, like Sly, he can only sustain the unfamiliar medium for a few speeches, and sinks back to his true milieu. Both tinker and soldier are innocent gulls, deceived but not deceiving. They lack the pretentiousness of a Parolles or a Pistol – or even an Autolycus, putting on the style to match

Florizel's borrowed clothes in three lines of verse, to assert his superiority over the shepherd and the clown (*Winter's Tale*, IV.iv.745ff.).

In these scenes where characters attempt to break out of their proper medium, the audience or reader should feel a sense of impropriety or disorder, as if some basic law were being denied. In some cases – Pistol and Fluellen, Cade and Iden – Shakespeare underlines the unnaturalness by confronting two characters each in a different medium, setting up a gap of ethos and style. Such 'split' scenes can achieve widely differing goals. When Benedick mocks love he does so in prose, naturally enough (*Much Ado*, II.iii.6–36), but as he overhears Don Pedro, Claudio, and Balthasar in verse, beginning the plot against him, we are conscious of the gap between mockery and romance. Benedick stays in prose, however, after the overhearing – perhaps there is something in him truly resistant to romance – whereas Beatrice moves up to verse after her duping (II.i.107–16). Together, the two wits tricked into love speak verse at the débâcle of Hero's wedding (IV.i.110ff.), but that is in response to the general seriousness. When they meet at the final masking, the atmosphere is again one of ceremony and solemnity, and they speak verse to each other (V.iv.72–83). But as they gently mock the truth of their attachment they relapse into prose, which in their mouths lacks many of the anti-romantic, realistic, mocking connotations it has elsewhere in Shakespeare. One of the great achievements of *Much Ado* is the transformation of prose to a medium in which romance can exist, aerated by wit. Beatrice and Benedick can speak verse, but their love seems much more natural in prose, neither limited nor coarsened by that vehicle. This new tool was honed still more sweetly for Rosalind.

The normal association of prose with the lower elements – no one could say in prose 'I am fire and air; my other elements/I give to baser life' (*Antony and Cleopatra*, V.ii.289f.) – is revealed most amusingly in the case of Bottom. Temporarily transformed into an ass, with Titania drugged into loving his new shape (Apuleius' *Golden Ass* must be somewhere in Shakespeare's mental world), Bottom persists in the good-humoured prose of *l'homme moyen sensuel*, utterly oblivious to the fact that the Queen of the fairies is in an erotic tizzy over him:

> TITANIA. Come sit thee down upon this flow'ry bed,
>   While I thy amiable cheeks do coy,
>   And stick musk-roses in thy sleek smooth head,
>   And kiss thy fair large ears, my gentle joy.
> (Midsummer Night's Dream, IV.i.1ff.)

After Titania's quatrains – the most artificial verse-form in drama, presupposing as it does that the speaker has four lines already prepared, with rhymes, confident of not being interrupted – Bottom's prose truly belongs to the world of unromantic everyday appetites:

BOTTOM. Mounsieur Cobweb, good mounsieur, get you your weapons in
your hand, and kill me a red-hipp'd humblebee on the top of a thistle;
and, good mounsieur, bring me the honey-bag.
... Give me your neaf, Mounsieur Mustardseed ... to help Cavalery
Cobweb to scratch ... I am such a tender ass, if my hair do but tickle
me, I must scratch.

(10ff.)

Bottom may have been 'translated' in shape, but nothing can elevate him to
verse and romance – apart, ironically enough, from his role as Pyramus, out
of whose Pistol-like doggerel he is ever ready to step in order to explain the
play: 'She is to enter now, and I am to spy her through the wall. You shall
see it will fall pat as I told you' (V.i.185ff.). Bottom is the antithesis not only
of romance but of any appeal to the imagination.

Troilus and Cressida is a kind of adult version of *Pyramus and Thisbe* (in
Dryden's adaptation Cressida is made to kill herself, indeed, as both vindication and punishment). The gap between Titania and Bottom, erotic
excitement and the matter-of-fact, recurs with much more force here:

TROILUS.   O gentle Pandar,
From Cupid's shoulder pluck his painted wings,
And fly with me to Cressid!
PANDARUS. Walk here i'th' orchard, I'll bring her straight.

(III.ii.13ff.)

The contrast is functional to the whole play, for from their first juxtaposition
(I.i) Troilus' super-charged verse (like the music of Richard Strauss or Scri-
abin at their most sensuous) shows that he over-dramatizes himself, in tune
with the whole excessively emotional Trojan ethos. Pandarus' prose not only
proves that he doesn't take Troilus seriously, so turning our reaction towards
a scepticism that stands off from full involvement, but in time it establishes
the speaker as a matter-of-fact fixer, who is not only alien to romance but
coarsens whatever he touches. At their first meeting his innuendo on such
words as 'fight', 'tame', 'deeds', 'activity' (III.ii.39–59) seems to be contagious,
for in an encounter unique in Shakespeare two lovers who have previously
spoken verse actually descend to prose for their first conversation, to exchange
bawdy double meanings on words like 'monster', 'monstrous', 'will', 'execution', 'act', and 'performance' (62–99). We recall Sonnet 129, with its bitter
puns on 'expence' and 'action', or the sniggers of Lucio or Pistol. Shakespeare
is making the same point as Donne – 'Love's not so pure, and abstract, as
they use/To say, which have no mistress but their muse'[9] – as he has done
obliquely in *Venus and Adonis* with the picture of the horse exuding desire
(259–324). Pandarus, who had instructed Troilus – 'You must be witty' –
seems to have infected the lovers with his fondness for dirty jokes (in him,
perhaps, a sign of impotence or disease), and seeing him again they are

reminded of this and go up to verse for their protestations of love and fidelity (113ff.). Pandarus, the 'pitiful goer-between' (200), remains in prose, though, here and at their parting (IV.iv.) He cannot transcend his limitations.

Nor can Thersites. One of the remarkable features of *Troilus and Cressida* is that Shakespeare has developed, out of sources as diverse as Chaucer and Chapman's Homer, two prose characters, one for the Trojan, one for the Greek camp, whose function it is to reduce the two great themes of epic, love and war, to their lowest common denominator: appetite. As in one of those *New Yorker* cartoons, when Pandarus sees a young couple together he has a mental image of a bed, organized by himself. When Thersites sees soldiers – we would have to change the modern parallel to those semi-pornographic animated cartoons like Ralph Bakshi's *Heavy Traffic* and *Fritz the Cat*, or sado-masochistic literature – he sees a degraded struggle over a whore by men running with disease. He who wants to 'see some issue of my spiteful execrations' (II.iii.6) – any word in Thersites' mouth can have distasteful implications, so here 'issue' is the pus from an infected wound – imagines Agamemnon as having boils over him, which 'did run ... Then would come some matter from him' (II.i.2ff.). To Ajax he says: 'I would thou didst itch from head to foot; an' I had the scratching of thee, I would make thee the loathsomest scab in Greece' (27ff.). Thersites is a walking manifestation of the 'leprous distillment' that Claudius poured into his brother's ears, a 'tetter' or scabby eruption 'bark'd about,/Most lazar-like' (*Hamlet*, I.v.64ff.). He is a scab on the play, a scab speaking prose. In peace-time Achilles and his cronies come down to his level of prose abuse and mockery (*Troilus and Cressida*, II.i.; II.iii; III.iii; V.i.), but when the fighting restarts Thersites takes no part in it, and is left alone to direct his poisoned breath straight at us. In fact, he increasingly leaves the stage after a prose-soliloquy, an unusually unresonant way to close a scene, especially given his sordid world-view (V.i; V.ii; V.iv. – which begins and ends with his soliloquies; and V.vii., where he is finally chased off by another bastard). A significant parallel, which says much about the degradation that Falstaff reaches, is that he, too, ends scenes with unheroic, self-satisfied prose soliloquies, if not so vicious (*1 Henry IV*, V.i.; V.iii.; *2 Henry IV*, III.ii.; IV.iii.; V.i.). No two prose characters exert so much influence on a play as do Pandarus and Thersites, and only one other play that I can think of (*King Lear*) makes so much use of a simultaneous gap between the two media. In both cases the result is discord, but in *Troilus* their joint influence adds to the effect of the whole play, which leaves no values standing. The difference between the two lowerers is that Pandarus cannot help speaking prose, since he is incapable of verse, heroism, or true love, being limited to 'handling' others' affairs. But whereas he merely wants to help people satisfy their baser appetites, Thersites would wish to reduce everyone to his poisonous and diseased state. A telling detail which his creator put in his mouth is the ending to one of his earlier soliloquies: 'I have said my prayers, and devil Envy say amen' (II.iii.20). What envy cannot have itself it wishes to destroy in others.

After *Troilus and Cressida* almost any play is a relief, even the brothel scenes of *Pericles*. Here we are in the world of Mistress Overdone and Pompey, with no Thersites, at least. Once again the 'split' use of verse and prose has the connotations of nobility versus degradation. Marina, having escaped being murdered due to the intervention of pirates, is sold to a brothel, her virginity to be auctioned to the highest bidder. By contrast with the calculating prose of the bawd, listing the attractions of his new acquisition, Marina's verse stands out with greater pathos (IV.ii.64–6). After a hundred lines of the coarsest prose the final juxtaposition shows a gap of ethos as wide as that between Troilus and Pandarus, but more threatening:

> MARINA. If fires be hot, knives sharp, or waters deep,
>   Untied I still my virgin knot will keep.
>   Diana aid my purpose!
> BAWD. What have we to do with Diana? Pray you will you go with us?
>
> (146ff.)

Her intended customer is the nobleman Lysimachus, and to begin with Marina speaks a docile prose with the bawds (IV.vi.51ff.), continuing with aggressive word-play in order to shame Lysimachus into naming the vice he is engaged upon (66–91). When he loses patience and wants to adjourn to 'some private place' she suddenly rises to verse: 'If you were born to honour, show it now' (92ff.). He, good man that he is, instantly returns to verse and to his better self: 'Had I brought hither a corrupted mind,/Thy speech had altered it' (104ff.). He has been so forcibly returned to his true ethos that when Boult returns, speaking prose, Lysimachus rebukes him in indignant verse (118ff.). His moral superiority over this 'damned door-keeper' re-established, Lysimachus leaves, and Marina remains in danger. While the bawds are deciding to have her forcibly raped she says little, but when Boult wants to lead her away she again rises to verse, her secret weapon, and appeals to his better sentiments. Over-awed, converted both by her persuasion and her gold, Boult remains in prose (any change would have been too great a transformation), yet agrees to help her. Verse is here the morally superior medium, but at least Boult redeems prose from its worst associations.

In *The Tempest* verse again stands for a superior ethos in stark juxtaposition with prose. Since Caliban is often performed in the modern theatre as if he were a later version of Thersites, we tend to expect him to be a prose-speaker. In fact, as a true 'salvage man' (a point well made in Giorgio Strehler's production), he belongs to a much higher niche in creation, albeit hating Prospero's forcible civilization or (depending on one's critical stance) colonization of the island. As such he is a natural verse-speaker, as we see from his first appearance (I.ii.321ff.) and from the soliloquy cursing Prospero during the storm (II.ii.1–17). Yet when he is confronted with Stephano and

Trinculo, the good-for-nothing drunken servants, Caliban is so frightened that he cowers and speaks prose (55ff.). This may seem paradoxical, but it represents a gesture of adaptation. When he speaks an aside to us, in his own person, it is in verse:

> These be fine things, an' if they be not sprites.
> That's a brave god, and bears celestial liquor.
> I will kneel to him.
>
> (116ff.)

He continues in their prose, but when he wants to express his respect for them and offer his services, he moves up to verse:[10] 'I'll show thee the best springs; I'll pluck thee berries;/I'll fish for thee, and get thee wood enough' (160f.). Caliban's affection is as misplaced as that of Titania for Bottom, yet it obeys the normal Shakespearian convention of moving from prose to verse to express respect. Stephano and Trinculo cannot go above prose, being 'below stairs' in every sense.

The juxtaposition of high and low recurs in their next scene. Caliban begins it in prose, at their level, and also slightly tipsy. But when Ariel intervenes, invisible, to accuse Caliban of lying, in indignant self-defence he moves up to verse:

> Thou liest, thou jesting monkey thou!
> I would my valiant master would destroy thee.
> I do not lie.
>
> (III.ii.45–7)

His naturally superior medium re-established, Caliban continues in verse, appropriately enough since his speech includes a plan of murder, and that marvellous description of the beauty of the island: 'Be not afeard, the isle is full of noises,/Sounds, and sweet airs, that give delight and hurt not' (135f.).

The limitations of Stephano and Trinculo are in part the limitations of their medium. This we see when they return. Caliban is in verse, as befits the dignity and danger of a killing, they in prose, easily side-tracked by a clothes-line of gaudy apparel (IV.i.194–257). Caliban's intelligence far exceeds theirs, to 'dote' as he puts it contemptuously, on such 'trash' and 'luggage'. In the proper mouths – Lafeu, Henry V, Duke Vincentio – Shakespeare's prose can be rhythmic and expressive. But for such degenerates as Cade, or these two, Shakespeare can also deprive his prose of rhythm, make it flaccid, shapeless, a difficult mouthful to get out:

STEPHANO. Every man shift for all the rest, and let no man take care for himself; for all is but fortune. *Coraggio*, bully-monster, *coraggio*!
TRINCULO. If these be true spies which I wear in my head, here's a goodly sight.

> (V.i.256ff.)

Caliban's verse stands out with the greater force, cured as he now is of his delusions:

> I'll be wise hereafter,
> And seek for grace. What a thrice-double ass
> Was I to take this drunkard for a god,
> And worship this dull fool!

(295ff.)

But – so at least the juxtaposition suggests – that is in part the judgement that verse can make over prose.

It is now time to confront my anthropological model with the experience of reading the plays. Obviously, the two do not wholly coincide, since the *rite de passage* is performed once only – no one, so far as I know, ever had to undergo an initiation ceremony twice! As a one-way passage the model clearly does not square with the repeated movements between verse and prose that we find in Shakespeare. While it is tempting to see Hal's rejection of Falstaff and his world as a rejection of prose, the issue is never as linear or straightforward as that; indeed in *Henry V* the King uses prose in four or five scenes, both for his nocturnal tour and for his wooing of Katherine. One can, perhaps, speak of a fall into prose followed by a recovery, as in the case of Lysimachus, or Caliban. This has the advantage of stressing that the two media, especially when simultaneously juxtaposed, can symbolize a vast difference in ethos, quite apart from the social differences mentioned earlier. It will not do to suggest that prose is always the inferior state, of course, since Edgar in prose is a better man than Edmund (*King Lear*), as he is in verse, and Iago (*Othello*) works equal havoc in both media. But the shifts between the two levels are often significant of shifts of value, or collisions between value-systems. Since anthropology is so much involved with recreating alien belief-worlds, with all the varied and competing value-systems that exist in other cultures, just as in our own, literary critics who would wish to acquire more flexibility in dealing with that collision of view-points which forms the basic experience of drama could do worse than to consult the anthropologists. The difference between verse and prose in Shakespeare, as in literary theory generally, it seems to me, can be helpfully understood in terms of such major cultural distinctions as those between male and female, right and left, the pure and the impure, the sacred and the profane.[11] These distinctions *are* hierarchical, but they are relative, not absolute. In many situations the male is thought to be superior to the female, but not in all; in some situations an object or person can be profane, in others sacred. The terms are complementary, but their relationship can shift from context to context.

In reflecting on the varying complementarities of verse and prose in Shakespeare, then, we might ponder over van Gennep's analysis of what he called 'the pivoting of the sacred'. As he shows, 'the presence of the sacred (and the performance of appropriate rites) is variable. Sacredness as an attribute is not absolute; it is brought into play by the nature of particular situations', existing in both space (such as the movement to and from town, or to a foreign country), and time (between birth and initiation, say). We can, then, apply his metaphor to our studies: 'Thus the "magic circles" pivot, shifting as a person moves from one place in society to another.'[12]

So the media of prose and verse 'pivot' too, shifting in value or significance as a character moves within the society of the play, or within its internal hierarchy of language and values. The anthropological model allows us to detect within the lived experience of the play a system of complementarities which obeys its own laws, creating at the level of style a scale of discriminations that reinforce those perceived, perhaps intuitively, at the level of action. The decision that Shakespeare faced hundreds of times – whether to put his words, as Dryden expressed it, into verse or into 'the other harmony of prose'[13] – is one that the reader ought always to be alert to, for each decision signals an element of dramatic meaning that we can yet recover.

Notes

1 See Arnold van Gennep, *The Rites of Passage*, trans. M. B. Vizedom and G. L. Caffee, introduction by S. T. Kimball (London, 1960). An excellent application of this concept to ancient Greece is P. Vidal-Naquet, 'The Black Hunter and the origin of the Athenian Ephebia', *Proceedings of the Cambridge Philological Society* 194 (1968): 49–64.

2 See Brian Vickers, *The Artistry of Shakespeare's Prose* (London, 1968; rev. edn London and New York, 1979), chapter 1 and the notes, pp. 432ff., for reference to older studies by R. W. David, Milton Crane, Traudl Eichhorn, and Elisabeth Tschopp.

3 For this distinction see Brian Vickers, 'Shakespeare's use of prose', in John Andrews (ed.) *William Shakespeare: His World, His Work, His Influence* (New York, 1985), vol. II, pp. 389–95.

4 See Vickers, *Artistry*, p. 319, and Mark Eccles (ed.) *Measure for Measure*, New Variorum Edition (New York, 1980), p. 148. For Spitzer, see 'Klassische Dämpfung in Racine', *Romanische Stil- und Literaturstudien*, 2 vols (Marburg, 1931).

5 'Continuities and discontinuities in Shakespearian prose', in *Shakespeare 1971*, ed. C. Leech and J. M. R. Margeson (Toronto, 1972), pp. 59–75, at pp. 63–5.

6 Milton Crane, *Shakespeare's Prose* (Chicago, 1951), p. 5.

7 See Brian Vickers, ' "The power of persuasion": images of the orator, Elyot to Shakespeare', in *Renaissance Eloquence*, ed. J. J. Murphy (Berkeley and Los Angeles, 1983), pp. 411–35, at pp. 424f.

8 This perverse interpretation is made by H. J. Oliver in his recent edition, *The Taming of the Shrew* (Oxford, 1982). See my critique of it in *Review of English Studies*, n.s.36 (1985): 415–18.

9 Donne, 'Love's Growth', lines 11–12.

10 I am not in agreement with G. B. Evans's Riverside text at this point, which prints

Caliban's lines as verse already at line 148: 'I'll show thee every fertile inch o'th'island;/And I will kiss thy foot. I prithee be my god.' These are not only extra-metrical, but unrhythmic. Similarly in the next scene, where he has Caliban in verse *before* Ariel speaks to him (a passage reminiscent of the opening of *As You Like It*):

> As I told thee before, I am subject to a tyrant,
> A sorcerer, that by his cunning hath
> Cheated me of the island

(III.ii.42–4)

If those are verse-lines they are extremely clumsy. Once again we see that editorial decisions depend not on 'scientific textual criticism' but on literary judgements.

11 See, e.g., such anthropological classics as Emile Durkheim, *Les Formes élément-aires de la vie religieuse* (Paris, 1912); Louis Moulinier, *Le Pur et l'impur dans la pensée des Grecs d'Homère à Aristote* (Paris, 1952); Robert Hertz, *Death and the Right Hand* (London, 1960), trans. R. and C. Needham from 'La prééminence de la main droite: étude sur la polarité religieuse', *Revue philosophique* 68 (1909): 553–80; R. Needham (ed.) *Right and Left: Essays on Dual Symbolic Classification* (Chicago, 1973). I am sorry to record that several contemporary Shakespearians feel an irrational antipathy to even a modest use of anthropology or sociology, rejecting them as 'unnecessary'. But any discipline that can 'let in new light on a subject', in Francis Bacon's phrase, is worth exploring – not mechanically, of course, but with tact and sensitivity in relating it to essentially literary discussions.

12 Van Gennep, *The Rites of Passage*, p. 12.

13 Dryden, 'Preface' to *Fables Ancient and Modern* (1700), in *Of Dramatic Poesy and Other Critical Essays*, ed. G. Watson, 2 vols (London, 1962), II.272.

2

'Mutual render':
I and *Thou* in the *Sonnets*

In his *Sonnets* Shakespeare achieved the rather remarkable feat of turning to new and individual ends a genre that had flourished throughout Europe for several centuries and was in effect beginning to die at the time when he wrote, in the mid 1590s. At the risk of stating the obvious, we could describe the situation presented in the Renaissance love-sonnet as one in which the poet adores, often from afar, a woman who either surpasses the worth of the poet to such a degree that union with her is inconceivable, or else rejects his advances with scorn and cruelty. This tradition had been reanimated by Sir Philip Sidney in his *Astrophil and Stella*, but even he, pioneer and inventor though he was, was content to reproduce the standard man–woman relationship while devoting his energies to creating an idiomatic English-speaking voice for Astrophil, and to filling out the persona of the frustrated lover, with all his follies and self-deceptions, hope and disappointment. One way out of this dead-end situation, denying as it did the possibility of a human relationship, was taken by Donne in his love-poems, where the woman is no longer on a pedestal but is discovered in bed with the poet. She is no longer desired, yearned after: she has been 'had', 'got', 'cast off', and in turn can have, get, and cast off the man. The situation in the traditional poem, as exemplified by Sidney, is an *I–She* one, where the pronouns reveal the gap between the lover and his mistress; in Donne, as I have shown elsewhere,[1] it is an *I–Thou*, and above all a *We/Us/Our* relationship, where the lovers exist, after the consummation, as a unit, a model to others, from which point Donne's wit takes off in a brilliant sequence of rhetorical strategies.

Shakespeare evidently shared Donne's dissatisfaction with the extant convention, agreed with him that unfulfilled love was a trope that could only lead to a limited number of stereotyped situations. I suggest that Shakespeare reacted critically against the whole European tradition of the sonnet as a form of impotent adoration or frustrated lament by striking out, like Donne, towards fulfilment. Like Donne, he wrote poems to a mistress with whom a relationship had been consummated, was continuing on a carnal basis, with many fluctuations of desire and love. (I had better say now that readers who identify the *I* of the *Sonnets* with Shakespeare's own personality not only encourage that futility of speculation about the identity of a real-life 'Friend' and 'Dark Lady' which has pestered discussions of these poems for so long, and is now in the last stages of senility; but in so doing they also destroy one of the essential principles of literary criticism in modern times, the independence of the *I* in lyric poetry, its existence as a persona or mask behind which the poet is free to impersonate any human situation without being identified with each or all of the mutations – often contradictory – taken on by his persona.) But while writing about a sexual relationship between a man and woman Shakespeare does not continue with Donne towards celebration of the beloved, effecting a union between sex and love. In another sharp break with convention, the protagonist of Sonnets 127–52 (I set aside 153 and 154, two sonnets on themes traditional since the *Greek Anthology*, which do not seem to belong to this sequence) gives his mistress not compliments but insults, or mock-compliments, and that at the level of the body alone: sex without love, as it were.

More remarkable than his treatment of the mistress as recipient or subject-matter of the sonnets is Shakespeare's treatment of the man who fills that role in the first 126 poems. Victorian editors, embarrassed by the imputation of homosexuality, argued that it was quite customary in the Renaissance for men to write sonnets to men. While we know of certain special cases (the sonnets of Michelangelo to Tommaso Cavalieri, for instance[2]), it is now clear that this was not at all customary, and that the imputation of homosexuality in the Renaissance could have as destructive an effect on a man's life as it has had until recently (if, indeed, there has been any real change of English attitudes in these supposedly liberal times). Of course, individual sonnets of compliment to a male friend or patron exist in Renaissance poetry, but, as J. W. Lever wrote, summing up previous researches, 'there is no parallel in the whole corpus of Renaissance poetry to Shakespeare's sustained exploration of the theme of friendship through more than a hundred and twenty sonnets'.[3] This radical break with tradition had far-reaching effects on the tone and substance of the poetry. These are, to state the obvious again, not homosexual poems. That much is made clear by Shakespeare, early on in the sequence, as if to forestall suspicion or criticism, in Sonnet 20, which his protagonist addresses to the deuteragonist (if I may borrow the terminology of the historians of drama to stress the fictive, dramatic status of the personae in these poems):

> A woman's face with nature's own hand painted
> Hast thou, the master-mistress of my passion;
>
> .   .   .   .
>
> And for a woman wert thou first created, –

Till nature as she wrought thee fell a-doting,
And by addition me of thee defeated,
By adding one thing to my purpose nothing.
  But since she prick'd thee out for women's pleasure,
  Mine be thy love and thy love's use their treasure.[4]

That is as clear a statement of the non-sexual relationship between the two personae as could be wished for, and a wittier one than most. Whereas the sonnets to the mistress express sex without love, those to the friend express love without sex.

That opposition is a neat one, and neatness in verbal formulations commonly arouses suspicion. Yet one of the striking characteristics of Shakespeare's *Sonnets* is that they exist on an almost universal level; they are generalized (with none of the depersonalization that usually goes with generalization); they are widely, perhaps indefinitely applicable. Here again Shakespeare challenges the Renaissance concept of the sonnet's content and function. While the norm was in effect a type of seduction poem, in which sexual love is frustrated and unrealized, Shakespeare drops that whole area of human behaviour yet shows that love-poetry is still possible – only a new kind of love. The 'Poet' cannot marry the 'Friend' (to use the conventional terms for our two personae), does not wish to seduce him: in the first seventeen sonnets he urges him to marry, indeed, but not (as elsewhere) choosing the writer of the poetry, but someone else, a woman (obviously!). And whereas other Renaissance examples of the exhortation to marriage dwell on the delight and solace of the married state, our poet's argument, by contrast, is directed to the friend's reproduction of himself for the benefit of posterity. (The woman is noticeable by her minimal status as co-agent of reproduction.) That is, the poet is concerned solely with the existence and perpetuation of the friend, is writing a peculiarly *selfless* form of love-poetry – 'peculiar', I mean, by comparison with the egoism and self-satisfaction inherent in the usual specimens of this genre. These poems offer, then, not care for the self but care of the other. As C. L. Barber once put it, in an essay remarkable for its sensitivity to the kinds of human relationship postulated or implied by the poems,

> the love expressed for the friend *is* love, a most important kind of love which is ordinarily part of a relationship but here becomes the whole and is expressed with an unparalleled fullness and intensity. It is love by *identification* rather than sexual possession. Such cherishing love is a leading part of full sexual love between men and women. And it is central in other relations of life, notably between parents and children.[5]

As Barber says, the 'universality of the part of love which here becomes the whole' makes these poems available to all readers. To report on my own experience, I have found a surprising number of English people outside the academic world who have lived with the *Sonnets*, have taken them into their own experience, can quote with ease 'To me, fair friend, you never can be old', or 'Shall I compare thee to a summer's day?', or 'When, in disgrace with Fortune and men's eyes', or 'Let me not to the marriage of true minds/Admit impediment'. C. S. Lewis noted the same phenomenon, writing of Sonnets 25 and 29 that they are

> poems that any man can walk into and make his own. And those must be few and fortunate who cannot do the same with 33 ('Full many a glorious morning have I seen') and 34 ('Why didst thou promise such a beauteous day').[6]

These poems are not only read but used, applied to individual lives.

It is at this stage that the specific aspect of the *Sonnets* which I wish to explore begins to emerge. These are generalized, universalized poems, which deal with love-situations in a way that transcends the limitations of poetry written to a special occasion or with a specific individual in mind. They are like blank cheques, or Christmas cards: the sender, or the receiver, can fill in the amount, or the name, just as he or she wishes. This is because they are fundamentally 'you and me' poems, and any *You* or any *Me* can be substituted for the personae. To make that point in another way, in terms of tradition, it is striking, when you come to Shakespeare's after a reading of other Renaissance sonnets, to note the absence of proper names. No Laura, no Beatrice, no Hélène, Cassandre, Marie, Stella, Mira, Delia, Licia, Diana, Geraldine, Phillis, not even Idea. True, there is a *Will* in Sonnets 135 and 136, and if the italicization in the 1609 Quarto is significant it can be seen to represent Shakespeare's own name, or that of the Friend, or even the Dark Lady's husband. (And it is in any case a singular unromantic name!) But otherwise the absence of specific characters defined in the third person under-lines the universality and also the particularity of these poems. C. S. Lewis saw this point too: the poems express 'simply love, the quintessential of all loves whether erotic, parental, filial, amicable, or feudal. Thus from extreme particularity there is a road to the highest universality.'[7] The particularity derives, I shall argue, from their being poems imagined for a series of concrete life-situations; in literary-critical terms they are examples of that minimal dramatic form, the monologue.[8] But the particularity, as Shakespeare for-mulates it, also creates intimacy. If a poet writes about 'Stella', what *she* does, what *her* attributes are, by the use of the third-person form he has acknowledged a certain distance separating himself from his beloved. She is going about her business, while he is writing about her to the world, and we are seeing her through his eyes. The relationship with the reader is a direct one, but that with the beloved is indirect. The *I–You* form, on the other hand, although the poetry is clearly written to be read by the public at large, presents the relationship directly, face to face. The beloved is not separate, absent, but present, at the moment of the poet's writing or speaking, as of the beloved's hearing or reading the poem – as, indeed, of the reader's reading, now and always: he or she is always there as we read. We can put ourselves in the place of the poet or the friend; we can be either the sender or the receiver.

My distinction between the effects of second-person and third-person pronouns can be made clearer, perhaps, with some diagrams. In the Sidneian sonnet form the relationship between poet, mistress, and reader is as follows (where a single-ended arrow denotes a one-sided relationship, a double-ended one mutuality):

$$[\text{Poet/Person loving}] \; I \rightarrow She \; [\text{Person loved}]$$
$$\downarrow \qquad \uparrow$$
$$You \; (\text{Reader})$$

In Shakespeare's sonnets to the friend, by contrast, the relationship is on one level only:

[Poet/Person loving and loved] *I↔Thou/You* [Reader/Person loved and loving]

That is, the reader is absorbed into the experience, does not stand outside it. In the sonnets involving the Dark Lady, however, with their tortuous triangular structure, the reader does stand apart, watching the poet's attempt to come to terms with deception and exclusion:

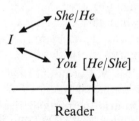

We can distinguish, then, between those Shakespeare sonnets addressing the recipient directly, in which writer and addressee form the couple defining a relationship, and poems addressing a recipient who is engaged in a triadic – or perhaps, better said, two dyadic relationships. The effect of this intense focus on modes of address is that personal pronouns become unusually prominent. I had often noted this characteristic in reading, but until I once calculated the extent to which the *Sonnets* depend on pronouns I had no idea of its magnitude. This is a case in which one turns to computation in order to verify an impression gained in reading, and in the Appendix (pp. 85–8) I have recorded the results of my count. Statistics alone are of little use in literary criticism, and I present the table more as a finding-list than anything else. By using it one can locate, for instance, the sonnets in which the *I* dominates, or those where the *You* overpowers the *I*. From that point onwards analysis and interpretation must take over. Yet a mere glance at the list will reveal the predominance of the *I* form (960 times in my count, taking all first-person forms: *I/me/my/myself/mine*) and the *You* or *Thou* form (890 times, including *thou/thee/thy/thine/thyself; you/ye/your/yours/yourself*), over the third-person forms, where these imply either a third-person account of the beloved (*He* in Sonnets 1–126: 51 times; *She* in Sonnets 127–52: 31 times) or a reference to some third party with whom the poet or his beloved is having a relationship (*She* in Sonnets 1–126: 11 instances; *He* in Sonnets 127–52: 22 instances; total 33). Extremely small are the figures for *We/Us/Our*, where this refers to an aspect of experience shared by the poet and his friend (Sonnets 1–126: 10 times) or mistress (Sonnets 127–52: twice); also the plural *You* or *Ye* (once only) and the plural *They* (twice). In other words, the *I* and *Thou* forms predominate over all other personal pronouns by a factor of more than 13 to 1. The statistics confirm what a detailed reading will tell us, that the majority of the *Sonnets* move with astonishing frequency on the axis from *I* to *You* and back again. They enact a transaction, one that is constantly being made, broken, and remade, coming under doubt and suspicion, collapsing with proof of infidelity or betrayal by either side, being slowly rebuilt as doubt gives way to confirmation. The phases of the relationship are reflected in the constellation of the pronouns – or rather, they are *created by* the pronouns. Critics vie with each other in discovering the dominant qualities of the *Sonnets:* one chooses imagery, another stresses repetition, or symmetry, or antithesis. But the truly dominant, characterizing feature is the use of pronouns and the movement between them: take those away and you destroy the relationship out of which the poems derive.

Discussion of Shakespeare's use of pronouns has been, so far, largely focused on the plays, in particular on the distinction within the second-person form between singular and plural, *Thou* and *You*. There are scattered remarks on this topic in the standard reference books on Shakespeare's grammar, an early American dissertation, and several articles of greater or lesser linguistic expertise.[9] To anyone familiar with the conventions of the second-person singular in modern European languages it is no surprise to learn that Shakespeare preserves the distinction *You/Thou* primarily to express the relationship far/near, as when a parent addresses a child (or a master a servant) as *Thou* and receives *You* in reply. These have been called the pronouns of power and solidarity respectively.[10] More interesting is the discovery that while *You* is the stylistically unmarked form, more matter-of-fact, 'not impolite' or 'not informal', *Thou* can express both intimacy and anger, or indeed any increase in the emotional tone of a conversation. We find scenes in which two characters on an equal footing move back and forth between *Thou* and *You* according to mood (Hal and Falstaff); others where both characters use *Thou,* one expressing affection, the other hostility (Richard III wooing Lady Anne); others where the shift from *You* to *Thou* expresses a crucial shift of intimacy (Goneril to Edmund) or acceptance (Brabantio to Roderigo).[11] The critic of the plays must pay attention to register, those variations in language

46

as used in particular social contexts, but also to rises and falls in the emotional temperature within a scene. Neither of these approaches is relevant to the *Sonnets*, obviously enough, but a third certainly is, namely the question of euphony, the difference between 'Do you think that they are threatening?' and 'Thinkst thou that they threaten?' As Vivian Salmon has shown, awkwardness in pronunciation, 'where the -*st* suffix of the *Thou*-form stood in close proximity to consonants whose assimilation was difficult, or would have resulted in syntactic ambiguity', led to a preference for the *You* form or for one retaining *Thou* but adding an unstressed *do*, as in 'What didst thou lose?' or 'It was ourself thou didst abuse'.[12]

The question of variations between *Thou* and *You* in the *Sonnets* has been discussed rather fruitlessly. Just as characters in the plays switch from *Thou* to *You* and back in a way that seems to us to have no evident rationale, so in the *Sonnets* Shakespeare uses both forms indifferently, and indeed switches from one to the other within one poem (Sonnet 24). Attempts have been made to distinguish the two forms by close reading of 'groups' or 'sequences' within the collection, but such attempts either to arrange the order of the 1609 Quarto into some new scheme, or to read a consistent development within it are equally misguided. It is not a coherent and steadily developing sequence but a collection of poems, including variations on themes which result in both repetitions and overlapping. Attempting to distinguish the two forms, Frances Berry arrived at the strange result that *Thou* in the *Sonnets* is 'remote' and 'betokens distant admiration', while *You* is 'more intimate'.[13] Andrew Gurr claimed to detect 'a rather remarkable pattern of shifts between "you" and "thou"', only to admit that the 'sequence' as a whole showed 'a remarkable display of inconsistency' and so concentrated on Sonnets 1–17. There he found a whole drama of 'switches' and changes, 'the first open declaration of a real intimacy' coming in Sonnet 13, with 'the humble poet' thereafter oscillating between *Thou* and *You* according to how things stood between him and his 'wealthy aristocrat'. By this close reading Gurr could claim that 'the phrase "your image" in 59 becomes "thy image" in 61, in a change marking a distinct chill in the relationship'.[14] These changes, switches, and sequences seem to be wholly illusory, caused by misapplying the linguistic criterion of register (not to mention the biographical fallacy). One criterion ignored by both critics is that of euphony, although its relevance to the *Sonnets* has long been clear.[15] Sonnet 13 begins:

> O that you were yourself, but love you are
> No longer yours than you yourself here live.
> Against this coming end you should prepare
> And your sweet semblance to some other give.

Recast this in the second-person singular and we have: 'O that thou werst thyself, but love thou art/No longer thine than thou thyself here livest.' Not only do we have an almost unpronounceable cluster of 'th' sounds but we ruin both rhymes. I can find no other principles for distinguishing *You* and *Thou* in the *Sonnets:* Shakespeare can use either without implying greater or lesser formality.

A more promising approach would be the comparative one, starting from the total distribution of pronouns in Shakespeare compared to other Elizabethan sonnet-writers. So far three critics have attempted this comparison (with varying statistics[16]), but none of them has done justice to the intensity and range of Shakespeare's pronouns. Giorgio Melchiori rightly sees pronouns as 'semiotic pointers' towards a 'network of relations', and notes the far greater proportion of second-person pronouns in Shakespeare (some 37.2 per cent compared to other poets' average of 20 per cent, with 40.3 per cent for the first person). He is the first critic in print to notice the 'balanced predominance of *I* and *thou*' in Shakespeare's *Sonnets*, in the proportion 51.1 per cent to 48.9 per cent.[17] However, he then interprets his statistics in rather dubious socio-literary historical terms,[18] seeing Shakespeare as 'breaking with the tradition of the sonneteer as a court poet or an aristocrat' by involving 'his interlocutors ... in debate' and dialogue. Melchiori then explains the 'balance between *I* and *thou*' reductively, as an instance of Shakespeare's 'dramatic and theatrical' genius: 'it is simply his profession as a playwright, as a man of the theatre' which places him 'on a totally different plane' in the social hierarchy of his time. This argument would deny Shakespeare any powers of invention, making him the creature of his profession, another version of the biographical fallacy. Melchiori in one place actually describes 'the *I*' as being 'the poet who voices his own feelings', and says that the absence of the *I* form in some sonnets 'is an impediment to the dialogue, to the theatrical quality', which he describes in disappointingly literal terms: 'Normally in Shakespeare's Sonnets we find a truly dramatic dialogue between two characters: the *persona* of the poet himself (the speaking I, not the man William Shakespeare)' – a welcome disclaimer! – 'and a 'you', the actor playing the role of a lovely boy, a worthy or unworthy mistress, possibly a rival poet'.[19]

Apart from the irrelevant actor there, it seems worth observing that the sonnets are not in fact dialogues, but either monologues or poems of direct address, and that their dramatic quality is due to a sustained effort of imagination rather than the conditioning of a career.

Melchiori uses statistics in attempting to define the 'norm' of *I–Thou* in Shakespeare and the exceptions, the twenty-one sonnets lacking *I*, and the twenty-five lacking *Thou* or *You* (he also sees no distinction between singular and plural forms). His particular interest, it turns out, is in the 'non-*You* Sonnets', the 'dramatic meditations' of his title, in other words the exception to the norm, to which he dedicates most of his space, studying in detail Sonnets 94, 121, 20, 129, and 146. Both in the exclusion of the *I–Thou* relationship and in the critical method, an uneasy union of formalist grammatical analysis, highly idiosyncratic diagrams, and a belief that his approach is 'scientific' or 'objective' when it rests on a whole series of unargued critical assumptions,[20] this remains a learned but peripheral book. David K. Weiser has been more consistently involved with the central *I – Thou* poems, although his analytical categories are derived from Martin Buber's essay on modern theology, 'I and Thou' (p. 107), rather than from Renaissance grammar. The absence of second-person pronouns may make a poem a 'soliloquy', but their presence in poems does not make them 'dialogues'.[21] Poems may be addressed to someone but, lacking a respondent, a lyric or sonnet remains, as Donne called one of his poems, 'this dialogue of one'.[22] Weiser divides the 112 sonnets using *I* and *Thou* into four groups: those using the pronouns infrequently, without the sense of a personal relationship, amount only to four poems. Second, those emphasizing *Thou* more than *I*, a larger group, sixteen in all, in thirteen of which the Other outnumbers the Self by more than two to one. Third, the opposed relationship, *I* dominating in twenty-seven sonnets, in nineteen of which by a ratio of at least two to one. Last, those balancing the two pronouns 'quantitatively while developing a reciprocal relation between them', the largest group, consisting of 'more than one third of all the sonnets: 57 of 154'.[23]

Weiser is the first critic to see the full significance of the pronouns in the *Sonnets*, and every reader will benefit from many pages of sensitive criticism in his book. Where I differ from him is on the nature of the collection as a whole, which to me seems a collection of poems differing in method and indeed quality, written over a period of years,[24] and having two distinct sequences, to the Friend and to the 'Dark Lady'. Beyond that I believe we cannot go, although there are occasionally tantalizing groups of poems on related themes, either brought together by the editor/printer or composed as deliberate variations on a theme, and perhaps copied out on a 'sheet' of paper, folio size, folded (which we know was a unit of composition and occasionally payment in Elizabethan poetry and drama). Weiser, however, claims to find 'a well-defined dramatic character' as speaker of the poems, with the arrangement of the 1609 Quarto reflecting 'a steady pattern of growth and final disintegration in the speaker's personality'. There is one sonnet sequence with such a coherent persona, of course: Sidney's *Astrophil and Stella*. But that is truly a narrative, including a series of songs that advance the action in definite stages before it collapses in the lover's rejection by his (married) mistress. All the stages that Weiser finds of 'advance in personal knowledge', a 'basic transition' here, a 'discovery' there, one which 'begins to dissolve' the speaker's 'coherent identity' (a development which the sceptic may see as a rationale for the failure of an analytical method) – stages of awareness that lead to a final collapse:[25] all this seems to me fictitious, revealing the critic's categories rather than the poet's. Similarly, when G. P. Jones moves from noting the greater prominence of pronouns in Shakespeare compared with other Elizabethans to the statement that his sonnets have 'a substantial autobiographical element', and that the 'fluctuation between *thou*

and *you*' shows 'the poet's uncertainty about his personal, social and professional connection with his patron is at its most acute',[26] then I feel that such
speculations deflect attention from the real focus of interest, the pronouns as
forms of relationship.

My own approach is not biographical, and assumes neither a clear-cut
persona nor a narrative sequence. Since the *Sonnets* are, in an important and
unique way, poems of direct address, we should start by considering them in
terms of the appropriate Renaissance genre. The literary form that they most
nearly resemble, or the situation in life that they come nearest to recreating,
is that of a letter. Each poem is a verse-epistle, as it were, and together they
consitute a whole collection of correspondence. Looking at them in this light
it is natural to turn to that Elizabethan model for letter-writing, Angel Day's
The English Secretorie (1586).[27] There we read the following definition:

> A letter therefore is that wherein is expreslye conveid in writing, the intent
> and meaning of one man, immediately to passe and be directed to another,
> and for the certaine respects thereof, is termed the messenger and familiar
> speeche of the absent.

Subsequently Day repeats this concept in terms that seem especially relevant
to the quiet tone and intimate atmosphere of the *Sonnets*. A letter is 'the
familiar and mutuall talke of one absent friend to another' (a definition taken
from Erasmus, who took it from Libanius), and ought therefore to be 'simple,
plaine, and of the lowest and meanest stile, utterly devoyde of anye shadowe
of hie and loftye speeches'. Day divides epistles into the categories 'general',
which are 'familiar letters' passing between people of 'long acquaintance or
auntient familiarity'; and 'speciall', which 'do admit both higher stile and
more orderlye deliverance', since they bear 'a resolute purpose and intend-
ment seriously to discourse, aunswere, implye or avoyde, any certain matter
or causes, importing the present affaires whereupon the direction is framed'.

In this second category we might place the first seventeen sonnets, with
their persuasion to marriage, a sequence that may in fact draw some of its
arguments and images from a model epistle, Erasmus's *Encomium Matri-
monii,* Englished by Sir Thomas Wilson as *An Epistle to perswade a yong
Gentleman to mariage, devised by Erasmus, in the behalfe of his freend.*[28] Angel
Day transposed the exercise for the opposite sex in *An Epistle Swasorie,
wherein a Gentlewoman is councelled to mariage.* These are clearly more formal
models than those which the modern letter-writer is used to, yet Shakespeare's
range stretches from the intimate and occasional to just such formal rhetorical
structures as Day's category of the 'Epistle Deliberative', which uses a mixture
of praise and criticism in its 'Hortatory' or 'Dehortatory' intent, and may
legitimately subject the recipient to moral pressure:

Likewise, if the state of the party do serve there unto, it shal not be amisse to put him in mind of his parentage, fortune, virtue, nobilitie, witte, towardnes of great expectation, and of all sorts generally well reputed, his discretion, abilitie, age, and conceipt.

Yet, while acknowledging the relevance of Day's treatise on letter-writing and its tactics of persuasion, we may note that in Shakespeare one of Day's categories is absent, namely the 'Responsory Epistle', which 'dependeth of the partes of a former letter' and must refer back to it.[29] The poet receives no replies: the *Sonnets* are one-half of a correspondence, as they represent one-half of a relationship. This one-way traffic gives them their uniqueness but also a certain poignant quality: the *I* is always striving towards the *Thou* or *You*, but the second person never replies.

Since so much emphasis falls on the pronouns, it seems to me natural to turn next to the basic grounding of education and humanity in the Renaissance, the *trivium* (grammar, logic, rhetoric) and to ask what these grammatical categories meant in Shakespeare's time, and what they mean today, so joining the history of grammar – a subject whose importance to the study of literature is seldom realized[30] – to modern linguistics. If we turn first to the best-known Tudor textbook, the so-called 'Royal Grammar' originally produced by Lily and Colet for St Paul's School, but becoming virtually ubiquitous after a proclamation by Edward VI in 1548 ordering its use in all grammar schools[31] – it was undoubtedly used by Shakespeare – we find that a pronoun is said to be 'a parte of speeche, much lyke to a noune, whyche is used in shewyng or rehersyng'. That is, pronouns which 'shew' are called 'Demonstratives, because they shew a thynge not spoken of before', while those that 'rehearse' are called 'relatives', because they relate or refer back to something already mentioned[32] – we would call them antecedents. Further, 'A pronoune hath thre persons':

The fyrst person speaketh of hym self: as *Ego*, I: *nos*, we. The second person is spoken to: as *Tu*, thou: *vos, ye*.
   And of this person is also every vocative case. The thirde person is spoken of: as *Ille*, he: *illi*, they. And therefore all nounes, pronounes, and participles be of the thirde person. (Sig. Bii r)

These are the traditional grammatical definitions of the pronoun, as first made by Dionysius Thrax in the second century BC, and systematized further by Priscian (*c.* AD 500), whose account Lily is quoting word for word.[33] Later English theorists of grammar bring out more clearly the implications of 'shewing' and 'rehearsing', distinguishing which of the pronoun's functions are substitutive ('rehearsing') and which not. As Ian Michael puts it in his admirable history of English grammar,

A speaker does not use the word *I* as a substitute for his own name; still less does he use *You* as a substitute for the name of the person he is addressing. In normal, unemphatic, face-to-face conversation the speaker will use *You* even when he knows the name of the person he is speaking to.

This function of pronouns, as John Wilkins saw in 1668, is to 'represent things ... *Immediately* and in kind, without respect to the names of those things'.[34] The *I* will 'represent to our thoughts the person speaking' without any loss of immediacy, or any deflection of address. What takes place between the *I* and the *You* is a human transaction which can also be thought of in terms of gesture. James Harris, writing in 1751, saw that 'all Conversation passes between *Particulars* or *Individuals*', and argued that when, at the formative stages of human language, a speaker met another whose name he did not know he addressed him by using 'δειχις, that is, *Pointing*, or *Indication by the Finger or Hand*, some traces of which are still to be observed as a part of that Action which naturally attends our speaking'. To point to myself I use the pronoun *I*, to point to '*the Party addrest*' I use *Thou*. Harris perceived that the *I–Thou* relationship is represented perfectly adequately by

> *a single Pronoun* to each person. ... But it is not so with respect to the *Third* Person. The various relations of the various Objects exhibited by this (I mean relations of near and distant, present and absent, same and different, definite and indefinite, &c.) made it necessary that there should not be one, but *many* Pronouns, such as *He, This, That, Other, Any, Some,* &c.[35]

By frequently limiting his scope to *I* and *Thou* Shakespeare is creating an interpersonal field which is so restricted that thoughts, ideas, feelings move back and forth between sender and receiver without the need for any other delimitation or definition. The rest of the world is excluded: these two are all that matter. The function of the pronoun, then, is neither to name nor to act as a substitute for a noun. As Michael says, these two main discoveries by English grammarians were both negative.[36] It seems to me, if a literary critic may be allowed a comment on these linguistic matters, that the function of the first– and second–person pronouns is rather to relate two people, to set up a plane of relationship which includes them and excludes all others. The pronouns do not 'stand for a noun', nor indeed for anything else, but map out paths of communication between human beings, transactions.

Yet, as we have seen by reference to epistolary theory in the Renaissance, the *Sonnets* are *I* utterances which receive no replies. To complete this brief survey of the linguistic status of the pronoun we need an account of its function that will do justice to the first-person perspective. For this purpose I draw on a wide-ranging survey by John Lyons, which carries on naturally from the analysis by James Harris that I have just quoted. Lyons writes,

> Every language-utterance is made in a particular place and at a particular

time. ... It is made by a particular person (the speaker) and is usually addressed to some other person (the hearer). ... The typical utterance includes a reference to some object or person, which may or may not be distinct from the speaker and hearer.

Lyons calls this 'the subject of discourse'.[37] In Shakespeare's *Sonnets*, we could say, the 'subject of discourse' is largely the speaker and hearer themselves; thus the field of discourse is identical with the two people constituting the language-utterance. The personal pronouns, according to Lyons, form part of 'the "deictic co-ordinates" of the typical situation of utterance'; that is, they help to define (along with such adverbs of place and time as *here, there, now, then*) the spatio-temporal location of the act of communication. Thus:

> The typical situation of utterance is *egocentric:* as the role of speaker is transferred from one participant to another in a conversation, so the 'centre' of the deictic system switches ... . The speaker is always at the centre, as it were, of the situation of utterance.[38]

Since the centre of the deictic system switches, personal pronouns are known as 'shifters', which 'means that they have a double structure, uniting conventional and existential bonds within the same sign'.[39] That is, the linguistic categories anchor communication in the real world and in the relationship between speaker and hearer/reader. As Lyons says, the grammatical 'category of *proximity* is typically determined in relation to the category of person. ... Both *this* and *here* are to be interpreted as "proximate" with respect to the speaker.' The speaker evaluates time, distance, and person from his own point of view. But of course he does not stand alone. Our two personae may have the roles of speaker and hearer, yet they 'may also stand in a certain linguistically-relevant relationship of *status* vis-à-vis one another (parent: child, master:servant, teacher:pupil, etc.).'[40] These status relations can interact with, reinforce, or undermine the speaker–hearer relationship. In the *Sonnets*, clearly, the speaker is sometimes placed in a respectful relationship, the disinterested friend advising a brilliant young man to marry; at other times he is an equal, celebrating a friendship or reproaching its betrayal; but he is never the superior.

I have described the difference between the *sonnets* of Shakespeare and those of Sidney, say, as being that between first-to-second person and first-to-third person poetry. My diagnosis of the increased gap between the participants implied by the Sidneian constellation is strengthened by Lyons's argument that 'whereas first and second person are the positive members of the category of person, third person is essentially a negative notion', because 'it does not necessarily refer to participants in the situation of utterance'. To me 'positive'/'negative' seemed too sharp a distinction, for which I should have preferred the category 'included'/'excluded'. Happily Lyons himself subsequently used the more moderate opposition in making the important suggestion

that 'first' (*ego*) and 'second' (*tu*) are not of equal status in the category of person: that the primary distinction is between 'first' (+*ego*: 'plus ego') and 'not-first' (−*ego*: 'minus ego') and that the distinction of 'second' and 'third' is secondary. If this is so, the correct syntactic analysis of the traditional singular pronouns of English in terms of their component deictic features would be as follows: *I* = [+*ego*]; *you* (singular) = [−*ego*, +*tu*]; *he, she, it* = [−*ego*, −*tu*].[41]

That formulation makes an interesting link between linguistics and phenomenology which more knowledgeable readers might care to pursue. For the moment it is enough to underline the relevance of this suggestion to the *Sonnets*, the whole experience of which is presented from the point of view of *ego* alone, from which perspective the third person is indeed a sign of a double absence, both of the *I* and the *Thou*. But Shakespeare is capable of more complex patterns. What if the *Thou* has gone over to the *She*: are the two then at the same level of estrangement from the *I*? And if the *I* joins the *She*, how will the *Thou* see it? This would be the appropriate point to call in some modern philosophers who have discussed these issues, and an excursus into the work of Edmund Husserl, Max Scheler, Alfred Schutz, Georg Simmel, and others would be of undoubted value. Suffice to suggest that the *ego*-experienced world of the *Sonnets*, despite the enormous time devoted to the *Thou*, creates what is essentially a single vision, a self-dedication to the other, which in effect results in an exposure and analysis, not only of the other but also of the self. One thing we experience in reading these poems is the many ways one human being can care about another.

Not all the personal pronouns in the *Sonnets*, of course, are significant of personal relationships, and for this reason it is not enough just to tot up the figures in a computer-made concordance.[42] *He* and *She* can refer to the third party in either of the triangular relationships, but in Sonnet 2 *He* refers to the Friend's future child, while in 3 *She* refers to the Friend's mother; in 50 and 51 *He* refers to the poet's horse! Both pronouns can be used to refer to 'a man' or 'a woman' in the abstract (e.g. Sonnets 3, 21, 32, 38, 41) and *They* can also refer to 'men, women, the world' (e.g. Sonnets 20, 25, 69, 121, 123, 124, 125). Similarly *We, Us, Our* can refer to the protagonists in the poems but it can also describe the opinions or reactions of mankind at large (59, 60, 116, 118). *Thou* or *You* forms are frequently used to address personifications, at which point the Friend or Mistress often slips into the third person, as part of an imagined triangle. Such are the sonnets which include addresses to Nature (11, 20, 67, 126), Time (12, 15, 19, 123, 126), Love (1, 137, 148), the Sun (7, 18), Night (27), Day (28), the Soul (146), or the Muse (100, 101).

In some poems the poet addresses parts of his body in the third person, the eyes or the mind (24, 113, 114), or his 'flesh' (151).

Some sonnets contain no pronouns at all; others do not refer to the poet's relationship with either party. But the absence of pronouns is not in itself proof of the absence of a relationship. In Sonnet 5, for example, when we read 'Those hours that with gentle work did frame/The lovely gaze where every eye doth dwell' we take the second line as meaning 'Thy lovely gaze' (similarly with 137, to the Mistress). Equally, the presence of a pronoun does not prove a relationship. Thus while we could take 123 as being about the Poet's constancy to his Friend, even though we have neither *Thou* nor *He* form referring to the Friend ('No, Time, thou shalt not boast that I do change/ ... I will be true despite thy scythe and thee'), in Sonnet 116 the Friend seems to have receded into the background while the poet stands up for all men;

> Let me not to the marriage of true minds
> Admit impediment: love is not love
> Which alters when it alteration finds,
> Or bends with the remover to remove ...
> Love's not Time's fool ...
> Love alters not ...
> > If this be error and upon me prov'd,
> > I never writ, nor no man ever lov'd.

Although the poet's love is included in the affirmation, I would agree with Ingram and Redpath in seeing the poem rather as 'a meditative attempt to define perfect love'.[43]

This said, the number of sonnets which are not specifically about a human relationship is remarkably small. The single philosophic-religious poem is 146:

> Poor soul, the centre of my sinful earth
>
> . . . .
>
> Why dost thou pine within and suffer dearth,
> Painting thy outward walls so costly gay?

While we can easily relate this sonnet to the meditative tradition, or to Stoic-Christian mortification patterns, it is an outsider in the *Sonnets*, which are otherwise a collection of love-poems. This poem is not even a palinode to love. The three other sonnets which present no personal relationships are all generalizations about love. They are 56: 'Sweet love, renew thy force; be it not said/Thy edge should blunter be than appetite' which expresses a feeling of temporarily spent force. It clearly might apply to the poet's relationship, but it is not specifically said to.

From love's satiety we move to an indifference to feeling: 'They that have power to hurt and will do none'. This is Sonnet 94, 'which at no point addresses the Friend directly, stands back from the group much as a con-templative soliloquy does from the dialogue of a play'.[44] However, its cal-culatedly oblique and enigmatic avoiding of a direct statement – a withholding made all the more tantalizing in that it includes no less than eighteen declara-tive verb forms – could have a remarkably powerful effect if we imagine it being read by the person whose unnatural behaviour it describes. 'How smart a lash that speech doth give my conscience!' he might say, with Claudius (*Hamlet*, II.i.150). An equally studied absence of *deixis* is sustained in the exceptionally rhetorically structured[45] Sonnet 129: 'The expense of spirit in a waste of shame/Is lust in action'. Of course, this could apply to the Mistress or to the poet, but in its absence of relationship it stands apart, as do the other sonnets of this type, as general observations on phases of human love, common at certain times to all men and women.

This group is the exception, and a very small one, for the *Sonnets* otherwise express personal relationships in a highly concrete manner. The sequence to the mistress is explicit in its various phases of relationship, Shakespeare making almost all possible permutations on *I/Thou/She/He/You*. Yet while we make this point we must immediately see that these pronouns do not characterize the relationship. The pronouns relate people, create a path of feeling, and vary as that feeling varies. Since the pronouns are used to express a human encounter they derive their nature and value from the human beings, and not vice versa. In the group to the mistress, as every reader has seen, the feelings expressed are bitter, cynical, degraded; so the pronouns suffer the same change. At times the degradation is not serious, more a quizzical down-valuing of the woman by comparison with conventional norms of 'fair' beauty (127, 130). But elsewhere she is seen to be 'black' in more than one sense. This might be in a direct indictment, as at the end of 147, where after twelve lines describing the poet's state of fever and madness ('frantic-mad with evermore unrest'), the couplet finally reveals the cause of his derangement: 'For *I* have sworn *thee* fair, and thought *thee* bright,/Who art as black as hell, as dark as night.' Or it might be by indirection, as in 131 with its apologia: 'In nothing art *thou* black save in *thy* deeds.' The linguistic form there appears to excuse but in fact indicts her, a rhetorical device found also in the sonnets to the Friend.[46]

But elsewhere the poet prefers direct attack, as in 152:

> In loving *thee thou* know'st *I* am forsworn;
> But *thou* art twice forsworn to *me* love swearing,
> In act *thy* bed-vow broke, and new faith torn
> In vowing new hate after new love bearing.

Obscure though the details may be (have both the Poet and the Mistress broken their marriage-vows? is the Friend implicated?), the man certainly vaunts over the woman. But his superiority is short-lived, for the next line shows a recoil against the self:

But why of two oaths' breach do *I* accuse *thee*,
When *I* break twenty? *I* am perjur'd most:
For all *my* vows are oaths but to misuse *thee*,
And all *my* honest faith in *thee* is lost.
For *I* have sworn deep oaths of *thy* deep kindness –
Oaths of *thy* love, *thy* truth, *thy* constancy;
And to enlighten *thee* gave eyes to blindness,
Or made them swear against the thing they see:
    For *I* have sworn *thee* fair, – more perjur'd eye,
    To swear against the truth so foul a lie!

In the penultimate line Shakespeare achieves a fine double effect, the spelling 'eye' linking up with the 'eyes' (*his* eyes, be it noted) in the preceding lines, while the heard sense, 'more perjur'd I' looks back to 'I am perjur'd most'. The final insult is that he has not only forfeited his 'honest faith' in taking up with her but that his eyes have even deceived him about her beauty: she is 'foul' in every sense. Thus we note that the recoil against the *I* in the second quatrain was merely a ploy, resulting in an even more bitter attack on the *Thou*.

In many of these sonnets the poet accuses himself of a gross failure in judgement in having formed a relationship with this woman. The opening of Sonnet 148 again criticizes his own powers of sight and discrimination:

    Oh me! what eyes hath love put in my head,
    Which have no correspondence with true sight?
    Or if they have, where is my judgment fled,
    That censures falsely what they see aright?

It is not only a failure in perception: as we have seen in 152, the eyes were merely agents or instruments of the will or judgement, from which self-deception flowed, forcing the organs of perception to see what they are told to see (as in the political conformity enforced in George Orwell's *Nineteen Eighty-Four*). In that bitter paradox, he has given 'eyes to blindness', made his eyes 'swear against the thing they see'; similarly here, his judgement 'censures falsely' what his eyes 'see aright'. The conceits point to a monstrous self-perversion, the forfeiting of integrity and the living out of a lie at which, moreover, his mind or heart knowingly connives. Not only does he connive, she does so too, as in that most disturbing poem, 138, where the second-person form is strikingly absent. The mistress is seen here in Sidneian terms, from without, her motives wholly opaque, with no access to her feelings. The poet's relationship with her is what a judge would call an 'intimate' one but quite lacking in openness, trust, or love.

    When *my love* swears that *she* is made of truth
    I do believe *her*, though *I* know *she* lies,
    That *she* might think *me* some untutor'd youth

Unlearn'd in the world's false subtleties.
Thus vainly thinking that *she* thinks *me* young,
Although *she* knows *my* days are past the best,
Simply *I* credit *her* false-speaking tongue:
On *both sides* thus is simple truth suppress'd.
But wherefore says *she* not *she* is unjust?
And wherefore say not *I* that *I* am old?
Oh, love's best habit is in seeming trust,
And age in love loves not to have years told.
      Therefore *I* lie with *her*, and *she* with *me*,
      And in *our* faults by lies *we* flatter'd be.

Italicizing the pronouns may help to indicate the remarkable symmetry of the poem, if we read it as three quatrains and a couplet: each pronoun balances the other in frequency, as each person matches the other in self-deception and deception of the other. It is a peculiarly appropriate irony that this should be the only poem in this group with the *Our/We* form, establishing on the grammatical plane a congruence with the semantic one: seen from the outside, held up for inspection, they are united – at the level of mutual deception.

Several of these poems express doubts about the Mistress's 'truth', that is, both honesty and chastity. He lies *with* her, as he lies *to* her, and she with and to him. The logical development of this suspicion is the series of sonnets presenting a triangular relationship. (Critics assume that the other man involved is the same man to whom Sonnets 1–126 have been addressed; and some also assume that the three people involved in this series (133, 134, 135, 143, 144) are the same three involved in the earlier series (41, 42). Although 133 refers to 'my friend', I see no way of settling this issue in either direction; but I do see the danger inherent in treating both groups as autobiographical.) These are evidently not the greatest sonnets by any criteria, but they are both ingenious and fleet. That is, if one were to attempt to visualize the three personae involved in terms of a novel or play one would need pages to describe the kinds of interchange that Shakespeare renders in a quatrain:

Me from *myself thy* cruel eye hath taken,
And *my* next *self thou* harder hast engross'd:
Of *him, my self,* and *thee I* am forsaken, –
A torment thrice threefold, thus to be cross'd.

(133. 5–8)

'Thrice threefold', too, are the number of lines taken up by editors trying to pin down the multiple shifts of identity which take place in these four lines. This shuttling back and forth between the personae could only be done so adroitly by a poet exceptionally sensitive to the status and function of pronouns. The sheer density of appearance of the three pronouns in this group is impressive (see Appendix), as is their distribution. They represent a triangle of forces, in which the movement of any one point affects the other two. Their frequency results from Shakespeare's imaginative involvement with the relationship that they mediate.

Sonnet 143 begins with a leisurely analogy involving a housewife putting her child down in order to pursue a runaway chicken. In the same way, the Poet tells his Mistress,

> So runn'st *thou* after that which flies from *thee*,
> Whilst *I thy babe* chase *thee* afar behind;-
> But if *thou* catch *thy* hope, turn back to *me*
> And play the mother's part, – kiss *me*, be kind:
> > So will *I* pray that *thou* mayst have *thy Will*,
> > If *thou* turn back and *my* loud crying still.

There, curiously enough, although the Mistress is pursuing the Friend, the Poet is pursuing the Mistress, not the Friend; he wants to be kissed and consoled by her. One could also argue that the Poet is using the Mistress as bait to induce the Friend to remain: this three-way relationship is as complex as that in Sartre's *Huis clos* (two women, one man) and in some ways equally claustrophobic and degrading. In the sonnet just quoted, for instance, Shakespeare presents the Poet in a humiliating situation, indifferent to the behaviour of the Mistress with other men just so long as he gets some share of the action.

In 144 the situation is even more degraded. The poem is egocentric both in the strictly linguistic sense in which John Lyons uses the word and in its normal sense. The speaker sees the world from his own perspective, praises his man friend and does his best to damn the woman:

> Two loves *I* have, of comfort and despair,
> Which like two spirits do suggest *me* still:
> The better angel is a man right fair,
> The worser spirit a woman colour'd ill.

The emotional tone increases, from this relatively cool opening (although 'suggest' has the sinister connotation of diabolic temptation) as the poet's indignation at the woman grows ('my female evil/Tempteth ... would corrupt ... with her foul pride') until he reveals the sexual suspicion which motivates his anger: 'I guess one angel in another's hell'. The allusion to the famous novella in the *Decameron* (3, 10), in which 'to put the devil back in hell' was a euphemism for sexual intercourse by using which a hermit seduced a young novice, is given an application quite the reverse of Boccaccio's warm-hearted celebration of the flesh: 'Yet this shall *I* ne'er know, but live in doubt/Till *my* bad angel fire *my* good one out.' This last line has the overt meaning 'till the woman casts off the man', but in fact it is far more savage. As Ingram and Redpath note, '"Fire out" was common usage for "infect with a venereal disease" ', so the line means that 'the poet will not know whether the Friend has slept with the woman until he sees whether he has contracted venereal disease'.[47] This is a sentiment worthy of Juvenal, or some Restoration satirist (indeed the deliberate transmission of the pox was known as a form of revenge in the court of Charles II). But whereas those satirists recreated a context with omniscience in such a way as to justify their final attack, the poet here can give us no such context. He is merely expressing a suspicion, and in a sense a hope ('when *she* has given *him* the clap, then *he*'ll come back to *me*', to modernize it somewhat). The appallingly self-centred nature of this conclusion can only rebound against the man who has uttered it, and Shakespeare was too sensitive a poet and human being to be blind to such a reader reaction. The revenge of the self on the others here (for assuredly the Friend will not enjoy the experience either) acts to lower the self to their level, or even beneath it.

It is sometimes a relief to leave the sonnets to the Mistress. We admire their brilliance of language and psychology, but we do not necessarily like them. This is not to say that only poetry with 'positive attitudes to life' is acceptable, since anyone who has thought about the representation of evil in literature, whether in satire or tragedy or in the novel, will know that an apparently negative attitude can be in fact profoundly positive. The sonnets to the Mistress, though, do not deal with evil in a profound way; they are often cynical, self-accusing, and self-mocking. Since the Poet indicts himself, we are tempted to reject his artefacts on the same basis, as being either sordid or trivial. The whole series is a tribute to Shakespeare's dramatic imagination, but it does not inspire affection.

The sonnets to the Friend, by contrast, elicit warmth in us by the warmth that they contain. As C. L. Barber has finely said, in these poems 'poetry is, in a special way, an action, something done for and to the beloved.... Many of the sonnets are wonderfully generous poems; they *give* meaning and beauty'[48] The generosity resides in the act of celebration, a process by which the Poet can fade himself out as an actor, reducing himself to the role of recording agent. In Sonnet 17, indeed, he seems quizzically aware that his dedication to panegyric may result in a loss of credibility: 'Who will believe my verse in time to come?'

The point, though, is not that his poetry exceeds the truth but that it fails to keep up with the truth, since it cannot fully express the Friend's merits:

> If it were fill'd with your most high deserts –
> Though yet heaven knows it is but as a tomb
> Which hides your life and shows not half your parts, –
> If I could write the beauty of your eyes,
> And in fresh numbers number all your graces,

> The age to come would say: 'This poet lies;
> Such heavenly touches ne'er touch'd earthly faces.'

No one was ever taken in by Shakespeare's disclaimers of ability,[49] and few people will imagine that, whoever the Friend was – if indeed there was a real-life Friend – Shakespeare has failed to do justice to him; if anything, rather the opposite.

But the celebration of the Friend, which sometimes takes the form of an apparent self-abasement by the Poet, has not been to everyone's liking. Yvor Winters pronounced, in characteristically forthright manner, that

> there is in a large number of the poems an attitude of servile weakness on the part of the poet in the face of the person addressed; the attitude is commonly so marked as to render a sympathetic approach to the subject all but impossible, in spite of any fragmentary brilliance which may be exhibited[50].

Even C. L. Barber found that 'sometimes the activity of the poetry alone makes endurable the passivity of the attitude expressed by the poet'.[51] As I see it, the 'passivity' is in one sense a consequence of the decision to write the sonnets from a man to a man – as Sonnet 20 made clear, no 'activity' is contemplated. But, more important, I believe that celebration of the other and devaluing of the self is one of the oldest, as it is one of the permanent ways by which human beings express love or admiration for each other. 'And John ... preached, saying, There cometh one mightier than I after me, the latchet of whose shoes I am not worthy to stoop down and unloose' (Mark 1:7). In Dante's *Purgatorio* XXVI, 117, Guinicelli points to Arnaut Daniel as 'miglior fabbro', an elevation of the other that Eliot appropriated to indicate his indebtedness to Pound. In acknowledging the greater value of the other one is giving away a part of oneself: that is surely neither servile nor passive, but active generosity.

In the opening sequence the Poet is so concerned with the Friend and his future existence that he seems to write himself out of the picture. Simple statistics are revealing. In Sonnets 1 to 17 the first-person forms appear twenty-five times; if we compute the second-person forms by treating *Thou* and *You* as of equal value they appear 161 times. Of the first seventeen poems those with the maximum possible abnegation of the self (that is, with no *I/me/my* forms at all) number no less than eleven; the first reference by the Poet to himself comes in Sonnet 10. This is poetry to, for, and about the Friend, and the Poet is merely *vox*. Yet despite the enormous preponderance of *Thou* and *You* forms the addressee is under constant criticism. The 'cherishing love' that Barber has spoken of here takes the form of arguing that the Friend should cherish posterity, the world at large, by begetting a child on some anonymous and otherwise unimportant woman! (I sometimes wonder whether there is not an element of satire addressed by Shakespeare against the persona of the poet here, who can argue with such single-mindedness a case that seems the height of egoism in its intention to exploit the other – a woman – merely in order to reproduce itself.) The criticism is at times sharp, and the Friend is indicted of self-love, 'the most inhibited sin in the canon', as the Clown says in *All's Well*, doubtless aware of the seriousness of his words.[52] So this poet attacks his Friend for hoarding his beauty until it will be 'self-kill'd' (6.4). In Sonnet 3 he asks 'who is so fond will be the tomb/Of his self-love to stop posterity?' (Of course, a ridiculous exaggeration: posterity will do fine without him!). The Friend is like a 'profitless usurer' (a violent paradox in the Renaissance, as today): 'For having traffic with *thyself* alone-/*Thou* of *thyself thy* sweet *self* dost deceive' (4.9f). The pronouns seem to turn in on themselves in a solipsist dead-end. The Friend is like the phoenix, yet without the life-giving or self-sacrificing qualities of that mythical creature:

> But *thou* contracted to *thine own* bright eyes,
> Feed'st *thy* light's flame with *self-substantial* fuel,
> Making a famine where abundance lies,
> *Thyself thy* foe, to *thy* sweet *self* too cruel.

(1.5ff.)

Again, 'thou consum'st thy self in single life': for Shakespeare images of self-division were always among the most potent signs of disorder. The pronouns describe a narcissism which is doomed to destroy itself.

But this is to concede the argument of Shakespeare's Poet without further thought. Surely the Friend would be justified in rejecting the case by saying that he was living in the present and that whatever happened in the future, whether he married and had a son or not, would be of doubtful relevance to his own mind or body now. 'What man in the whole world', C. S. Lewis asked, 'except a father or a potential father-in-law, cares whether any other man gets married?' and he partly answered his own question by saying that the 'self-abnegation' and 'anxiety' of the Poet for his Friend's good was 'more like a parent's than a lover's'.[53] The persuasion to marriage, then, is a criticism of the Friend (whose reasons for not marrying may have been honourable or dishonourable), but it tells us something about the Poet. As I have already indicated, I am not sure whether there may perhaps be some mockery of the over-solicitousness of the Poet's desire for this marriage and the begetting of a (boy-)child, as indeed of the appeal to the egoist's desire to perpetuate himself. I see no way of deciding this issue, but it shows again the point made earlier, that the self in dealing with the other defines the other and itself reciprocally and simultaneously. What I want you to have tells you what I value, tells you – and me, perhaps – what kind of a person I am. To write a biography of another can involve one in autobiography.

This first sequence is problematic, even though the generosity seems overwhelming and unquestionably sincere. For the most part the later sonnets of celebration of the Friend impute no such extraordinary motives to the Poet.

One way of getting at the varieties of relationship in these poems is to group them, not too dogmatically, into poems where the *I* dominates, and those where the *Thou* carries more weight. Statistics are not always a reliable guide since, as every reader knows, frequency of utterance is not the same as intensity. Further, if one makes such a rough-and-ready division then one finds that the same categories of relationship occur in both groups. There are poems of celebration of the other where the *I* dominates, and others where the *Thou* does; there are poems of criticism of the Friend in both groups. Yet certain distinctions do emerge, certain patterns of relationship.

For instance, adoration of the Friend without – to give, for the moment, a hostage to Yvor Winters – the Poet abasing himself, but retaining instead his own dignity, is expressed more often in poems where *Thou* forms dominate. It is as if the Poet were concentrating so strongly on giving an adequate image of the Friend that he ceases to think about himself and his own unworthiness by comparison. Such is 53:

> What is your substance, whereof are you made,
> That millions of strange shadows on you tend?
> Since every one hath, every one, one shade,
> And you, but one, can every shadow lend:
> Describe Adonis, and the counterfeit
> Is poorly imitated after you;
> On Helen's cheek all art of beauty set,
> And you in Grecian tires are painted new:
> Speak of the spring and foison of the year, –
> The one doth shadow of your beauty show,
> The other as your bounty doth appear;
> And you in every blessèd shape we know:
>> In all external grace you have some part,
>> But you like none, none you, for constant heart.

The reader will have noticed the complete absence of the first person, as the Poet, fully caught up in his task, existed merely as vehicle for the other's praise. In the sonnet following the *I* appears only in the last line: 'And so of you, beauteous and lovely youth,/When that shall vade, my verse distils your truth.'[54]

In two other sonnets, 77 ('Thy glass will shew thee how thy beauties wear') and 84 ('Who is it that says most which can say more/Than this rich praise, – that you alone are you') the *I* is also totally absent. If we were now to consider the many sonnets of celebration of the Friend where the *Thou* outweighs the *I* we would find a similar dedication to the other without, I feel, any disabling – by modern tastes – self-abnegation. This would be the relationship that we find in 104 ('To me, fair friend, you never can be old') or 106 ('When in the chronicle of wasted time').

Turning now to the poems where the *I* dominates we find some instances of apparent self-abnegation. But they are not all to be interpreted literally: in some the imagery is conventional, in others the self-abasement is ironic. In the sonnets on the Rival Poet, for instance, whether the first or second person dominates, the technique of praising the other poet while denigrating oneself is clearly ironic, as J. W. Lever's discussion has shown. As he says of 80 ('Oh how I faint when I of you do write'), 'the lavish praise of the rival ... serves to destroy this writer's reputation by its very hyperbole'.[55] In this poem, as in 85, the Poet claims that his Muse is 'tongue-tied'; in 76, 102, 103 and 105 he gives conflicting reasons, all ingenious, why he writes such repetitive or uninspired poetry. By the conceit he is making a serious point: his poetry is repetitive because the virtues of the Friend are *semper eadem*. As 105 puts it:

> 'Fair, kind, and true' is all my argument –
> 'Fair, kind, and true' varying to other words;
> And in this change is my invention spent –
> Three themes in one, which wondrous scope affords.

It is hard to miss the wit in such poems, or in the earlier profession of incompetence:

> As an unperfect actor on the stage,
> Who with his fear is put besides his part,
>
> .   .   .   .
>
> So I for fear of trust forget to say
> The perfect ceremony of love's rite.

(23. 1–2, 5–6)

It would be a dull-witted reader who interpreted such poems literally, or who took *au pied de la lettre* such conventional statements of bondage as this:

> Lord of my love, to whom in vassalage
> Thy merit hath my duty strongly knit,
> To thee I send this written ambassage
> To witness duty, not to shew my wit, –
> Duty so great, which wit so poor as mine
> May make seem bare, in wanting words to shew it....

(26)

Self-depreciation (sometimes called 'the modesty topos'[56] has been a rhetorical device since the beginnings of literature and continues in full flourish today.

There is one poem in which the *I* dominates to a remarkable extent and which, since it has been read literally, might seem an exception to my argument, namely 62:

> Sin of self-love possesseth all mine eye,
> And all my soul, and all my every part;
> And for this sin there is no remedy,
> It is so grounded inward in my heart.
> Methinks no face so gracious is as mine,
> No shape so true, no truth of such account,
> And for myself mine own worth do define
> As I all other in all worths surmount.

If one reads only as far as this point, or reads the rest of the poem inattentively, one might indeed take this as an attack by the poet on his own narcissism. But it at once destroys such a reading:

> But when my glass shews me my self indeed,
> Beated and chopp'd with tann'd antiquity,
> Mine own self-love quite contrary I read –
> Self so self-loving were iniquity:
> > 'Tis thee (my self) that for myself I praise,
> > Painting my age with beauty of thy days.

And now it is clear that as in other sonnets (20, 36, 39), the Poet's best or true 'self' is the Friend. It begins to seem as if Winters's 'servile weakness' was rather over-stated.

To be faithful to the over-all impression of the celebratory poems we ought to note that the effect is often the reverse of abnegation. Particularly in the sonnets where the Poet confronts time and age, we find the affirmation that his verse will perpetuate the Friend's memory to eternity, and it follows – as history has indeed shown – that his verse itself, and the poet who wrote it, are also guaranteed immortality. In celebrating the Friend the Poet is celebrating himself and his own power:

> Not marble, nor the gilded monuments
> Of princes shall outlive this powerful rhyme;
> But you shall shine more bright in these contents
> Than unswept stone besmear'd with sluttish time.

> (55)

Here again Shakespeare has personalized the Friend while depersonalizing the Poet. He does not write 'my rhyme' but 'this', 'these contents'; his poem is 'The living record of your memory', 'You live in this'. Slightly more personal is 60 ('Like as the waves make toward the pebbled shore'), but only at the very last gasp, as it were, defeating time: 'And yet to times in hope my verse shall stand,/Praising thy worth, despite his cruel hand.' Indeed, a striking quality of the sonnets against time is their less personal quality. In some of them the Friend is described in the third person (often as 'my love') and time addressed as *Thou*.[57] It is as if the Poet were tackling time face to

65

face, confronting, wrestling with time, with his Friend standing apart as the prize in the competition. The poet's aggression towards time is marked in 19:

> Devouring Time, blunt thou the lion's paws
>
> . . . . . .
>
> But I forbid thee one most heinous crime: –
> Oh carve not with thy hours my love's fair brow,
>
> . . . . . .
>
> > Yet do thy worst, old Time: despite thy wrong
> > My love shall in my verse ever live young.

It is a challenge 'in the teeth', as an Elizabethan might have put it. Elsewhere time is also in the third person, and the field of utterance is concentrated on the Poet alone, his fears and hopes: experience has taught him 'That Time will come and take my love away' (64.12). In the matching sonnets, 63 and 65, Shakespeare calls up great reserves of language and feeling to create the corroding power of age and 'sad mortality': 'Against my love shall be as I am now/With Time's injurious hand crush'd and o'erworn' (63). The Friend is now no longer the hearer but the subject of discourse. The Poet's care for him is manifested in his absence, not to his face; there can be no suspicion of flattery. What is so touching about these poems is the contrast that they express. On one side is the shattering power of time:

> Oh how shall summer's honey breath hold out
> Against the wrackful siege of battering days,
> When rocks impregnable are not so stout
> Nor gates of steel so strong but time decays?

This feeling of inevitability becomes so strong that it makes the poem comment on itself in surprised awareness – 'Oh fearful meditation!' – and pushes on to an apparently unanswerable climax: 'Or what strong hand can hold his swift foot back?/ Or who his spoil of beauty can forbid?' The contrast is between all that unstoppable force, irresistible depredation, and the fragility of a poem: 'Oh none, unless this miracle have might – /That in black ink my love may still shine bright.'

All poets need self-confidence, but not all of them justify their belief in themselves. What Shakespeare had, in addition, was the self-confidence of a generation, indeed of the whole Humanist ethos, with its belief in the 'miraculous' power of works of literature – ink on paper – to survive the ravages of time. Reading this group of sonnets is to be reminded of the noble conclusion to the first book of Bacon's *Advancement of Learning*:

> We see then how far the monuments of wit and learning are more durable than the monuments of power or of the hands. For have not the verses of Homer continued twenty-five hundred years or more, without the loss of a syllable or letter; during which time infinite palaces, temples, castles,

cities, have been decayed and demolished? ... the images of men's wits and knowledges remain in books, exempted from the wrong of time and capable of perpetual renovation.[58]

In describing his Friend as *my love* or *He* the Poet could be seen as using the third-person form in order to place him apart, perhaps to place him outside the sphere of time's influence. If one accepts this interpretation then the third-person form would not have the negative connotations defined so sharply by John Lyons. Yet in other sonnets it does have those connotations of exclusion and separation. If we regard *He* as representing [− *ego*, − *tu*], then we have a valuable insight with which to read those sonnets where the Friend's behaviour is criticized by the Poet from a position of detachment. Such is 67:

> Ah, wherefore with infection should he live
> And with his presence gain impiety,
> That sin by him advantage should achieve
> And lace itself with his society?

The detail in much of this poem remains enigmatic, but here as in 68 I cannot think that the references to false ornament and cosmetics (including wigs made of hair taken from the scalp of corpses) are favourable to the Friend, who seems to be encouraging corruption by his own example or presence in this milieu.[59] It is noticeable that the *He* in these two poems represents a *'minus ego, minus tu'* situation in literal truth, since neither first- nor second-person form occurs. The Poet evidently wants to detach himself totally from the Friend, stand away from him as if he might suffer corruption or contagion by going any nearer. Similarly in 69, which has eleven instances of *Thou* and none of *I*, the analysis of the Friend's misbehaviour focuses on the discrepancy between his outward beauty ('thy fair flower') and his mind and action ('the rank smell of weeds'), an inconsistency given more biting expression by the double pun in the couplet: 'But why thy odour matcheth not thy show,/The soil is this – that thou dost common grow.' By this suppression of the *ego* the Poet has disowned the Friend, washed his hands of him, for the moment.

There are other poems attacking the Friend in which the Poet writes from a closer perspective. Here, indeed, we can see another facet of the relationship, to analyse which Shakespeare uses all possible permutations of dominant pronouns, approaching it now from this viewpoint, now that, and moving between direct attack and ironic excuse. The third-person form, in its rather more personal state as 'my love', is used in 33 to smooth over the Friend's faults. 'Full many a glorious morning' has been ruined and disgraced by 'the basest clouds':

> Even so my sun one early morn did shine
> With all triumphant splendour on my brow;
> But out alack, he was but one hour mine –

> The region cloud hath mask'd him from me now.
> Yet him for this my love no whit disdaineth:
> Suns of the world may stain, when heaven's sun staineth.

They 'may' stain: the ambiguity of the verb ('it can happen'; 'it is allowed') points up the ambivalence of feeling, for the poem is clearly another example of a strategy we have already found in the Mistress poems, an apparent exculpation which is in fact an indictment. In 87 ('Farewell – Thou art too dear for my possessing') the Friend's inconstancy and betrayal are excused as a simple error of judgement:

> *Thy self thou* gav'st, *thy own* worth then not knowing;
> Or *me,* to whom *thou* gav'st it, else mistaking:
> So *thy* great gift, upon misprision growing,
> Comes home again on better judgment making.

Here, though, Shakespeare is not content to let the irony stand, for the couplet, with its sarcastic double-rhyme, dispels both illusion and self-deception: 'Thus have *I* had *thee* as a dream doth flatter –/In sleep a king, but waking no such matter.'

The *I–Thou* relationship in these poems is poisoned by the Friend's behaviour, so it follows that the Poet's attempt to excuse it degrades himself still further. This judgement applies to the *I*-dominant poems (88, 89) as to the *Thou*-dominant ones, such as 35, where after the first quatrain excusing the Friend's faults ('No more be griev'd at that which thou hast done') the second suddenly recoils on itself:

> All men make faults, and even *I* in this,
> Authórizing *thy* trespass with compare,
> *Myself* corrupting salving *thy* amiss,
> Excusing *thy* sins more than *thy* sins are.[60]

This is indeed to bring a plea "gainst myself', to become an accomplice or 'accessory', plunging oneself in 'civil war'. So that when we subsequently read 70: 'That thou art blam'd shall not be thy defect,/For slander's mark was ever yet the fair', with its conclusion that the suspicion of the Friend's evil is in fact desirable since otherwise the whole world would be in love with him, then we can supply our own ironic commentary.

In this mode of complaint the *Thou*-dominated poems are the more powerful. Entire focus on the second person is elsewhere a mark of affection and respect: now it throws a spotlight on the Friend's degradation, isolated so that we can 'mark' it better. As in that sequence (1–17), so in this (67, 68, 69, 70) the *I* is suppressed altogether, the *Thou* has fallen from a pedestal to the gutter. A later (later in terms of the Quarto numbering, that is) example of this type of sonnet, with its disgusted 'withdrawal of the Poet' gesture, is 95:

How sweet and lovely dost *thou* make the shame
Which like a canker in the fragrant rose
Doth spot the beauty of *thy* budding name!
Oh, in what sweets dost *thou thy* sins enclose!

The exclamatory style, the notably affectionate gestures, the epithets of praise ('sweet and lovely', 'sweets', 'beauty's veil' in line 11) almost convince us that the Friend's personal attractiveness can somehow transmute evil to good, a form of paradoxical hyperbole that Shakespeare gives to Lepidus, attempting to excuse Antony's faults to Caesar: 'His faults in him seem as the spots of heaven,/More fiery by night's blackness' (*Antony and Cleopatra*, I.iv.13f). But just as that excuse failed, so does this, and the couplet emerges with a direct warning: 'Take heed'. In the following sonnet (one of numerous matched pairs) the excuses come from the world at large:

Some say thy fault is youth, some wantonness;
Some say thy grace is youth and gentle sport;
Both grace and faults are lov'd of more, and less, –
Thou mak'st faults graces that to thee resort.

What is the charming, or sinister, power that can turn faults into graces? As we have already seen by juxtaposing Sonnets 35 and 70, after we have read a poem in which the attempt at exculpation is exploded by the Poet, either by irony or by direct criticism, when we subsequently read one in which the exculpation is made again but with no recoil on itself, then the second poem seems hollow. So Sonnet 96 ends with a notably weak – I suggest, deliberately weak – couplet: 'I love thee in such sort/As, thou being mine, mine is thy good report.' Then the more fool you, we are likely to say. Two other matched pairs in which the *Thou* dominates as a focus of shameful action are 57 and 58, 92 and 93. In both pairs we find a sarcastic 'overlooking of the beloved's faults' which draws our attention unerringly towards them. Sonnet 57 begins: 'Being your slave, what should I do but tend/Upon the hours and times of your desire?' After ten more lines of self-abasement to 'my sovereign' from 'a sad slave' it ends with the biting couplet: 'So true a fool is love that in your will,/Though you do anything, he thinks no ill.' This gives a *carte blanche* to sin.

In 58 'your slave', 'your vassal' is ready to swallow any insult or neglect, the poem concluding:

Be where *you* list, *your* charter is so strong
That *you yourself* may privilege *your* time
To what *you* will, to *you* it doth belong
Yourself to pardon of *self*-doing crime:
    I am to wait, though waiting so be hell, –
    Not blame *your* pleasure, be it ill or well.

The second-person pronouns come so thick and fast here that we cannot miss the bitter criticism of the Friend setting himself up as a law unto himself, becoming so entirely obsessed with his own pleasures that he betrays their relationship. The passivity of the Poet here is pathetic. In 93, by contrast, the sense of isolation and suspicion of infidelity (92 ends with the line 'Thou mayst be false and yet I know it not') takes on that most bitter form, knowing self-deception: 'So shall I live supposing thou art true,/Like a deceivèd husband' – that is, a cuckold. It is all too fitting that this anatomy of 'the false heart's history' should end with a comparison of the Friend's beauty to 'Eve's apple': this sequence describes another grave discrepancy between substance and show, another Fall of man.

Yet the fault is not the Friend's alone. As if conscious of the damaging effect this group must have on the imagined relationship between the Poet and the Friend, damaging to the Poet and damaging to the reader's view of both the Friend and the Poet ('why does he persevere?' readers may ask in some irritation when confronted with such a catalogue of the Friend's faults), Shakespeare sets matters even by writing what seems to be a related group where the Poet describes his own faults (109, 110, 111, 112; 117, 118, 119, 120). In these poems the *I* far exceeds the *Thou* in frequency (nearly three times), and presents as many complexities of attitude. In 110 we find straightforward confession:

> Alas, 'tis true, I have gone here and there
> And made myself a motley to the view,
> Gor'd mine own thoughts, sold cheap what is most dear,
> Made old offences of affections new....

Yet in the same sentence we find specious self-excuses: 'but, by all above', – this unusual oath, calling the heavens to witness, is an anticipatory giveaway –

> These blenches gave my heart another youth,
> And worse essays prov'd thee my best of love.
> Now all is done, have what shall have no end:
> Mine appetite I never more will grind....

Well, the disbelieving reader will say, to claim that you betrayed your partner merely to test your love for him, which has supposedly been increased by the experiment – this is to add insult to injury. Who would be so naïve as to believe that? Evidently the Poet's estimate of the Friend's credulity is rather higher than ours.

The *I* of these poems is placed in a deliberately false and weak position. It can only appeal to be welcomed to the Friend's breast (110), to seek 'pity' for its harmful deeds (111). But worse still, just as the Poet and the Mistress connived at each other's deception in 138, just as the Poet connived at the Friend's deception in 93, so in 112 the Poet is inviting the Friend to complete

70

the circle: 'For what care I who calls me well or ill,/So you o'er-green my bad, my good allow?' The metaphor is unusual, drawing attention to the invitation to whitewash, cover up, turn a blind eye to evil.[61] It is varied, later in the sonnet, with the traditional image of the adder, which is believed to be able to block its hearing ('my adder's sense/To critic and to flatterer stoppèd are'), but does so in order not to be deflected by charm or blandishments from destroying its prey. Whether or not Shakespeare was aware of that piece of lore, the corrupt nature of the invitation is made only too clear. In the second two pairs devoted to this relationship the same pattern emerges. The Poet acknowledges that he has betrayed the relationship, but this time claims that he was testing the Friend(!): 'I did strive to prove/The constancy and virtue of your love' (117).

But in the very next poem he says that he did it for a change of diet, a bout of 'physic' as it were, needed after over-indulgence: 'being full of your ne'er cloying sweetness,/To bitter sauces did I frame my feeding' (118). If 'ne'er cloying', why does he need physic? It was 'policy in love', 'policy' being one of the Elizabethans' two or three most derogatory words, denoting hyper-cunning and treachery. The reader can only reject both the excuses and the man who makes them, tearful and repentant though he seems in 119.

The final poem in this sequence provides a natural transition to one of the most puzzling and problematic aspects of the *Sonnets* revealed by this analysis of pronoun and relationship, and that is the status of *We/Us/Our*. Sonnet 120 begins: 'That you were once unkind befriends me now'. In other words, the recollection that the Friend had once been guilty of the same fault is a consolation to the Poet, for he now knows how the other must have 'bowed' under his own 'transgression':

> For if *you* were by *my* unkindness shaken
> As *I* by *yours, you* have pass'd a hell of time;
> And *I*, a tyrant, have no leisure taken
> To weigh how once *I* suffer'd in *your* crime.

They are equal, then – but more, they are united: 'Oh, that *our* night of woe might have remember'd/*My* deepest sense how hard true sorrow hits.' He ought to have been reminded of their joint suffering before he committed his fault. Now at least they are in the same boat, and the balancing of the pronouns in the last four lines declares their equality:

> And soon to *you* as *you* to *me* then tender'd
> The humble salve which wounded bosoms fits!
> But that *your* trespass now becomes a fee:
> *Mine* ransoms *yours*, and *yours* must ransom *me*.

I have quoted extensively from that sonnet in order to give the full context for this *Our*: what they have in common is that they have sinned, each has betrayed the other. They finally come together at the lowest level of their relationship. Precisely the same union in disgrace happens in the series to the Mistress, as we saw in discussing 138: 'Therefore I lie with her, and she with me,/And in our faults by lies we flatter'd be.' The curious nature of the first-person plural relationship in the *Sonnets* [+ *ego*, + *tu*] is that it is so infrequent (twelve times only) and that even when it occurs it is tenuous, fragile, or, as here, stands for a union in falseness. The first time that we find it is in 36:

> Let me confess that *we two* must be twain
> Although *our* undivided loves are one:
> So shall those blots that do with *me* remain
> Without *thy* help by *me* be borne alone.

They are a *We* unit, but at once they are split up into two incompatible halves: 'In *our* two loves there is but one respect/Though in *our* lives a separable spite' – that is, some malicious act of fortune keeps them separate.

> *I* may not evermore acknowledge *thee*,
> Lest *my* bewailèd guilt should do *thee* shame;
> Nor *thou* with public kindness honour *me*,
> Unless *thou* take that honour from *thy* name.

Each is to the other a source not of delight and solace but of shame and guilt.

It is difficult to work out the 'plot' of this sonnet, and one is not sure to what extent it is meant to suggest a consistent relationship. But the fact is that all the other instances of union are just as swiftly broken up, disunited. A similar, and equally enigmatic poem is 39:

> Oh how *thy* worth with manners may *I* sing
> When *thou* art all the better part of *me*?
> What can *mine own* praise to *mine own* self bring?
> And what is't but *mine own* when *I* praise *thee*?
> Even for this let *us* divided live,
> And *our* dear love lose name of single one,
> That by this separation *I* may give
> That due to *thee* which *thou* deserv'st alone.

One can understand parts of this poem in terms of the punning elsewhere on *Me* = *Myself* = *Thee*, but still the insistence on their having to remain separate seems to move outside the context of this poem. The matching poem of the pair (40) performs even more dazzling feats of Self/Other identification:

> Take all *my* loves, *my* love, yea, take them all:
> What hast *thou* then more than *thou* hadst before?
> No love, *my* love, that *thou* mayst true love call –
> All *mine* was *thine*, before *thou* hadst this more.

But from this fairly innocuous interchange of terms the mood darkens, as can be seen most economically by isolating the rhyme-words of the next two quatrains: 'receivest – usest – deceivest – refusest – thief – poverty – grief – injury'. The couplet is both resentful of the Friend's sexual betrayal and appealing: 'Lascivious grace, in whom all ill well shows,/Kill *me* with spites, yet *we* must not be foes.' But the double oxymoron in line 13 suggests that they are already foes, that the poem has either been written to try and restore a lost harmony, or to draw attention to the fact that it cannot be restored.

The only other two references to a *We* relationship both place it in the past. In 89, a poem of infidelity ('Say that thou didst forsake me for some fault'), the Poet abases himself, vowing to perform all kinds of penance in order to win the Friend back, including never mentioning his name again in case he 'haply of our old acquaintance tell': it is over, in the past. Less discordant, but just as remote, is the recollection in 102: '*Our* love was new, and then but in the spring,/When *I* was wont to greet it with *my* lays.'

'All the true paradises are lost paradises', perhaps. Or perhaps the Poet and Friend are separated by unbridgeable gaps of sex and social position, and cannot ever form a unit. Or Shakespeare may not be making any such point at all, despite the apparent evidence of 36 and 38. It could be said that the *We/Us/Our* form is rather a mode of self-description when the poet wishes to present his beloved and himself to the world (as shown by Donne in the *Songs and Sonnets*), and that Shakespeare prefers to keep the relationship on an interpersonal level. In this case one could argue that *I* and *Thou* automatically imply *We*, since the two of us are sharing between ourselves the field of discourse. It is ours and no one else's.

This linguistic phenomenon, like so many others, is susceptible to several interpretations, even completely opposed ones. How we judge will depend on how we see the sequence as a whole, and whether we think of it as a sequence, in fact, or as a collection of poems. If the former, then the scarcity of the *We* would merely represent a personal whim of Shakespeare, of no particular significance. If the latter, and if we took Sonnet 20 as a key declaration of intent, then the paucity of the *We* might indeed imply that the two halves of this relationship are irredeemably twain.

The massive evidence of the repetition of first- and second-person pronouns entitles us to describe the *Sonnets* as moving forwards and backwards between *I* and *Thou*. Yet the weak or anomalous *We* forms may point to a further truth, that Shakespeare conceives of the relationship between two friends as both united and separated. In this case what keeps them apart is not belonging to the same sex, rather, it is simply a condition of life that in no human relationship can two persons 'fuse' into one. Two separate people are essential for any exchange to take place: you cannot give presents to yourself, just as you cannot give yourself to yourself. Georg Simmel's analysis of a *Zweierverbindung*, a 'union of two' or 'dyad' as it is usually translated, defines it as the minimal social unit, which depends always on 'immediacy of interaction', there being no super-individual unit to which either party can also belong (as with larger group-structures). The two members, Simmel emphasized, are interdependent, for 'the secession of either would destroy the whole' social unit, and its 'affective structure is based on what each of the two participants gives or shows only to the one other person and to nobody else'. Yet, despite this intimacy, the fact that they exist as a couple with a unique value in each other's eyes (a point marvellously grasped in Donne's love-poetry[62]), they remain separate, even when man and woman strive to overcome the fundamental dualism of life. As 'something essentially unattainable', their dualism

> stands in the way of the most passionate craving for convergence and fusion. The fact that, in any real and absolute sense, the 'I' can *not* seize the 'not-I', is felt nowhere more deeply than here, where their mutual supplementation and fusion seem to be the very reason for the opposites to exist at all. Passion seeks to tear down the borders of the ego and to absorb 'I' and 'thou' in one another.

But it cannot be, their 'nearness ... must remain a distance', this 'distance which nevertheless to an infinite degree approaches their becoming-one' – remains a distance.[63] While phenomenology can describe in philosophical terms the impossibility of entering another person's mind, language, memory, value-system, Shakespeare's sonnets long ago grasped the point that *I* and *You* communicate with each other from essentially separate positions.

The striking quality of the final group of poems that I want to discuss is their mutuality and reciprocity. We have already seen many instances of this, but there are more. In 22 the Poet is so much a part of the Friend that he cannot age, himself, 'So long as youth and thou are of one date'. But when the Friend begins to age the Poet would wish to die:

> For all the beauty that doth cover *thee*
> Is but the seemly raiment of *my* heart,
> Which in *thy* breast doth live, as *thine* in *mine*, –
> How can *I* then be elder than *thou* art?

Here the motif of giving and receiving love, central to this group, uses the traditional metaphor of exchanging hearts, but reanimates it by the particularity with which the trope is extended. The Poet will protect the Friend's heart 'As tender nurse her babe from faring ill', but after his death then the Friend's heart may also be in jeopardy: 'Presume not on *thy* heart when *mine* is slain;/*Thou* gav'st me *thine* not to give back again.' That is, the exchange of hearts was permanent, irreversible: if one dies the other must too. Such an *in*vestment cannot be *di*vested. Given Shakespeare's unlimited verbal energies it is no surprise to find him culling ingenuity from this idea of giving and receiving, as in the dazzling wit of 24:

Mine eye hath play'd the painter and hath steel'd
Thy beauty's form in table of *my heart*;
My body is the frame wherein 'tis held,
And perspective it is best painter's art –
For through the painter must *you* see *his* skill
To find where *your* true image pictur'd lies,
Which in *my bosom's* shop is hanging still,
That hath *his* windows glazèd with *thine* eyes:
Now see what good turns eyes for eyes have done: –
Mine eyes have drawn *thy* shape, and *thine* for *me*
Are windows to *my breast*, wherethrough the sun
Delights to peep, to gaze therein on *thee*:
    Yet eyes this cunning want to grace their art, –
    They draw but what *they* see, know not the heart.

(I have italicized *his* in line 5 since it refers to the Poet; *his* in line 8 since it refers to his bosom; and *They* in line 14 as referring to his eyes.) Not many modern readers like this sonnet – it is too clever for our tastes. We are by temperament more favourable to such a simple statement of mutuality as the conclusion to 25: 'Then happy I that love and am belov'd,/Where I may not remove nor be remov'd.'

    Yet the Poet does 'remove', in the sense that he takes a journey, or is parted from the Friend, and a whole series of sonnets records the separation. While separation can give the occasion elsewhere for infidelity and betrayal, in this series we find a serene confidence in the other's faith, the security of mutual trust. The separation may be more mental than physical, as in the much-loved pair 29 and 30, where the Poet's despair and sadness are dispelled merely by recalling the Friend: 'For thy sweet love rememb'red' and 'But if the while I think on thee, dear friend', couplets which once read it is impossible to forget. In physical absence, being separated by 'injurious distance', the theme of nine or ten consecutive sonnets (43 to 51 or perhaps 52), to think of the Friend is again a consolation against misery, since he is 'present-absent' (45) in thought or image:[64]

So, either by *thy* picture or *my* love,
Thyself away, art present still with *me*:
For *thou* not farther than *my* thoughts canst move
And *I* am still with *them* and *they* with *thee*;
    Or if *they* sleep, *thy* picture in *my* sight
    Awakes *my* heart to heart's and eye's delight.   (47)

After the parting, the reunion (97):

How like a winter hath my absence been
From thee, the pleasure of the fleeting year!
What freezings have I felt, what dark days seen! –

What old December's bareness everywhere!
And yet this time remov'd was summer's time....

Now the poet juxtaposes with great deliberation 'actual time' and 'actual weather' against personal climate, those subjective feelings which are controlled not by the calendar but by our individual experience. The last four lines of this sonnet are seldom quoted, but to me they represent Shakespeare at his best, that intimate tone and unforced style of which Angel Day's account of the personal letter is so apt a description: 'the familiar and mutuall talke of one absent friend to another ... simple, plaine, and of the lowest and meanest stile'[65] – yet how expressive:

For summer and his pleasure wait on thee,
And thou away the very birds are mute:
Or if they sing, 'tis with so dull a cheer
That leaves look pale, dreading the winter's near.

It is rare, even in his poetry, to find traditional tropes reanimated with such freshness and simplicity. Shakespeare is even able to repeat the trick for 98, the other sonnet of the pair, 'From you have I been absent in the spring'.[66] If I am forced to select it must be the conclusion:

Nor did I wonder at the lily's white,
Nor praise the deep vermilion in the rose;
They were but sweet, but figures of delight
Drawn after you, you pattern of all those.
Yet seem'd it winter still; and, you away,
As with your shadow I with these did play.

Any critic who quotes these sonnets runs the risk of putting himself out of business. Whereas readers often focus on the text of a critical work and skip through the quotations, here the eye is drawn to the poetry and resents the distraction of the critic's argument. Indeed, analysis is almost superfluous, since if any poems can speak for themselves these can. Yet I can perhaps perform a minimal interpretative function by putting together some of these 'mutual' sonnets which deal with the act of writing poetry, and in which Shakespeare seems more than usually sensitive to the weight of pronouns. First, two sonnets on the theme that the poetry will survive the poet's death, 71 ('No longer mourn for me when I am dead') and 74. The earlier of the two identifies the poet with his poetry, praying that after his death he should be forgotten:

Nay, if *you* read this line, remember not
The hand that writ it, for *I* love *you* so
That *I* in *your* sweet thoughts would be forgot
If thinking on *me* then should make *you* woe.

76

Sonnet 74 draws a different line, separating the Poet from his work:

> But he contented when that fell arrest
> Without all bail shall carry me away:
> My life hath in this line some interest
> Which for memorial still with thee shall stay.

The point to be stressed at this juncture – forgive the interruption! – is the turning of the other into the self and of the self into poetry, which is at the same time the turning of life into art and of transience into immortality:

> When *thou* reviewest this, *thou* dost review
> The very part was consecrate to *thee*:
> The earth can have but earth, which is his due;
> *My* spirit is *thine*, the better part of *me*:
> So then *thou* hast but lost the dregs of life,
> The prey of worms, *my* body being dead,
> The coward conquest of a wretch's knife,
> Too base of *thee* to be rememberèd:
> > The worth of that is that which it contains,
> > And that is this, and this with *thee* remains.

This marvellous poem can be linked, no doubt, to the series attacking time and proclaiming the certainty of the poet's survival. Yet to me it is more quietly impressive than all the grand 'exegi monumentum' gestures, since it refuses to turn outward to time, or the world, but addresses itself with complete absorption to its subject. As C. S. Lewis wrote so memorably, 'this transference of the whole self into another self without the demand for a return [has] hardly a precedent in profane literature'.[67] It is a gesture which is simultaneously human, literary, and religious. The *I* gives itself to the *Thou*, makes a complete act of dedication, links the two persons through the poetry.

Yet the two remain separate. For 'The Phoenix and the Turtle', another poem, a different problem, Shakespeare could celebrate the union of those two birds on an emblematic, almost mystical level:

> So they lov'd as love in twain
> Had the essence but in one;
> Two distincts, division none:
> Number there in love was slain.

The paradoxes are as bewildering as the mystery of the Holy Trinity:

> Property was thus appalled,
> That the self was not the same;
> Single nature's double name,
> Neither two nor one was called.
>
> Reason, in itself confounded,
> Saw division grow together,

To themselves yet either neither,
Simple were so well compounded;

That it cried, how true a twain
Seemeth this concordant one!

Mysterious and desirable though such a union may be, it is not given to human beings, and in the *Sonnets* it does not take place. To the last – from whichever point you begin, and wherever you end – these poems present an irreducibly double experience, where one admires, and one is admired. This is Shakespeare's truth about life, and love. The Poet himself is aware that his situation may seem repetitive, and in 76 answers the question, 'Why write I still all one, ever the same ...?' Like a good Renaissance poet he replies that this is the principle of decorum; his form merely recreates his subject-matter:

Oh know, sweet love, I always write of you,
And you and love are still my argument;
So all my best is dressing old words new,
Spending again what is already spent.

We are inclined to smile at the self-depreciation, as we are at the similar joke in 105:

Let not my love be call'd idolatry,
Nor my belovèd as an idol show,
Since all alike my songs and praises be
To one, of one, still such, and ever so.
Kind is my love today, tomorrow kind,
Still constant in a wondrous excellence:
Therefore my verse, to constancy confin'd,
One thing expressing, leaves out difference.

He has no need for other forms, other themes.

The repetitiveness of such poems is an obstacle to critics committed to the idea of an ever-developing narrative, and they are not often taken seriously.[68] I suggest that we take them not only seriously but literally, since they represent the very root of the relationship around which the *Sonnets* are structured. 'Nuns fret not at their convent's narrow-room' was Wordsworth's explanation why he willingly bound himself 'Within the Sonnet's scanty plot of ground'.[69] In contrast to some critics who would rather see the collection as a one-directional story, with its 'phases' and 'developments', I recall readers to the essentially, inherently repetitive or ongoing nature of this as of all deep and long-lived human relationships. It is the rhythm of exchange, like day and night, sun and moon, systole and diastole. Simmel refers to the inevitable 'repetition of the same contents, situations, excitations' within a relationship, yet together with the repetition there is 'the consciousness that ... the value

of this content depends on its very opposite – a certain measure of rarity'.[70]
Sonnet 108 challenges abruptly all the founts of invention:

> What's in the brain that ink may character
> Which hath not figur'd to *thee my* true spirit?
> What's new to speak, what now to register,
> That may express *my* love or *thy* dear merit?

The answer is predictable, inevitable, *right*:

> Nothing, sweet boy; but yet like prayers divine
> *I* must each day say o'er the very same,
> Counting no old things old, – *thou mine, I thine* –
> Even as when first *I* hallow'd *thy* fair name.

Those four lines could stand as a motto for the whole sequence, with their reworking from a fresh direction of the desire to celebrate the other from which Shakespeare started. The last line of that quotation inescapably echoes the Lord's Prayer – 'Hallow'd be Thy name' – and religious language has been in the background to other sonnets of this kind ('consecrate', 'spirit', and 'memorial' in 74, 'idolatry' in 105, 'The perfect ceremony of love's rite' in 23). All in all, then, the most fitting place to end might be 125, which rejects the glories of a canopy of state, a desire for eternity, or a profitable life at court. Instead, the Poet offers the Friend a gift as one would offer a sacrifice to a god, pagan or Christian (Shakespeare used the religious term 'oblation' just once in all his writings, for this poem). It is the ultimate gift that a human being can wish to make:

> No, let *me* be obsequious in *thy* heart,
> And take *thou my* oblation, poor but free, –
> Which is not mix'd with seconds, knows no art
> But mutual render, only *me* for *thee*.

Notes

1 Brian Vickers, 'The "Songs and Sonnets" and the rhetoric of hyperbole', in A. J. Smith (ed.) *John Donne: Essays in Celebration* (London, 1972), pp. 132–74. This essay on Shakespeare's *Sonnets* was first planned in 1971, and written in 1972–3, but I never got round to publishing it. I have revised it to take note of recent work but have not otherwise changed its emphasis.
2 See, e.g., John C. Nelson, 'The poetry of Michelangelo', in B. S. Levy (ed.) *Developments in the Early Renaissance* (Albany, NY, 1972), pp. 25ff. I discount as not worth serious consideration Joseph Pequigney's homosexual interpretation, *Such Is My Love: a Study of Shakespeare's Sonnets* (Chicago, 1985), which attempts to document a 'copious ... detailing [of] physical intimacies', which apparently involves taking the word 'ride' (as in 137, where the Friend's eyes, turned towards the Mistress, are said to be 'anchor'd in the bay where all men ride') in a literally sexual sense, so that the sun in 33, permitting 'the basest clouds

to ride/With ugly rack on his celestial face', must be an allusion to 'oral-genital carnality engaged in with some low type', and 'he upon your soundless deep doth ride' in 80 'refers to anal intercourse'. See the comments by Kenneth Muir, *Modern Language Review* 83 (1988): 405–6, and Ronald Levas, *Renaissance Quarterly* 40 (1987): 818–19. One wonders which will be the next word to be anachronistically violated. As Mistress Quickly says, 'these villains will make the word ["captain"] as odious as the word "occupy", which was an excellent good word before it was ill-sorted.'

3 J.W. Lever, *The Elizabethan Love Sonnet* (London, 1956, 1966), p. 165. Lever considers that the sonnets to the Mistress, which he well describes as 'a kind of sub-plot to the main series', represent the more startling break with tradition: 'in its negation of conventional values, this second series defied tradition even more outspokenly than the first' (p. 163). While I cannot agree with this relative evaluation it does at least present a meaningful historical viewpoint such as is lacking, for instance, in Stephen Booth's contention that *neither* series represents a break with tradition:

> Shakespeare's dark lady is traditionally cited as contrary to the traditional beloved, but the very impropriety of a technically unattractive and morally vicious beloved is a *consistent enlargement* on the standard rhetorical principle of the convention; and, whatever other significance there may be, certainly addressing love sonnets to a man is an *all but predictable extreme* of a courtly love technique.
> (*An Essay on Shakespeare's Sonnets* (New Haven, Conn., 1969), p. 180 (my italics))

If so predictable, why did no poet before Shakespeare attempt either 'extension' of the convention?

4 All quotations are from W. G. Ingram and Theodore Redpath (eds) *Shakespeare's Sonnets* (London, 1964). I have occasionally italicized the pronouns in quotations for the sake of emphasis.

5 C. L. Barber, 'An essay on the *Sonnets*', Introduction to The Laurel Shakespeare edition of the *Sonnets* (New York, 1960), p. 21.

6 C. S. Lewis, *English Literature in the Sixteenth Century, Excluding Drama* (Oxford, 1954), p. 504.

7 ibid., p. 505.

8 See the stimulating article by G. K. Hunter, 'The dramatic technique of Shakespeare's *Sonnets*', *Essays in Criticism* 3 (1953): 152–64.

9 E. A. Abbott, *A Shakespearian Grammar. An Attempt To Illustrate Some Of The Differences Between Elizabethan And Modern English*, 3rd edn (London, 1886), para. 231–6, pp. 153–60; Wilhelm Franz, *Shakespeare-Grammatik* (Heidelberg, 1909), pp. 252–62; Sister St Geraldine Byrne, *Shakespeare's Use of the Pronoun of Address, its Significance in Characterization and Motivation* (Washington, DC, 1936); A. McIntosh, '"As You Like It": a grammatical clue to character', *Review of English Literature* 4 (1963): 68–81, repr. with additional notes in A. McIntosh and M. A. K. Halliday, *Patterns of Language. Papers in General, Descriptive and Applied Linguistics* (London, 1966), pp. 70–82; Joan Mulholland, ' "Thou" and "You" in Shakespeare: a study in the second person pronoun', *English Studies* 48 (1967): 34–43; Charles Barber, '"You" and "Thou" in Shakespeare's *Richard III*', *Leeds Studies in English* 12 (1981): 273–89. These last two essays are reprinted in the useful collection by Vivian Salmon and Edwina Burness (eds) *A Reader in the Language of Shakespearean Drama* (Amsterdam and Philadelphia, 1987), pp. 153–61 (Mulholland) and 163–79 (Barber). This reader also includes brief but helpful

remarks on Shakespeare's use of pronouns by Randoph Quirk (pp. 7–10), V. Salmon (pp. 59, 67–8), and R. D. Eagleson (p. 142). A reliable general study is T. Finkenstaedt, *You and Thou: Studien zur Anrede im Englischen* (Berlin, 1963).

10 Roger Brown and Albert Gilman, 'The pronouns of power and solidarity', in T. A. Sebeok (ed.) *Style in Language* (Cambridge, Mass., 1960), pp. 253–76. A stimulating and suggestive study of the whole linguistic phenomenon of encoding the person, time, and place involved in communication acts (where 'person deixis' is effected by pronouns) is Charles J. Fillmore, 'Toward a theory of deixis', *Working Papers in Linguistics, University of Hawaii* 3 (1971): 219–42, with a useful bibliography (see especially the items by Bühler, Frei, and Weinreich).

11 See Quirk, 'Shakespeare and the English language'; Barber, ' "You" and "Thou" in Shakespeare's *Richard III*'; and R. D. Eagleson, 'Propertied as all the tuned spheres: aspects of Shakespeare's language'; all in Salmon and Burness, *A Reader:* pp. 7–8, pp. 168ff., and p. 142 respectively.

12. V. Salmon, 'Elizabethan colloquial English in the Falstaff plays', in Salmon and Burness, *A Reader*, pp. 67–8, citing also Charles Williams, 'The use of the second person in *Twelfth Night*', *English* 9 (1952): 125–8.

13 Frances Berry, ' "Thou" and "You" in Shakespeare's *Sonnets*', *Essays in Criticism* 8 (1958): 138–46; repr. in Frances Berry, *Poets' Grammar. Person, Time and Mood in Poetry* (London, 1958), pp. 36–46.

14 Andrew Gurr, 'You and Thou in Shakespeare's Sonnets', *Essays in Criticism* 32 (1982): 9–25.

15 See C. Archer, ' "Thou" and "You" in the Sonnets', *Times Literary Supplement*, 27 June 1936, p. 544, who notes that 'the use of the plural forms ... greatly enlarges the field of choice in rhyming', citing 13 (with its couplet rhyming 'you know/You had a father: let your son say so'), and ten other instances of the *you* form affecting the rhyme-word. As for euphony, he notes that the use of the plural 'obviates stumbling-blocks or positive cacophonies', as in 104, in which the Friend is addressed as *you* up to the couplet when the poet speaks to posterity: 'For fear of which, hear this, *thou* age unbred:/Ere *you* were born was beauty's summer dead.' Here the avoidance of 'the sibilant tautology' ('Ere thou wast born was beauty's summer') is made even at the price of a slight ambiguity, for the *you* in the last line refers not to the Friend but to the individuals constituting posterity. Elsewhere, however, choice of *thou* produces its own crop of rhyme-words and its own range of tonal emphases. In 'Pronouns in poetry', *Essays in Criticism* 8 (1958): 456–7, Thomas Finkenstaedt invoked Archer's article in response to Berry, and also rebuked her for ignoring the preponderant evidence from prose usage for *thou* being more intimate – or, as linguists would now say, representing the marked form.

16 See, e.g., Giorgio Melchiori, *Shakespeare's Dramatic Meditations. An Experiment in Criticism* (Oxford, 1976), especially pp. 5–18 and 197–9, giving statistics derived from Herbert Donow, *Concordance to the Sonnet Sequences of Daniel, Drayton, Shakespeare, Sidney and Spenser* (Carbondale, Ill., 1969); David K. Weiser, ' "I" and "Thou" in Shakespeare's *Sonnets*', *Journal of English and Germanic Philology* 76 (1977): 506–23, at pp. 510–11, repr. in David K. Weiser, *Mind in Character. Shakespeare's Speaker in the Sonnets* (Columbia, Mo., 1987), pp. 105–6; G. P. Jones, 'You, Thou, He or She? The Master–Mistress in Shakespearian and Elizabethan sonnet sequences', *Cahiers Elisabéthains* 9 (1981): 73–84. Melchiori computes 351 uses of *I* and 974 total uses of the *I* form (including *Me, My, Mine*) on p. 19, yet on p. 197 the total for *I* is given as 344; Weiser computes for whole sonnets (which is less helpful), according to his own rather peculiar Buberian categories: 'Impersonal' – using *It* (five poems); 'Self-Effacing' – *Thou–It*, but not

I (seventeen); 'Soliloquy' – *I–It/He/She* (twenty), and 'Dialogue' – *I–Thou* (112), which he then subdivides into four types. G. P. Jones computes according to another system, sonnets characterized by *Thou* forms (sixty-nine to the 'Fair Youth'; seventeen to the 'Dark Mistress'), *You* forms (thirty-four; none); *She* forms (six; five); *Zero* (fifteen; five); and *Mixed* (one: Sonnet 24). It would be helpful if commentators could use agreed terms and methods.

17 Melchiori, *Shakespeare's Dramatic Meditations*, pp. 9, 15, 16, 20.
18 Melchiori tends too often to propose superficial socio-economic explanations for literature: 'new economic mechanisms created by the birth of modern capitalism' (ibid., p. 26), 'the encroaching middle class' (ibid., p. 27), 'the rise of capitalism which was radically transforming the social structures' (ibid., p. 54), and so on (ibid., pp. 66–7, 68, 69, and *passim*). To see 'they' in 94 ('They that have power to hurt and will do none') as referring to 'the mighty' in society (ibid., pp. 55ff.) is to reduce the scope and meaning of the poem, which is about all people who enjoy power in a relationship and abuse it. And to call it a 'meditative' poem (ibid., p. 63), not addressed to anyone, is arbitrarily to limit its possible application.
19 ibid., pp. 15–16, 10, 28, 29, 132.
20 For passages quoted in this paragraph, see ibid., pp. 19, 28, 20 (note). For passages of formalist grammatical and phonological analysis, ignoring or suspending questions of meaning, see, e.g., ibid., pp. 40, 61, 73–4, 79, 80, 82, 114, 133, 136, 137, 138, 140, 165ff., 181. For his strange 'diagrams' or 'semantic patterns' of sonnets, see ibid., pp. 59, 61, 78, 80, 85, 103, 119, 143, 147, 168, 172, 184. In connection with the last of these, a 'gyre' form, or 'double cone' (ibid., p. 186), whatever Yeats may have done with his 'esoteric notions' there is no evidence for the claim that Francis Bacon was 'an adept' of the Rosicrucians. See Brian Vickers, 'Frances Yates and the writing of history', *Journal of Modern History* 51 (1979): 287–316. For instances of the biographical fallacy, see ibid., pp. 98, 152, 157. The section on 'Shakespeare's God' (pp. 93–101) seems especially dubious, while the discussion of 'Sonnet 146 and the ethics of religion' (pp. 161–96, 'The soul as vampyre'; 'The body as servant and the soul as Coriolanus') is bizarre.
21 Weiser, *Mind in Character*, pp. 107, 59, 99–138.
22 *The Ecstasy*, line 74.
23 Weiser, *Mind in Character*, pp. 109, 113, 117, 121–2.
24 Dating the *Sonnets* is notoriously difficult. The best discussion remains that of Hyder E. Rollins in his New Variorum edition of the *Sonnets*, 2 vols (Philadelphia, 1944). Incidentally, the fact that this masterpiece of historical scholarship should have been out of print for so many years is a sad comment on the apathy of the body holding the copyright, namely the President and Fellows of Harvard University.
25 See Weiser, *Mind in Character*, pp. xii, 13, 40. Weiser groups together, as if related, Sonnets 15, 29, and 104 – selecting sonnets according to his own analytical categories, reasonably enough – but finds that 104 'brings us to the third and final stage of awareness in dramatic irony' (ibid., p. 43) – as if Shakespeare had made a tidy three-part plan. He divides the 'sonnet-soliloquies' into three groups, then comments: 'such patterning may be relegated to chance, but it seems rather to reveal a definite process of psychological growth' (ibid., p. 60). Elsewhere he finds 'a more revealing pattern' (ibid., p. 74), and separates the last twenty-eight sonnets from the others ('a vulnerable but by no means arbitrary decision' (p. 139)), the later Dialogues leading to 'The Final Breakdown' (p. 169). It begins to sound like a novelette.
26 Jones, 'You, Thou, He or She?', pp. 81–2, sees Shakespeare as a court poet walking 'a tight-rope between flattery and familiarity, between commercialism and

affection', involved with his patron in 'an ambivalent relationship that is almost sexual.' As the author adds, 'Unfortunately these observations do not lead very far.'

27 Quotations from Angel Day, *The English Secretorie,* are from the Scolar Press facsimile (Menston, 1967), pp. 1, 18–19; u/v and ʃ/s are modernized.

28 The parallels have been noted, *inter alia,* by J.W. Lever, *The Elizabethan Love Sonnet,* pp. 190ff., but I would argue that the differences between Shakespeare's argument and Erasmus's are more important than the resemblances. See Sir Thomas Wilson's *Arte of Rhetorique* (1560, 1585) ed. G. H. Mair (Oxford, 1909), pp. 39–63; or, with helpful annotations, the new critical edition by T. J. Derrick (New York, 1982), pp. 95–140.

29 Day, *The English Secretorie,* pp. 122–6 (see also comments on pp. 138–9), 85, 105.

30 On the importance of grammar, a useful starting-point is the erudite survey by Aldo Scaglione, *Ars Grammatica* (The Hague/Paris, 1970). See also W. K. Percival, 'Grammar and rhetoric in the Renaissance', in J. J. Murphy (ed.) *Renaissance Eloquence* (Berkeley and Los Angeles, 1983), pp. 303–30.

31 On the influence of this grammar, see T. W. Baldwin, *William Shakspere's Small Latine & Lesse Greeke* (Urbana, Ill., 1944), 2 vols, index: II, pp. 756–7.

32 Quotations from *A Short Introduction of Grammar, generally to be used in the Kynges Maiesties dominions, for the bryngynge up of all those that entende to atteyne the Knowlege of the Latine tongue* (1549); Scolar Press facsimile (Menston, 1970), Sig.A$_{viii}$^v.

33 See R. H. Robins, *Ancient & Medieval Grammatical Theory in Europe* (London, 1951), and Ian Michael, *English Grammatical Categories and the Tradition to 1800* (Cambridge, 1970), pp. 69f., 99, 101.

34 Michael, *English Grammatical Categories,* p. 322.

35 ibid., pp. 323, 324.

36 ibid., p. 325.

37 John Lyons, *Introduction to Theoretical Linguistics* (Cambridge, 1968), p. 275.

38 ibid., pp. 275–6.

39 Raymond Tallis, *Not Saussure* (London, 1988), p. 152.

40 Lyons, *Introduction to Theoretical Linguistics,* pp. 278, 276.

41 ibid., pp. 277–8.

42 The most useful concordance to the *Sonnets* is that by Marvin Spevack, *A Complete and Systematic Concordance to the Works of Shakespeare,* vol. 2 (Hildesheim, 1968), pp. 1255–87.

43 Ingram and Redpath, *Shakespeare's Sonnets,* p. 268.

44 Lever, *op. cit.* pp. 210–11.

45 I made a brief rhetorical analysis of this poem in Brian Vickers, *Classical Rhetoric in English Poetry* (London, 1970), pp. 160–3. Returning to the topic in more detail some years later I found the rhetoric less convincing: see 'Rhetoric and feeling in Shakespeare's Sonnets', in Keir Elam (ed.) *Shakespeare Today: Directions and Methods of Research* (Florence, 1984), pp. 53–98, at 83–5.

46 See Vickers, 'Rhetoric and feeling', pp. 86–94. This essay includes extended analyses of Sonnets 8, 105, 116, 35, 40, 42, and 138.

47 Ingram and Redpath, *Shakespeare's Sonnets,* p. 332.

48 Barber, 'An essay on the Sonnets', p. 11.

49 This is perhaps too optimistic: some critics have indeed taken Shakespeare's tropes at face value. When the poet writes of his 'tongue-tied patience' in 140, some editors deduce that Shakespeare stammered; when he describes himself as 'Beated and chopp'd with tann'd antiquity' in 62, that is used as a key to date the *Sonnets.* When he writes of his 'rude ignorance' in 78, Patrick Crutwell seriously adds a

footnote: 'It is interesting to see, so early and in Shakespeare himself, a recognition of what was to become the critical commonplace: that he "wanted art" (as Jonson put it) and was unlearned' (*The Shakespearean Moment* (London, 1955), p. 10).

50 Yvor Winters, 'Poetic styles, old and new', in D.C. Allen (ed.) *Four Poets on Poetry* (Baltimore, Md., 1959); repr. and quoted from Barbara Herrnstein (ed.) *Discussion of Shakespeare's Sonnets* (Boston, Mass., 1965), p. 107. Melchiori similarly describes Sonnets 1–17 as being written in a 'hierarchical tone' expressing 'almost masochistic humility' (*Shakespeare's Dramatic Meditations*, p. 20).

51 Barber, 'An essay on the Sonnets', p. 11.

52 I.i.157f.: see the New Arden edition by G.K. Hunter. In Erasmus's *Moriae Encomium*, Self-love (*Philautia*) is a follower of Folly, nursed by Drunkenness and Ignorance. A.H.T. Levi notes in the Penguin edition (*The Praise of Folly*, trans. B. Radice, 1971) that Erasmus took the word 'from Plutarch and Horace, both of whom emphasize the blindness it causes', while in Rabelais Panurge's *philautie* makes him unable to act (pp. 59f.): presumably because he has isolated himself from his fellow men.

53 Lewis, *English Literature*, pp. 503, 505.

54 Here I differ from Ingram and Redpath who accept the Quarto reading, 'by verse'; the emendation 'my' derives from Capell and Malone.

55 Lever, *The Elizabethan Love Sonnet*, pp. 227ff.

56 See, e.g., E.R. Curtius, *European Literature and the Latin Middle Ages*, trans. W.R. Trask (New York, 1953), p. 83.

57 As Charles Barber noted, in Shakespeare as in other Elizabethan writers, 'invocations or apostrophes to a supernatural being, or to an inanimate object, or to a personified abstraction, regularly make use of *Thou*' (' "You" and "Thou" ', p. 278/168).

58 Bacon, *Works*, eds J. Spedding, R.L. Ellis, and D.D. Heath, 14 vols (London, 1857–74), 3.318.

59 See Lever, *The Elizabethan Love Sonnet*, pp. 209ff.

60 Ingram and Redpath retain the Quarto reading 'their sins ... their sins'. While it can be made to yield a sense, as they show, 'thy' seems more appropriate to the rhetorical structure of the sonnet, and its interpersonal relationship.

61 I am reminded of an equally unusual, though far more sinister metaphor, Macbeth's 'This my hand will rather/The multitudinous seas incarnadine,/Making the green one red' (II.ii.61ff.).

62 See Vickers, 'The "Songs and Sonnets" ', pp. 148ff.

63 Kurt H. Wolff (ed. and trans.) *The Sociology of Georg Simmel* (New York, 1950), pp. 122–8.

64 Compare the treatment of separation in *Antony and Cleopatra*, I.v. and II.v.

65 Day, *The English Secretorie*, p. 18.

66 It is worth noting, perhaps, that 97 is a *Thou* poem, and 98 a *You* poem. Who will say that there is a drop in intensity or intimacy from one to the other?

67 Lewis, *English Literature*, p. 505.

68 Melchiori says of 105:

this sonnet, a monotonous sequence of deliberate variations on 'three theames in one' ... has a false ring, due to the conventional use of the word kindness (= generosity, courtesy, the granting of favour by the lady) in love-poetry ... an elegant conceit, soon exhausted.

(*Shakespeare's Dramatic Meditations*, p. 110)

Weiser writes: 'Accepting monotony as its very theme, 105 does not escape the consequences. ... The sonnet shifts to a rather idolatrous praise centering on three key words that are repeated three times: "Fair, kind, and true".' To Weiser

> that repeated claim is disturbing because it contradicts the powerful criticisms previously directed against *the same person* [my italics]. Turning to other sonnets, we recall the many censures of the youth's misconduct in matters of love and sex. If now he remains 'fair', that quality is often reduced to a misleading cover.

Weiser quotes negative comments on the youth from 69, 92, and 120, concluding that 'there is ample evidence, then, that the youth is not entirely "fair, kind, and true".' (*Mind in Character*, pp. 75–6.) One can hardly hope for a better example of the way in which constructed theories of sequence and personality judgements can harden into an *idée fixe* that prevents a critic from seeing the value of the poem before him. Weiser goes on to observe that 'in Shakespeare's time "idolatry" was often used as a synonym for Roman Catholicism by its opponents', and insinuates that the sonnet actually strengthens this unpleasant analogy with the veneration of the saints. The speaker expresses 'one thing' and 'the sonnet displays the unhappy effects of that restriction. . . . It is a programmatic soliloquy, clearly setting forth intentions that it cannot fulfill. Its rhetoric is far more appropriate to the shallow-minded Lorenzo in *The Merchant of Venice*' (ibid., p. 76). This seems to miss every point.

69 Wordsworth's Poems, ed. Philip Wayne, 3 vols (London, 1955), I.183.
70 Wolff, *Simmel*, p. 125.

Appendix: A word-count of personal pronouns in the *Sonnets*

In Table 2.1 I have grouped together all manifestations of the first-person form (I, Me, My, Myself, Mine); similarly for the second person (Thou, Thee, Thine, Thy, Thyself; You, Yours, Yourself), the third person (He, Him, His; She, Her, Hers); and the first-person plural (We, Us, Ours).

I have excluded uses of He, She, We, etc., when they refer to 'a man', or mankind in general; similarly, I have omitted 'Thou' when addressed to a non-human personification. In cases where the first-person forms including the possessive (I, Mine) are used for imagined speech by the 'Thou' of the poem (as in Sonnet 2) I have counted them as second person; and where the third person is used by the 'I' of the poem in imagined speech (as in 139) I have counted it as part of the second-person form otherwise used in that poem. Under the first person are found some figures in square brackets (e.g. Sonnets 24, 113, 114, 137, 151). These represent instances where the 'I' of the poem refers to his body (or parts of it) in the third person, and they have been added into the general total.

Although I have done my best to be accurate, there are borderline cases where opinions might differ as to whether a 'my friend' or 'my self' are to be counted as 'I', 'Thou', or 'He' forms (see 65, line 14, for instance). This depends on the interpretation of each context, and for that reason this list ought to be regarded as a personal evaluation of the pattern, not as a piece of hard-and-fast statistics.

Forms and meanings

Sonnet	I	Thou/You	He	She	We	You (plural)	They
1	0	10	0	0	0	0	0
2	0	15	0	0	0	0	0
3	0	14	0	0	0	0	0
4	0	14	0	0	0	0	0
5	0	0	0	0	0	0	0
6	0	14	0	0	0	0	0
7	0	4	0	0	0	0	0
8	0	9	0	0	0	0	0
9	0	7	0	0	0	0	0
10	3	15	0	0	0	0	0
11	0	11	0	0	0	0	0
12	4	3	0	0	0	0	0
13	0	18	0	0	0	0	0
14	8	5	0	0	0	0	0
15	4	5	0	0	0	0	0
16	2	12	0	0	0	0	0
17	4	8	0	0	0	0	0
18	1	7	0	0	0	0	0
19	4	0	3	0	0	0	0
20	4	7	0	0	0	0	0
21	4	0	1	0	0	0	0
22	12	12	0	0	0	0	0
23	5	0	0	0	0	0	0
24	6[+3]	7	0	0	0	0	0
25	4	0	0	0	0	0	0
26	14	6	0	0	0	0	0
27	12	2	0	0	0	0	0
28	6	3	0	0	0	0	0
29	12	2	0	0	0	0	0
30	8	1	0	0	0	0	0
31	8	7	0	0	0	0	0
32	6	2	0	0	0	0	0
33	6	0	3	0	0	0	0
34	7	6	0	0	0	0	0
35	6	7	0	0	0	0	0
36	8	9	0	0	4	0	0
37	9	4	0	0	0	0	0
38	5	10	0	0	0	0	0
39	8	5	1	0	2	0	0
40	10	15	0	0	1	0	0
41	4	16	0	2	0	0	0
42	19	5	0	9	0	1	3
43	7	8	0	0	0	0	0
44	8	3	0	0	0	0	0
45	7	4	0	0	0	0	0
46	8	6	0	0	0	0	0
47	16	6	0	0	0	0	0
48	10	7	0	0	0	0	0
49	9	6	0	0	0	0	0
50	11	1	0	0	0	0	0
51	12	4	0	0	0	0	0
52	2	2	0	0	0	0	0
53	0	12	0	0	0	0	0
54	1	2	0	0	0	0	0
55	0	6	0	0	0	0	0
56	0	0	0	0	0	0	0

'Mutual render': *I* and *Thou* in the *Sonnets*

Sonnet	I	Thou/You	He	She	We	You (plural)	They
57	6	12	0	0	0	0	0
58	4	18	0	0	0	0	0
59	3	2	0	0	0	0	0
60	1	1	0	0	0	0	0
61	11	12	0	0	0	0	0
62	21	2	0	0	0	0	0
63	2	0	10	0	0	0	0
64	5	0	1	0	0	0	0
65	[1]*	0	[1]*	0	0	0	0
66	3	0	1	0	0	0	0
67	0	0	10	0	0	0	0
68	0	0	3	0	0	0	0
69	0	11	0	0	0	0	0
70	0	10	0	0	0	0	0
71	12	9	0	0	0	0	0
72	13	9	0	0	0	0	0
73	3	6	0	0	0	0	0
74	5	9	0	0	0	0	0
75	4	5	0	0	0	0	0
76	8	3	0	0	0	0	0
77	0	18	0	0	0	0	0
78	7	8	0	0	0	0	0
79	5	16	[9]†	0	0	0	0
80	9	7	[6]†	0	0	0	0
81	7	8	0	0	0	0	0
82	3	7	0	0	0	0	0
83	5	10	0	0	0	0	0
84	0	10	0	0	0	0	0
85	5	3	0	0	0	0	0
86	8	2	8	0	0	0	0
87	8	14	0	0	0	0	0
88	16	10	0	0	0	0	0
89	13	8	0	0	1	0	0
90	7	3	0	0	0	0	0
91	5	3	0	0	0	0	0
92	9	10	0	0	0	0	0
93	4	13	0	0	0	0	0
94	0	0	0	0	0	0	0
95	0	10	0	0	0	0	0
96	3	11	0	0	0	0	0
97	3	3	0	0	0	0	0
98	4	5	0	0	0	0	0
99	4	6	0	0	0	0	0
100	0	0	2	0	0	0	0
101	2	0	4	0	0	0	0
102	8	1	0	0	1	0	0
103	9	6	0	0	0	0	0
104	6	8	0	0	0	0	0
105	5	2	0	0	0	0	0
106	2	3	0	0	0	0	0
107	4	3	0	0	0	0	0
108	6	6	0	0	0	0	0
109	14	3	0	0	0	0	0
110	11	1	0	0	0	0	0
111	13	4	0	0	0	0	0
112	17	5	0	0	0	0	0
113	6[+7]	3	0	0	0	0	0

Forms and meanings

Sonnet	I	Thou/You	He	She	We	You (plural)	They
114	7[+3]	3	0	0	0	0	0
115	8	2	0	0	0	0	0
116	[3]‡	0	0	0	0	0	0
117	12	7	0	0	0	0	0
118	2	2	0	0	0	0	0
119	9	0	0	0	0	0	0
120	13	10	0	0	1	0	0
121	8	0	0	0	0	0	0
122	5	7	0	0	0	0	0
123	5	0	0	0	0	0	0
124	2	0	4	0	0	0	0
125	7	2	0	0	0	0	0
126	1	9	0	0	0	0	0
127	0	0	0	2	0	0	0
128	5	8	0	0	0	0	0
129	0	0	0	0	0	0	0
130	11	0	0	6	0	0	0
131	7	10	0	0	0	0	0
132	5	7	0	0	0	0	0
133	16	8	5	0	0	0	0
134	14	9	10	0	0	0	0
135	5	8	[7]§	0	0	0	0
136	11	11	[3]§	0	0	0	0
137	6[+4]	0	0	0	0	0	0
138	10	0	0	11	2	0	0
139	15	10	0	0	0	0	0
140	9	6	0	0	0	0	0
141	11	7	0	0	0	0	0
142	6	15	0	0	0	0	0
143	5	9	0	0	0	0	0
144	14	0	7	7	0	0	2
145	7	0	0	5	0	0	0
146	1	0	0	0	0	0	0
147	9	2	0	0	0	0	0
148	7	0	0	0	0	0	0
149	17	13	0	0	0	0	0
150	10	9	0	0	0	0	0
151	10[+3]	8	0	0	0	0	0
152	9	13	0	0	0	0	0
153	2	0	0	2	0	0	0
154	2	0	0	1	0	0	0
Total	960	890	73	42	12	1	2

* Line 14: 'my love' – could be either *Ego* or *Thou* or both.
† The rival Poet: is this a relationship?
‡ *Ego* as example of mankind.
§ References to *Will*.

3

Shakespeare's hypocrites

L'hypocrisie est un hommage que le vice rend à la vertu.[1]

La Rochefoucauld's famous maxim challenges by the precision with which it is formulated. On further reflection, however, we may apply to it T. W. Baldwin's criticism of the genre as a whole: 'A brilliant aphorism is a dangerous thing. It is always a lie and never the truth.'[2] Questionable though that judgement may be on the aphorism in general, it does seem to me to catch the half-formed nature of this observation – or perhaps, better speaking, its lack of a frame. La Rochefoucauld gives us an observation on behaviour, but withholds speculation on the causes of that behaviour. If we consider why people become hypocrites – as far as I know, no one is ever born one – then we would have to suggest a variety of motives. Shame at what one has done, or is doing, may cause someone to cover his or her vice with the appearance of holiness: this, I suppose, is what is meant by giving homage or paying tribute, to virtue. Hypocrisy of this kind derives from the agent's conscience telling him of his evil, while his desire not to appear evil causes him to feign goodness. His goal is no more than to conceal from others the discrepancy he feels between his own behaviour and what he knows to be the standards of his group, wider society, or religion. Hypocrisy of this kind is familiar to us all, from our own practice of it and from our knowledge of it in others, whether real people or fictional characters, such as the puritan ministers in Ben Jonson's *The Alchemist*. This type of hypocrisy is often backward-looking, designed to retain or consolidate what one already owns – I think of Bulstrode in George Eliot's *Middlemarch*, before his encounter with Will Ladislaw. Yet, in both life and literature – and especially in drama – such static hypocrisy, while condemned (if discovered or exposed), generates neither the energy nor the interest produced by a more dynamic dissimulation. Here the pretence of good is not merely a cover for the continuing practice of one's own faults, whether grave or trifling, but is the method by which a person develops new ones, tries to reach some clearly defined goal. It is a pretence or imposture adopted in order to achieve power, or riches, or sensual gratification, all types of the fulfilment of desire.

In traditional moral thought hypocrisy, like lying, has always been detested as a sin against the fundamental principle of human communication, namely that language was given to mankind so that we may express our thoughts and feelings openly, honestly. The standard accounts in the rhetorical tradition of the divine gift of speech associate language with justice and virtue, sincerity and truth.[3] The liar and the hypocrite are enemies of society since they pervert language to their own gain and other people's harm. In classical literature and ethics hypocrisy is condemned as undermining the essential distinction between good and evil. Juvenal warned:

> *frontis nulla fides; quis enim non vicus abundat*
> *tristibus obscaenis?*

(Men's faces are not to be trusted; does not every street abound in gloomy-visaged debauchees?)

Some men show their passions openly, and may be pardoned. 'Far worse are those who denounce evil ways in the language of a Hercules; and after discoursing on virtue, prepare to practise vice.'[4] In his moral-philosophical works Cicero frequently denounces pretence. In *De Officiis* he describes two ways that men can do wrong, 'by force or by fraud', and says that

> both are bestial: fraud seems to belong to the cunning fox, force to the lion; both are wholly unworthy of man, but fraud is the more contemptible. But of all forms of injustice, none is more flagrant than that of the hypocrite who, at the very moment when he is most false, makes it his business to appear virtuous.

In order to guard against such destructiveness Cicero urges that 'pretence and concealment [*simulatio dissimulatioque*] should be done away with in all departments of our daily life'. In his second oration against Verres Cicero describes hypocrisy in terms which sound like a scenario for Iago's undermining of Othello:

> No acts of treachery are harder to detect than those which lurk under the false show of loyal service [*in simulatione officii*], or some nominal fidelity to a personal obligation. With an open enemy, it is easy to be on your guard and escape him; but this hidden peril, in your own circle and under your own roof, not only does not reveal itself, but overwhelms you before you have time to think how to deal with it.

In the *Academica* he attacks the *simulatio* of virtue which is assumed not out of duty but in pursuit of pleasure, and in *De Finibus* he denounces those whose actions are motivated by personal desire for pleasure rather than respect for the moral law. Such people 'will assuredly prefer the reputation without the reality of goodness [*iustitia simulationem*] to the reality without the reputation'. Yet in one of his letters he comments, 'how far from easy a thing is virtue, how difficult its simulation for any length of time!'[5] This suggests that hypocrisy cannot be sustained indefinitely, or only at great personal cost. Quintilian, as ever more complacent about the orator being a *vir bonus*, declares that

> however we strive to conceal it, insincerity [*simulatio*] will always betray itself, and there was never in any man so great eloquence as would not begin to stumble and hesitate so soon as his words ran counter to his inmost thoughts. Now a bad man cannot help speaking things other than he feels. On the other hand, the good will never be at a loss for honourable words.[6]

Such moral optimism is hard to square with history.

In Christianity denunciations of hypocrisy are a constant in all ages. The Old Testament contains memorable diatribes in the Book of Job, including a similarly optimistic assurance of its brevity: 'Knowest thou not this of old, ... That the triumphing of the wicked is short, and the joy of the hypocrite but for a moment? ... Though wickedness be sweet in his mouth, though he hide it under his tongue', yet it shall turn sour and be 'the gall of asps within him'.[7] Christ attacked the hypocrites in two long and rhetorically structured sequences (as recorded by Matthew), first in the Sermon on the Mount, denouncing their ostentatious alms-giving, praying, fasting, all actions done in public so 'that they may have glory of men'. In the temple he launched another violent attack, punctuated with the ritual curse, seven times repeated, 'Woe unto you, scribes and Pharisees, hypocrites!', including this devastating metaphor: 'for ye are like unto whited sepulchres, which indeed appear beautiful outward, but are within full of dead men's bones, and of all uncleanness'.[8] In another place Christ, too, forecast that hypocrisy would eventually be exposed:

> Beware ye of the leaven of the Pharisees, which is hypocrisy. For there is nothing covered, that shall not be revealed; neither hid, that shall not be known. Therefore whatsoever ye have spoken in darkness shall be heard in the light; and that which ye have spoken in the ear in closets shall be proclaimed upon the housetops.[9]

The Church Fathers inveighed bitterly against hypocrisy, associating it with all forms of evil, depravity, and the work of the devil. As Gregory wrote, '*hypocritarum corda diabolus tacitus tenet, & quasi ipse quietus ibi dormit, ubi eos quos possidet, quiescere non permittit.*'[10] In Dante's *Inferno* the hypocrites are punished by wearing cloaks which are 'whited sepulchres' indeed, 'so gilded outside that they dazzle, but within, all of lead, and so heavy' that they can barely walk: 'O toilsome mantle for eternity!'[11]

The real threat of hypocrisy to the Christian community, as indeed to all others, is the impenetrability with which it conceals evil. Fear of this confusion of values was still so real for the Reverend Alexander Cruden in the late eighteenth century that, not content with defining and illustrating the term from biblical texts, he added two paragraphs of solemn warning:

> This sin of *hypocrisy* is difficultly cured, in that it is not easily discovered by men, and does not expose to shame, but is subservient to many carnal ends. Men cannot dive into the hearts of others, and cannot discern between the paint of *hypocrisy* and the life of holiness. *Hypocrisy* also turns the means of salvation into poison; for the frequent exercise of religious duties, which is the means to sanctify others, confirms and hardens *hypocrites*.

Yet there is a cure, if men recognize divine omniscience:

> The effectual means to cure it, is a stedfast belief of the pure and all-seeing eye of God; who sees sin wherever it is, and will bring it into judgment. A *hypocrite* may hide his sin from the eyes of the others, and sometimes from his own conscience, but can never impose upon God. The stedfast belief of this truth will cause frequent and solemn thoughts of God, as our Inspector and Judge.[12]

Cruden is echoing Christ's words in Luke's gospel, as Milton had done in *Paradise Lost*, after describing how Satan's disguise deceived the archangel Uriel:

> So spake the false dissembler unperceived;
> For neither man nor angel can discern
> Hypocrisy, the only evil that walks
> Invisible, except to God alone.[13]

Drawing on a pagan tradition, Montaigne passed a similar judgement on lying: *'To say that a man lieth, is as much as to say ... that he is brave towards God, and a Coward towards Men.'* 'For', Francis Bacon added, 'a *Lie* faces God, and shrinkes from Man'.[14]

Yet the paradox is that we only use the word hypocrisy when we have reasons for believing that we have found the thing itself. Hypocrisy is curiously associated with its own exposure: concealment is simultaneously effected yet discovered. In works of literature the exposure works on two levels, first in the very act of creation, by which the hypocrite is seen and known to the audience or reader. But on the second level, in most novels and plays there is a sequence of exposure within the literary work itself. It is never the case that a writer creates a hypocrite without giving us some clue, however subtle, to his dissimulation; and it is seldom the case that he is not exposed within the bounds of the artwork. This may sound like a special aesthetic law, but in fact I believe it is implicit in the very act of pronouncing, or thinking, the word 'hypocrite': you only use it when you have caught one. So many of the literary works having *hypocrisy* in their title add to it the word *exposed*, or a synonym. Ten minutes with a good library catalogue will yield plentiful examples: *Hypocrisie Unvail'd and Jesuitisme Unmaskt* (1662) by Robert Boreman, *Hypocrisis Marci Antonii de Dominis detecta* (1620) by John Floyd, *Hypocrisie Alamode, Expos'd in a True Picture of [Jeremy Collier]* (1704) by Thomas Brown, or *Hypocrisie Unmasked*, the title of two works with American associations, one published in 1646 by Edward Winslow relating grievances by *the Governor and Company of Massachusetts against Samuel Gordon of Rhode Island*, the other published in 1776 with the subtitle *or, A short inquiry into the religious complaints of our American colonies*.[15] 'Hypocrisy displayed', then, is a two-stage process, a masking followed by an unmasking.

In drama one might revise Bacon's dictum to read, 'a lie shrinks from men but faces the audience'. While some hypocrites may be known from their outer appearance – Ananias and Tribulation in *The Alchemist*, say – the dramatist must normally establish a two-level process of communication between the hypocritical character and the audience. One way of doing this is to use the soliloquy or aside, such flexible resources on the Elizabethan stage. The aside is a piece of direct address to the audience: it takes place simultaneously with the dramatic action, is produced by, and directed towards, that action, yet stands a little outside it. We might conceive of the aside as occupying a zone midway between the play and the audience; we continue to experience the play, but we do so via the new information or attitudes given us by the character or characters speaking the asides. If used frequently, or if used in conjunction with the soliloquy, this mode of direct presentation brings us into closer contact with that person, so that we in part share his or her hopes and fears, become more closely involved with their desire to control the world. (It seems to me an odd misuse of modern theatre aesthetics to believe that asides and soliloquies are 'distancing' or 'alienating' devices: rather the opposite.)

A significant point about Shakespeare's use of asides and soliloquies in the tragedies based on hypocrisy concerns the allocation of these passages of direct address. In the comedies that expose hypocrisy (Malvolio in *Twelfth Night*, Parolles in *All's Well that Ends Well*), we typically see the hypocrite through the eyes of the group of people exposing him – Sir Toby, Maria, and company; the soldiers trying to make Bertram see his favourite's falseness. The exposers form the moral perspective that defines, and reveals, pretence. In the tragedies, though, Shakespeare gives the direct address to the hypocrites, not their exposers. We see the social group from the viewpoint of the person out to exploit and deceive it. We are made to share his view, and with it his plans and hopes to gain at the expense of good. So, willingly or not, we become the privileged sharers of his dissimulating techniques. This relationship may be expressed in a simple diagram:

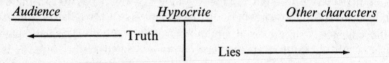

The hypocrite is nearer, his dupes farther off, and this in-between position allows him to exploit his skilful two-facedness. In *Othello*, it is no accident that Iago swears 'by Janus'. Since the hypocrite (it is usually a he: there are few women hypocrites in Elizabethan drama, which may be a comfort to the feminists) tells us the truth, we are able to judge the extent of his lies, his success in duping others. This set-up can indeed create a moral problem for the audience, for our awareness of the hypocrite's skills may easily pass over into admiration of his performance. He becomes an entertainer, a manipulator whose victories we watch as if hypnotized, seeing both the tricks and the mesmeric effect that they have on the innocent. Our enjoyment of his resourcefulness can (temporarily!) blind us to the moral significance of his actions.

Further, since we see his victims through his eyes it becomes harder to keep our own perspective, and judgement, clear. For the dynamic hypocrite other people are either victims or accomplices. The victims are people who stand between him and the desired goal, usually some form of power, and who must be set aside, disbarred, or killed. His superiority over them cannot but make them seem to us inferior, innocent, or naïve, dupes who trust too easily and are soon outwitted. Apart from the victims are the accomplices, who – knowingly or unknowingly – help the hypocrite to achieve his goals. Either way they risk being swept aside in turn when he succeeds, when they also seem stupid. At this point, unless the dramatist is going to allow hypocrisy to triumph, he must bring in some external power to penetrate the hypocrite's disguise. In *The Alchemist* Subtle and Face use all the obfuscations of the spagyrical art to deceive a whole cross-section of Jacobean society, from the tradesman Abel Drugger, anxious to establish his business, to Sir Epicure Mammon, that decadent blend of Marlovian hero and would-be Roman emperor. The hypocrites could continue their spiel for ever, but are destroyed by forces from outside, notably the unexpected return of the master of the house in which they have set up shop. The roles needed for this kind of plot, then, are Hypocrite, Dupe, and Exposer.

Shakespeare brings hypocrisy and dissembling into several comedies – Proteus in *The Two Gentlemen*, Don John in *Much Ado*, Parolles, Malvolio – and uses counter-plots to expose them. Deception is set against pretence, and the hypocrite, once exposed, is punished, exiled, or forgiven. *Measure for Measure* takes this basic pattern and develops it in a new direction. Comparison with the earlier comedies shows that there imposture is usually adopted consciously, deliberately – a man *becomes* a hypocrite for his own gain or/and the ruin of others. But some men, besides achieving hypocrisy, have it thrust upon them. At the beginning of the play Angelo, the deputy judge who rules over Vienna in the Duke's absence, is a man of severe habits, whose austerity suppresses desire in himself and would utterly eradicate it in others. As Lucio, part villain, part commentator, describes him, he is 'one who never feels/The wanton stings and motions of the sense' (I.iv.57ff.). Angelo's judgement on Claudio, a death sentence for having got his bride with child, is severe but consistent with his principles, and he can affirm without hypocrisy, although self-righteously,

> When I that censure him do so offend,
> Let mine own judgement pattern out my death,
> And nothing come in partial.
>
> (II.i.29ff.)

Yet the confrontation with Isabella, come to appeal on her brother's behalf, fills Angelo with desire for the first time in his life, and a soliloquy gives us this crucial information about his new state:

> What's this? What's this? Is this her fault or mine?
> The tempter or the tempted, who sins most, ha?
> Not she; nor doth she tempt; but it is I
> That, lying by the violet in the sun,
> Do as the carrion does, not as the flow'r,
> Corrupt with virtuous season.
>
> (II.ii.162ff.)

Shakespeare there presents Angelo in a soliloquy nearer the mode of tragedy than comedy. Like some hypocrites in tragedy, Angelo's readiness to dissemble could be checked by his conscience. Here he is aware of his fall into corruption, but as yet draws neither conclusion nor consequence from it.

But when we see him next, sexual desire has begun to eat away his conscience, and he feels possessed by 'the strong and swelling evil/Of my conception' (II.iv.6f.). In the great tempting scene between Angelo and Isabella the deputy hypocritically exclaims on other men's sins – 'Ha, fie, these filthy vices!' (II.iv.42) – but proceeds to proposition her with a debased contract, that she should exchange her chastity for her brother's life. Since he is in truth 'now, the voice of the recorded law' (61), he can afford to ignore Isabella's outburst against his 'most pernicious purpose': 'Seeming, seeming!/I will proclaim thee, Angelo; look for't!' (150f.). Whereas hypocrisy in the tragic mode is usually revealed to the audience directly, in advance of the action, here Shakespeare makes Angelo declare himself to a second person, Isabella, confident that – as Falstaff says when he is planning his pretence of having killed Hotspur in battle – 'Nothing confutes me but eyes, and nobody sees me' (*1 Henry IV*, V.iv.125f.):[16]

> Who will believe thee, Isabel?
> My unsoil'd name, th' austereness of my life,
> My vouch against you, and my place i' th' state,
> Will so your accusation overweigh
> That you shall stifle in your own report,
> And smell of calumny....
>   – As for you,
> Say what you can, my false o'erweighs your true.
>
>   (*Measure for Measure*, II.iv.154ff.)

And indeed, Angelo's position is impregnable, unless some force from outside, with superior knowledge, can expose him.

At this point Shakespeare brings back the Duke, disguised as a Friar, who sets in motion a complex plot involving several substitutions: of Mariana for Isabella, in Angelo's bed; of the head of Ragozine, 'a most notorious pirate', for Claudio's (IV.iii.69). The final substitution is of the Duke for the Friar, returning in his own person to act as a tribunal for complaints against Angelo. This 'outward-sainted deputy', as Isabella calls him (in words that recall Christ's 'whited sepulchres'), who imagines that he has enjoyed the sister and killed the brother – thus breaking even the corrupt contract he had himself proposed – listens with composure to Isabella's accusation that he is 'a murderer, ... an adulterous thief,/An hypocrite, a virgin-violator' (V.i.39ff). Isabella does not know that the Duke had played the role of the Friar instructing her in the foiling of Angelo's plots, and so, lacking any independent evidence, she realizes how feeble her case must seem; yet she still affirms that

>   the wicked'st caitiff on the ground,
> May seem as shy, as grave, as just, as absolute
> As Angelo.
>
>   (V.i.53ff.)

But the Duke, behaving as Angelo had predicted, and as he would have to behave if he had no evidence, sweeps aside her complaint, leaving her with only heaven to appeal to:

> Then, O you blessèd ministers above,
> Keep me in patience, and with ripened time
> Unfold the evil which is here wrapp'd up
> In countenance!
>
>   (V.i.115ff.)

The evil is indeed finally 'unfolded', not by heaven but by the Duke, although Angelo (as if recalling that passage in Luke's gospel) ascribes divine omniscience to him:

O my dread lord,
I should be guiltier than my guiltiness
To think I can be undiscernible,
When I perceive your grace, like pow'r divine,
Hath look'd upon my passes.

(363ff.)

But the Duke has only used deception and disguise, legitimately, as Shakespeare makes him say: 'Craft against vice I must apply' (III.ii.270).

Although one might not realize it from some modern accounts, *Measure for Measure* is a comedy, and Angelo can be dismissed at the end to marry his contracted wife, since his hypocrisy had no evil effects. In the history plays and tragedies the consequences of hypocrisy are more serious. Here the hypocrite is often connected with the actor in that peculiar process by which Shakespeare, within a play performed by actors in a theatre, could make those actors refer to acting in terms of insincerity. This metaphor of the stage or the world as a place for performance and pretence is familiar, but it is often misinterpreted as a criticism of the theatre. In fact theatrical imagery is, and always has been derogatory, used to expose human pretence, or the futility of secular life compared to some other existence or system.[17] The metaphor does not in itself debase the theatre, and although Shakespeare is using plays and actors to present insincerity or hypocrisy that does not make him or them corrupt: the medium is not the same as the message. Rather, the second-level falseness of the role that the dramatic persona adopts serves to legitimize the first-level status of the actor. When, in the last play of the *Henry VI* trilogy, the future Richard III is presenting to the audience his capabilities – as if auditioning for the role of hypocrite – he exults at being able to

wet my cheeks with artificial tears,
And frame my face to all occasions. . . .
I'll play the orator as well as Nestor,
Deceive more slily than Ulysses could,
And, like a Sinon, take another Troy.
I can add colours to the chameleon,
Change shapes with Proteus for advantages,
And set the murderous Machiavel to school.

(*3 Henry VI*, III.ii.184ff.)

By grouping all those *exempla* of deceit Shakespeare makes us unconscious of the initial role-playing of the actor involved, alerting us to the deceptions he is about to foist on others.

Richard III is the first full-scale hypocrite in Shakespeare, using the dramatic structure I have described, based on the dichotomies near/far, truth/lies, with supreme energy and skill. In the opening soliloquy he declares his true intent:

> I am determinéd to prove a villain....
> Plots have I laid, inductions dangerous,
> By drunken prophecies, libels and dreams,
> To set my brother Clarence and the King
> In deadly hate the one against the other:
> And if King Edward be as true and just
> As I am subtle, false and treacherous,

then Clarence will go to prison this day. – And pat, like the catastrophe in the old comedy, Clarence is seen approaching guarded, on his way to the Tower. At this point an aside from Richard marks the turning-point between truth and concealment: 'Dive, thoughts, down to my soul – here Clarence comes!' (*Richard III*, I.i.30–41). The two-facedness of the hypocrite is expressed not only by his privileged relationship to the audience in his dealings with others but by means of equivocation, a doubleness of language in which an innocuous level of meaning is visible to the dupe, sinister undertones to us. So Richard assures Clarence that his 'imprisonment shall not be long;/I will deliver you, else *lie* for you' (I.i.114–15). Clarence hears the sense 'go to prison on your behalf', and we that of untruth. In the brief soliloquy following Clarence's exit Richard keeps up the equivocation: 'I will shortly send thy soul to heaven,/If heaven will take the present at our hands' (119–20). In one place Shakespeare stretches the hypocrite's resourcefulness to the limits, when an aside about the wisdom of the young Prince meant only for the audience – 'So wise, so young, they say do never live long' – is overheard by the Prince himself – 'What say you uncle?' – forcing Richard to improvise brilliantly:

> I say, without characters, fame lives long.
> [*Aside*] Thus, like the formal vice Iniquity,
> I moralize two meanings in one word.
>
> (III.i.79ff.)

But this superiority of wit places the audience in any uneasy position: if we laugh with the deceiver we could share his dehumanizing of the dupe. Laughter here might anaesthetize our feelings, deaden us to the moral issue.

The opening scene has no less than three of Richard's ten soliloquies, which inform us at every stage of his dissimulation. The normal dramatic sequence for this mode of communication is triple:

Prediction	–	Action	–	Commentary
(aside, soliloquy)		(public speech)		(aside, soliloquy)

So in the third and last soliloquy Richard reminds us of his concealed plot, his 'deep intent' to kill Clarence – deep to the rest of the world, visible to us – and tells us of his further plan to marry Lady Anne ('What though I kill'd her husband and her father?'). He is at pains to assure us that he will do so

> not all so much for love
> As for another secret close intent
> By marrying her which I must reach unto.

(149ff.)

We are privileged to share in these Machiavellian plans (the word 'reach' has such connotations: 'overreach' is when the Machiavel attempts too much), and we see them fulfilled in the brilliant wooing scene that follows. This second stage is carried out in public speech to which we have been given the decoding key, and from our privileged perspective the success of the hypocrite has unfortunate consequences for the dupe. As the history of Shakespeare criticism has shown, Lady Anne has all too often been seen either as a particularly silly person or as representing the weak and malleable sex.[18]

After the Action comes the Commentary, again addressed exclusively to us:

> Was ever woman in this humour wooed?
> Was ever woman in this humour won?
> I'll have her; but I will not keep her long.

Shakespeare indeed emphasizes the excellence of the performance, as if from a purely aesthetic point of view, with Richard simultaneously producer, actor, and audience celebrating his skill:

> What! I, that killed her husband and his father,
> To take her in her heart's extremest hate,
> With curses in her mouth, tears in her eyes,
> The bleeding witness of my hatred by;
> Having God, her conscience, and these bars against me,
> And I no friends to back my suit at all,
> But the plain and dissembling looks. –

'Tis well done, indeed! – Yet, as the continuation makes clear, success for the hypocrite implies contempt for the dupe:

> Hath she forgot already that brave prince,
> Edward, her lord, ...
> And will she yet abase her eyes on me...?

(I.ii.227ff.)

Richard's combination of gloating self-admiration and criticism of his victim makes Lady Anne doubly unfortunate, both gulled and guilty of disloyalty to her dead husband.

Richard's second victim, Clarence, is also taken in by the hypocrite's feigned concern, but since the real plot against him has been done through intermediaries he may seem less blameworthy. Richard's other dupes seem

99

culpably naïve, deceived by false appearances. Hastings affirms his loyalty to 'my master's heirs in true descent', despite being explicitly told that Richard intends to be king (III.ii.36–55), and in the face of ominous dreams and omens (III.ii.10ff., III.iv.81ff.). There is a moment of high comedy, almost, in Hastings' comments at the council scene when Richard has gone out with Buckingham (to plot Hastings' death, as it happens), that

> I think there's never a man in Christendom
> Can lesser hide his love, or hate, than he,
> For by his face straight shall you know his heart.
>
> (III.iv.51ff.)

As Hasting soon realizes, he has been 'too fond' (or foolish) to penetrate Richard's deceit (III.iv.80). Despite being exercised at such length, Crookback's histrionic powers show no abatement. Deciding that he must marry Elizabeth, the daughter of his dead brother Edward, he woos her mother on her behalf in a scene which repeats the wooing of Lady Anne, his enormous energies finally overcoming all of her well-merited opposition (IV.iv.199–430). Once she has capitulated and goes off to gain her daughter's assent he switches faces, turning to us in the middle of a line: 'Bear her my true love's kiss; and so, farewell/Relenting fool, and shallow-changing woman!' (431–2). The manipulator's contempt for his victims is hard to ignore.[19]

  Richard's accomplice in all this is Buckingham, who shares the same two-faced split between open good and concealed evil. As he says to one of their tools:

> Come Catesby, thou art sworn
> As deeply to effect what we intend,
> As closely to conceal what we impart.
>
> (III.i.157ff.)

When Buckingham presents his credentials for deceiving the London citizens it is in the same theatrical-Machiavellian terms as Richard:

> Tut, I can counterfeit the deep tragedian,
> Speak, and look back, and pry on every side,
> Tremble and start at wagging of a straw,
>   ... ghastly looks
> Are at my service, like enforcèd smiles,
> And both are ready in their offices
> At any time to grace my stratagems.
>
> (III.v.5ff.)

But Buckingham himself is deceived, as we realized long ago in the flurry of insincere praise that Richard heaped upon him:

My other self, my counsel's consistory,
My oracle, my prophet, my dear cousin!
I, as a child, will go by thy direction.

(II.ii.151–3)

Buckingham should have known that such effusiveness from a hypocrite can only bode ill. Given the dichotomous speech model that Richard uses, one need only invert the sense to discover the true meaning.

The sticking-point for Buckingham is the murder of the princes in the Tower, and in two brief soliloquies Richard resolves to break with this half-hearted Machiavellian – 'High-reaching Buckingham grows circumspect' (IV.ii.31). The accomplice becomes an enemy, and in due course a victim, at which point he can only salute the irony of his being executed on All Souls' Day: 'This is the day wherein I wished to fall/By the false faith of him whom most I trusted' (V.i.16f.). Richard has gained power by the successful interchange of the two resources that Machiavelli (as so often, drawing on Cicero but ignoring his moral scheme) singled out as the means by which legitimate rule could be overcome, force and fraud:

it seldom happens that men rise from low condition to high rank without employing either force or fraud. ... Nor do I believe that force alone will ever be found to suffice, whilst it will often be the case that cunning alone serves the purpose.[20]

So he recommended that the Prince who wishes to succeed must not only unite the attributes of the fox and the lion, fraud and force, but in addition

must know how to whitewash [*colorire*] these attributes perfectly, to be a liar and a hypocrite [*simulatore e dissimulatore*]. Men are inexperienced [*semplici*], and are so bound to the needs of the moment that the deceiver will always find someone who will let himself be deceived.[21]

Richard's achievement of the throne necessarily brings him out into the open, where fraud and concealment are of no use and force alone can preserve him. Once seen and known, he is vulnerable to attack, and the forces of legitimacy under Richmond duly muster against him. Yet Shakespeare also undermines him from within, in the great scene where the ghosts of all the people he has murdered appear in turn, cursing him and blessing Richmond (V.iii.118–206). In his anguished soliloquy on awaking from what he thinks has only been a dream, we see that the hypocrite has lost for ever the advantage he has had over other people. There is no longer any dichotomy of truth and lies that he can manipulate from midway between the audience and the other characters. He is now wholly caught up in his own sufferings, in a new dichotomy, an agonizing split within himself:

Richard loves Richard; that is, I am I.
Is there a murderer here? No – yes, I am:
Then fly. What, from myself? Great reason why –
Lest I revenge. Myself upon myself?
Alack, I love myself. For any good
That I myself have done unto myself?
O, no! Alas, I rather hate myself
For hateful deeds committed by myself!

(V.iii.179ff.)

Although he rejects conscience as 'but a word that cowards use,/Devised at first to keep the strong in awe' (309f.), the duality between truth and lies proves too great for Richard to sustain. The role of the hypocrite becomes too much for him: he is, in the end, 'o'er-parted'. As Cicero said, it is difficult to maintain *simulatio* for any length of time.

The optimism of the secular moralists that hypocrisy will reveal itself, the conviction of a Christian that God can penetrate it, these are reassuring attitudes in the long term. Yet they are of no consolation to Richard's victims, and as we look back over his career of slaughter we see that for Shakespeare hypocrisy is a particularly sinister vice, often associated with ruthless egoism. Here, as in the mature tragedies, the hypocrite is ready to destroy anyone if he can benefit from it. There can be few writers who have so closely linked pretence with destructiveness. I feign: I gain: you've lost.

In *Macbeth* the first hypocrite we hear of, the Thane of Cawdor, has already been exposed. Like Juvenal, Duncan realizes

There's no art
To find the mind's construction in the face:
He was a gentleman on whom I built
An absolute trust.

(I.iv.11ff.)

At this point enters Macbeth, the new Thane of Cawdor, a double irony that critics have long relished. Macbeth resembles Angelo in many ways, his hypocrisy being similarly fed by desire yet opposed by conscience. His desire is for the crown, and the way he starts at the witches' double prophecy shows that he already has it in mind. His reaction puzzles Banquo, but Macbeth explains it to us in an aside:

Two truths are told
As happy prologues to the swelling act
Of the imperial theme.

(I.iii.126f.)

The word 'swelling' is sometimes glossed by comparison with a stage thronged with people, but it also suggests pregnancy, and we may recall Angelo's sense of 'the strong and swelling evil/Of my conception'. Macbeth also judges himself, and his many asides and soliloquies (structurally as important as in *Richard III*, although vastly more compressed) bring us into close contact with his divided claims of desire and conscience ('This supernatural solic-iting/Cannot be ill; cannot be good'). Our closeness to him involves us in his struggle. Yet, together with the involvement, his own moral sense establishes a detached, judging position. So we share his horror as he observes in himself, experiences almost passively – as if it were happening to someone else – the emergence of the tempting desire to murder Duncan ('suggestion' still had the sense of diabolic temptation):

> If good, why do I yield to that suggestion
> Whose horrid image doth unfix my hair
> And make my seated heart knock at my ribs
> Against the use of nature? Present fears
> Are less than horrible imaginings.
> My thought, whose murder yet is but fantastical,
> Shakes so my single state of man that function
> Is smothered by surmise, and nothing is
> But what is not.
>
> (I.iii.133ff.)

There, with amazing speed, and as if parenthetically ('whose murder yet') we become privy to the secret that sets him apart from the others on stage, the goal to which all his energies will ultimately be directed.

Knowledge of Macbeth's intentions gives us the superior insight to gauge the false appearances that he assumes. One of the least often discussed aspects of Shakespeare's mastery of language is his ability to present insincerity: whenever anyone in his plays is being insincere, the style shows it. So Macbeth thanks Duncan's messengers with this affected metaphor: 'Kind gentlemen, your pains/Are registered where every day I turn/The leaf to read them' (149ff.). In similarly insincere terms he thanks Duncan for the honours he has received from him:

> The service and the loyalty I owe,
> In doing it, pays itself. Your highness' part
> Is to receive our duties, and our duties
> Are to your throne and state children and servants;
> Which do but what they should, by doing everything
> Safe toward your love and honour.
>
> (I.iv.22ff.)

These speeches are subtly calculated by Shakespeare, for their insincerity is obvious to us (the affected metaphors, the flabby repetitions) but not to the recipients. Macbeth is using language on two levels, one of which rebukes the other. Once Duncan has created his eldest son Prince of Cumberland, and named him his successor, we see the real language, the accents of desire:

> [*Aside*] The Prince of Cumberland! – that is a step
> On which I must fall down, or else o'erleap,
> For in my way it lies. Stars, hide your fires,
> Let not light see my black and deep desires.

> (48ff.)

The paradox of these invocations of darkness and deception is that they are being made to the audience: the lies hide from men but face us, and in that respect we enjoy the privilege of God.

The structure of deception takes on another layer when Lady Macbeth learns of the prophecies. Where Macbeth had been concealed or opaque to Duncan, and was thus in a superior position, manipulating him by pretence, we now see Lady Macbeth putting herself in the dominant position, planning to manipulate her husband:

> Glamis thou art, and Cawdor, and shalt be
> What thou art promised: yet do I fear thy nature,
> It is too full o' th' milk of human kindness
> To catch the nearest way....
>
>   Hie thee hither,
> That I may pour my spirits in thine ear.

> (I.v.14ff., 24ff.)

Macbeth is now transparent to her, and she to us. His ignorance of what she feels about his 'human kindness' – she rejects any 'compunctious visiting of nature' (44) – makes him a victim, or accomplice, who has to be instructed in hypocrisy:

> Your face, my thane, is as a book, where men
> May read strange matters. To beguile the time,
> Look like the time, bear welcome in your eye,
> Your hand, your tongue: look like th' innocent flower,
> But be the serpent under 't.

> (61ff.)

One of Shakespeare's problems in having to develop an evil conspiracy in the absence of any vocal moral commentary on it is to make it judge or condemn itself. This is done here, partly directly, as in the injunction to be like the serpent, and partly indirectly, in her perversion of such words as 'milk' or 'nature'. Her parting injunction to him is to 'look up clear' (71), 'clear' meaning 'innocent, spotless': the stress must fall on the verb, 'look' or 'seem'.

The dichotomy between appearance and reality, the continuity of metaphors for usurpation applied to Macbeth, the incredible number of antitheses (some 400 odd): these are aspects of the play that have been well studied in modern criticism, and all show its persistent operation on two linguistic levels. It is a textbook for the study of dramatic irony in all its forms. But irony is always double-edged. When Lady Macbeth welcomes Duncan, the fulsome insincerity of her verse is by now unmistakable to us:

> All our service
> In every point twice done, and then done double,
> Were poor and single business to contend
> Against those honours deep and broad, wherewith
> Your majesty loads our house.
>
> (I.vi.14ff.)

Yet, while feigning gratitude she is also expressing exactly the reasons why she ought to feel gratitude:

> For those of old,
> And the late dignities heaped up to them,
> We rest your hermits.
>
> (18ff.)

The unusual and affected word 'hermits' points up her insincerity, while the content of the speech establishes the good they have received from Duncan. Shakespeare shows her feigning, but simultaneously condemns her. In the next scene Macbeth, speaking alone and with no need to deceive anyone (given the convention in Elizabethan drama that what characters say in soliloquy is true), admits the evil of their 'deep intent':

> He's here in double trust:
> First, as I am his kinsman and his subject,
> Strong both against the deed: then, as his host,
> Who should against his murderer shut the door,
> Not bear the knife myself. Besides, this Duncan
> Hath borne his faculties so meek, hath been
> So clear in his great office.
>
> (I.vii.12ff.)

Duncan is 'clear', really has that freedom from guilt or stain that his wife had urged Macbeth to assume: in a sense he tries to do so here, in his defence of Duncan's right to be treated with love and respect, and in his invocation of 'pity', that constant test of humanity in Shakespeare. Yet when he expresses this moral sense to his wife – 'We will proceed no further in this business./He hath honoured me of late (31f.) – she is able to sweep his scruples aside by mocking his cowardice and by showing her own readiness to be the accomplice in this 'terrible feat'.

Once the murder is done the hypocrisy must continue: in Marvell's version of Machiavelli, 'The same *Arts* that did *gain*/A *Pow'r* must it *maintain*'.[22] The same insincere welcome is used by Macbeth to Macduff: 'The labour we delight in physics pain' (II.iii.48f.), and at the news of Duncan's murder Lady Macbeth is given one of the most brilliant pieces of hypocrisy Shakespeare ever invented: 'Woe, alas!/What, in our house?' (II.iii.86ff.). This is what any innocent hostess would say in those circumstances: Lady Macbeth knows exactly how things ought to look (*scheinheilig*, as one says in German). Her husband makes a veritable meal of professing his regrets:

> Had I but died an hour before this chance,
> I had lived a blessed time; for from this instant
> There's nothing serious in mortality:
> All is but toys: renown and grace is dead,
> The wine of life is drawn ....

(90ff.)

The multiple functions of dramatic irony are apparent here, for this speech is both self-fulfilling – Macbeth will not enjoy any 'blessed time' from this point onwards – and literally true, since 'grace is dead', and Macbeth has killed it (one of its forms is sleep, which he has also murdered). 'The spring, the head, the fountain of your blood/Is stopped', he says to the king's sons, but as Shakespeare soon makes clear, the lifeblood of the whole state has been dammed and perverted.

The effects of hypocrisy in *Macbeth*, compared to *Richard III*, are far greater, spreading outwards from the king's murder, creating correspondent perversions in the whole realm of nature. The hypocrisy of the murderers, then, is the means by which they both gained trust – 'Fair and noble hostess,/We are your guest tonight' were among Duncan's last words – and destroyed it. The breakdown of trust which they effect is graphically represented by Shakespeare, first by the way in which the king's sons, fleeing the country, are suspected to have been his killers; second, in the scene where Macduff, who has finally fled Scotland (his wife and children are murdered by Macbeth in his absence), is confronted and tested by Malcolm. The king's son feigns all manner of vice, exceeding even Macbeth –

> I grant him bloody,
> Luxurious, avaricious, false, deceitful,
> Sudden, malicious, smacking of every sin
> That has a name.

(IV.iii.57ff.)

– but professing for himself a list of vices so horrible that Macduff is forced to exclaim that if he succeeds to the throne, Scotland will receive a far worse tyrant. At which point Malcolm explains that he was merely pretending, in order to test his countryman, who might have been an emissary of Macbeth's:

> Macduff, this noble passion,
> Child of integrity, hath from my soul
> Wiped the black scruples, reconciled my thoughts
> To thy good truth and honour. Devilish Macbeth
> By many of these trains hath sought to win me
> Into his power; and modest wisdom plucks me
> From over-credulous haste.

(114ff.)

Duncan had trusted his kinsman, and host, and been murdered for his pains. If trust is to establish itself again, it has to do so by such devious and long-winded means, and it has to use the tools of its antitype. Paradoxically, only through deception, now, can sincerity be distinguished from hypocrisy. Malcolm might say, with the Duke in *Measure for Measure*, 'Craft against vice I must apply'.

Consideration of the nature of hypocrisy in *Macbeth* reinforces our awareness that Shakespeare connects it with all other forms of evil, the initial dissimulation leading to treason, regicide, and the never-ending chain of murder by which Macbeth destroys the whole of Scotland:

> Alas, poor country, ...
> ... It cannot
> Be called our mother, but our grave;
> ... the dead man's knell
> Is there scarce asked for who, and good men's lives
> Expire before the flowers in their caps,
> Dying or ere they sicken.

(IV.iii.164ff.)

Macbeth, having used fraud and force to obtain power, must now use force openly. The function of hypocrisy in the initial stage of usurping legitimacy is now clear; once it has gained its desires, evil can afford to declare itself. Yet in Macbeth's case that declaration was not voluntary, or the result of carelessness. His guilt has been exposed by his own actions. The insecurity he feels, knowing that Banquo's children are prophesied to become the lineal kings of Scotland, makes him plan to kill Banquo. In his professed concern for Banquo's welfare (III.i.11–38), as in his urging on of the murderers (III.i.73–139), Macbeth displayed some of his earlier resource in hypocrisy, although the scene with the murderers is laboured, I believe deliberately, to show how energy and invention are gradually deserting him.

Macbeth's explanation of why they must kill Banquo for him is a perfect description of the tribute that vice pays to virtue: because of

> certain friends that are both his and mine.
> Whose loves I may not drop, but wail his fall
> Who I myself struck down: and thence it is

> That I to your assistance do make love,
> Masking the business from the common eye,
> For sundry weighty reasons.
>
> (III.i.119ff.)

That is almost too explicit in its description of the gap between false surface and his true feelings, and in its affected, forced language ('to your assistance do make love'). But the level of pretence he sustains after the murder is penetrated and exposed by the arrival of the very being whose absence he so insincerely deplores: 'Here had we now our country's honour roofed,/Were the graced person of our Banquo present' (III.iv.40ff.). To accuse Banquo of 'unkindness', unnatural ingratitude, in not attending, having just had him murdered, is one of the greatest perversions of truth and goodness in Shakespeare, and is immediately answered by the appearance of the ghost. Macbeth defends but at the same time accuses himself; 'Thou canst not say I did it: never shake/Thy gory locks at me' (50f.). Lady Macbeth succeeds in calming him by her usual tactics of scornful reductivism: 'When all's done,/You look but on a stool' (67f.), and mockery of his cowardice: 'What! quite unmanned in folly?' (73). So he tries again, but is instinctively led toward his own fatal, self-revealing hypocrisy:

> I drink to th' general joy o' th' whole table,
> And to our dear friend Banquo, whom we miss;
> Would he were here! to all, and him, we thirst,
> And all to all!
> LORDS [*drinking*]. Our duties, and the pledge.
> MACBETH [*turns to his seat*]. Avaunt! and quit my sight! let the earth hide thee!
>
> (III.iv.89ff.)

The appearance of the ghost to unmask Macbeth's hypocritical greetings in the very moment when he utters them is Shakespeare's most brilliant device in the 'exposure' sequence. (In *Siegfried* Wagner achieved a comparable brilliance in that Siegfried, having been splashed by the blood of the dragon he has killed, wins the ability to penetrate the hypocrisy of Mime, who is made to profess good while simultaneously revealing the real evil he intends.)

The workings of some obscure principle of retribution, Macbeth believes – 'It will have blood, they say; blood will have blood' (122) – have here 'brought forth/The secret'st man of blood' (125f.). The exposure of his hypocrisy has been made by an innate moral principle in the universe. The same principle is at work in the other great invention in this play, Lady Macbeth's sleep-walking. That she, who has always denied any further consequences of their evil – 'A little water clears us of this deed:/How easy is it then!' (II.ii.67f.) – should now collapse under it, seems to vindicate the powers of good, operating in so many different ways in the second half of this play. This 'great perturbation in nature' (V.i.9f.) causes her to reveal all their deeds, an effect made much more intense in the theatre by the Doctor writing down all that she says, so that hypocrisy is not only detected but recorded.

> LADY MACBETH. Yet who would have thought the old man to have had so
>   much blood in him?
> DOCTOR. Do you mark that?
>
> (V.i.38ff.)

As she reveals more, the Doctor turns to rebuke Lady Macbeth's gentle-woman for having heard these secrets of state:

> DOCTOR. Go to, go to; you have known what you should not.
> GENTLEWOMAN. She has spoke what she should not, I am sure of that:
>   heaven knows what she has known.
>
> (45ff.)

Yet the audience, divine in that, has known all along. As the Doctor gives the conventional lore of his day, a blend of ethics and medicine:

> unnatural deeds
> Do breed unnatural troubles: infected minds
> To their deaf pillows will discharge their secrets.
> More needs she the divine than the physician.
>
> (70ff.)

we see that we are also those 'deaf pillows', that the masking and unmasking has been all for our sake. The superiority of *Macbeth* over *Measure for Measure* in this respect is that it needs no external moral force, such as the Duke, to 'Unfold the evil, which is here wrapp'd up/In countenance.' Evil expresses and exposes *itself* now, as an organic extension of its own workings. In the moral optimism informing this play, evil may corrode trust, but it also destroys the healthy functioning of all who give themselves over to it. The Ghost of Banquo is more than a figment of Macbeth's imagination: it stands in some way in relation to his conscience. It lacks the grandeur of Macbeth's earlier apocalyptic image of pity,

> like a naked new-born babe,
> Striding the blast, or Heaven's cherubim, horsed
> Upon the sightless couriers of the air.
>
> (*Macbeth*, I.vii.21ff.)

Yet it is no less the response to what Macbeth knows to be his 'horrid deed'. Devastating though it is in its presentation of the destructive power of guilt, *Macbeth* may be thought a comforting play, finally, in that hypocrisy exposes itself.

No such comforts can be gleaned from *Othello*. Indeed, it remains the most uncomfortable play in the English language. Everyone must admire it as a supreme example of the unremitting development of one basic situation, Iago's destruction of Othello, with a claustrophilic refusal to digress or vary from its path, yet no one is known to have enjoyed it. Every time I start to read it my spirits sink. But neither Shakespeare's tragedies nor life itself can be fully understood unless we are prepared to take Iago fully into our consciousness, and make our own attempt to come to terms with what Shakespeare created. (What hand or eye, we may well ask, could afford to gestate such a thing for the six to nine months Shakespeare usually took to write a play? To live with Iago as a reader, or in the theatre, is bad enough; to create him shows an ability to conceive evil that almost strikes us as perverse and unnatural. Except....)

I define the basic situation as that of Iago destroying Othello, since I believe that much modern criticism of the play has gone wrong through beginning with Othello, or through not giving Iago his full measure of dominance. This is not the place to show the history of this misinterpretation, so I will merely suggest that discussions of the play ought to start from the beginning, as Shakespeare did, with the presence of Iago. It is a presence that dominates the action, first of all in its intimacy with the audience. No one else in the tragedies has as many soliloquies as Iago does (not even Hamlet). Hamlet is given soliloquies for reflection, self-criticism, and for resolves to act, some of which are carried out; Iago has them for self-presentation and for announcements of his actions which – like Richard III in his self-confidence – are first described, then performed, and subsequently commented on. He is forever telling us what he will do and why, forever taking us into his confidence. Now, there is no one in the world whose confidence I would rather share less than Iago's, and that is one of the reasons for the discomfort I feel each time I experience this play. We are confronted with a man whose sole aim in life is to manipulate and destroy others, a dedication to evil that even Macbeth and his wife do not match. They want power, and will destroy to gain it; Iago wants the power to destroy. They can work by fraud and open force; he only by fraud, through which his gulls are made to use force. Whereas they expose themselves by coming to power, he can remain concealed indefinitely. Every word Iago speaks to us is a demonstration, an exposure, and a revelling in his own hypocrisy, which remains completely concealed from all the other characters in the play.

They only person in the play to whom he reveals some of his real feelings is Roderigo, but only while using him as a tool, spending his money, and working him up to be the accomplice in his attack on Othello. Iago's first stated reason for hating his master is that he has been passed over in favour of 'a great arithmetician', a 'counter-caster', Michael Cassio (*Othello*, I.i.19–31). Iago's contempt for the new breed of Renaissance soldier, necessarily more technical given the increasingly scientific development of warfare in the sixteenth century, may be intended to show that his complaint is the predictable and irrelevant grumble of the old-fashioned soldier made obsolete by new technology. There is not enough evidence to decide this issue, but there is enough to be sure what we should feel about the conclusions he draws concerning Othello:

> I follow him to serve my turn upon him.
> We cannot all be masters, nor all masters
> Cannot be truly followed.
>
> (I.i.42ff.)

One part of this antithesis follows – some men must be servants – but not the other: why cannot all masters be served 'truly'? Iago describes those who serve 'duteously' with a series of contemptuous images, ending 'Whip me such honest knaves' (44–9). He then holds up his own ideal, a calculated inversion which in a normal man might be the text for a denunciation of what Cicero called the treachery 'lurking under the false show of loyal service':

> Others there are
> Who, trimmed in forms and visages of duty,
> Keep yet their hearts attending on themselves;
> And, throwing but shows of service on their lords,
> Do well thrive by them; and, when they've lined their coats,
> Do themselves homage.
>
> (I.i.49ff.)

At this point, normally, the attack on evil would be made; but Iago unconcernedly identifies himself with this group: 'These fellows have some soul,/And such a one do I profess myself' (53ff.). The elevation of false appearance is made by no one in Shakespeare with the same fanaticism as Iago, for whom it becomes a principle of life. He does not serve out of 'love and duty', but only 'seeming so', for his own ends. And he exults, like Richard III, in his abilities in deception, which have indeed supplanted his real self:

> For when my outward action doth demonstrate
> The native act and figure of my heart
> In complement extern, 'tis not long after
> But I will wear my heart upon my sleeve
> For daws to peck at. I am not what I am.
>
> (62ff.)

It is difficult for a modern audience, which has lost that sense of reverence attaching to 'service' that animated Renaissance society, from the glorification of the *vita activa* down to the duties of bondsmen and tenants, to appreciate fully the shock that these self-revelations would have had. Iago systematically inverts all the great positives of dedication and loyalty, offers

111

in their place an unnatural egoism. (Note the awkward self-reflexive phrasing of such men having 'their hearts attending on themselves', doing 'themselves homage', or in Iago saying 'I follow but myself'. All three phrases describe forms of impossibility: language can say it, but a man cannot do it – unless he has two selves.)

This first scene establishes Iago as a hypocrite and as a rapacious egoist, the same combination that we observed in *Macbeth*, the one state creating and supporting the other. Having declared to Roderigo his true feelings about Othello, Iago later explains why he pays tribute to virtue: personal gain.

> Though I do hate him as I do hell-pains,
> Yet, for necessity of present life,
> I must show out a flag and sign of love,
> Which is indeed but sign.

(I.i.155ff.)

Immediately afterwards we see Iago telling Othello of Brabantio's anger, and claiming that 'I lack iniquity/Sometimes to do me service', else, 'with the little godliness' he had, he would have attacked Roderigo (I.ii.3ff.). That total reversal of the truth is prophetic of Iago's methods. He deceives those near to him by his professions of love – 'A man he is of honesty and trust', Othello says (I.iii.284); Iago calls Roderigo 'noble heart' (I.iii.302) and swears fidelity to him:

RODERIGO. Wilt thou be fast to my hopes if I depend on the issue?
IAGO. Thou art sure of me.

(I.iii.360ff.)

– yet as soon as they have left the scene he turns to us and shows his loathing and contempt:

> Thus do I ever make my fool my purse;
> For I mine own gained knowledge should profane
> If I would time expend with such a snipe
> But for my sport and profit.

(I.iii.381ff.)

That Othello should trust him, merely makes him a gull: 'He holds me well;/The better shall my purpose work on him' (392f.). The cumulative effect of these direct revelations of his intentions is to make us highly alert to Iago's language when he is with other people. Since we know that he is out to deceive and destroy, everything he says has a second meaning to us. If the normal description of the linguistic sign, following Saussure, is Signified over Signifier, then when Iago speaks we have to enclose that whole sign in another bracket, which would invert it, opposing surface and real meaning.[23] (This is a necessarily more complicated formulation than Saussure's, since linguistics is usually concerned with 'normal' communication, not with irony, hypocrisy, or lying.) Listening to Iago is a double process of decoding: deciphering his utterance in the way that his dupes understand it, and decoding it again to understand how he meant it. The two signals are discrepant, on a scale ranging from partial to total incongruence. We are somehow able to perform both operations simultaneously.

A clear-cut instance of these inversions of meaning is the sequence in Act II where Iago engineers the downfall of Cassio. He instructs Roderigo to 'find some occasion to anger Cassio': 'Sir, he's rash and very sudden in choler, and haply may strike at you – provoke him that he may; for even out of that will I cause these of Cyprus to mutiny' (II.i.261ff.). (These are the same tactics by which the tribunes eject Coriolanus from office and from society.) When Roderigo, 'this poor trash of Venice', leaves, Iago tells us that his plan is still vague, but that he intends to bring Othello to the point where surface and reality are so inverted that he will 'thank' Iago for making him an ass,

> And practising upon his peace and quiet
> Even to madness. 'Tis here, but yet confused;
> Knavery's plain face is never seen till used.
>
> (II.i.302ff.)

In the event, Iago succeeds in making Cassio drunk, proceeds to 'put' him into an 'action' that – just like the tribunes' manipulation – degrades him yet 'approves my dream' (II.iii.58ff.) – his fantasy or plan of success. To Montano, Iago lies that Cassio is always drunk, and professes to 'fear the trust Othello puts him in' (121–31). Montano reacts to this inversion of the truth with the correct response (assuming it to be true) which Iago has elicited from him, namely that Othello ought to be told; at which point Iago demurs, with the pretence of friendship:

> Not I, for this fair island:
> I do love Cassio well, and would do much
> To cure him of this evil.
>
> (II.iii.143ff.)

From that declaration, after the ensuing brawl, Iago has built himself a platform from which he can now act the perfect friend:

> I had rather have this tongue cut from my mouth
> Than it should do offence to Michael Cassio;
> Yet, I persuade myself, to speak the truth
> Shall nothing wrong him.
>
> (217ff.)

As we alone know, to get the truth from what Iago says about Cassio one must simply invert everything he says. The climax of his tale is to profess to excuse Cassio – 'But men are men; the best sometimes forget' (237) – an extremely effective way of indicting him in the eyes of those present. If

113

hypocrisy formally resembles irony in operating on two levels in its systematic inversion of the truth, Iago here uses an old form of irony, the mock-apologia, which is really an attack. Othello, who only has Iago's word to go on, falls into the trap:

> I know, Iago,
> Thy honesty and love doth mince this matter,
> Making it light to Cassio.

(II.iii.243ff.)

So Cassio is displaced. But something else is being minced here.

Our feelings for Iago are a mixture of loathing and respect, or fear, at the resource of his deceptions, for there seem to be no limits to his skill. Only a few moments later he is being sympathetic with Cassio – 'What, are you hurt, lieutenant? . . . Marry, heaven forbid!' – and gradually winning his confidence (259–328) until he can, tentatively, enquire whether he is being trusted: 'I think you think I love you'. We can better understand this speech by setting out the levels of deception in parentheses: (I think [you think] {I love you}). Cassio answers 'I have well approved it, sir' (304ff.). Caught! When Iago outlines his plan to regain Othello's respect through the intervention of Desdemona, Cassio is grateful:

> CASSIO. You advise me well.
> IAGO. I protest, in the sincerity of love and honest kindness.
> CASSIO. I think it freely. . . .

(II.iii.319ff.)

The point that this sequence establishes is that Cassio, like Roderigo before him, and like Othello, and Desdemona after him, trusts Iago and believes that he has appeared in the nick of time, solely in order to help him. Iago seems to be acting wholly for the others' good, since, as he challenges us to deny, 'this advice I give is free and honest./Probal to thinking' (330f.). The gulls can see the help and benefit they receive from Iago's service, but cannot see, or conceive, that Iago could be benefiting himself at the same time; and no one could possibly see that Iago is in fact benefiting himself by destroying them. As he explains to us his brilliant plot to tell Othello that Desdemona wants Cassio recalled only to satisfy 'her body's lust', we see that the more she strives on behalf of Cassio the more she will damage herself. Iago not only knows no altruism in himself, he blocks and destroys it in others:

> So will I turn her virtue into pitch,
> And out of her own goodness make the net
> That shall enmesh them all.

(II.iii.350ff.)

Iago's practice of inversion, by which he destroys Cassio while making him and others believe him to be Cassio's friend, and by which he turns

114

Desdemona's purity into a black, viscous liquid that will catch his victims like birds in quicklime, has been fully established by Shakespeare and shown to be successful. Whatever Iago predicts he will do, he performs. Setting Cassio up for his plots, he so manages to present the image of the faithful friend that – as he predicted Othello would – the dupe actually thanks him: 'I humbly thank you for 't. I never knew/A Florentine more kind and honest' (III.i.39f.). Even Emilia is deceived by his concern on behalf of Cassio: 'I warrant it grieves my husband/As if the case were his' – 'O, that's an honest fellow', agrees Desdemona (III.iii.3ff.). In *Much Ado about Nothing* the villainous Borachio, tool of the malcontent Don John, exults at the success of his deception: 'I have deceived even your very eyes' (V.i.238f.). This is what Iago now does to Othello. He uses the same methods as with the other five people he has so far deceived, his 'outward action' being the opposite of the 'native act and figure' of his heart, but he carries the principle of inversion much further. Whereas the hypocrite normally deceives other people's vision of himself, making them see good where he means evil, Iago manages to transmit that doubleness into their vision of the rest of the world. He has convinced Roderigo that Othello's attraction for Desdemona is purely sensual, will soon be satiated, and that then Desdemona will love him; even though the dupe is constantly doubting that vision, Iago manages to sustain it for as long as he needs to. He convinces Roderigo that Cassio is a rival likely to seduce Desdemona, and makes Othello and Montano see Cassio as a drunken and irresponsible officer. All these, we know, are inversions of the truth, yet by using himself as a reference point, Iago can convince people to the stage where they accept his view unquestioningly. He is like the filter used in film-making to reverse daylight and night effects, a technique known as 'day for night'. Or, as he puts it himself, in words that recall the Christian association of hypocrisy with the devil's 'suggestion' or tempting:

> Divinity of hell!
> When devils will the blackest sins put on,
> They do suggest at first with heavenly shows,
> As I do now.
>
> (II.iii.343ff.)

Iago's most brilliant inversion of vision is reserved for Othello – to which, indeed, all the other inversions have been preliminary. The sequence begins when Cassio, brought to Desdemona by Emilia (the unwitting intermediary of evil), leaves in some embarrassment when he sees Othello and Iago approach:

IAGO. Ha! I like not that.
OTHELLO.   What dost thou say?
IAGO. Nothing, my lord; or if – I know not what.
OTHELLO. Was not that Cassio parted from my wife?
IAGO. Cassio, my lord! No, sure, I cannot think it,

That he would steal away so guilty-like,
Seeing you coming.

OTHELLO.   I do believe 'twas he.

(III.iii.35ff.)

Iago moves from an upper plane (Signifier) to a lower (Signified), from perception to interpretation: subtly doubting the former – *Was that Cassio leaving your wife?* – so that Othello, who thinks he can trust his own eyes, takes the latter – *so guiltily* – with it, accepting a – false! – linguistic sign. Iago returns to the process, with a series of hints and insinuations, having asked whether Cassio knew of Othello's love for Desdemona:

OTHELLO. He did, from first to last. Why dost thou ask?
IAGO. But for a satisfaction of my thought;
    No further harm.

(III.iii.96ff.)

(thus insinuating the possibility of harm). As Othello tells him that Cassio had even acted as a go-between in their courtship, Iago appears surprised – 'Indeed!' – and takes refuge behind a series of evasive answers – 'Honest, my lord?' 'My lord, for aught I know' – 'Think, my lord?' (101ff.). 'Discern'st thou aught in that?' Othello asks, seeing that Iago (*is transmitting the signal that he*) has something on his mind. (It would be tedious to write it out each time, but the italicized phrase in brackets represents our recognition of the constructed signal that Iago emits.) Othello sees the surface doubts, is made to suspect that there is something behind them, is led on to discover – what Iago wants him to discover. The hypocrite offers the gull a surface falseness which he penetrates to discover 'a truth', but which we know is another falseness. Iago's technique of holding off exacerbates Othello's curiosity, arouses his suspicions, and destroys his trust in appearance, in his own perception of reality. The reason why (to answer an old critical fallacy) he does not go and ask Desdemona whether she is Cassio's lover is that, by the end of this scene, he no longer believes what she – or anyone but Iago – would tell him. And to answer a more recent fallacy, it is not the case that Othello *wants* to believe what Iago tells him, or is an accomplice in this destruction of the truth. He is an accomplice, in the sense that everyone who joins another in decoding a linguistic sign co-operates with them in the establishment of its meaning; but we can see that the sign Iago offers him is just the opposite of what Othello wants to believe, or has believed till now. (Of course, no utterances are safe from the post-Freudian trick of claiming that they mean the opposite of what they say, but in the interpretation of literary texts we must be given additional, fairly unequivocal evidence of a discrepancy between speech and meaning, as we are given for Iago, but not for Othello.)

What Iago does is to prove that, in the right context, anyone can be made to believe anything. Even a slight knowledge of modern political or social or religious history will make us accept this truth, sadly. Iago works on Othello's vision-interpretation until he replaces it with his own. It is a form of brain-washing, or what that pioneer in the study of learning processes, Gregory Bateson, called corrective learning, that information-seeking activity whereby a person attempts to 'achieve a congruence between "something in his head" and the external world ... by altering what is in his head'[24] – only in this case it is what is in Iago's head. 'If thou dost love me', Othello says to Iago, 'Show me thy thought'; earlier he had said that Iago hesitated, 'As if there were some monster in thy thought/Too hideous to be shown. Thou dost mean something' (III.iii.110ff.). By being *shown* Iago's thought, Othello comes to *think* it. The whole process is a transference of vision by which, under the pressure of negative feedback, Othello learns to see, and think, like Iago: 'I prithee, speak to me as to thy thinkings/As thou dost ruminate', he begs him, 'give thy worst of thoughts/The worst of words' (134ff.). The irony of this and similar appeals (145ff., 149ff., 164f.) is painful, knowing what we do of Iago's purpose and methods. Having brought Othello to the point where he proclaims 'I'll see before I doubt', and when he knows, 'Away at once with love or jealousy!' (191ff.), Iago can take a stand with every appearance of confidence:

> I am glad of it; for now I shall have reason
> To show the love and duty that I bear you
> With franker spirit. Therefore, as I am bound,
> Receive it from me.

> (195ff.)

Yet from that firm-sounding position he lapses into uncertainty – 'I speak not yet of proof' (ironically true!) – but an uncertainty that suggests far more than it states, with its rash of words for perception and deception ('look', 'observe', 'wear your eye thus', 'not ... secure', 'abused', 'look', 'know', 'see ... pranks', 'show', 'conscience', 'keep't unknown'). 'If you dissemble sometimes your knowledge of that you are thought to know', wrote Francis Bacon, 'you shall be thought another time, to know that you know not.'[25] Othello's vision of Iago gives him total credit:

> This honest creature doubtless
> Sees and knows more, much more, than he unfolds

> (III.iii.244ff.)

With the vision of Iago, Othello also takes over his language, as critics have long noted, with its bestial images, but also his attitudes, especially a generalized distrust of women. (Iago's misogyny has deep roots in his psyche.)

Iago's transplantation of his own inverted values to Othello is Shake-speare's most remarkable development of the inherent dynamic of hypocrisy. Iago continues in other, more familiar postures, professing love to Othello and Desdemona (III.iii.119ff., 136ff., 196ff., 213ff., 218f., 225) and feigning a sympathy for their sufferings which we know to be a covert expression of his gloating:

> IAGO. I see this hath a little dashed your spirits.
> OTHELLO. Not a jot, not a jot.
> IAGO   In faith, I fear it has.
>
> (216ff..)

As Cicero said, there is no more flagrant injustice than 'that of the hypocrite who, at the very moment when he is most false, makes it his business to appear virtuous'.

'I am sorry to hear this' (346), Iago says, having just exulted to us, *en clair*, that

> The Moor already changes with my poison:
> Dangerous conceits are in their natures poisons
>
> .   .   .   .   .   .
>
> Look where he comes! Not poppy, nor mandragora

will ever restore to him his peace and quiet (328ff.). The inversion technique works, too, by suggestion. When Othello swears revenge, Iago offers himself to 'obey . . . without remorse,/What bloody business ever' (469f.) – that is, he means, the bloodier the better. Inversion also works by forbidding what you want the other to do: Iago will kill Cassio, but as for Desdemona – 'let her live', he suggests, knowing that Othello will immediately say 'Damn her, lewd minx!' and look for 'some swift means of death/For the fair devil' (475ff.). Iago can turn anything into its opposite: under his tuition even Othello becomes a hypocrite, with difficulty – 'O, hardness to dissemble!' he says (III.iv.34), like Coriolanus, feigning 'a salt and sorry rheum' so that Desdemona will give him the handkerchief (III.iv.51f.). Since she has lost it, she is forced to lie, too (85ff.). Iago turns them all into hypocrites.

Iago's technique of offering a false surface, designed to appear false and encourage his dupe to penetrate to what is only another false bottom, reaches its climax at the opening of Act IV, where master and pupil enter, already engaged in conversation:

> IAGO. Will you think so?
> OTHELLO.   Think so, Iago!
> IAGO.   What,
>   To kiss in private?
> OTHELLO.   An unauthorized kiss.
> IAGO. Or to be naked with her friend in bed

An hour or more, not meaning any harm?
OTHELLO. Naked in bed, Iago, and not mean harm!
It is hypocrisy against the devil.

(IV.i.1ff.)

That Othello should be accusing Cassio and Desdemona of hypocrisy, the devil's weapon, is the sign of Iago's total triumph in creating false perception. Here there is not even anything to perceive, just words that purport to represent deeds. 'Hath he said anything?' asks Othello about Cassio, and Iago replies yes, but

No more than he'll unswear.
OTHELLO.   What hath he said?
IAGO. Faith, that he did – I know not what he did.
OTHELLO. What? What?
IAGO. Lie –
OTHELLO.   With her?
IAGO.   With her, on her; what you will.
OTHELLO. Lie with her! lie on her! – We say lie on her, when they belie her – Lie with her! 'Zounds, that's fulsome!

(29ff.)

Othello's collapse into prose, and madness, comes when his worst suspicions, aroused by Iago, are given verbal form. Iago's manipulation of the verbal sign was never more brilliant, for he has only to offer the Signifier, 'Lie' – which could mean 'tell an untruth' – for Othello to snatch the Signified, 'lie with', which has been planted in his consciousness so remorselessly. It is indeed a case of 'what you will' in decoding this and all other linguistic signs, but it is Iago who has made Othello construe it in that manner, and will continue to do so. Shakespeare makes the point about interpretation that modern research in theories of vision and the education of young children has confirmed – that we are all taught to see – by Iago's prediction of the view that Othello, hidden in the normally superior position of the eaves-dropper, will take of his imminent conversation with Cassio:

As he shall smile, Othello shall go mad;
And his unbookish jealousy must construe
Poor Cassio's smiles, gestures, and light behaviours,
Quite in the wrong.

(100ff.)

After the scene has turned out exactly as predicted, Iago checks on his victim's responses:

IAGO. Did you perceive how he laughed at his vice?
OTHELLO. O Iago!
IAGO. And did you see the handkerchief?

119

OTHELLO. Was that mine?
IAGO. Yours, by this hand –

(170ff.)

The Signifier here, the handkerchief, has been made by Iago to yield a meaning which is totally false, but which he has put upon it with so much circumstantial detail – Shakespeare's diligence in this point risks pushing his plot into the incredible – that Othello can only see it as a present that Cassio has received from Desdemona and has 'given ... his whore'.

Iago's dominance of Othello's eyes and brain is total; indeed he now begins to destroy his memory. We see Othello clutching at the last flickers of his memory of Desdemona as she was, for him (*and as of course she still is*):

OTHELLO. A fine woman! a fair woman! a sweet woman!
IAGO. Nay, you must forget that.
OTHELLO. Ay, let her rot, and perish, and be damned tonight....
    O, the world hath not a sweeter creature....
IAGO. Nay, that's not your way.

(178ff.)

Not your way, because not my way. Iago soon brings him back to the 'foul' image: 'I will chop her into messes – cuckold me!' Othello ends up with the same poisoned suspicions as Iago, who had earlier confessed that he suspects both Othello and Cassio of having cuckolded him with Emilia (II.i.285ff.). Is there any other instance of a man transferring to another his own sexual paranoia? From Iago, too, Othello has caught the habit of repeating a word, dwelling on it to debase it or bring out a sinister double meaning (compare Iago on 'virtue' and 'blest': I.iii.318ff.; II.i.245ff.). So Othello seizes on Lodovico's request that Desdemona should return with a series of puns on 'turn' in its sexual sense (IV.i.254ff.), and, more painfully, on 'committed' (IV.ii.71ff.). Othello cannot now see anything but dirt, Iago's dirt. When he had been keeping Desdemona company, awaiting Othello's arrival from Venice, Iago had entertained them with impromptu (and bitter) rhymes, describing his imagination's preliminary working (the rhetorical process of *inventio*) in these terms:

I am about it; but indeed my invention
Comes from my pate as birdlime does from frieze –
It plucks out brains and all.

(II.i.125ff.)

Frieze is a coarse woollen cloth, birdlime a viscous stuff used to entangle: the destructive collocation of the two seems an apt metaphor for Iago's 'invention'.

Shakespeare's remorselessness in *Othello*, his refusal to be deflected from

120

his single path, is reinforced by the obsessive nature of his characters. Iago only ever talks about destroying Othello and Desdemona, has even forgotten about his own career, and Othello takes over his obsessions. When Cassio has been attacked by Iago, apparently murdered, Othello lauds his master's example:

> O brave Iago, honest and just,
> That has such noble sense of thy friend's wrong!
> Thou teachest me: minion, your dear lies dead,
> And your unblest fate hies! Strumpet, I come!

(V.i.31ff.)

The murder scene, with its marvellously wrought language, a ceremony that Othello thinks of as a sacrifice, is the most deluded, most fictitious scene in Shakespeare – not a word in it that Othello says is true. Desdemona is not a whore, he is not 'Justice' (V.ii.17), and when he kills her – 'I that am cruel am yet merciful' (90) – we see that he has even learned Iago's trick of euphemism (cf. Roderigo's reaction to being urged to effect 'the removing of Cassio' (IV.ii.228ff.)). Iago has led Othello to where he had predicted, caused the people he hates to destroy each other. His revenge (whatever the provocation) seems complete! But just at this point Iago makes his single mistake. Following the Machiavellian rule of killing your catspaws before they can betray you, he stabs Roderigo, exclaiming the while, 'Kill men i' th' dark! Where be these bloody thieves?' (that still has something of Richard III's panache), and protests that 'Here's Cassio hurt by villains' (V.i.62ff.) – namely himself and Roderigo – while offering Cassio hypocritical sympathy. But Iago's hypocrisy, like Macbeth's, causes his own undoing. He puts himself too completely into the role of the good man here, behaving, like Lady Macbeth, as one ought to behave, for he sends his wife on an errand: 'Emilia, run you to the citadel,/And tell my lord and lady what hath happed' (V.i.126f.). Perhaps he has forgotten that his lord ought to be murdering his lady just at this juncture; or perhaps he thinks Emilia is as corrupt as himself; or perhaps he does not understand love. The error is great, since Emilia is the only person who knows the truth about the handkerchief. She has already suspected that Othello's erroneous view of Desdemona is a malicious fiction put out by some Machiavel:

> I will be hanged, if some eternal villain
>
> .   .   .   .
>
> Some cogging, cozening slave, to get some office,
> Have not devised this slander;

(IV.ii.131ff.)

and – as we know, but Iago evidently does not – she loves her mistress. Sent by Iago, coming upon Othello just after the murder, Emilia's love and integrity cause her to denounce her husband, even at the cost of her own life.

121

It is ironic that the hypocrite, who is seen throughout with a neurotic distrust of women, and whose every second word to his wife is an insult, should finally be exposed by a woman he had trusted, from whom he had snatched the handkerchief without even thinking her worth swearing to secrecy (III.iii.320ff.). Iago's hatred of women undoes him. He has not managed to destroy trust.

In the final reckoning, truth is restored. Emilia reveals that she found the handkerchief ('Villainous whore!' and 'Filth', he calls her), and with her dying breath – that most crucial of all utterances to Renaissance beliefs – proclaims her integrity: 'So come my soul to bliss, as I speak true;/So speaking as I think, alas, I die' (V.ii.253f.). The agony of Othello's realization that he has been duped into killing Desdemona is one of the two or three most intense sequences in Shakespeare. Lodovico gives an external judgement on him that is essentially right: 'O thou Othello, that wert once so good,/Fallen in the practice of a damned slave' (293f.). Yet Othello has the integrity not to make excuses for his error but to accept his responsibility, equate himself with the 'malignant and turbaned Turk', and execute himself. Now and not before, he is Justice with its sword. Iago, that 'Spartan dog', is given his final share of responsibility:

> Look on the tragic loading of this bed –
> This is thy work. The object poisons sight;
> Let it be hid.

(364ff.)

Just as Iago poisoned sight, so do the fruits of his action. In Shakespearian tragedy, hypocrisy is not only a poison in itself but the cause of ever greater destruction.

Two last points need to be made about *Othello*, the first concerning the hypocrite's superiority over his dupes. As we have observed with Richard III, the power gained by the deceiver's *simulatio* makes the dupes seem naïve or silly – 'Relenting fool, and shallow-changing woman!' was Richard's parting comment on Queen Elizabeth. Iago's superiority over the six people he directly deceives (and behind them, of course, the whole of society) is so marked that we risk endorsing his contempt for whichever 'snipe', 'knave', or 'ass' he happens to be manipulating. For characters like Roderigo such contempt may not be unjust. But I suspect that unawareness of this structural effect within hypocrisy plots lies behind the disparaging attitude, so common in modern criticism, towards Othello and, to a lesser extent, Desdemona. Critics of the play have failed to notice that, since everything pivots around Iago's plotting, we tend to accept – unless we are very careful – Iago's version of events, and his attitude to his victims. In some perhaps not fully conscious way critics tend to look for faults in Othello, errors of personality or upbringing (to neo-Freudians his sexual hang-ups), that will explain why he believes Iago and murders Desdemona. But Iago's 'practice' is so assured, his control of surface and perspective so total, that we have to put him in the highest class of hypocrites, along with Satan. What could he not accomplish? Since, as Alexander Cruden put it, 'men cannot dive into the hearts of others', critics should be careful not to abuse the privileged vision they enjoy, compared to the false and occluded images that the characters in the play have to go on, and judge them disparagingly.

Second, Iago's terrible silence once his deceptions have been exposed: 'Demand me nothing, what you know, you know,/From this time forth I never will speak word' (V.ii.304f.): this refusal of language is the logical outcome of the destructive egoism with which Iago has put himself outside, and in his own eyes above, society. His violations of truth and trust make him, for anyone who conceives of the human community as being based on mutual help, guilty of ingratitude, of breaking those bonds of reciprocity which make life possible. Iago is 'hardened', as Cruden put it, in his hypocrisy, so that his refusal to repent or explain shows great psychological insight on Shakespeare's part. Expounding Seneca's moral philosophy, towards the end of the seventeenth century, Roger L'Estrange begins by emphasizing the importance of 'the theme of *Benefits*, *Gratitude*, and *Ingratitude*' to the author of *De Beneficiis*. Then he links pagan philosophy with Christianity, recalling the 'Apostasie' of the angels and the feelings of hatred, the 'Implacable Malice' which Lucifer and co. expressed against the other angels. The two vices, he points out, are connected, for

> What could *Ingratitude* do, without *Hypocrisie*, the Inseparable Companion of it; and, in Effect, the Bolder, and the Blacker Devil of the Two? ... 'Tis not for nothing, that the *Holy Ghost* has denounc'd so many *Woes*, and redoubled so many *Cautions* against *Hypocrites*, plainly intimating at once how dangerous a Snare they are to Mankind, and no less odious to God himself: Which is sufficiently denoted in the force of that dreadful Expression, '*And your Portion shall be with Hypocrites*'. You will find in the Holy Scriptures ... that God has given the Grace of *Repentance* to *Persecutors*, *Idolaters*, *Murtherers*, *Adulterers*, &c. But I am mistaken, if the whole *Bible* affords you any one Instance of a *Converted Hypocrite*.[26]

That seems to me a fitting explanation for the resolutely 'Implacable Malice' of Iago. And in any case, the hypocrite has abused language so much that, if he offered a show of remorse, who could believe him?

The challenge of integrity against hypocrisy, made by Emilia at the very end of *Othello*, is placed first in *King Lear*. As the king abdicates, he divides up his kingdom as a dower for his three daughters, and orders them – 'Tell me, my daughters' – to declare the quantity of their love: 'Which of you shall we say doth love us most?' (*King Lear*, I.i.48ff.). Lear speaks again at line 62, and in the meantime not one but two of his daughters speak, one to him and one to the audience. Goneril declares an absolute love, beyond expression:

> Sir, I love you more than word can wield the matter;
> Dearer than eye-sight, space and liberty;
> Beyond what can be valued rich or rare;
> No less than life, with grace, health, beauty, honour
>
> (55ff.)

and so forth. It is a speech of effusive praise, which if it were true, would make her an exceptionally loving child. Its tone is such that Cordelia tells us, alone, that she cannot compete with it: 'What shall Cordelia speak? Love, and be silent' (62). Already we have that dichotomy between words and deeds that typifies hypocrisy, and which runs throughout the play. Cordelia equates her sisters' words with falseness, her own silence with love, and we have no reason to disagree.

Lear is evidently pleased with what Goneril has said, since he awards her a rich part of England, and moves on to the second movement, where again two daughters speak. Regan declares her love to be identical with Goneril's, only that she has understated it (we had scarce thought it possible to go beyond Goneril):

> Only she comes too short: that I profess
> Myself an enemy to all other joys
> Which the most precious square of sense possesses,
> And find I am alone felicitate
> In your dear highness' love.
>
> (69ff.)

To claim that your love for your father exceeds all the joys which can be derived from the senses – with your newly wedded husband standing by – is to claim too much. Cordelia again comments to us, criticizing that profession:

> Then poor Cordelia!
> And yet not so; since I am sure my love's
> More ponderous than my tongue.
>
> (76ff.)

Deeds against words, truth against fiction, integrity against hypocrisy: that is the position of Cordelia. Her father's loving- (or lying-) competition, designed though it may be to give her the best part of England (which he is also giving himself, of course, since he intends to live in retirement with her), and revealing, in a way, his love for her, is nevertheless so constructed that she would have to compete with hypocrisy in order to win. Lear is quantifying love, confusing it with other things that can be measured, weighed, counted. Cordelia, like Coriolanus, is being forced into a ceremony in which she would have to be false to her own nature. Lear pretends to be offering a gift, but is in fact extorting a bribe. She refuses to play the game according to these rules, professing 'Nothing'.

As we experience Act I, Scene i, of *King Lear* for the first time, it may not be easy to see that Cordelia is right, the others wrong. By the time we reach the end of the scene we see that this is how it is, for the fulsome praisers of their father put aside their hypocrisy and, left alone with each other, and with us, reveal their true nature, moving down from inflated verse to coldly pragmatic prose:

> GONERIL. You see how full of changes his age is; the observation we have made of it hath not been little: he always lov'd our sister most; and with what poor judgement he hath now cast her off appears too grossly.
> REGAN. 'Tis the infirmity of his age; yet he hath ever but slenderly known himself.
>
> (I.i.288f.)

They are not only cold and censorious – 'unruly waywardness ... infirm and choleric years ... unconstant starts' – but end by planning some form of counteraction: 'We shall further think on it' – 'We must do something, and i' th' heat' (307f.). Structurally, left alone on-stage after the main figures have left, plotting behind Lear's back, they are exactly in the position of Iago, or the tribunes in *Coriolanus*. We see that Cordelia's judgement of them was correct:

> I know you what you are;
> And like a sister am most loth to call
> Your faults as they are named. Love well our father;
> To your professed bosoms I commit him.
>
> (I.i.269ff.)

As they taunt her for her disobedience she replies, 'Time shall unfold what plighted cunning hides;/Who covers faults, at last with shame derides' (280f.).

The metaphor of covering and exposing falseness (as used by Isabella, we recall) describes the whole career of the hypocrite within literary form. By her stand we judge them, and we see that Cordelia's calm statement of her love for her father, her refusal to compete in extravagant adulation, was the result not of some inherent coldness but of integrity under unusual and unnatural pressure. She was only like this in response to Lear's perverted claim: the rest of the play shows that there is no one more loving. As Kent tells Lear,

> Thy youngest daughter does not love thee least;
> Nor are those empty-hearted whose low sounds
> Reverb no hollowness.
>
> (152ff.)

Sent into banishment for opposing his master, Kent can give his moral support to Cordelia (in terms that echo Emilia's dying words):

> The Gods to their dear shelter take thee, maid,
> That justly think'st and has most rightly said!
> [*To Goneril and Regan*] And your large speeches may your deeds approve,
> That good effects may spring from words of love.

(182ff.)

The division is clear-cut, and it is right.

The first scene in the main plot of *King Lear* opposes and discriminates its protagonists. Cordelia, Kent, and France, who stand up to Lear, and whose judgement mutually reinforces one another, are right then, and are shown to be right by the way the action develops. Lear himself soon regrets his decision. Two scenes later we see Goneril instructing her servant Oswald to be rude to Lear, put on 'weary negligence', and bring the issue to a violent state: 'What grows of it, no matter ... I would breed from hence occasions' (I.iii.8–26). The tactics of Iago against Cassio, the tribunes against Coriolanus, work, as they must always work, given human nature and the will to manipulate it. Lear is offended by Oswald's negligence (I.iv.47ff.), and his new servant (Kent, returned in disguise) shows his loyalty by tripping up this 'clotpoll'. Goneril thereby gains the pretext she had wanted to 'speak', and accuses Lear and his knights of all manner of disorder, 'epicurism and lust' (209–22, 245–59). Immediately angry, manipulated by these evidently false accusations (like Coriolanus, Lear cannot see that the whole purpose of them is to make him angry), Lear regrets the 'most small fault' that had caused him to disown Cordelia (275ff.), curses Goneril with appalling violence (284ff.), and sweeps off to Regan. But as we know in advance, the two sisters are in communication by letter, and have established a joint policy of provocation. Face to face with him (the first time since receiving their inheritance from him), they attack his claimed need for a hundred knights. Although at one point Lear is willing to return to Goneril, since she seems to be allowing him fifty knights, Regan only twenty-five, so that 'Thy fifty yet doth double five-and-twenty,/And thou art twice her love' (II.iv.260ff.) – a quantification of love that would be comic were its effects not so awful – Lear becomes enraged by the two of them, and prefers 'To wage against the enmity o' th' air' than live with them. So he goes out into the storm and into wild nature, together with 'the wolf and the owl', while his daughters and son-in-law close their doors on him (306ff.).

The development of this part of the plot is swift, Lear's impatient anger leading him from one self-imposed crisis to another. His methods of computation may be ridiculous, but he is right to think that they do not love him, and his sense of bitter ingratitude causes his madness. They, for their part, attempt to justify their actions to each other, hypocrisy apparently continuing by habit, having become a way of life (since there is no one on-stage whom they need to deceive, perhaps they have come to believe their own lies):

126

REGAN. This house is little: the old man and's people
    Cannot be well bestow'd.
GONERIL. 'Tis his own blame; hath put himself from rest,
    And must needs taste his folly.
REGAN. For his particular, I'll receive him gladly,
    But not one follower.
GONERIL.   So am I purpos'd.

                                                (II.iv.290ff.)

The truth is transparent, however; indeed, when Gloucester reports that the king is leaving, Goneril says, 'My Lord, entreat him by no means to stay' (301). Having just received the whole kingdom from him, they can't wait to get rid of him. Lear is now experiencing the truth of La Rochefoucauld's maxim that 'So long as a man is still in a position to help others he will rarely encounter ingratitude.'[27] Yet, although sinned against, Lear is also sinning. He had devised a purely verbal test of his daughters' love, and while a devotee of Practical Criticism could soon have told him what was wrong with Goneril and Regan from their speeches alone, there was apparently no way in which he could discriminate them from Cordelia. But, as Iago says, 'Knavery's plain face is never seen till used' (*Othello*, II.i.306). Goneril and Regan used fraud to gain power, and now that they have it, no longer need to dissimulate. Their false show, like that of Iago, is the pivot on which the whole action turns. Yet while Iago had to start from scratch, foment hatred, poison sight, and invert reality to set his chosen enemies against each other, all that Goneril and Regan have to do to get a third of Britain is to make the kind of noises Lear expects to hear; indeed, since Cordelia won't flatter, they get her part too, and even her coronet as an unlooked-for bonus, Lear's only 'free gift', to use the language of modern advertising promotions ('This coronet part between you' (*King Lear*, I.i.139)). The hypocrites take, or are given, all, and once they have it, show their real selves. No other hypocrites in Shakespeare gain so much so quickly, so easily, and can afford to drop pretence so fast.

The first scene of the subplot also opposes and discriminates its protagonists. Whereas Goneril and Regan had been shown to us first in disguise, and then in reality, Edmund begins in reality, and only adopts disguise when his father enters. Hypocrisy is a key element in this plot, too, with the difference that while they started near the top of society and were on the verge of receiving power at the very beginning, he – as a bastard son who is only just back from having spent nine years abroad (the typical occupation for one who has no prospect of inheritance in his own country) and is due to go again – starts very much lower down in society, virtually at the bottom. He has to do more than they do, and he has to keep it up for much longer. From his first soliloquy (I.ii.) to his last (V.i.), Edmund's hypocrisy stretches across the play, a freewheeling career of pretence in the service of egoism. Like Iago, like Goneril and Regan, he pretends in order to acquire. Since he is well built, and inventive, he argues (in a travesty of logic that echoes Iago's at a similar point, the thinness of the pretext revealing the strength of the desire), he has a right to the land reserved for the son born 'by order of law':

> Well then,
> Legitimate Edgar, I must have your land:
> Our father's love is to the bastard Edmund
> As to th' legitimate.

(King Lear, I.ii.15ff.)

Since Gloucester loves both sons equally, that means that both by birth and by nature (to the Renaissance the terms were synonymous) he cannot discriminate good from bad. His love for Edmund is a trust that the bastard exploits, planting a false letter, which he backs up with false testimony, alleging that Edgar would wish to oust his father, a hypocrite's typical inversion of the truth. It is a convention in Elizabethan drama that slander is always believed, which can be explained perhaps from the necessities of the limited time available, or is perhaps a truth about life (how many of us instantly *dis*believe bad report?). But we are at liberty to form our own judgement of the person doing so. Lear is to be blamed for believing Goneril and Regan, yet since they were merely flattering his debased scale of values, in a test which he had himself devised, it is not surprising that he did so. But Gloucester believes Edmund instantly, in the absence of Edgar, and even engages the bastard son to spy on the legitimate. As Edmund says, ending the scene as he had begun it, with a soliloquy, how lucky he is to have

> A credulous father, and a brother noble,
> Whose nature is so far from doing harms
> That he suspects none; on whose foolish honesty
> My practices ride easy! I see the business.
> Let me, if not by birth, have lands by wit:
> All with me's meet that I can fashion fit.

(I.ii.187ff.)

The naked statement of self-seeking reminds us of Iago, as does the confidence with which he approaches the task – 'easy' ('For 'tis most easy/Th' inclining Desdemona to subdue/In any honest suit' (*Othello*, II.iii.332ff.)) – and the scorn for those taken in by his traps ('Thus credulous fools are caught!' (*Othello*, IV.i.45)). Shakespeare's villains have it too easy, one sometimes feels.

Edmund's predictions of the success of his plots are, like Iago's, accurate. The 'credulous father' Gloucester is easily manipulated into setting a guard to catch Edgar (*King Lear*, II.i.17), and Edmund, who has been 'sheltering' Edgar (that is, keeping him locked up, where he cannot confront his father), dupes him into fleeing, so that Gloucester can order him to be pursued and killed (56–63). The systematic inversion practised by the hypocrite is brought out by Shakespeare, almost with an admiration for its trickery. Edmund reports to Gloucester how,

> When I dissuaded him from his intent,
> And found him pight to do it, with curst speech
> I threaten'd to discover him: he replied,
> 'Thou unpossessing bastard! ... though thou didst produce
> My very character – I'd turn it all
> To thy suggestion, plot, and damned practice.'
>
> (II.i.64ff.)

Since it is all, in truth, Edmund's 'suggestion, plot, and damned practice', the inversion is so apparent to us as to make him seem cheeky. Edmund displays throughout a relaxed, almost dapper manner, far removed from the obsessive Iago, eaten up by the suspicions in his own innards. Yet their deeds have the same perverted outcome. Gloucester exclaims 'O strange and fast'ned villain! ... I never got him' (77f.), and promises to take the necessary legal steps to make Edmund capable of inheriting his patrimony, otherwise closed to a bastard: 'Loyal and natural boy, I'll work the means/To make thee capable' (84f.). Edmund now has Edgar's lands.

I earlier described the form of hypocrisy that Shakespeare was most interested in as dynamic, acting on its own behalf to achieve some definite goal. Yet in the tragedies these villains are never satisfied: Macbeth goes on killing like some automaton, Iago goes on destroying until he has brought everyone down. The principle of rapacious egoism, Shakespeare shows, does not let up once it has achieved its first-formulated goal. We see this from Edmund both as subject and object. As subject, acting for his own interests, the later confusion of events – with Cordelia returned from France with soldiers to seek her father and secret letters passing to and fro – suddenly puts Gloucester in a dilemma. He is loyal to Cornwall, but he is also loyal to Lear, and is outraged at the way the King has been treated: 'Most savage and unnatural', Edmund agrees (III.iii.1ff.). Telling Edmund of the letter, Gloucester makes him his trusted accomplice: 'We must incline to the King. I will seek him and privily relieve him; go you and maintain talk with the Duke, that my charity be not of him perceiv'd' (III.iii.14ff.).

No sooner has he left than Edmund moves up to verse to show that he is *semper idem*:

> This courtesy, forbid thee, shall the Duke
> Instantly know; and of that letter too:
> This seems a fair deserving, and must draw me
> That which my father loses; no less than all;
> The younger rises when the old doth fall.
>
> (23ff.)

Edmund shares Goneril and Regan's contempt for old age, but he goes beyond them even, in betraying his own father, knowing that the penalty for helping Lear may be death. Loathsome as he now is, he becomes still more so as he hypocritically professes to Cornwall his filial embarrassment: 'How, my lord, I may be censured, that nature thus gives way to loyalty, something fears me to think of.... O Heavens! that this treason were not, or not I the detector!' (III.v.2ff.).

Yet when Cornwall pronounces him the new Earl of Gloucester, and orders him to seek his father out, Edmund has yet another layer of pretence at hand:

> [*Aside*] If I find him comforting the King, it will stuff his suspicion more fully. [*Aloud*] I will persevere in my course of loyalty, though the conflict be sore between that and my blood.

> (17ff.)

Edmund's perversion of such words as 'nature', 'loyalty', and 'blood' is grimly evident to us, but not to Cornwall – who may not understand those terms, in any case – and who now puts himself into the position of an adopted father to Edmund: 'I will lay trust upon thee; and thou shalt find a dearer father in my love' (24f.). Knowing what Edmund has done to his real father might have given Cornwall pause before proclaiming himself the next one.

As subject, Edmund acts for himself, doing anything that will advance him: Goneril and Regan live by the same principle. When Edmund is sent off with Goneril (since, Cornwall tells him, 'the revenges we are bound to take upon your traitorous father are not fit for your beholding' (III.vii.6ff.)), he comes into the final stage of his career, moving from subject to object, first of Goneril's love, then of Regan's. Arriving home, Goneril pronounces herself his mistress, and promises him speedy advancement – which can only mean by the murder of her husband, Albany (IV.ii.17ff.). To her, as to Edmund, the question of legitimacy is a nuisance to be subverted:

> Oh! the difference of man and man.
> To thee a woman's services are due:
> My Fool usurps my body.

> (IV.ii.26ff.)

When Goneril's 'trusty servant', Oswald, bears a letter from her to Edmund, Regan attempts to corrupt him into giving it to her (IV.v.20ff.). All trust has now been destroyed by these seemers. Having declared her desire for Edmund to Oswald (28ff.), Regan declares it to the man himself (V.i.6ff.), as the egoism they each pursue turns the two sisters into deadly rivals (15f., 18f.). Left alone, Edmund is rather amused by the situation:

> To both these sisters have I sworn my love;
> Each jealous of the other, as the stung
> Are of the adder. Which of them shall I take?
> Both? one? or neither?

> (V.i.55ff.)

Rather like Iago, in a soliloquy at a similar stage of the action (*Othello*, V.i.11–22), Edmund concludes that he will win anyway. But in fact he has already been exposed. Oswald, carrying Goneril's letter, and with the added instructions to kill Gloucester should he find him, tried to do so but was killed by Edgar, who discovered their secret plans to kill Albany (*King Lear*, IV.vi.227–80). Immediately before Edmund's soliloquy, Edgar, still in disguise, has given the letter to Albany (40–50), and for the first time the forces of good have a superior knowledge over the hypocrites. As a result, Albany can arrest Edmund after their victory in battle, and prevent Goneril's marriage plot (V.iii.83ff.). Then Edgar appears, disguised as a poor knight whose 'name is lost;/By treason's tooth bare-gnawn, and canker-bit' (121f.), and by defeating him in single combat, completes the exposure of Edmund, the bastard being displayed as a hypocrite and pretender (162–74), who in a fair contest – according to Renaissance optimism about the superiority of right – is bound to be defeated by the legitimate.

The egoistic destructiveness represented by Goneril and Regan destroys itself: one poisons the other, and then kills herself. Goneril's letter declaring her desire to Edmund is the means by which the truth is finally revealed: again appetite destroys itself. Yet before it does so it destroys much else, and the devastation at the end of *King Lear* is a sufficient proof of the destructiveness of hypocrisy, once it is believed. Trusting hypocrites such as these is like offering oneself as a test-bed for the cultivation of some deadly bacillus. Once established, it will not be got rid of save at the cost of the organism on which it has bred; like Iago's 'invention', it 'plucks out brains and all'.

Looking back over this chronicle of destruction we are struck by Shakespeare's revelation of the unsuspected depths of evil connected with hypocrisy. After Falstaff or Malvolio or Parolles, we might be tempted to think that dissimulation can be known, exposed, or controlled, without much harm being done. But after Richard III we would have second thoughts; after Iago we might begin to doubt whether anyone could ever be trusted again. Not all the hypocrites are equally resourceful, but they all exploit positions of trust in order to gain at the expense of others. Goneril and Regan almost have hypocrisy thrust upon them, in that Lear's invitations to flatter for instant profit do impose an intolerable burden on anyone of a less than firm integrity. Yet once they have collaborated in this verbal insincerity they reveal an extent of human viciousness no one could have expected. Having shut Lear out in the storm, Goneril and Regan lay 'a plot of death upon him' (III.vi.92ff.). In Shakespeare's tragedies hypocrisy is no mere quirk of human nature but the sign of a propensity towards deep and ultimately inexplicable evil. No one attempts to answer Lear's question, 'Is there any cause in nature that make these hard hearts?' (III.vi.78f.), because no one could answer it, then or now. Iago's exploitation of trust enables him to make Othello kill

Desdemona: all that Othello can say at the end is, 'Will you, I pray, demand that demi-devil/Why he hath thus ensnared my soul and body?' (*Othello*, V.ii.303f.). Iago's refusal to answer that question puts him outside human society for ever. The hypocrite, presented in asides and soliloquies, is given the theatrical medium that suits exactly his isolation over and against his fellow men. In Shakespeare, hypocrisy is linked inseparably with that rapacious egoism that is willing to destroy all in order to advance itself. We might attempt to complete La Rochefoucauld's maxim by saying that hypocrisy is the tribute that vice pays to virtue, in order to destroy it.

Notes

1 La Rochefoucauld, *Les Maximes* (1665), no. 218.
2 T. W. Baldwin, *Shakspere's Small Latine and Lesse Greeke*, 2 vols (Urbana, Ill., 1944), vol. 1, p. 1.
3 See, e.g., Brian Vickers, *In Defence of Rhetoric* (Oxford, 1988), pp. 10–11; and Inga-Stina Ewbank, 'Shakespeare's liars', *Proceedings of the British Academy* 69 (1984): 137–68, at pp. 137, 141, and 146 for apposite quotations from Montaigne on the belief that whoever lies 'betraieth publik society'.
4 Juvenal, *Satire* ii.8f., 19ff., in G. G. Ramsay (trans.) *Juvenal and Persius* (Loeb Classical Library; London, 1928), p. 19. See also Persius, v. 115ff., ibid., p. 381.
5 The Cicero references (translations from the Loeb editions) are: *De Off.*, 1.13.41, 3.15.61; *Verr.*, 2.15.39; *Acad.*, 2.46.140; *De Fin.*, 2.22.71; *Ad Att.*, 7.1, in D. R. Shackleton Bailey (trans.) *Cicero's Letters to Atticus* (Harmondsworth, 1978), p. 260.
6 *Institutes of Oratory*, 12.1.29f., in H. E. Butler (trans.) *Quintilian*, 4 vols (Loeb Classical Library; London, 1922), 4.371.
7 Job 20:4ff.; see also Job 8:13; 13:16; 15:34; 17:8; 27:8; 34:30; 36:13; etc. See also Isaiah 9:17; 10:6; 33:14.
8 Matthew 6:1–18; 23:13–33.
9 Luke 12:1–3.
10 Gregory, *Moralia*, Book 8: one of the 'Patrum Sententiae' in the eight-column assembly of quotations under 'Hypocriseos', in D. N. Mirabellius *et al.*, *Florilegii Magni, seu Polyantheae Floribus Novissimis Sparsae, Libri XX* (Frankfurt, 1628), cols. 1337–44.
11 *Inferno*, xxiii.58ff., C. S. Singleton (trans.) *The Divine Comedy* (Princeton, NJ, 1970) 1.239: the translation here is virtually identical with that by John D. Sinclair (London, 1939), 1.285, who notes that in a Latin lexicon available to Dante, *hypocrite* is said to mean *gilded over* (p. 291).
12 *A Complete Concordance to the Holy Scriptures of the Old and New Testament*, the Ninth Edition (London, 1828), p. 356.
13 John Milton, *Paradise Lost*, III, 681–4.
14 Bacon, 'Of Truth', *The Essayes or Counsels, Civill and Morall*, ed. Michael Kiernan (Oxford, 1985), pp. 8–9. Bacon is quoting from Montaigne's *Essays*, II.xviii, who is himself drawing on Plutarch's *Life of Lysander*, ch. 8.
15 Compare also William Prynne, *The Hypocrites Unmasking. Or a Cleare Discovery of the Grosse Hypocrisy of the Officers and Agitators in the Army* ... (1647); Anon., *The Hypocritical Christian; or The Conventicling Citizen Displayed* ... (1682);

Anon., *The Hypocritical Whigg Displayed* (1682); W. Winstanley, *The Hypocrite Unmask'd; a Comedy* ... (New York, 1801); G. P. R. James, *The Convict; or The Hypocrite Unmasked. A Tale* (New York, 1847); etc.

16 For a fuller commentary on this scene, see Brian Vickers, *The Artistry of Shakespeare's Prose* (London, 1968), pp. 116f.

17 See Brian Vickers, 'Francis Bacon's use of theatrical imagery', *Studies in the Literary Imagination* 4 (1971): 189–226; and Jonas Barish, *The Anti-Theatrical Prejudice* (Berkeley and Los Angeles, 1981), especially pp. 91–2, 125, 196–7, 258, 277–80. For a useful commentary on the resources of the hypocrite as itemized by Richard, see Barish's index, s.v. 'Chameleon; Change; Machiavelli; Proteus'.

18 William Richardson, for instance, writing in 1779, judged the scene only comprehensible by keeping

> in view the character of *Lady Anne*. ... She is represented of a mind altogether frivolous, the prey of vanity, her prevailing, over-ruling passion; susceptible, however, of every feeling and emotion ... but hardly capable of distinguishing the propriety of one more than another; or, if able to employ such discernment, totally unaccustomed and unable to obey her moral faculty as a principle of action; and thus exposed alike to the authority of good or bad impressions.
> (Brian Vickers (ed.) *Shakespeare, the Critical Heritage, vol. 6, 1774–1801*
> (London, 1981), p. 209)

See also ibid., pp. 19–20, 357, 452.

19 A. P. Rossiter has well described Richard's inheritance of the tricks of 'the old Vice of the Moralities ... the generators of roars of laughter at wickedness (whether of deed or word) which the audience would immediately condemn in real life'. But he has also fallen into the trap of seeing the victims through Richard's dehumanizing eyes:

> a good third of the play is a kind of grisly *comedy*, in which we meet the fools to be taken in on Richard's terms, see them with his mind, and rejoice with him in their stultification (in which execution is the ultimate and unanswerable practical joke, the absolutely final laugh this side of the Day of Judgement).

Richard 'inhabits a world where everyone deserves everything he can do to them; and in his murderous practical jokes he is *inclusively* the comic exposer of the mental shortcomings (the intellectual and moral deformities) of this world of beings depraved and besotted.' See '"Angel with horns": the unity of *Richard III*', in A. P. Rossiter, *Angel with Horns*, ed. G. Storey (London, 1961), pp. 1–22; quoted from W. A. Armstrong (ed.), *Shakespeare's Histories. An Anthology of Modern Criticism* (Harmondsworth, 1972), pp. 136–7.

20 Machiavelli, *Discorsi*, II, xiii, C. Detmold (trans.) *The Prince and Discourses*, intro. M. Lerner (New York, 1950), p. 318.

21 J. B. Atkinson (trans.) *The Prince* (Indianapolis, Ind., 1976), p. 281. Machiavelli notes here that

> there are two ways to fight: by using laws, and by using force. The former is characteristic of man; the latter, of animals. But frequently the former is inadequate and one must resort to the latter. Consequently a prince must perfect his knowledge of how to use the attributes of both animals and men.

He thus unites the strong points of the fox and the lion (p. 279). Machiavelli is recalling Cicero's distinction (*De Officiis*, 1.11.34) between the two ways of settling a dispute, by discussion or by physical force: 'the former is characteristic of man, the latter of the brute', with the corollary that both force and fraud are bestial

(1.13.4). Shakespeare uses the dichotomy between force and fraud several times: *1 Henry VI*, IV.iv.36; *3 Henry VI*, IV.iv.33; *Rape of Lucrece*, 1243. My point about Machiavelli drawing on Cicero's categories while ignoring their moral structure has been confirmed by the perceptive analysis of J. N. Stephens, 'Ciceronian rhetoric and the immorality of Machiavelli's *Prince*', *Renaissance Studies* 2 (1988), 258–67.

22 Andrew Marvell, 'An Horatian Ode upon Cromwell's return from Ireland', *Poems of Andrew Marvell*, ed. H. Macdonald (London, 1952), p. 121; Brian Vickers, 'Machiavelli and Marvell's *Horatian Ode*', *Notes and Queries* 36 (1989): 32–8.

23 F. de Saussure, *Course in General Linguistics*, trans. W. Baskin (New York, 1959), pp. 65–7.

24 Gregory Bateson and J. Reusch, *Communication: the Social Matrix of Psychiatry* (New York, 1951), p. 179.

25 Bacon, 'Of Discourse', *The Essayes or Counsels, Civill and Morall*, cd. Michael Kiernan (Oxford, 1985), pp. 104–5.

26 *Seneca's Morals By way of Abstract*, the Ninth Edition (London, 1705), Sig. A_4^v–A_5^r.

27 La Rochefoucauld, *Les Maximes*, no. 306, in C. Fitzgibbon (trans.) *The Maxims of the Duc de la Rochefoucauld* (London, 1957).

28 Edmund has perverted the meaning of 'nature' and 'loyalty', of course, so that his phrase becomes another instance of the destructive processes of egoism. Compare his 'gives way' with the words of the third servant after Gloucester's blinding: 'If she live long,/And in the end meet the old course of death,/Women will all turn monsters' (*King Lear*, III.vii.100ff.), and with Gloucester's prediction of discord: 'love cools, friendship falls off, brothers divide' (I.ii.115ff.). It is this sense of the *process* of evil, the actual moments of change, transformation, or self-revelation, that gives *King Lear* its unique quality. As Gloucester says, 'Our flesh and blood, my lord, is grown so vile/That it doth hate what gets it' (III.iv.137f.). Albany calls Goneril 'Thou changed and self-cover'd thing' (IV.i.62).

4

Coriolanus and the demons of politics

The early Christians knew full well that the world is governed by demons and that he who lets himself in for politics, that is, for power and force as means, contracts with diabolical powers.... Anyone who fails to see this is a political infant.

Max Weber[1]

Coriolanus is Shakespeare's most difficult, most complex play. It has often been misunderstood and has never been very popular. A. C. Bradley, writing in 1912, observed that it was 'seldom acted, and perhaps no reader ever called it his favourite play'.[2] T. S. Eliot's riposte, in 1919, when he bracketed it with *Antony and Cleopatra* as 'Shakespeare's most assured artistic success',[3] has been largely dismissed as a puzzling gesture of defiance which Eliot was never able to elaborate on. Recently T. J. B. Spencer has said that 'to write *Coriolanus* was one of the great feats of the historical imagination in Renaissance Europe',[4] and although this is a just comment the play is far more than a historical feat. It is Shakespeare's most detailed analysis of politics, an analysis carried out both at the public level – the formal political manoeuvring between the patricians and the plebeians over the rulers' attempt to have Coriolanus elected consul; and, at the personal level, within the family, in the relationship between Coriolanus and his mother, Volumnia. In both spheres the analysis is presented by Shakespeare but is not explicitly judged by him. All the information is given to us, but the dramatist does not vote for one side or the other. He votes, I shall argue, against both sides, but this is an interpretation of the play that has not often been made. Critics have usually sided with the people, or with the rulers; but whatever their position on this issue they have mostly sided against Coriolanus.

One reason for the great divergence of opinion over this tragedy – greater than for any other of Shakespeare's mature plays – is its withholding of explicit judgement; another is the subtlety with which Shakespeare worked, a subtlety that has been lost on many of his commentators. While it will always be a difficult play, 'caviar to the general', and may never mean much to people who have not been accustomed to think critically about politics and about such issues as the manipulation of a democracy and the pressurization of the individual, one could at least have expected that trained scholars and critics would perceive the subtlety with which Shakespeare balanced his hero's virtues and faults. Yet the dominant reaction of his critics in this century (to go no further back) has been unfavourable. To A. C. Bradley, who conceded him some 'nobleness of nature', Coriolanus was none the less 'the proudest man in Shakespeare', 'an impossible person', whose 'faults are repellent and chill our sympathy'.[5] He has been described as 'a schoolboy, crazed with notions of privilege and social distinction, incapable of thinking';[6] as 'essentially the splendid oaf who has never come to maturity',[7] or as 'inordinately proud, and as something of a schoolboy'.[8] If not proud or adolescent he has been accused of being too much the soldier, dehumanizing himself in the pursuit of military success: one critic described him as a 'human war-machine', a 'mechanical warrior, a man turned into an instrument of war';[9] another saw him as a 'mechanical Juggernaut',[10] yet another as 'an automaton in fight, a slaying-machine of mechanic excellence'.[11] Implicit in all these accounts is an unsympathetic attitude to the hero; one critic, indeed, suggested that Coriolanus was in fact alienated from us by Shakespeare, as a deliberate effect of tragic satire.[12]

Yet, fashionable though 'alienation' may be as an aesthetic concept, it does not seem relevant to Shakespearian tragedy in general, nor does it apply to this play. In none of the mature tragedies are we asked to remain wholly detached from the central tragic character, uninvolved with his goals, their frustration, and his suffering; nor are we expected to be detached from Coriolanus. If we entirely fail to sympathize with him, we have misunderstood the play.[13] I shall argue that he is a character, and his is a situation, which are fully tragic because they exist in a context in which a profound conflict of values renders individual action, and finally existence itself, impossible and pointless.

In order to do justice to Shakespeare's subtlety we have to separate and define each of the areas of pressure on Coriolanus which he has fused so organically; we must see each area for what it represents in itself, before putting it back into the fluid movement of the play as a whole. Two great critical errors in reading *Coriolanus* have been to take a person or social group either at their own estimate of themselves or at others' estimate of them. Another error has been to take a character out of its social context, and to attribute to it alone ideas or attitudes which are in fact the responsibility of the class to which it belongs. Lump those three errors together, I suggest, and you have an explanation for the generally unsympathetic response to Coriolanus. His pride, arrogance, unfeelingness, machine-like military destructiveness, ingratitude, and so forth, the qualities harped on by many modern critics, are all misconceptions loosely derived from what people *say* about Coriolanus, not what he *does*.

This play makes a deep analysis of action and value; so do all Shakespeare's tragedies, and indeed all major works of literature. What is exceptional about *Coriolanus* is that it also analyses the evaluation of action and value, the processes by which human behaviour is seen by others, reported on by them, given an agreed status or meaning. In other plays Shakespeare had used dramatic situations in which action was made to seem other than it was: in *Much Ado About Nothing* Claudio is made to see his wife-to-be, Hero, as a false, corrupt deceiver of him, and in *Othello* Iago imposes on Othello a vision and an evaluation of Desdemona that is a creation of fantasy and malice. In other plays, too, Shakespeare had presented critical moments of evaluation, from Portia's choice of the caskets to the discussions in *Troilus and Cressida* of value as a subjective, individual reaction and as an objective, social one. To Troilus' question 'What's aught but as 'tis valued?' Hector replies:

> But value dwells not in particular will.
> It holds his estimate and dignity
> As well wherein 'tis precious of itself
> As in the prizer.

(II.ii.52ff.)

Coriolanus pushes that debate further, deeper into the issue, both at the individual and the social levels. How does a man learn values? What do they mean to him? What happens if you ask him to change them? Those are some of the questions that will face Coriolanus. For his society the questions are more disturbing: how can you best create a value? To what extent can an image of value be manipulated? If each political group has its own interpretation of events, which one is right? Whom can we trust?

In approaching *Coriolanus*, then, I urge that we consider its evaluations of human action as we would do in real life. To evaluate human behaviour we tend to use a scale running from 'good' to 'bad', but we know that different people will give different evaluations of the same act. We know that values are personal, and that other people may have entirely different categories to ours. When person A tells us something nice, or nasty, about person B, we do not mechanically accept it as an objective fact: we know that it has been coloured by the personality and values of person A, and we will accept or reject it according to our evaluation of them. We all know, furthermore, that people do not communicate with us in total openness, honesty, and candour, addressing themselves purely to the matter in hand in itself and for itself.

They often speak or act in the present with an eye to some future state or event; they wish us to see or think or do something according to their wills or plans, not ours. They have, as we say, a 'design' on us. If we subsequently realize that the design was a harmless one which resulted in mutual pleasure and profit with no evil effects, then we are not likely to mind. But if we realize that we have been made to do something that we did not wish to do, and especially if we have been made to do something degrading or humiliating to ourselves and others, then we will feel cheated, exploited, manipulated.

I have written that very simple account of evaluation, presentation, and manipulation in real life partly because I feel that modern criticism is in danger of severing its links with ordinary human behaviour, and partly because *Coriolanus* presents just these patterns of action as they affect a hero who lives in a state of pristine innocence. This will be Coriolanus' first experience of a conflict of values or an opposition between loyalties; his first experience of manipulation; and, above all, his first experience of politics. What makes the play so complicated and so hard to evaluate, is that on to my simple model of human behaviour Shakespeare has superimposed the whole system of political evaluation, political presentation, and political manipulation. This not only complicates the issue but makes it more uncertain, unstable. For in addition to the inevitable clash between individual value-judgements, we have the clash between those of political parties, with their 'agreed values', values which can nevertheless be changed or abandoned if politically expedient; 'agreed fictions', we might call them, images which are created precisely in order to manipulate. Political parties are supposed to address themselves to immediate issues; they are supposed to work for the good of the whole community. This play shows the opposite practices, action addressed to some concealed aim, and action designed to secure and advance the power of a party in itself and for itself, if necessary against the community.

Politics is one of the areas of existence in which Coriolanus is made to act, and his actions observed, evaluated, and reported on, sometimes to one end, sometimes to another. There are three other areas in which the same process of action, report, and evaluation are carried out: Coriolanus in war and fighting; Coriolanus in relation to his class; Coriolanus in relation to his family. In all four Coriolanus is the focus of action and commentary. If we use the familiar division between 'individual' and 'society' we would have to say that the individual here is not merely juxtaposed with society but that the pressures of this society – above all the conflicting demands of class, politics, and family – are not only seen acting on Coriolanus but *can only express themselves in and through him*. They conflict with each other not face to face but through him. The central experience of the play is of a man caught in the various social roles that we all hold, simultaneously, each with its own loyalties – as son, husband, father, to the family; as soldier, to his comrades and his social rank; as political man to the party of his class – a man caught in these roles and destroyed by the conflict between them. At the end of the

138

play all the social groups – aristocrats, plebeians, the family, the army, the enemy – are recognizably the same as they were at the beginning: only Coriolanus is dead.

Coriolanus is the centre of the play, the focal point towards which every pressure converges. For this reason his character is under constant discussion from all groups, and a mass of conflicting evaluations of him can soon be assembled. Yet it is not enough to say that Shakespeare intends there to be a final 'mystery' about him. Each evaluation tells us as much, if not more, about the person or group making it as about Coriolanus himself. There are no unbiased opinions about him, each is the product of an implicit social attitude or an explicit social goal. Finally the only evaluation of him that matters is his own: what he values, how he acts, and how he evaluates his own action, are, in the last resort, the most important human judgements. As Kierkegaard said, 'a man lives his values'. But even here we cannot accept his perspective alone, for neither his actions nor his evaluations of them are purely personal discoveries. At the crisis of the play, when he is vainly trying to deny his instinctual love and loyalty to his family, he cries out

> I'll never
> Be such a gosling to obey instinct, but stand
> As if a man were author of himself
> And knew no other kin.
>
> (V.iii.34ff.)

But the linguistic formulation itself ('As if ... were') denies its own validity. Coriolanus, like any other man, is in part a product of his society and his family, with all their ideals and prejudices, inhibitions and taboos, evasions and self-flattery. Critics who isolate Coriolanus from his social nexus fail to see how much of his character has been learned, acquired. Yet, before we start to examine that social nexus, let us guard against falling into the opposite error, of making him entirely homogeneous with the values of his class and family. Coriolanus has learned much from them, but the more he sees what they have made of him the more he tries to unlearn it. One of the least commented on aspects of the play, and the one that, in my view, gives Coriolanus an independent and tragic existence, is the process by which he frees himself to the point where he is no longer of any use either to his class or to his family, so that they can afford to sacrifice him in order to preserve themselves.

Class war

The Rome of *Coriolanus* is a society at war, both externally, against the Volscians, and internally, against itself. Given this rift, it is not surprising that the values of the ruling class should be exclusively aggressive, self-defending, and self-perpetuating. In reading Plutarch, and to a lesser extent

Livy,[14] Shakespeare found a political conflict, unconnected with a family conflict. In Livy the political struggle is clearly defined in terms of class war, starting from the challenge to the consuls' authority made by a group of plebeians who, led by 'the persuasion of one *Sicinius*', left the city and encamped themselves as if ready for war, thus arousing much fear in Rome: 'The commons forlorne of their fellow commoners doubted the violence of the Senatours: the Senatours againe stood in feare and jelousie of the commons that remained stil behind'.

To settle this discord the senators send out Menenius Agrippa to reconcile the citizens, which he does with his belly fable (some details of which are drawn only from Livy's version), but not without the split between the two sides in Rome being institutionalized in a new office. It was granted that 'the Communaltie should have certaine sacred and inviolable magistrates of their owne among themselves, such as might have power to assist the Commons against the Consuls', so five tribunes were elected, including '*Sicinius*, the author of the sedition or insurrection'. There is no doubt as to which side Livy supports!

Of Coriolanus and his background Livy says no more than that he was 'among the flowre of gallant youths, ... right politicke of advise, active besides'. But he is soon marked out as 'an utter and capitall enemie to the Tribunes power and authoritie', urging the Senate to use the supply of corn to recover their previous dominance. Livy is doubtful whether the senators, by following his advice, 'might have eased themselves of the Tribunes authoritie over them', but he gives a vivid account of how the Commons regarded Coriolanus' policies as a threat to their very existence. They would have killed him as he left the Council-house had the tribunes not prevented them, insisting on a public trial. Coriolanus rejects the tribunes' authority over the Senate, 'But so spightfully were the Commons bent, and all so set upon mischief, that there was no other remedie, but one man must pay for it, to save and excuse the rest of the Nobles.' Coriolanus becomes the victim of the class struggle, a scapegoat for the patricians, and is banished, vowing revenge. The rest of the story is essentially as in Shakespeare, with special emphasis on the fact that he was dissuaded from his revenge on Rome by the intervention of his mother, wife, and children. The emotional emphasis, however, is different, for when he hears of their approach

> *Coriolanus*, faring like a man well neare beside himselfe, arose from his seate, and ran to meete his mother, and to embrace her. But the woman falling in steede of praiers into a fit of choller: 'Let me know (quoth she) before I suffer thee to embrace me, whether I am come to an enemie or to a sonne, whether I be in thy campe as a captive prisoner, or as a natural mother'.

When she has finished berating him, 'his wife and children hung about him, and clipped him; whereat the women fell a weeping on all sides, bewailing their owne case and the state of their countrey. So as at length the man was overcome.'

In Livy we only hear of Coriolanus' mother at the very end, family and political conflicts existing on separate levels. Plutarch starts by discussing the psychological consequences of how Coriolanus 'being left an orphan by his father, was brought up under his mother a widowe'. Such a man would not be 'well brought up and taught that were meete', the unfortunate result being that

> a rare and excellent witte untaught, doth bring forth many good and evill thinges together.... For this Martius' naturall wit and great harte dyd marvelously sturre up his corage, to doe and attempt noble acts. But on the other side for lacke of education, he was so chollericke and impacient, that he would yeld to no living creature; which made him churlishe, uncivill, and altogether unfit for any mans conversation.

('Conversation' here means 'society'.) Plutarch's particular diagnosis of the effect of orphanage is also useful to Shakespeare. Whereas for other Roman soldiers

> the only respect that made them valliant, was they hoped to have honour: but touching Martius, the only thing that made him to love honour, was the joye he saw his mother dyd take of him. For he thought nothing made him so happie and honorable, as that his mother might heare every bodie praise and commend him, that she might allwayes see him returne with a crowne upon his head, and that she might still embrace him with teares running downe her cheekes for joye.

Shakespeare does not actually develop that scene (indeed he drastically changes Coriolanus' attitude to glory) but the relationship is significant, and so is the further domestic detail that

> Martius thinking all due to his mother, that had bene also due to his father if he had lived: dyd not only content himselfe to rejoyce and honour her, but at her desire tooke a wife also, by whom he had two children, and yet never left his mothers house therefore.

A marginal note at this point signals 'The obedience of Coriolanus to his mother'. Shakespeare will retain the son's respect for his mother, but complicate it with resentment and criticism; and while showing Virgilia as the dutiful resident daughter-in-law, he will also give her a mind of her own. These are the familiar tactics of a writer who hated simple contrasts, always created a complex balancing of character and motive.

As for the political situation, Plutarch extends the discord he had found in Livy and in a more detailed source, the *Roman Antiquities* of Dionysius Halicarnassus.[15] In Plutarch the main conflict is between the people and the patricians, with the tribunes sometimes causally involved, at other times the people acting alone. The plebeians have more initiative than Shakespeare grants them, and more admirable qualities. They fight willingly 'for defence of their countrie and common wealth', and once their grievances have been met 'the people immediately went to the warres, shewing that they had a good will to doe better than ever they dyd'. Indeed, Coriolanus is moved to 'persuade the Patricians to shew themselves no less forward and willing to fight for their countrie, than the common people were', in order to prove their superior 'nobilitie and valliantnes'. However, in the battle of Corioles the people show both greed in looting, and cowardice in not following Martius into the city, negative qualities which Shakespeare will develop and unify. In Plutarch, again, when Martius stands for Consul, 'the common people favored his sute, thinking it would be a shame' to refuse the man 'that had done so great service and good to the commonwealth'. Coriolanus goes among them, following the old 'custome, [shewing] many woundes and cuttes apon his bodie', with none of the repugnance at this practice that Shakespeare ascribes him. It is only when he appears 'with great pompe' at the election, accompanied by the Senate and 'the whole Nobilitie of the Cittie about him', that the 'love and good will of the common people turned straight to an hate and envie toward him, fearing to put this office of soveraine authoritie into his handes, being a man somewhat partiall toward the nobilitie'. That is, only at this point do the plebeians recognize Coriolanus as a member of the patrician class, sharing their hatred of the people: in Shakespeare that point is made in the very first scene (I.i.5).

In Shakespeare, too, the rejection of Coriolanus is not the spontaneous reaction of the people but is brought about by the tribunes (II.iii.177–258).[16] For Plutarch, as for Livy, the tribunes are 'the flatterers of the people', who can be relied upon 'to sturre up sedition'. They are 'busie pratlers that sought the peoples good will', and cause 'a second insurrection against the Nobilitie and Patricians' by 'spreading abroad false tales and rumours against the Nobilitie', that they had actually caused the dearth of corn. But in Plutarch we seldom see them directly manipulating the people, who still have the power to act on their own initiative. The tribunes are rather presented as personal enemies of Coriolanus, who 'openly spake against these flattering Tribunes' in the Senate, and again calls them 'people pleasers, and traitours to the nobilitie', having nourished 'insolencie and sedition'. Coriolanus urges that their tribuneship be taken from them, at which the tribunes rush to the people for help, so provoking a tumult (cf. *Coriolanus*, III.i.180–228). When Martius appears next day to answer the articles that the tribunes have prepared against him, he 'gave him selfe in his words to thunder', defending himself stoutly, which 'stirred coales among the people, who were in wonderfull furie at it'. At this point 'Sicinius, the cruellest and stowtest of the Tribunes, after he had whispered a little with his companions, dyd openly pronounce ... Martius as condemned by the Tribunes to dye'. But at this, as the Aediles are preparing to throw him off the Tarpeian rock, 'divers of the people themselves thought it too cruell and violent a deed', and the tribunes' 'owne friends and kinsemen ... dyd persuade and advise not to proceede in so violent and extraordinary a sort' as to kill him without a lawful trial.

In Shakespeare the people are both less admirable and more docile, thus easily manipulated by the tribunes. In Plutarch Shakespeare found a continuing emphasis on civil dissension, including the speech of Appius Clodius, 'one that was taken ever as an heavie enemie to the people', and the people's not unjustified sense of being 'contemned and hated of the nobilitie'. The division within Rome is partially healed by the expulsion of Coriolanus, the plebeians rejoicing, the patricians sorrowing, but it resurges long after his banishment. Plutarch's Coriolanus actively plots against his enemies, with a 'craftie accusation' and a 'device' used against Rome 'to increase still the malice and dissention between the nobilitie and the communaltie'. And while his exploits and fame 'ranne through all Italie ... all went still to wracke at Rome', where 'they were one so much against another, and full of seditious wordes', that they could not put an army into the field. It is only the imminence of his attack on Rome that appeases, for the time being, 'the sedition and dissention between the Nobilitie and the people'.

As we read Plutarch's account of the political dissension in Rome we are struck by the absence in it of any reference to Coriolanus' family. True, the capitulation scene before his mother is dealt with at great length, North's English translation even amplifying some details from Amyot's Plutarch. But after the early mention of his mother the only other time the family appears in the story is at Coriolanus' banishment, when he has gone home to

> take leave of his mother and wife, finding them weeping, and shreeking out for sorrowe, and had also comforted and persuaded them to be content with his chance: he went immediately to the gate of the cittie, accompanied with a great number of Patricians.

Shakespeare dramatizes that moment (IV.i.) but he also invents a number of important scenes for Volumnia in order to give reality to the effects of the mother's upbringing mentioned by Plutarch, and he then interweaves the family conflict with the political. In Act I, scene iii, he shows Volumnia and Virgilia sewing, with the mother recalling how she had sent her son to the army to prove 'himself a man', passing on to him her highest value of service to the state: 'had I a dozen sons ... I had rather eleven die nobly for the country than one voluptuously surfeit out of action' (I.iii.22ff.). Here Shakespeare brilliantly characterizes the kind of ethos that would produce mothers ready to sacrifice their own children, giving Volumnia a visionary scene. They have been talking in prose, but when Virgilia wishes to 'retire myself' Volumnia refuses permission and – as if to breathe some martial spirit into this too-tender wife – launches into verse with an auto-suggested vision of battle and aggressive defiance:

> Methinks I hear hither thy husband's drum;
> See him pluck Aufidius down by th'hair;
> As children from a bear, the Volsces shunning him.
> Methinks I see him stamp thus, and call thus:
> 'Come on, you cowards! you were got in fear,
> Though you were born in Rome'.

(I.iii.31ff.)

This is just the taunt that Volumnia will make to him when he returns to destroy Rome: she, too, knows how to provoke a man of honour.

Volumnia's exultation uses analogies that confuse growth and death, Shakespeare's way of suggesting her perversion of nature:

> His bloody brow
> With his mailed hand then wiping, forth he goes,
> Like to a harvest-man that's tasked to mow
> Or all or lose his hire.

This is bad enough, but worse follows as Virgilia exclaims in horror 'His bloody brow? O Jupiter, no blood!' and Volumnia scorns her:

> Away, you fool! It more becomes a man
> Than gilt his trophy. The breasts of Hecuba,
> When she did suckle Hector, looked not lovelier
> Than Hector's forehead when it spit forth blood
> At Grecian sword, contemning.

(40ff.)

I can hardly think of a more devastating way of showing Volumnia's militaristic subordination of all values, even the most tender emotions of giving suck, to the glorification of blood and battle. To put the values of *patria* first, Shakespeare suggests, can have disastrous consequences for natural relationships.

Having established the idea of the women enduring Martius' absence in Corioli, Shakespeare then places Volumnia, Virgilia, and Valeria among the crowd in Rome awaiting his return (II.i.94–202), where Volumnia for the first time openly declares her ambition that he become consul (II.i.195–9). After the fiasco of the first confrontation with the tribunes (III.i.), which ends in confusion, Shakespeare weaves Volumnia still more closely into the plot by giving her, rather than the patricians (as in Plutarch), the task of persuading Coriolanus to return and beg the plebeians' votes (III.ii.), a crucial scene in making his political behaviour dependent on the sanctions of his mother. When this second stage fails, and Coriolanus is banished, Shakespeare not only brings Volumnia and Virgilia on for the parting, but also shows Volumnia confronting the tribunes in a scene which begins comically, as they try to avoid meeting her (IV.ii.7ff.), and continues with her blistering attack on them: 'Hadst thou foxship/To banish him that struck more blows for Rome/ Than thou hast spoken words?' (IV.ii.18ff.).

In these five invented scenes, only two of them suggested by Plutarch, Shakespeare built up the character of Volumnia as ferociously determined to defend her values, ready to sacrifice anyone who should challenge them. (In the same desire for plot coherence and unification Shakespeare introduces Aufidius in I.x., long before Plutarch mentions him.) The values of Volumnia are those of the patricians, militaristic and patriotic, only too appropriate to Rome in its early days, surrounded by enemies. In Plutarch, Shakespeare found an explanation of Roman society at that period which he built into the play to characterize a whole class strikingly lacking in any other qualities but those designed to give immediate and continuing success in combat, military or civil: 'Now in those dayes, valliantness was honoured in Rome above all other vertues: which they called *Virtus*, by the name of vertue selfe, as including in that generall name, all other speciall vertues besides.' In the play these sentiments are given to Cominius, at the start of his formal panegyric on Coriolanus' achievements at Corioli:

> It is held
> That valour is the chiefest virtue, *and*
> *Most dignifies the haver.*

> (II.ii.81ff.; my italics)

This scale of values would undoubtedly seem to Shakespeare, as to Plutarch, a perversion of classical and Christian concepts of virtue, where man's 'excellence or proper function was the use of reason'.[17] What Shakespeare has added to Plutarch is the attitude often expressed by the patricians in this play, their awareness of appearances, of the beneficial results of heroism, how a man's image – and so his political bargaining power – will be enhanced by fame or glory, how these will 'become' him. That is, the patricians tend to evaluate action not so much in itself but for its future benefits to them. They always have an eye to what they can get out of it.

Coriolanus has certainly taken over from his class a belief in the value of the soldier and of such military virtues as courage, loyalty, and comradeship. But for Coriolanus valour is not the chief, nor the only virtue, and even valour is pursued by him in an idealistic, non-materialistic way. He fights not because fighting is an end in itself, nor for his own profit, but out of love for his country, service to the state. This is made clear to us in the sequence of scenes presenting the battle for Corioli, and its aftermath (especially I.vi. and I.ix.).

Highlighting this part of the play reveals a fairly simple, unproblematic relationship. Coriolanus could go on fighting for the good of Rome for just as long as he can stand. Yet this Rome is not a united and self-balancing society, but one divided by famine and social unrest. Shakespeare chooses to begin the play with a mob, up in arms and angry for food, convinced that the patricians are withholding grain from them. The patricians send Menenius to them in his role as friend of the people, as they have done before, and he manages to placate them once again with the old story about the belly, a part of the body which *appears* to do no work – like the senators of Rome, he argues – but in fact supports the rest of the organism or state (I.i.85ff.). It is, as Menenius says, a tale that 'serves my purpose', but this is the last time that he will be able to fob the people off, for under the pressure of their protests, we learn, the patricians have just granted the people five tribunes to represent their case (I.i.213ff.). When told of this by Coriolanus, Menenius comments, 'This is strange': evidently so liberal a gesture puzzles the more reactionary party.

We are here at the beginning, in Rome, of an experiment in democracy and political representation. It goes hideously wrong, and although we must place the blame for this on the self-seeking nature of the tribunes and the stupidity of the people, a large element in the social discord – and just the one that the tribunes can exploit for their ends – is the patricians' general loathing of the people. Coriolanus' first words in the play constitute the most unattractive opening lines of any Shakespeare character:

> What's the matter, you dissentious rogues
> That, rubbing the poor itch of your opinion,
> Make yourselves scabs?

> (I.i.162ff.)

It is undeniable that Coriolanus loathes the populace. But before we dismiss him as 'proud' or 'arrogant' we should consider two other factors that Shakespeare has rather carefully worked up throughout the play, sometimes in contradiction to his sources: first, the general patrician attitude to the plebs, and second, the plebs' actual behaviour in battle.

The leading patricians are Cominius, Menenius, and Volumnia: they are a coherent group ('us o'th' right-hand file' is how Menenius describes them (II.i.22), '*Enter Coriolanus ... [and] all the gentry*' is how Shakespeare puts it in the stage direction to Act III, scene i), and they express a coherent attitude, one of disgust and contempt for the plebeians. Menenius calls them 'my countrymen' and 'friends' to their faces, avows that the patricians 'care for you like fathers' (I.i.53, 63, 75f.), yet when the quarrelsome first citizen challenges him his real feelings break out: 'Rome and her rats are at the point of battle./The one side must have bale' (I.i.160f.).

There is no doubt which side will 'have bale', or be destroyed. The metaphor of 'rats' to describe the people is used to introduce the desired reflex: 'exterminate them'. Menenius dismisses the tribunes with a similarly insulting reduction of the people to the level of animals: they are 'the herdsmen of the beastly plebeians' (II.i.93). By this point in the play we have few illusions about the goodness of the citizens, yet all the same Menenius' contempt is nauseating, as when he describes the people as 'multiplying spawn' (II.ii.78).

Here person A's evaluation of group B can only reduce our sympathy for the speaker. Yet members of this patrician class support one another in these attitudes: when Coriolanus rages at the people Menenius calls it a 'worthy rage' (III.i.240); a nobleman approves of Coriolanus' refusal to compromise: 'You do the nobler' (III.ii.6); Volumnia says that Coriolanus is 'too absolute', although therein he 'can never be too noble' (III.ii.40f.). Even the more restrained Cominius describes the people as a 'tag', or rabble (III.i.247), and Menenius sees this class as 'the grains', the tribunes as 'the musty chaff' (V.i.30f.).

The most revealing expression of the patricians' hatred for the people comes out when Coriolanus puzzles over Volumnia's eagerness that he should flatter the people in order to gain their votes for the consulship:

> I muse my mother
> Does not approve me further, who was wont
> To call them woollen vassals, things created
> To buy and sell with groats; to show bare heads
> In congregations, to yawn, be still, and wonder,
> When one but of my ordinance stood up
> To speak of peace or war.
>
> (III.ii.6ff.)

This sequence creates an effect which we experience several times in this play, that of a sudden insight into past or future behaviour: people are recorded, unawares, in some peculiarly revealing posture. There we have the whole ethos of aristocratic superiority that Coriolanus has been born into and moulded by. Volumnia in the present is just as violent, for when her son says of the people, 'Let them hang', she adds 'Ay, and burn too' (III.ii.22f.). At Coriolanus' banishment she calls down the typhus on them: 'Now the red pestilence strike all trades in Rome,/And occupations perish!' (IV.i.13f.). Added to the violence of the wish is the unpleasant aristocrat's definition of its enemies as being all those who have to work for a living ('occupations'). Surely we cannot endorse the patricians on this issue.

As for Coriolanus' attitude to the people, it is the same as the rest of his class, only expressed with the energy and vehemence that he brings to all his activities. It bulks larger, then, both in quantity and intensity, than that of the other patricians. The people, he says, 'would feed on one another' if their rulers did not keep them under control (I.i.186). 'Hang 'em!' is his remedy (I.i.180, 203). He describes them as 'fragments' (I.i.221), 'Our musty super-fluity' (226), 'rats' (247); he loathes their dirty faces and stinking breath (II.iii.61f.), they are the 'rank-scented meinie' (III.i.70), 'measles' or scabs 'Which we disdain should tetter us' (82f.); they are 'The beast/With many heads' (IV.i.1f.). The culmination of all his feelings towards them is his speech after they have banished him:

147

You common cry of curs! whose breath I hate
As reek o'th' rotten fens, whose loves I prize
As the dead carcasses of unburied men
That do corrupt my air – I banish you.

(III.iii.120ff.)

It is hard to think of many more unpleasant similes than that.

It would be a failure of humanity if the reader, spectator, or critic did not register at this point an unequivocal distaste for the patricians' violent feelings against the citizens who, after all, represent the bulk of their country and on whose work and services they rely in order to support their own positions of privilege. If Shakespeare were now to show the people as not having the faults ascribed to them, but as being honest, sober, responsible craftsmen, workers of integrity – then we could safely dismiss the patricians as the villains of the piece. But he does no such thing. He presents them as muddled and confused, as in the scene where a group of them on stage together, with neither patricians to abuse nor tribunes to organize them, are made to undermine their own pretensions to having a coherent collective identity:

1 CITIZEN. . . . [Coriolanus] stuck not to call us the many-headed multitude.
3 CITIZEN. We have been called so of many; not that our heads are some
    brown, some black, some abram, some bald, but that our wits are so
    diversely coloured; and truly I think, if all our wits were to issue out
    of one skull, they would fly east, west, north, south, and their consent
    of one direct way should be at once to all the points o'th' compass.

(II.iii.15ff.)

Evidently Shakespeare does not intend us to think very highly of the mob. (Where Plutarch records that their protest against the famine took the form of a peaceful and religious gesture, leaving the town to go as suppliants to a sacred hill, Shakespeare will allow them no contact with the sacred, and makes them mutinous, not peaceful.) Even the tribunes, their own leaders, despise them – whenever, that is, they do not do exactly what the tribunes expect of them. So Brutus describes the people's welcome to Coriolanus with such contempt that one might be forgiven for recalling the lines as having been spoken by one of the patricians. The mob is so eager to see him, he reports, that the 'prattling nurse' neglects her child to gossip about him,

the kitchen malkin pins
Her richest lockram 'bout her reechy neck,
Clamb'ring the walls to eye him. Stalls, bulks, windows,
Are smothered up, leads filled and ridges horsed
With variable complexions, all agreeing
In earnestness to see him.

(II.i.205ff.)

The images of dirt and commotion, the sardonic oxymoron of 'richest lock-ram', the contemptuous punning sound (richest/reechy), the deliberately ugly and undignified verbs to describe the crowd's movement (clamb'ring, smothered up, horsed) – the language reduces their own supporters to an animal-like jumble. From this and other comments by the tribunes it becomes impossible to take the people seriously as an alternative to the patricians: we cannot prefer either.

The really telling factor in the disvaluing of the people, and one that relates mose closely to Coriolanus' own set of values, involves, as we have seen, a reshaping of the source material. In Plutarch the people of Rome are not, perhaps, such dedicated soldiers as Coriolanus but they fight alongside him, rallying to his calls. Although there are 'very fewe men to helpe him' in Corioli they do fight on with him, and his subsequent exhortation moves the whole army to fight once more. His only criticism of them is directed against the looters. In Shakespeare the people are much less reliable. Even before the battle of Corioli, Martius sums up their previous behaviour in terms which make it clear to us that they stand as polar opposites to all his values: they are 'curs', who are frightened by war but in peacetime become 'proud' (that is, referring to animals, 'quarrelsome, high-mettled, ungovernable').

> He that trusts to you,
> Where he should find you lions, finds you hares, ...
> He that depends
> Upon your favours swims with fins of lead
> And hews down oaks with rushes. Hang ye! Trust ye?
> With every minute you do change a mind,
> And call him noble that was now your hate,
> Him vile that was your garland.
>
> (I.i.168ff., 177ff.)

Although it is excessively violent, as usual, the inescapable fact about that speech is that Shakespeare has so planned the play that every criticism in it is justified. The mob are cowardly; they go to war not out of Coriolanus' ideals of service to their country but only when they cannot avoid the duty. When Coriolanus and the other patricians are about to leave for the wars Shakespeare makes the populace slink off: '*citizens steal away*' is his stage direction, and Coriolanus comments with sarcasm: 'Worshipful mutineers,/ Your valour puts well forth' (I.i.250f.) – that is, it 'makes a fine show'. Finally at the wars, if the plebeians can make any profit by looting, they will; and in peacetime they are fickle and unreliable.

They are so constructed by Shakespeare as to form an anti-type to Coriolanus' values – or he is so built up as to be their opposite. When the Roman soldiers are beaten back ignominiously – a detail invented by Shakespeare – he attacks them as 'geese':

> how have you run
> From slaves that apes would beat! Pluto and hell!
> All hurt behind! Backs red, and faces pale
> With flight and agued fear!

(I.iv.35ff.)

He tries to rally them with his favourite idea of 'standing': 'If you'll stand fast, we'll beat them to their wives' (41). But they take 'stand' literally, remaining where they are outside Corioli while Martius breaks into the city alone. 'Mark me, and do the like', he cries, and they reply:

> 1 SOLDIER. Foolhardiness, not I.
> 2 SOLDIER. Nor I.   [*Martius is shut in*
> 1 SOLDIER. See, they have shut him in.
> ALL.   To th'pot, I warrant him.

(I.iv.46ff.)

The callousness of that final image – leaving him to be chopped up in the stew-pot – is observed by us, and not by Coriolanus, so that when the mob of soldiers descend to looting instead of fighting we can hardly not endorse his attack on their greed for trash:

> See here these movers that do prize their honours
> At a cracked drachma! Cushions, leaden spoons,
> Irons of a doit, doublets that hangmen would
> Bury with those that wore them, these base slaves,
> Ere yet the fight be done, pack up.

(I.v.4ff.)

Nor can we quarrel with his later description of the people's cowardice: 'The mouse ne'er shunned the cat as they did budge/From rascals worse than they' (I.vi.44f.). Commentators have praised Shakespeare for his refusal to take sides, and Coleridge enthused over the 'wonderful impartiality in Shakespeare's politics'.[18] What needs to be said, however, is that Shakespeare has downgraded both sides, successively eliminating each party as an object of our sympathy or concern.

Political image-making

Moving now from the opposed social groups to the individual who is the focus of their conflict, we begin to notice that when set against his family or class Coriolanus exists not as a free individual but as a man with a role to play on behalf of others. His mother claims credit for the self-sacrifice by which she sent him, when still a boy, to 'a cruel war' in order to 'find fame' (I.iii.13), and she refers possessively to him as 'my boy Martius... my good soldier.... My gentle Martius' (II.i.98, 169f.). After Coriolanus has gone to see the patricians on his return from Corioli, Volumnia reveals her long-standing ambition that her son should become consul:

> I have lived
> To see inherited my very wishes,
> And the buildings of my fancy: only
> There's one thing wanting, which I doubt not but
> Our Rome will cast upon thee.

(II.i.195ff.)

She has 'long dreamed of an inheritance', as the editors gloss the second line: the fantasy which she has indulged in is about to come true. Yet she speaks as if the inheritance will be hers, not his; and the disproportion in the pronouns (four 'I' or 'my' to one 'our' and one 'thee') reflects the sense we receive that Coriolanus has been groomed for success for her sake, not his own. He will fulfil the desires which she, as a woman, could not fulfil.[19] As he says, with some resentment, at the moment of banishment: 'Mother, you wot well/My hazards still have been your solace' (IV.i.28f.). Whatever he imagines he is doing, he is in effect a puppet, being controlled by her.

Within the patrician class he is also a puppet. In this rather confused political situation, where power has been given to the people and its representatives, yet with no clear division of responsibility for the legislature and the executive, the sole strategy of the patricians is to have Coriolanus elected consul, from which position, they imagine, he will be able to exert their traditional downward pressure over the people. The main justification for his election being his military feats on behalf of the state, we see the patricians again and again building up an image of Coriolanus as an invincible fighter. Modern critics have noted the presence of these passages but have mostly failed to see their significance as political propaganda in an election campaign. As a result such critics describe Coriolanus as a juggernaut or tank, as if that were the evaluation Shakespeare were making of him. In fact, however, Shakespeare evidently evaluates him favourably as a charismatic leader, a soldier who fights for his country to the limits of endurance, and just as clearly indicates the gap between a balanced evaluation of Coriolanus and the extraordinary reports that the patricians give of him. In the mouths of the patricians any chance to report on Coriolanus' deeds becomes the occasion for shameless panegyrics, encomia produced with an eye to his vote-catching power as superhero.

When Martius is shut up alone inside Corioli, seemingly lost, Lartius pronounces a premature epitaph over him which shows the instinctive patrician desire to exaggerate his exploits:

> Thou wast a soldier
> Even to Cato's wish, not fierce and terrible
> Only in strokes, but with thy grim looks and

151

The thunder-like percussion of thy sounds
Thou mad'st thine enemies shake, as if the world
Were feverous and did tremble.

(I.iv.57ff.)

The magnification of Coriolanus by the patricians results always in a kind of
gigantism: his voice is now like thunder, enemies quake before him as if he
gave the whole world the jitters. All these 'enormous and disgusting hyperboles' (as Dr Johnson described the Metaphysicals' conceits) are quite dis-
proportionate to what we see of Coriolanus, or indeed of any man. The
political function of it all is nakedly revealed just after the battle, where
Cominius looks forward to 'reporting' his exploits precisely for the social
and political effect they will have. Each section of society (he hopes) will react
with admiration and gratitude:

If I should tell thee o'er this thy day's work
Thou't not believe thy deeds. But I'll report it
Where senators shall mingle tears with smiles,
Where great patricians shall attend, and shrug,
I'th' end admire; where ladies shall be frighted
And, gladly quaked, hear more; where the dull tribunes,
That with the fusty plebeians hate thine honours,
Shall say against their hearts 'We thank the gods
Our Rome hath such a soldier'.

(I.ix.1ff.)

Before we see the triumph-scene, and before we know whether or not
Cominius' report will have the effect he hopes for, Shakespeare brings
together Menenius and Volumnia, who have received news of Coriolanus'
success in the battle. As they discuss his fortunes the patrician concept of his
'person' or body as an investment-object is rendered literal, quantified before
our eyes; wounds, like honour, 'become' him, not just in themselves but for
their vote-catching power.

MENENIUS. Is he not wounded? He was wont to come home wounded.
VIRGILIA. O, no, no, no!
VOLUMNIA. O, he is wounded, I thank the gods for't.
MENENIUS. So do I too, if it be not too much. Brings a' victory in his
pocket, the wounds become him. ... Where is he wounded?
VOLUMNIA. I'th'shoulder and i'th'left arm. There will be large cicatrices to
show the people, when he shall stand for his place.

(II.i.116ff., 143ff.)

Volumnia truly has Coriolanus' body, and his career, mapped out for him,
and to her the fact that he now has twenty-seven visible scars proves his
invincibility in war and peace. As I have written elsewhere, 'they count his

scars, each one fatal to the enemy, with the same intention as that of the soldier or confirmed killer making notches on the handle of a gun or a knife. Coriolanus is their human liquidator.'[20]

In the triumph-scene itself we can observe the formation of a marketable political image, for Cominius' panegyric to Coriolanus takes on a unity and identity in itself which has less and less connection with the man we have observed. Menenius formally invites Cominius 'to report/A little of that worthy work performed' by Coriolanus (II.ii.44ff.), but his 'little' is swept aside by a Senator, who urges Cominius to 'Leave nothing out for length' (49ff.). The purpose of this zealous invitation is again made explicit by Shakespeare as the senator addresses the tribunes:

> We do request your kindest ears and, after,
> Your loving motion toward the common body
> To yield what passes here.
>
> (50ff.)

The patricians are naïve enough to think that the tribunes will pass on their panegyrics as reported: that is one of the weak links in their strategy.

Thus prompted, Cominius launches into a forty-line speech reviewing Coriolanus' glowing career down to the present. (Coriolanus has left the scene in disgust: 'I had rather have my wounds to heal again/Than hear say how I got them. . . ./When blows have made me stay, I fled from words'.) If we pick out the account of the battle of Corioli we will see the disproportion between the event and the analogies used to describe it, in which a man is elevated to the level of some principle of death by being depersonalized, successively treated as a ship, a tool for stamping a mark on some softer material, a blood-covered machine:

> as weeds before
> A vessel under sail, so men obeyed,
> And fell below his stem. His sword, death's stamp,
> Where it did mark, it took; from face to foot
> He was a thing of blood, whose every motion
> Was timed with dying cries.
>
> (II.ii.103ff.)

The unity of attitude and intention among the patricians is shown again by the similarity between this and the scene just before, where Volumnia and Menenius created their image of Coriolanus as death-machine.

MENENIUS. Now it's twenty-seven [wounds]. Every gash was an enemy's grave. – Hark! the trumpets.
VOLUMNIA. These are the ushers of Martius. Before him he carries noise, and behind him he leaves tears.
  Death, that dark spirit, in's nervy arm doth lie,

Which being advanced, declines; and then men die.

(II.i.151ff.)

The antithesis and paradox in Volumnia's militarist jingle creates the same impression as Cominius' 'every motion ... timed with dying cries', the impression of a stiff, unstoppable machine, with a jerky action, 'up: down: dead!', each movement a killing one. But this is to coin an image of Coriolanus as some supernatural force with whom death is in league, while we know that Coriolanus is only a man. In other words the visions tell us more about the patricians and their need to create a gigantic, frightening image of Coriolanus to represent their own power, their own wished-for deterrent. Cominius even describes him as running 'reeking o'er the lives of men, as if/'Twere a perpetual spoil' (II.ii.117ff.), that is, at once a stream of blood swallowing up the men in his path and a predatory animal massacring deer. The image of Coriolanus created by the patricians is nauseating, disclosing their pathological delight in blood and death, and their desire to have a superman figure on their side.

In this way the two areas of society closest to Coriolanus, the family and the patricians, see him as performing the major role in their own triumphs, and in order to give this role a prestige matching their ambitions they do not hesitate to inflate 'report' until it overtowers reality. How does Coriolanus react? If he were the proud and arrogant figure described by some modern critics he would presumably revel in all this, gloat over his defeated enemies, bask in adulation.[21] In fact he does quite the opposite. I have made the general claim that Coriolanus, on some major issues, stands outside the values of his class, and this is one of them. He does not at all share the ambition that Volumnia has for him. After her speech looking forward to the fulfilment of her greatest desire he affirms that his values are more important to him than the power, and values, of others:

> Know, good mother,
> I had rather be their servant in my way
> Than sway with them in theirs.

(II.i.199f.)

As a reply to a mother in her ecstasy of longing that is cool enough: indeed, if we watch Coriolanus each time he refers to his mother we will find him not lacking in duty, of course, but often expressing a certain resentment at her demands on him and on his behalf. One of the most carefully developed pieces of characterization that Shakespeare ever made is Coriolanus' loathing of adulation. At his first appearance Menenius welcomes him fervently: 'Hail, noble Martius!', and gets as reply the laconic 'Thanks' (I.i.162f.). When Lartius expresses concern at his wounds the reply is simply, 'Sir, praise me not' (I.v.16). Later, the battle successful, Lartius embarks on a panegyric, with Coriolanus as 'the steed, we the caparison' only to be cut short with:

154

> Pray now, no more. My mother,
> Who has a charter to extol her blood,
> When she does praise me grieves me.
>
> (I.ix.13ff.)

The sarcasm in that remark ('my mother has taken out a licence to praise her own family') is repeated when he is welcomed by her at the triumph:

> ALL. Welcome to Rome, renownéd Coriolanus!
> CORIOLANUS. No more of this, it does offend my heart;
>   Pray now, no more.
> COMINIUS.   Look, sir, your mother!
> CORIOLANUS.   O,   [*Kneels*
>   You have, I know, petitioned all the gods
>   For my prosperity!
>
> (II.i.165ff.)

'That's what you've been up to again': the note of disapproval of her vociferousness on behalf of her own family is unmistakable. Coriolanus shares the sense of social superiority common to his whole class, but he does not share their pride, ambition, or liking for adulation. It is hard to see how critics can have failed to note the quantity and intensity of anti-panegyrical feelings given to Coriolanus. At every point where his deeds are vaunted he responds with violent disapproval. His characteristic reaction to praise is embarrassment – he blushes; at the same time he tries to minimize his exploits and deflate the praise-situation. In the scene after Corioli, Cominius urges him not to be 'the grave' of his 'deserving'; Coriolanus' reply is a brief disclaimer:

> I have some wounds upon me, and they smart
> To hear themselves remembered.
>
> (I.x.28f.)

But for once Shakespeare is not ready to let it go at that. Since this sequence
      < action : evaluation : report : adulation : advantage >
is crucial to the political manoeuvring in the play he devotes eighty lines of this scene to a debate on the morality of praise and reward. Cominius offers Coriolanus a tenth of the spoils as a reward for his bravery, and when the offer is refused as unnecessary the soldiers give their hero a great acclamation.[22] The army's reactions to Coriolanus' integrity may seem perfectly reasonable to us: if so, we will be quite unprepared for the violence, the almost religious feeling of sacrilege with which Coriolanus attacks his comrades:

> May these same instruments which you profane
> Never sound more! When drums and trumpets shall
> I'th'field prove flatterers, let courts and cities be
> Made all of false-faced soothing!
>
> (41ff.)

This shows a truly deep loathing, a suspicion of panegyric as expressing flattery and lies, an inherently false genre:

> You shout me forth
> In acclamations hyperbolical;
> As if I loved my little should be dieted
> In praises sauced with lies.

(50ff.)

They do 'cry him up', and their hyperboles indeed topple over into fiction and fantasy.

With great insistence Shakespeare builds up this picture of a soldier embarrassed and nauseated by praise, who tends in response to undervalue his own exploits. Coriolanus does not seem to be aware why his class praises him so much, but he finds their praise out of proportion to his deeds. He is not, then, a 'proud' man, in terms of his personal achievements. Indeed when Cominius delivers his formal panegyric Coriolanus cannot bear to listen to what he accurately predicts to monstrous exaggeration:

> I had rather have one scratch my head i'th'sun
> When the alarum were struck than idly sit
> To hear my nothings monstered.   [*Exit*

(II.ii.75ff.)

If not proud, neither is he ambitious. Having engaged to serve with Cominius he is ready to honour his promise, and accepts his place below him (I.i.236ff.). As we have seen, he would rather be a servant of Rome on his terms than have power on theirs (II.i.199ff.). He does not in the least wish to be consul, and tries several times to get released from the task – but the patricians insist.[23]

All this is perfectly clear. Yet in the play he is called proud and ambitious, and some modern critics have taken over those criticisms without realizing that Shakespeare has disvalued them by giving them to the enemies of Coriolanus. Those people who resent him wish to abuse him, and therefore call him proud. The tribunes even accuse him of ambition, but Shakespeare makes them do so immediately after we have seen him gladly accept the post subordinate to Cominius:

> BRUTUS. The present wars devour him! He is grown
>   Too proud to be so valiant.
> SICINIUS.   Such a nature,
>   Tickled with good success, disdains the shadow
>   Which he treads on at noon. But I do wonder
>   His insolence can brook to be commanded
>   Under Cominius.
> BRUTUS.   Fame, at the which he aims –

and so on, speculating how Martius will rob Cominius of his merits (I.i.257ff.). The tribunes are inventing this greed for fame and precedence, which does not square with anything we have seen of Coriolanus.[24] What this scene shows is that they, too, are constructing an agreed image of Coriolanus for their own purposes. In order to succeed with the people they have to create a figure that will focus all the class-hatred and resentment of the plebeians. Of course, given Martius' personally violent endorsement of the patricians' sense of superiority, that is not a difficult task. Yet their manner of executing it involves constant distortions. After we have seen the vehemence with which Coriolanus has rejected the army's tributes to him at Corioli and the nausea he revealed at their boasting about him, the tribunes' account of him is exposed as the product of cheap malice:

> BRUTUS. He's poor in no one fault, but stored with all.
> SICINIUS. Especially in pride.
> BRUTUS. And topping all others in boasting.
>
> (II.i.18ff.)

Their Coriolanus is a caricature of all 'anti-democratic attitudes'. It is the creation, as are all the other images of Coriolanus in the play, of immediate needs and long-term political ambition. Their underlying political motives emerge in their dialogue at the end of the scene where he returns in triumph to Rome:

> SICINIUS.   On the sudden,
>   I warrant him consul.
> BRUTUS.   Then our office may
>   During his power go sleep.
>
> (II.i.218ff.)

To preserve their power they will try to destroy his – that being one of the operative principles in politics, then as now. Their 'identikit' picture of Coriolanus is almost a parody of the clichés about the upper classes so necessary to the continuance of class hatred. It is one of the sharper, and sadder, insights of this play that social divisions based on class enmity need to create ever more violent images of the enemy if the class struggle is to continue. These are tragic fictions.

Rehearsals and performance

In any political situation where conflicting interpretations of events oppose each other in the struggle for immediate power, the resulting actions can be described as a sequence of consolidation, manipulation, and direct attack. Each group has to unify its endeavours; each has to persuade its supporters that the cause is just; each has to rehearse its candidates in the appropriate role; and each has to exert prolonged and increasing pressure on the candidate and supporters of the other side. The central sequence in Acts II and III of *Coriolanus* resembles a gigantic two-party election, fought according to the usual political rules of magnification of one's own party and denigration of the other. Coriolanus is the protagonist on one side, organized and rehearsed by the patricians, while on the other the tribunes groom their protagonist, the mob. (As well as resembling an election campaign this sequence recalls two rival theatre-productions.)

As we have seen from their estimation of the bargaining-power of Coriolanus' wounds, the patricians are not lacking in calculation. But, more important, neither are the tribunes, and throughout Acts II and III Brutus and Sicinius dominate the action, manipulating it all from behind the scenes. That is, 'behind the scenes' as far as the patricians are concerned, but 'before them' as far as we are, for in this play Shakespeare makes a brilliantly sustained exploitation of drama's ability to mount separate presentation. Individual units of action presented on-stage are experienced by some characters but not by others. We, the privileged spectators, see every stage in every group's preparations, but Coriolanus sees none of them. Once he has left the battlefield, where action is immediate and significant on its own terms, he enters a political arena in which every action that reaches him has been planned, rehearsed, set up entirely in terms of the effect it will have on his role or behaviour. He does not see his mother exulting over his bloody deeds (I.iii.), nor Volumnia and Menenius computing his wounds (II.i.); he does not hear the comments and evaluations made of him by the citizens (I.i.), by the two officers laying cushions in the Capitol (II.ii.), by the patricians in his temporary absence (III.i.), by Aufidius (I.x.; IV.vii.). So much of the action of the play *goes on behind Coriolanus' back* – we may say, dropping the conventions of literary criticism for a moment, and restoring the point of view of life – that it is no wonder if he seems completely puzzled by it all, unprepared to cope with what people say and do to him. In addition, each issue is no simple one, but always a crisis.

For much of the time (much more than for perhaps any character in any other play) Coriolanus is the focus of discussion and calculation. If two people meet in this play they will talk about him. In Act II, scene i, as a sinister epilogue to his triumph-scene, the two tribunes discuss for over sixty lines the tactics with which they will attack him when he stands for consul. The election ceremony consists of the candidate having to go among the people in the market-place, wearing a specially humble dress, 'the napless vesture of humility', and, stripping his war wounds to testify his services, effectively solicit the people's 'voices' for him. The tribunes realize that Coriolanus will loathe having to display his wounds (a practice of Elizabethan cast-off soldiers and beggars, often showing self-inflicted wounds – compare Edgar as 'Poor Tom' in *King Lear*, II.iii.14ff., and Falstaff's tricks in *1 Henry IV*, II.iv.299ff.). In order to preserve their own 'authorities', Brutus argues,

'We must suggest the people in what hatred/He still hath held them' (II.i.242ff.). 'Suggest', meaning to insinuate or tempt, is a word that Shakespeare associates with hypocrites and their ruling genius, the devil. The tribunes are in effect planning a hypocritical performance, in a scene of private 'complots' which recalls those between Richard III and Buckingham, or Iago and Roderigo. Like those assured hypocrites they use the future tense, confidently predicting the outcome:

> Doubt not
> The commoners for whom we stand, but they
> Upon their ancient malice will forget
> With the least cause these his new honours

(a devastating comment on the people's ingratitude!). Coriolanus 'will give' them cause; ' 'Tis most like he will' retain his disgust at the people's 'stinking breaths'; 'It shall be to him then as our good wills:/A sure destruction' (II.i.224ff.). Our good: his destruction – just like Shakespeare's other hypocrites, they are setting up what modern games theorists call a 'zero-sum game', where one player wins, the other loses. Their superiority over their dupe resembles Iago's over his, 'easy' meat. Coriolanus' hatred of the people must be 'suggested/At some time when his soaring insolence' provokes them:

> – which time shall not want,
> If he be put upon't, and that's as easy
> As to set dogs on sheep.

> (II.i.250ff.)

It is bad enough to have one Iago to deal with; two such destructive hypocrites are invincible.

Throughout this sequence I keep thinking of Max Weber's bitter analysis of politics, and the qualities needed for success in it. The politician, he writes, must have passion, but 'passion in the sense of matter-of-factness, of passionate devotion to a cause', joined with a sense of proportion, the 'ability to let realities work upon him with inner concentration and calmness'. Coriolanus is strikingly lacking in both qualities. But this does not mean that the tribunes, demagogues that they are, represent an ideal pragmatic – let alone ethical – version of politics. As Weber writes, the demagogue lacks objectivity and responsibility, enjoys 'power for power's sake without a substantive purpose' (such as a genuine commitment to social good), and has no solid core: 'from the sudden inner collapse of typical representatives of this mentality, we can see what inner weakness and impatience lies behind this boastful but empty' façade.[25] Events in this play bear out Weber's diagnosis. Later scenes will show us the tribunes quailing before Volumnia (IV.ii.8ff.), feebly disclaiming responsibility for Coriolanus' banishment (IV.vi.122), cringing to the patricians and trying to allay the people's fears, and their own (IV.vi.140–62), begging Menenius (of all people!) to intercede

(V.i.33–63), and finally being 'haled' up and down by the plebeians, angry and frightened at Coriolanus' impending attack (V.iv.34ff.). They are hollow and unheroic, but their collapse is yet to come: for the moment they seem to control events.

The election ceremony takes place in the Forum (II.iii.): I call it a ceremony because it seems more like a rite than a truly open political choice. Coriolanus is the only candidate, supposedly representing the whole of Rome, but, in effect, standing for only part of it. In the intentions of the patricians the people are to be fobbed off with an upper-class candidate who will strengthen their own side and repress the plebs. They regard it as a mere formality for the people to endorse their candidate, and so ensure their future power, but Coriolanus sees it in the present, for what it does to his values, and he goes through with it in a mood of bitter jesting. He is standing for the office, he tells them, for his 'desert' but not his 'desire': ' 'twas never my desire yet to trouble the poor with begging' (65ff.). In a soliloquy – for once he speaks behind somebody else's back, but to the opposite effect of the hypocrites' concealment, revealing only what we already know about him – Coriolanus exposes the absurdity of the ceremony: if he has already 'deserved' or earned the reward why should he now have to 'crave' it? To do so suggests that the honours were not truly his in the first place, which is an insult, and it also suggests that the mob is a more valuable arbiter of honour than the standards of bravery and loyalty on the battlefield. The ceremony is a meaningless piece of ritual which serves only to confuse the true relationship between service and reward (II.iii.112–24).

The people are expected to endorse the patricians' candidate, and although they presumably have a right to give a veto the ruling party never expects that they will exercise it. In the sequence between the tribunes and people that follows (II.iii.155–263) Shakespeare suddenly shows us how the tribunes carry out the political sequence which I have called consolidation, manipulation, and direct attack. It appears that the ceremony ought to have gone off quite differently, for the people had already been manipulated and rehearsed as to how they should have attacked. Whereas normally in this play we, the privileged spectators, see people and actions that Coriolanus does not see, here not even *we* have been allowed to attend this political rehearsal:

> BRUTUS.   Could you not have told him –
>   As you were lessoned....
>   You should have said....
> SICINIUS.   Thus to have said
>   As you were fore-advised, had touched his spirit
>   And tried his inclination....

(II.iii.176f., 185, 190ff.)

And just like Richard III, Iago, Goneril, and Regan, the tribunes spell out the 'advantages' to be gained by exploiting the victim's weakness:

> So, putting him to rage,
> You should have ta'enth' advantage of his choler,
> And passed him unelected.

(197ff.)

This perversion of politics is bad enough; worse still is their urging the people to blame their tribunes for having persuaded them to vote for Coriolanus:

> BRUTUS. Lay
> A fault on us, your tribunes, that we laboured,
> No impediment between, but that you must
> Cast your election on him.
> SICINIUS. Say you chose him
> More after our commandment.... Lay the fault on us.
> BRUTUS. Ay, spare us not. Say we read lectures to you,
> How youngly he began to serve his country,
> How long continued....

(II.iii.225ff.)

This is so far from the truth that we are appalled at their hypocrisy, revealed 'in private', as it were, which would make a mockery of democracy. As with Shakespeare's other hypocrites, their concealment of their plots from others makes them all the more transparent, and disgusting, to us.

The tribunes, having dismissed the people and 'put in hazard' a 'mutiny', bank on Coriolanus' tendency to 'fall in rage' and resolve again to take 'vantage of his anger'. As they say, this proceeding 'shall seem, as partly 'tis, [the people's] own,/Which we have goaded onward' (255ff.). The plebs are the unwitting accomplices, the tribunes the hypocrites ('seem' is one of their words) who manipulate them but have to keep in the background at supposed elections. They 'goad' the people like cattle.

The first stage of the open confrontation between the people and the patricians, a confrontation to be expressed in and through the person of Coriolanus, takes place in Act III, scene i. The whole sequence of political plot and counterplot has been set out so clearly by Shakespeare, individual and party perspectives defined so sharply, that we watch their interlocking with a sense of *déjà vu*. It is clear that the tribunes have the superior strategy and the more reliable actors. All that the patricians can do is nominate Coriolanus, hope that he will not anger the people, and trust that he will be elected. In the discussion that follows, although he takes the usual patrician attitude, with violent contempt for the people, Coriolanus – alone among his class – sees the absurdity of a situation in which the tribunes have power but no seat on the executive, while the senators supposedly have power but cannot control the tribunes (93ff.). More important, he sees, almost for the first time, where a given pattern of action could lead to:

> my soul aches
> To know, when two authorities are up,
> Neither supreme, how soon confusion
> May enter 'twixt the gap of both and take
> The one by th' other.
>
> (III.i.109ff.)

That is an impressive diagnosis of what social discord could do to Rome, and Shakespeare follows Plutarch in making Coriolanus the only man of the patrician class who has a grasp of the total political situation.[26] (All that Cominius can do is to say, 'Well, on to th' market-place.') He sees, too, that the peculiarly vague distribution of power must mean that no government can continue: 'Purpose so barred, it follows/Nothing is done to purpose' (151f.). Once again he is alone among the patricians in realizing that they are involved in a crucial power-struggle:

> Your dishonour
> Mangles true judgement and bereaves the state
> Of that integrity which should become't;
> Not having the power to do the good it would,
> For th'ill which doth control 't.
>
> (157ff.)

Coriolanus is reaching political maturity fast. This is a penetrating series of comments on the current situation, the more praiseworthy given the silence of the rest of the patricians. Yet his remedies, as opposed to his diagnoses, are the old patrician extremist ones of more violence, starting with the abolition of the tribunes' office: 'at once pluck out/The multitudinous tongue', 'throw their power i'th'dust' (155f., 170). Openly challenged, the tribunes use their weapon against him by calling him a traitor (irony!) and calling for the aediles to arrest him. At this '*a rabble of Plebeians*' as Shakespeare's derogatory stage direction has it, comes pouring in and '*all bustle about Coriolanus*', while civil war seems to be at hand. As Menenius says: 'What is about to be?... Confusion's near' (188f.). The civil violence implicit in the disorder becomes real when Coriolanus draws his sword and in the fighting (or '*this mutiny*', as the stage direction calls it) the tribunes, aediles, and people are beaten away and the patricians hold the stage again. Coriolanus regards this as a military engagement: 'Stand fast; We have as many friends as enemies.' He has now, alas, no thought as to its future consequences for the state. It is left to Menenius to ask 'Shall it be put to that?' – 'The gods forbid', a senator answers. Coriolanus having been the focus of all the violence so far, the patricians are relieved when they finally persuade him to go back to his house.

Coriolanus has left the stage but he is still the centre of discussion. The tribunes return, '*with the rabble again*', and Menenius must somehow try to save the situation. The metaphors used by both sides are revealing. In contrast to Coriolanus' integrity and refusal to compromise, Menenius says that the rent in society 'must be patched/With cloth of any colour' (251f.), and he tells Coriolanus that ' 'tis a sore upon us/You cannot tent [heal] yourself' (234f.). At this stage of Menenius' argument the 'sore' is something on society as a whole, distinct from Coriolanus: yet the metaphor of the body politic is a dangerous one to use, as we may have noticed from the silent trans-formations of the belly fable – mostly damaging to the patricians – that have been going on since Menenius used it. Once under attack from the tribunes Menenius is forced to revise his metaphor:

> SICINIUS. He's a disease that must be cut away.
> MENENIUS. O, he's a limb that has but a disease;
>   Mortal to cut it off, to cure it easy.
>
>   (III.i.296ff.)

On the defensive, Menenius concedes that Coriolanus *is* the sore, the centre of disease in the commonwealth. This is the first patrician betrayal of Cori-olanus, for by conceding the tribunes' metaphor of him as the source of the disease in the body politic, they are powerless to argue against any extensions of that metaphor, such as Coriolanus as a 'gangrened' foot, which must be amputated to save the rest of the body, or as the source of a contagious disease (307ff.). Faced with intolerance and violence, the patricians' only tactic seems to be to try and apply 'tact' and calmness, but to do so is futile, since they have lost the initiative and have no positive ideas to offer. In the end they merely concede their position to the tribunes. So proud and confident in advance of the election, they are now revealed as men of straw. All that Menenius manages to achieve is to have the tribunes drop the punishment of instant death and to allow Coriolanus to stand trial and 'answer by a lawful form,/In peace, to his utmost peril' (322ff.).

So far the power-conflict has been located in Coriolanus' struggle (along with the other patricians) against the plebeians. The women of the play have been absent from the political arena, as not having any right to be there. Now, however, sent off by the would-be placatory patricians, Coriolanus returns to his house, hoping to solve this crisis of behaviour in the political arena before he has to return to stand trial.

Shakespeare has controlled both the tempo and the level of the conflict during Act II so that Coriolanus has been confronted with relatively unprob-lematical issues. He was faced with a quick and urgent crisis that gave him no time to think of the issues involved: he had to act, and fell back on instinctively violent responses. The level at which the action existed was public rather than private, and the enemies were familiar ones, the people and their tribunes. Now, though, in his own house, away from the civil strife in the city, he is trying to understand the crisis, and turns to his mother for help. The problem he faces, without knowing it, is to find out how much his mother cares for him, whether she respects his integrity. This is in many ways the most decisive scene in the play.

In a brief soliloquy Coriolanus reveals that he is puzzled at the events, and that his mother does not support his open intransigence. When he had been told the first time to beg the people's votes, he had objected: 'It is a part/That I shall blush in acting' (II.ii.145f.). Now he confronts Volumnia with the same equation of political role-playing with corruption:

> Why did you wish me milder? Would you have me
> False to my nature? Rather say I play
> The man I am.
>
> (III.ii.13ff.)

As the immediately preceding lines make clear, Volumnia has indoctrinated Coriolanus with her hatred of the people; yet, in order to maintain his 'power' (17) she shows that she can temporize:

> I have a heart as little apt as yours,
> But yet a brain that leads my use of anger
> To better vantage.
>
> (28ff.)

The use of anger for advantage is exactly the method of the tribunes: the awful effect of this scene is to make us realize that the patricians' methods are just as corrupt as their opponents'. One of the most detested words in Renaissance English was 'policy', which had acquired, through the outraged propaganda against Machiavelli during the sixteenth century, all the negative senses of unscrupulous manipulation, dissimulation, and treachery, the achieving of one's political aims by any means.[27] Volumnia gives her son a belated lesson in politics, starting, cleverly enough, with an argument from war:

> I have heard you say,
> Honour and policy, like unsevered friends,
> I'th'war do grow together.
>
> (42ff.)

We may doubt whether Coriolanus ever thought in such abstractions, or so deviously – it sounds more like what she would say to him. One could accept that in a state of national emergency stratagems are permissible; yet Volumnia sees no difference between war and peace:

> If it be honour in your wars to seem
> The same you are not, which for your best ends
> You adopt your policy, how is it less or worse
> That it shall hold companionship in peace

> With honour, as in war, since that to both
> It stands in like request?

(47ff.)

The only proper reply to this suggestion is Cavour's famous remark: 'If we did for ourselves the things we do for Italy, what scoundrels we should be!' Everyone must recognize Volumnia's perversion of ethics: if one were to argue that for one's 'best ends' or future advantage any 'policy' is acceptable, this would permit absolutely all forms of evil, violence, or destructiveness. Volumnia's appeal to naked self-interest – unknowingly echoing the tribunes ('as our good wills') – is just as degraded as their readiness to preserve their power at whatever cost. (If she had been more subtle she would not have argued that the same behaviour is justified in peace as in war, but rather that Rome is at this present in a state of war.)

In her advice to 'seem the same you are not', Volumnia touches on the nerve-centre of Coriolanus' values. He has been told often enough by his class to dissimulate or conceal his real feelings about the people; now he is being urged to simulate affection for them, to effect a split between language and values. He should go to them not guided by his own feelings,

> Nor by th' matter which your heart prompts you,
> But with such words that are but roted in
> Your tongue, though but bastards and syllables
> Of no allowance to your bosom's truth. . . .

(53ff.)

Volumnia recommends the separation between language and value, language and truth, with no compunction: it cannot 'dishonour' him to do this, and she herself would go much further.

> I would dissemble with my nature, where
> My fortunes and my friends at stake required
> I should do so in honour.

(62ff.)

Having held the issue of integrity in reserve for so long Shakespeare now articulates it with the sharpest clarity. We know how antipathetic all this must be to Coriolanus, yet Volumnia seems neither to know nor care. The gap between them is greater than ever, and there can be no doubt as to which side has our sympathies. For Shakespeare not only articulates the issue but judges it. Volumnia is damned out of her own mouth by her corrupt advocacy of policy, by her sophistic and specious use of such words as 'honour' and 'truth', and by several negative details of language. To call successful political words 'bastards' (illegitimate words, whose parentage one can disown without damaging one's 'bosom's truth') is an attempt to devalue language which

165

instead devalues her; and to offer to 'dissemble with my nature' is to make an extraordinarily unnatural effect. How could one do it?

Volumnia, however, has it all worked out. Coriolanus should go to the people, take his hat off to them, even kneel to them (for the Elizabethans two symbolic gestures for acknowledging the superiority of another party – one's parent, one's sovereign). He should beg their love, and feign love for them, a hypocritical procedure which she presents throughout in terms of the theatre, but which links up inescapably with the world of the politician. At this stage in our experience of this play there comes a tremendous shock as we realize that we have seen the hypocrite and the politician at work together earlier on. Volumnia's rehearsing of Coriolanus for a false political campaign is an exact parallel to the tribunes' rehearsal of the people. Both sides of society are using the same methods to gain political power. Coriolanus, silent for a long time, reaches a moment of decision:

> Must I go show them my unbarbéd sconce?
> With my base tongue give to my noble heart
> A lie that it must bear? Well, I will do 't: ...
> To th' market-place!
> You have put me now to such a part which never
> I shall discharge to th' life.

(III.ii.99ff.)

It is not in him to play this role. Coriolanus sees precisely what her dichotomy between language and truth will mean for him: he will forfeit both integrity and authenticity.

Cominius offers – in a fine piece of linguistic irony – to 'prompt' Coriolanus, and Volumnia promises her son more maternal praise if he will 'perform a part/Thou hast not done before' (106ff.). The theatrical analogy is becoming more insistent, and all the insulting implications of insincerity and deceit that have always been connected with the image of the actor well up into Coriolanus' great outburst:

> Well, I must do't.
> Away, my disposition; and possess me
> Some harlot's spirit! My throat of war be turned,
> Which choiréd with my drum, into a pipe
> Small as an eunuch or the virgin voice
> That babies lulls asleep! The smiles of knaves
> Tent in my cheeks, and schoolboys' tears take up
> The glasses of my sight! A beggar's tongue
> Make motion through my lips, and my armed knees,
> Who bowed but in my stirrup, bend like his
> That hath received an alms!

(III.ii.110ff.)

This is one of the two most agonized speeches in the play (both come from Coriolanus), a series of images of perversion and travesty of the self: in doing this he will be like a eunuch, a knave, a schoolboy, a beggar, all nauseating opposites to his true self. Most telling of all is the image of the beggar's tongue moving 'through' his lips, as if it were some other person's, or one manipulated by a puppeteer – but it would be his own. These are all the tricks of the Machiavellian hypocrite as described by Richard III and Buckingham. It is no wonder that, as he itemizes them and realizes what it will do to his integrity if he obeys his mother, Coriolanus should finally burst out:

> I will not do 't,
> Lest I surcease to honour mine own truth,
> And by my body's action teach my mind
> A most inherent baseness.
>
> (III.ii.120ff.)

One can only admire Coriolanus at this point. Exposed for the first time to political manoeuvring, first in practice, now in theory, he sees with great force – with all the freshness of innocence – the extent of personal corruption involved in projecting a false political image. He is right, too, to see that the 'body's action' and the mind are organically related: debase one and you debase the other. Shakespeare has organized this ethical crisis in a deliberate, clear-cut intensity such as life seldom offers, for the emotional agony of Coriolanus derives from the realization, in pristine terms, of what we might call an absolute ethical concept: integrity is like virginity, you only have it once. The intensity of Coriolanus' perception of corruption derives from it being an absolute novelty to him. Although father of a son, he retains the naïvety of a boy (not yet disillusioned by experience) about the importance of truth. Writing of *Huckleberry Finn*, Lionel Trilling praised Mark Twain's realization that

> No one ... sets a higher value on truth than a boy. Truth is the whole of a boy's conscious demand upon the world of adults. He is likely to believe that the adult world is in a conspiracy to lie, to him, and it is this belief ... that arouses ... boys to their moral sensitivity, their everlasting concern with justice, which they call fairness.[28]

Coriolanus is learning for the first time that in politics an ability to lie convincingly is more important than telling the truth.

When Coriolanus began the scene by appealing to his conception of integrity Volumnia quickly deflected him to questions of power and dissimulation. Now that he has reached this absolute affirmation of integrity she can evidently no longer hope to sidetrack him. What she does is revelatory of the process by which she has so far trained and moulded him. To punish the recalcitrant child the mother withdraws her love, freezes him by isolation, works up his dependence on her until he is ready to abandon his own opinions and creep back into her approval and warmth (123ff.). In the last few scenes Coriolanus has made an impressive breakthrough in his awareness of the nature of the political struggle in Rome and of the role that the patricians are expecting him to play in that struggle. We could have hoped that here he would be strong – or cold – enough to affirm his independence. But as Volumnia withdraws her love and projects her disapproval he cracks under it:

> Pray be content:
> Mother, I am going to the market-place.
> Chide me no more.
>
> (130ff.)

The humiliation of the last appeal ('please don't scold!') is pathetic, but at least as a chastised son Coriolanus realizes what the alternative for him now is, expressed in biting sarcasm:

> I'll mountebank their loves,
> Cog their hearts from them, ... I'll return consul,
> Or never trust to what my tongue can do
> I'th'way of flattery further.
>
> (132ff.)

The language forcibly expresses his disgust. The mountebank is the most deceitful salesman in the market-place, associated elsewhere in Shakespeare with deception and corrupt deeds: 'Disguised cheaters, prating mountebanks' (*Comedy of Errors*, I.ii.101); 'a mountebank,/A threadbare juggler' (ibid., V.i.238); 'Corrupted/By spells and medicines bought of mountebanks' (*Othello*, I.iii.61). To 'cog' means to wheedle, with the associations of cheating, being interequated with 'to prate', 'lie', 'dissemble' (*Merry Wives of Windsor*, III.iii.50; *Much Ado*, V.i.95; *Timon of Athens*, V.i.98). Most significant, in view of the links with Shakespeare's other hypocrites, are Richard III's claim that 'I cannot flatter and look fair,/Smile in men's faces, smooth, deceive and cog' (*Richard III*, I.iii.46f.) – abilities that he in fact excels in – and Emilia's suspicion that 'Some busy and insinuating rogue,/Some cogging, cozening slave, to get some office', devised the slander of Desdemona (*Othello*, IV.ii.130ff.). Coriolanus is everything that Iago is not. But his disgust at hypocrisy is now self-disgust, since Volumnia has left him no alternative. She has destroyed his integrity, pushed him back into the political arena where he can only be damaged further.

The confrontation in *Coriolanus*, Act III, scene iii, when it finally takes place, fulfils our expectations with depressing accuracy. Shakespeare even prepares us for the event once more, although he has already written two long sequences in which the tribunes rehearsed the people. Leaving nothing to chance, they are at it again, manufacturing their image of the enemy:

> BRUTUS. In this point charge him home, that he affects
> Tyrannical power. If he evade us there,
> Enforce him with his envy to the people,
> And that the spoil got on the Antiates
> Was ne'er distributed.
>
> (III.iii.1ff.)

The people are again rehearsed in how to shout exactly what their leaders tell them to shout, 'either/For death, for fine, or banishment' (12ff.).

The political behaviour being rehearsed once again is of the most loathsome kind, for, if their manipulation of the people should succeed, a newly conceived democratic process will have given up its very identity, forfeited its integrity as a free and individual expression of opinion, and reduced itself to an indiscriminate support for any policy proposed by its leaders, however inhuman or arbitrary. It is as disgusting as Volumnia's advice to adopt any policy that serves 'Your best ends'. They repeat that the people must say whatever they are told to (19ff.), and lay great stress on the need to make Coriolanus angry: once he speaks his mind he will break his neck (25ff.). Credit must be given the tribunes for their political shrewdness ('know your enemy'), and for their careful preparation – what might be called today 'efficient campaigning'. (There seems hardly much point in stressing how eternally relevant this play is, when modern history offers us so many instances, from so many countries, of corrupt electioneering.)

The outcome is exactly according to the tribunes' plans. They call him a tyrant and a traitor, he erupts with anger (III.iii.68ff.), and the well-drilled mob sentences him to be banished. The patricians have been routed, and Coriolanus' unwilling attempt to pervert his own integrity has failed; yet he is not defeated. This individual, expelled by society, replies:

> I banish you.... Despising
> For you the city, thus I turn my back.
> There is a world elsewhere.
>
> (123, 133ff.)

Some critics describe these words as arrogant, but it seems to me that in such a situation the individual is right to reject a corrupt society and to affirm the authenticity of his own values. As Coriolanus takes leave of Rome he compares his future existence to that of 'a lonely dragon that his fen/Makes feared and talked of more than seen' (IV.i.31f.). The analogy with the dragon has been treated by some critics in the same way that they treat the references to Coriolanus as a fighting machine, that is, as if both represented criticisms of his inhumanity made by Shakespeare. What the image in fact means is that he is discouraging anyone from following or trying to approach him: the dragon is talked about rather than seen, since people are afraid to go near it. Just as society shuns the dragon, they have shunned him, and he will shun them. His intention is to isolate himself, and if he is an exceptionally strong – or cold – person then he might be able to sustain the isolation, become self-sufficient.

For the present, victory is to the tribunes. Having achieved their goal, Shakespeare reveals them donning the mask of humility again, a bitter 'before/after' effect:

> Now we have shown our power,
> Let us seem humbler after it is done
> Than when it was a-doing.

> (IV.ii.3ff.)

When attacked by Volumnia their hypocrisy even claims that Coriolanus 'unknit himself/The noble knot he made', a point made only for her to reject it: ' 'Twas you incensed the rabble' (31ff.). In a later scene, the last moment of peace before Coriolanus returns with the Volscian army to take his revenge on Rome, the tribunes receive the citizens' gratitude with a hypocrisy as stunning as that of Richard III:

> BRUTUS. Farewell, kind neighbours. We wished Coriolanus
>   Had loved you as we did....
> SICINIUS. This is a happier and more comely time
>   Than when those fellows ran about the streets
>   Crying confusion.

> (IV.vi.23ff.)

As if they had not engineered the whole chaos for their own advantage! The final irony is that at the end of the play all the hypocrites, all the manipulators of public life, patrician or plebeian, remain alive. The only person to die is the man who challenged that system and its values. He exposed the hypocrisy in his own party, but only the audience was privileged to see the full range of dissimulation that goes on in politics all the time, 'behind the scenes', as we still say.

Breaking point

Rejected by Rome, Coriolanus resolves to live outside society, a drastic transformation for any man. Yet he fails to do so, since he finds that he is not a dragon, that he needs human society and human action. After a short scene between a Roman and a Volsce (IV.iii.) which tells us that civil disorder is growing in Rome and that the patricians seem likely to follow Coriolanus' violent policies and deprive the tribunes of their power, we find Martius '*in mean apparel, disguised and muffled*' (IV.iv.S.D.), standing outside Aufidius' house. As he reflects on what it means for him to be in Antium we notice a quality of feeling in him which puts him apart from everyone else in the play, except Virgilia:

> A goodly city is this Antium. City,
> 'Tis I that made thy widows. Many an heir
> Of these fair edifices 'fore my wars
> Have I heard groan and drop.

(IV.iv.1ff.)

This quality in Coriolanus, hardly commented on by any student of the play (an exception was the late Una Ellis-Fermor[29]), is Coriolanus' sensitivity to the feelings, and especially the sufferings, of others. No one else, Roman or Volscian – with the exception of Virgilia in her wifely love for him – evinces the slightest concern for the losses or sorrow of anyone other than him or herself. Yet Shakespeare has shown Coriolanus' responsiveness in several places, such as his desire to repay the poor man in Corioli who needed his help and had once helped him (I.ix.82ff.), or his deep sympathy for the women whose sons or husbands will not return from the war (II.i.174ff.), or his attempt to soften his friends' suffering at the parting scene (IV.i.19ff.).

The compassion and tenderness of Coriolanus represents a human value entirely absent from the Roman public world, as from his mother's attitude to him. The only other person in this world capable of experiencing or valuing such feelings is, significantly enough, Virgilia. If it is generally true that a man's choice of his wife reflects his own values found in her, or at least some of the attributes he values most, then Virgilia is an extension of Coriolanus' personality. With this as with other values Shakespeare stresses how Martius conflicts with the ethos of his class by constantly juxtaposing Virgilia and Volumnia, from their important first scene together (I.iii.) onwards. Virgilia's love is made by Shakespeare into a source of warmth and loyalty that is, however, felt rather than verbalized. She is the least articulate of all the major figures in the tragedies. This is in part due to the dominating presence of Volumnia, whose gigantic personality seems to reduce Virgilia to silence. But also, I think, it shows how out of place the tenderness of the Coriolanus–Virgilia relationship is in this ethos. Virgilia's characteristic utterance is a single sentence of exclamation for the safety or fortune of her husband, at the furthest remove from Volumnia's unfeeling gloating that 'he is wounded; I thank the gods for't'. In contrast, Virgilia can only say, 'O, no, no, no' (II.i.116ff.). In the scene of parting Virgilia is made to speak twice only: 'O heavens! O heavens!' and 'O the gods!' is all that she can utter (IV.i.12, 38). This discrepancy between speech and feelings serves almost to increase our admiration for Virgilia, since so much of the language in this play is used to deceive and manipulate that at times we feel a certain distrust of language. Feeling not put into words can at least not be falsified.

Love outraged, denied its focus and fulfilment, can legitimately turn to hate. That is the experience of Virgilia (IV.ii.26ff.): it is also the experience of Coriolanus. For in going to Antium he is not merely returning from the wilderness back to society but is instinctively looking for a way to revenge himself on Rome. The people of Rome repaid his service not with love but with ingratitude, and he will repay their hate not with love but with more hate. Some critics attack Coriolanus for wanting revenge on Rome, describing this as part of his colossal egoism. Perhaps on this issue modern critics should let themselves be guided by the view of that great exponent of the individual's contract with and debt to society, Thomas Hobbes. 'A man that by asperity of nature' will not co-operate with others, he declares, 'and for the stubbornness of his passions cannot be corrected, is to be left or cast out of society, as cumbersome thereunto'.[30] Yet, once exiled, such a man no longer owes any services to his country: 'For a banished man is a lawful enemy of the commonwealth that banished him; as being no more a member of the same'.[31]

After a sardonic scene with Aufidius' servants, who, like everyone else in this play, seize their chance to discuss Coriolanus and the political situation, Coriolanus finally comes face to face with his great rival Aufidius, and in a long speech (IV.v.66ff.) offers his services in the destruction of Rome. Aufidius suppresses any resentment that he may feel about the past in his delight at having his most feared enemy transformed into an ally, and the atmosphere changes to one of harmony and co-operation. Yet no sooner have Aufidius and Coriolanus gone in to the banquet than the report by the servingmen of what took place there sows the first seeds of discord in this new alliance. At once Aufidius' prestige is reduced, since the Volscian leaders have divided his command with Coriolanus: 'the bottom of the news is, our general is cut i'th' middle, and but one half of what he was yesterday, for the other has half by the entreaty and grant of the whole table' (IV.v.202ff.). Coriolanus' instant success with the Volscians is now presented as a threat to Aufidius' power, so motivating any jealousy or resentment from him.

In the sequence leading up to Act V, scene iii, the climax of the play, Shakespeare develops two dramatic movements which act, in effect, in opposed directions. From the perspective of Antium, Coriolanus' increasing success with the Volscian soldiers leads to jealousy, hatred, and a desire for revenge. These reactions (as usual hidden from the source and focus of them, Coriolanus himself) serve to undermine the general's apparent success, for Aufidius' envy takes the form of planning to allow Coriolanus to defeat Rome and then to destroy him: 'When, Caius, Rome is thine,/Thou art poor'st of all; then shortly art thou mine' (IV.vii.56f.). In Aufidius' eyes, then, Coriolanus' future is limited, and once he has performed a convenient task for the Volscians, his present strength will be cut off. But on either side of this scene Shakespeare gives us the perspective of Rome, in which Coriolanus' strength seems enormous and threatening. The second view is of course correct, since Aufidius will wait until after the victory before taking revenge.

172

The two perspectives offer us, in effect, a scale of power of descending magnitude, which, using the symbol >('greater than') can be set out as: Aufidius > Coriolanus > Rome. If we think back to the beginning of the play we will remember that the power-structure then was just the reverse: Rome > Coriolanus > Aufidius. In a number of details the final stages of the play reverse the initial ones, as we will see if we think for a moment in terms of such general concepts involved in much human action as the pressurizer (or influencer); the agent; the goal; and the obstacles to achieving that goal. The play has, so far as we can see at the moment, three movements, War (Acts I–II); Politics (Acts II–IV); and Revenge (Acts IV–V). Set out as a diagram the following structure can be seen:

Stage	Pressurizer	Agent	Goal	Obstacles	Outcome
I	Rome	Coriolanus	Defeat Aufidius	The citizens	Success
II	Volumnia and patricians	Coriolanus	Gain consulship	Tribunes and citizens	Failure
III	Aufidius	Coriolanus	Defeat Rome	Volumnia and patricians	

In all three movements so far Coriolanus is pressurized, acted upon ('put upon') in order to act. Individuals and groups use him to effect their own ends, and in each case he could say, as he says to the soldiers who take him as their leader against Corioli, 'Make you a sword of me?' (I.vii.76). But although the pressurizer and goal have become interchanged from stage I to stage III the situation is still the same in that Coriolanus is being manipulated without realizing it. He is always the agent, willing or unwilling, knowing or unknowing.

To the Romans, however, all this is as obscure as it is to him. Writing with undiminished fullness and energy at the end of what has already been a long and dense play, Shakespeare develops the perspective of Rome in full detail. In doing so he not only shows their present situation, but sheds fresh light on the events of the past. When the news of Coriolanus' march on Rome is confirmed the tribunes collapse abjectly, denying that they were responsible for his banishment. Yet Menenius, in attacking them, also indicts the patricians:

> We loved him, but, like beasts
> And cowardly nobles, gave way unto your clusters,
> Who did hoot him out o'th'city.

> (IV.vi.122ff.)

So Coriolanus' complaint that he has been betrayed by the patricians is validated. They would not risk their own skin but gladly sacrificed their candidate, and in this respect the aristocracy were just as monstrous as the people.

Rome seems on the verge of destruction. The patricians do what they can to save it, and in a sequence of scenes each of the major characters goes in turn to Coriolanus as a suppliant. We learn about Cominius' embassy after the event, as, unsuccessful, he explains to Menenius and the tribunes how coldly he was treated, he who 'was sometime his general, who loved him/In a most dear particular' (V.i.2f.). Coriolanus did not seem even to know Cominius, and dismissed him with no sympathy. Menenius' supplication (V.ii.) is both comic and pathetic. To begin with he cannot even get past the watchmen, under orders to admit no one from Rome. In order to impress them, Menenius describes his past relationship with Coriolanus, and in so doing Shakespeare makes him illuminate retrospectively the whole rationale of the patricians' representation of Coriolanus, the sequence that I have described as

<action: evaluation: report: adulation: advantage>

Here the truth behind the image-making finally appears:

> I tell thee, fellow,
> Thy general is my lover. I have been
> The book of his good acts, whence men have read
> His fame unparallel'd, haply amplified;
> For I have ever varnishéd my friends,[32]
> (Of whom he's chief), with all the size that verity
> Would without lapsing suffer. Nay, sometimes,
> Like to a bowl upon a subtle ground,
> I have tumbled past the throw, and in his praise
> Have almost stamped the leasing....

$$(V.ii.15ff.)$$

This is an astonishingly revealing speech, which seems to have no immediate dramatic function. Indeed its central human relationship is obsolete, for there can be no future for Menenius as a panegyrist for Coriolanus. Perhaps he thinks that Coriolanus owes him a debt of gratitude for all his efforts in compiling 'the book of his good acts' – but Coriolanus never wanted them. The actual function of the speech seems to be to recall how the patricians acted as if they owned Coriolanus, as if he represented, in the language of Hollywood, a 'property' (a word that is applied both to a performer and a script), a property that becomes more valuable the more it is hyped. Menenius confesses that he may have amplifed him too much but that in general he 'laid on as much praise as would stick', but without 'verity' suffering a lapse. Yet, to be perfectly honest (damaging to him though that will be), and using a self-excusing metaphor from bowls, in the exercise of panegyric he has sometimes inadvertently gone too far and given falsehood the stamp of truth (19ff.). So, Menenius claims, he has a right to pass. The soldiers substitute for Menenius' euphemisms a frank description which echoes Coriolanus' own (I.ix.50ff.): Menenius has uttered 'lies in his behalf', has been not the general's 'lover' but his 'liar' – as if that were a permanent office, such as cup-bearer or treasurer. (Under the later Roman emperors panegyrists were indeed employed full-time and enjoyed great status and vast rewards, rather like a modern promotion or advertising agency.)

Despite the watchmen's efforts the meeting takes place, and we observe with embarrassment how Menenius becomes cloyingly sentimental, weeping with joy, affirming that the gods 'love thee no worse than thy old father Menenius does! O my son, my son!' (V.ii.69ff.) – and so on in a fast and incoherent prose speech. All the more cutting, then, is Coriolanus' reply, stylistically distanced by being in verse:

> CORIOLANUS. Away!
> MENENIUS. How? away?
> CORIOLANUS. Wife, mother, child, I know not. My affairs
> Are servanted to others. Though I owe
> My revenge properly, my remission lies
> In Volscian breasts.
>
> (V.ii.80ff.)

That is, his revenge is his own, but the power to pardon belongs entirely to the Volscians. For him, Shakespeare reminds us again, pardon is impossible since his natural pity has been killed by Rome's ungrateful forgetting of his services to them (85ff.).

At this stage Coriolanus seems completely in control of himself and others. Yet he has just made a mistake. He thinks that it was Rome's 'latest refuge', or last resort, to send Menenius, but in the preceding scene Shakespeare alerted us, through Cominius, that Rome's single remaining hope consists of

> his noble mother, and his wife –
> Who, as I hear, mean to solicit him
> For mercy to his country.
>
> (V.i.70ff.)

Rome hangs on this thread, and so does Coriolanus. For across the apparently final sequence of the play, Aufidius' move against Rome, Shakespeare has spaced out three contrasting counter-moves:

Stage	Pressurizer	Agent	Goal	Obstacle	Outcome
III	Aufidius	Coriolanus	Defeat Rome	Volumnia and patricians	
IIIa	Rome	Cominius	Spare Rome	Coriolanus	Failure
IIIb	Rome	Menenius	Spare Rome	Coriolanus	Failure
IIIc	Rome	Volumnia, Virgilia, Young Martius	Spare Rome	Coriolanus	

These three counter-moves are treated contrastingly, too, in ascending order of proximity to Coriolanus. We heard about Cominius' encounter only after the event, and by a report; we saw Menenius and Coriolanus face to face; and finally Coriolanus is not only confronted immediately by his family but is given a long aside, a virtual soliloquy, to tell us directly what he is feeling. We come closer to him, as he to them.

Coriolanus hears shouting. He does not know who is coming but, curiously enough, anticipates that he is about to be put under pressure. 'Shall I be tempted to infringe my vow/In the same time 'tis made? I will not' (V.iii.20f.). He needs to stiffen himself already. Hard and inflexible as he has been to the patricians, he is now exposed to his whole family, dressed in mourning. He has perhaps dismissed the possibility of their intercession because on the Roman political stage women have played no part. Now they approach him, as he sits in a chair of state – with Aufidius standing by him – and for sixteen lines we see through his eyes and feelings what they mean to him.

> My wife comes foremost, then the honoured mould
> Wherein this trunk was framed, and in her hand
> The grandchild to her blood. But out, affection!
> All bond and privilege of nature, break!
> Let it be virtuous to be obstinate.

(22f.)

He acts as a quasi-neutral commentator describing their arrival, yet his personal feelings keep breaking through. He records their impression on him and at once fights against it, denying his love. He attempts a perversion of himself, and in the language Shakespeare gives him we see him making an effort to reject his fundamental nature which, were it to succeed, would be just as unnatural as if he were to try to fawn, flatter, and dissemble. Words like 'affection', 'nature', and 'virtuous' cannot be deprived of their positive, creative connotations, at least not by someone as patently natural and lacking in guile as Coriolanus.

The great paradox of this scene is the struggle within Coriolanus and the consequent split in the reader's or spectator's sympathies. He is trying to be hard-hearted, so that he can go through with his revenge on Rome. Since he has our sympathies for the way in which the Romans have treated him we might want him to succeed in this revenge. Yet our wish for revenge is confronted with all those feelings of love and tenderness towards those closest to him that have been so impressive throughout the play. (To speak personally, I cannot wish him to close up and deny those feelings. I would rather he expressed them, even though it may mean his death.) He had meant to remain seated, distanced from all the suppliants by his formal position in his chair of state. Yet the pressure of feeling is so great that he realizes that this is another unnatural role that he simply cannot sustain. He has to go to Virgilia:

> Like a dull actor now
> I have forgot my part, and I am out
> Even to a full disgrace. [Rising] Best of my flesh,

Forgive my tyranny, but do not say
For that 'Forgive our Romans.' [*Kisses her*] O, a kiss
Long as my exile, sweet as my revenge!

(41ff.)

He welcomes his mother with great reverence, acknowledging his inferiority
to her (like a molehill to Olympus, as he puts it) and kneels down before her.
And from this point on Volumnia dominates the scene, both as producer and
as chief actor.

In a sense this scene defies criticism. Shakespeare has built everything up
towards this point, has made the forces of pressure so clear that the collision
between them becomes totally explicit. The scene does not need to be expli-
cated: it needs to be felt.

Coriolanus tries to prohibit them from making any requests on him (82ff.),
but Volumnia will not be deterred, and forces him to allow her to supplicate.
At this point the scene is transformed from a private back into a public
action. Coriolanus sits on his throne of state again and bids Aufidius and the
Volsces to observe his behaviour: 'mark', he says (92), as if confident of giving
a demonstration of a strong and cold man rejecting attempts to weaken his
will. Volumnia's first speech (of thirty lines) is a carefully structured piece of
rhetoric, beginning by describing their costume, drawing attention to his
family's rags and emaciated condition, juxtaposing their present state of 'fear
and sorrow' with their normal feelings in the past on being reunited with
him, when their eyes would 'flow with joy, hearts dance with comforts' (94ff.).
Her most important tactic is to stress the triple relationship that binds
Coriolanus, as Shakespeare makes still more clear by putting it into cor-
relative verse:

Making the mother, wife, and child, to see
The son, the husband, and the father, tearing
His country's bowels out.

(101ff.)

Coriolanus had always rejected the idea that he could play an unnatural role,
so it is ironic that he should now be trapped by the three natural roles that
he cannot help playing. Having started with her main claim on him Volumnia
now shifts to the claims of the state, ringing the changes, with much elaborate
rhetorical parallelism, on their dilemma of having to pray both for their
country and for his person (105ff.). She claims that he can hardly destroy the
city without also shedding his 'wife and children's blood' (116ff.). Characteristically, Volumnia seizes that point to exert all possible pressure, and in
so doing produces one of the most tragic moments in the play:

VOLUMNIA.   thou shalt no sooner
March to assault thy country than to tread –
Trust to't, thou shalt not – on thy mother's womb,

That brought thee to this world.
VIRGILIA.   Ay, and mine,
That brought you forth this boy, to keep your name
Living to time.

                                                                    (122ff.)

It is only to be expected that Volumnia will use the most emotive weapons
possible. As with 'tearing his country's bowels out' earlier, she goes straight
for the soft middle of the body, using a rhetoric calculated to make the enemy
seem a monster and a pervert: this is another belly fable. But it is a terrible
moment when Virgilia follows Volumnia's cue, when she betrays her husband
and sides with the values of the patrician class. This is the last time that she
speaks to him in the play, an awful note for their relationship to end on.

Stung by these pressures Coriolanus tries to escape from the situation by
ending the interview, getting down from his throne to symbolize that the
audience is over:

Not of a woman's tenderness to be,
Requires nor child nor woman's face to see.
I have sat too long.   [*Rising*]
                                                                    (129ff.)

Yet this, too, is a futile attempt to deny his own nature, that tenderness that
is not womanish but essentially human. Undeterred, Volumnia continues
with more arguments, and as he remains silent she urges him to speak: 'speak
to me, son' (149), she says, invoking natural relationships only so that he will
give in to her, 'Why dost not speak?' (154). She knows that 'His heart's his
mouth:/What his breast forges, that his tongue must vent' (III.i.257f.), and
that if he can be brought to speak then he will give way. So she urges Virgilia
and young Martius to speak: 'Daughter, speak you:/He cares not for your
weeping. Speak thou, boy' (156f.). But important as those relationships are
to Coriolanus they are relationships of love, not power. They cannot be made
to bend or break him, since they would first break themselves. Volumnia is
the only one with the big pull, and she exerts it.

There's no man in the world
More bound to 's mother, yet here he lets me prate
Like one i' th' stocks. Thou hast never in thy life
Showed thy dear mother any courtesy....

                                                                    (V.iii.158ff.)

Surprisingly to her, perhaps, he still hasn't given in; but he '*turns away*',
which might mean that he is wavering, or trying to hide his feelings. So she
stage-manages another use of gesture as pressure:

178

> Down, ladies, let us shame him with our knees.
> To his surname Coriolanus 'longs more pride
> Than pity to our prayers. Down! An end.
>
> > [*The four all kneel*
> > (169ff.)

Yet even this gesture fails. He neither raises them up nor relents. Volumnia's failure, though, means that she and her fellow actors have to go through the indignity of standing up again, and as they prepare to leave in defeat she throws her last weapon:

> Come, let us go.   [*They rise*
> This fellow had a Volscian to his mother;
> His wife is in Corioles, and his child
> Like him by chance.
>
> > (178ff.)

Here Volumnia plays her last card, that withdrawal of a mother's love which had worked so well in the past. But now she even cancels her relationship with him, disowns him, and thus denies 'nature' and 'affection'. Coriolanus had attempted to deny these concepts earlier, in the long soliloquy as his family had approached, but he had failed: Volumnia succeeds. In his mouth words such as 'affection' or 'nature' refused to take on a sophistic sense, rebounded rather as the fixed points by which his attempted alternatives were tested and found lacking:

> my young boy
> Hath an aspect of intercession which
> Great nature cries 'Deny not.' Let the Volsces
> Plough Rome and harrow Italy: I'll never
> Be such a gosling to obey instinct, but stand
> As if a man were author of himself
> And knew no other kin.
>
> > (V.iii.31ff.)

'Stand' he has done, throughout this scene, attempting to 'stick i'th'wars/Like a great sea-mark', withstanding every pressure. Yet the whole attempt to 'stand', in this context, is a perversion, against which 'Great Nature cries "Deny not"', for 'instinct' knows that a man is not author of himself, cannot be 'a lonely dragon'. When Volumnia disclaims him, then, denies the 'bond and privilege of nature', it seems finally to snap Coriolanus' denial, changing him from a man who stands alone to one who puts out his hand, in acknowledgement of nature and relationship. In one of the most poignantly expressive stage directions in all drama, he *Holds her by the hand, silent* (V.iii.183). It is the moment of victory for her, agonizing defeat for him. And for once he seems to know it:

179

> O mother, mother!
> What have you done? Behold, the heavens do ope,
> The gods look down, and this unnatural scene
> They laugh at. O my mother, mother! O!
> You have won a happy victory to Rome;
> But for your son, believe it, O, believe it,
> Most dangerously you have with him prevailed,
> If not most mortal to him.

(183ff.)

The laughter of the gods, beholding the follies of man on the stage of the *theatrum mundi*, is a finely ironic summation of the theatrical nature of this scene, the costume, tableau, gestures, and speeches of which were all controlled by Volumnia. For a moment Coriolanus speaks with his old bitterness to her as he regards this 'unnatural scene', on which his mother has played the most unnatural role. But feelings of waste and regret dominate him, as they must us.

Since the pressure has broken his attempt to play an unnatural role, has shown him to be fundamentally true to his private world, he can now only be false to his public one and to 'good Aufidius', as he calls him rather entreatingly. Announcing that he intends to make peace he appeals to his new colleague to understand, and forgive, his collapse into feeling (191ff.). Aufidius is non-committal, but gives his real reaction to the scene in an aside to us, another crucial utterance that takes place behind Coriolanus' back:

> I am glad thou hast set thy mercy and thy honour
> At difference in thee. Out of that I'll work
> Myself a former fortune.

(200ff.)

The collapse or 'melting' of Coriolanus' honour to his pity is action in the present which will have great future advantage for Volumnia, for the patricians, and for Rome in general; it will also be of great benefit to Aufidius, who can now manipulate Coriolanus in such a way as to regain his 'former fortune', all his earlier prestige. Everyone benefits, then, except Coriolanus. From being the agent in the assault of Aufidius on Rome Coriolanus has been transformed, by the successful supplication of Volumnia, into the obstacle that frustrated that assault. He has been pressurized, once again, turned from an active to a passive role, his will and desires smashed by his own mother, acting on behalf of his own class.

Death of a puppet

Having presented the events leading up to his climax from the twin perspectives of Antium and Rome, Shakespeare, not skimping in either length or detail, deals with the after-effects of the climax from both points of view. The confrontation took place at the tent of Coriolanus, in the Volscian camp outside Rome, from which Menenius had been dismissed in the scene before. When the scene shifts back to Rome, therefore, it is just in time to find Menenius meeting Sicinius and telling him the outcome of the embassy which the tribunes had entreated him to perform (V.i.40ff., 47ff., 60ff.). Since Menenius was dismissed from Coriolanus' tent before the women reached there he does not know the result of their embassy. News travels slowly for the people of Rome, but more quickly for the spectators of the play, who realize that the situation Menenius is about to describe is already out of date. Menenius is not cast down by his news but positively exults in the approaching destruction, since the tribunes were responsible for it. The terms in which he reports his interview will remind us of other passages in the play:

> MENENIUS. . . . This Martius is grown from man to dragon. He has wings, he's more than a creeping thing.
> SICINIUS. He loved his mother dearly.
> MENENIUS. So did he me, and he no more remembers his mother now than an eight-year-old horse. The tartness of his face sours ripe grapes. When he walks, he moves like an engine, and the ground shrinks before his treading. He is able to pierce a corslet with his eye, talks like a knell, and his hum is a battery. He sits in his state as a thing made for Alexander. What he bids be done is finished with his bidding. He wants nothing of a god but eternity and a heaven to throne in.
>
> (V.iv.12ff.)

There are all the familiar processes of the patricians' propaganda for Coriolanus, turning him into a colossus, a war-machine with an eye like a laser-beam, a 'hum' like the noise of an artillery battery, his gait like a battering-ram. Once again he is made into an image of unnature or anti-nature: his face sours grapes, his speech is a 'knell' – the sound of a bell at a funeral – the ground shrinks before him, 'there is no more mercy in him than there is milk in a male tiger' (28f.). Yet, as everyone must now see, these are merely false images created for a deterrent effect, increasingly improbable analogies for this man whom we have just seen break down and weep, 'melt', his 'honour' drowned by the flow of his 'mercy' and 'pity'. The last ironic comment on their tactics of over-inflated report ('varnished' up to the maximum, we remember), is Sicinius' rejoinder: 'Yes, mercy, if you report him truly.' Menenius claims, 'I paint him in the character' (27f.) but is soon proved totally, comprehensively wrong by the return of the women bringing peace and 'love'.

From triumph in Rome we move to conspiracy in Corioli, with Aufidius delivering an indictment of Coriolanus to the nobles and anticipating how his enemy 'Intends t'appear before the people, hoping/To purge himself with words' (V.vi.5ff.).

There is yet another reversal accomplished by these closing stages, now of everything that Coriolanus has stood for. He no longer has deeds to offer but only words, and those false ones. But his behaviour is being observed and predicted, once again, as a new group of people, Aufidius with '*three or four Conspirators*', construct a scenario in which Coriolanus is again to play the central and pressurized role. Here, too, the manipulators pretend to respect the mind of 'the people', but conclude that they will be so indiscriminate or fickle as to follow whichever faction destroys the other. All that is now lacking is a party manifesto, and Audifius promptly produces one, in which Coriolanus is presented as a hypocrite and a flatterer who had seduced Aufidius' friends away from him (21ff.). The picture is so amazingly false that one of Aufidius' own supporters is moved to protest, recalling 'his stoutness/When he did stand for consul, which he lost/By lack of stooping' (26ff.). That, however, is no longer part of official history. We see that this anti-Coriolanus party, like the others, is creating an image of him for their own purposes. To the patricians a depersonalized fighting machine, to the tribunes arrogant and ambitious, to Volumnia proud and ungrateful, to Aufidius and his supporters he is now a corrupt flatterer. And, as with the other enemies of Coriolanus, Shakespeare makes it perfectly clear that what is driving their manipulation of him is their own self-interest:

> AUFIDIUS. At a few drops of women's rheum, which are
> As cheap as lies, he sold the blood and labour
> Of our great action; therefore shall he die,
> And I'll renew me in his fall.

> (45ff.)

Wherever he turns Coriolanus seems to be either the agent in one group's plot or the obstacle in the way of some other group. All the political and personal pressures of the play meet in him.

For what seems like the umpteenth time, Coriolanus enters on to a scene in complete ignorance of the plot which we have seen hatched to manipulate him. One other lie that the conspirators attempt to plant is that Martius threw away the whole cost of raising the army and brought the Volsces nothing in return (64ff.). This economic aspect of war is one that has never appealed to him (we recall that Cominius shrewdly offered his soldiers the spoils of battle as incentive, but that Coriolanus offered service and self-sacrifice), so it comes as a surprise to us when Coriolanus answers the lie by stating that his audited accounts declare a more than 30 per cent profit! It is also a surprise to find him praising his own achievements. At last he sounds like the conquering hero or politic soldier:

> Hail, lords! I am returned your soldier;
> No more infected with my country's love
> Than when I parted hence, but still subsisting

Under your great command. You are to know
That prosperously I have attempted, and
With bloody passage led your wars even to
The gates of Rome. Our spoils we have brought home
Doth more than counterpoise a full third part
The charges of the action. We have made peace
With no less honour to the Antiates
Than shame to th' Romans. . . .

(71ff.)

The style of that speech would bear detailed comparison with the vauntings of Cominius in Act II, with its abrupt and assertive rhythms, its self-confident proclamatory syntax, its generalissimo's plural, its formalized inversions ('prosperously I have attempted', 'With bloody passage led'). More important than the style is our discovery that, like other successful soldiers, Coriolanus has finally learned the trick of presenting his actions in a more favourable light than they actually deserve. He did not capture the city: true, but he led his army 'even to/The gates of Rome'; he did not defeat the Romans: true, but he made a peace with 'shame' to them. . . . He makes his failures look like successes, a most useful ability in a general.

But it is an accomplishment that debases him, and we are almost relieved that he has learned it too late. For Aufidius' attack on him, Shakespeare writes a speech with all his astonishing skill in projecting himself into individual human perspectives, a speech that presents the whole of the suppliant scene in the most distorted and malicious light imaginable:

He has betrayed your business, and given up,
For certain drops of salt, your city, Rome –
I say 'your city' – to his wife and mother;
Breaking his oath and resolution like
A twist of rotten silk; never admitting
Counsel o' th' war. But at his nurse's tears
He whined and roared away your victory;
That pages blushed at him, and men of heart
Looked wond'ring each at other.

(94ff.)

Having seen the original action that is now reported and evaluated here, we can appreciate the brilliant ingenuity of the distortion; yet we have to admit the underlying truths, that he did give up Rome to his 'wife and mother', that he did break his 'oath and resolution', that he did not take 'counsel' from his fellow officers. But none of these, perhaps, is as painful as the final shameful image of a man whining and blubbering so much that boys are made to blush (blushing is Coriolanus' own instinctive reaction to embarrassment). Now, if Coriolanus had learned anything from his confrontation with the

183

tribunes, he might think 'Ah, yes, that's just what I expected him to do: he's trying to provoke me, but I shan't let him, for I can see where all this is leading.' However, still innocent of the future, evaluating action and speech for what they represent when performed, he bursts under this pressure on his honour: – 'Hear'st thou, Mars?' – an exclamation that Aufidius seizes on for the most cutting insult yet: 'Name not the god, thou boy of tears!' (102f.).[33]

When Coriolanus had reviewed the types of self-perversion which he would suffer by fawning to the mob they included that in which 'schoolboys' tears take up/The glasses of my sight!' (III.ii.116f.). Having created his hero Shakespeare knows just how to hurt him most, and at this provocation his real nature asserts itself, no longer dressing up words to disguise the deeds recorded by them but speaking what he feels: 'Measureless liar, thou hast made my heart/Too great for what contains it' (104f.). He can neither dissemble nor repress his natural, instinctual feelings for long: out they must come, directly. This was the great redeeming factor in the suppliant scene, and it is the quality that his enemies can always exploit to destroy him. Faced with a distortion of his true 'report', which is as extreme as either the undervaluation of the tribunes or the overvaluation of the patricians, Coriolanus – like Othello at the last moment of his tragedy – affirms his true worth and report:

> 'Boy'! False hound!
> If you have writ your annals true, 'tis there,
> That, like an eagle in a dove-cote, I
> Fluttered your Volscians in Corioli.
> Alone I did it. 'Boy!'

(113ff.)

And as with Othello, the hero has to make his own self-validation because no one else will do it for him: those who love him are absent or dead. Both tragic heroes reach their greatness again, but both do so only by retrospective narration, and only for a moment. Despite the protests of one of the Volscian lords, who wishes Coriolanus to have a judicial hearing (126f.), the conspirators, egged on by the insults of Aufidius ('unholy braggart', 'Insolent villain'), descend on him with the mob's shout: 'Kill, kill, kill, kill, kill him!' In a play remarkable for graphic and explicit authorial stage directions the Folio's instructions to the actors here sum up Coriolanus's final reversal: '*Draw all the* Conspirators, *and kill* MARTIUS, *who falles.* AUFIDIUS *stands on him.*' Not only does that deed project Coriolanus all the way down from his first moment of greatness in Corioli to his last indignity – once again he is the only Roman in the city – but it catches up and reverses the terms of Volumnia's bloodthirsty prediction: 'He'll beat Aufidius' head below his knee/And tread upon his neck' (I.iii.48f.). This whole sequence creates in us, once more, that feeling of predictability. Yet again a conspiratorial plot has succeeded in dislodging Coriolanus. He has not learned – but then he has not had much time to learn, and he has no one to teach him. The coaching by the patricians on the presentation of the self have been oddly lacking in instruction on how to avoid being manipulated by others.

What is new about this scene is that the enemies of Coriolanus not only express their hatred openly, but follow it with apparent regret. Aufidius falsely claims that Coriolanus offered a great threat to the Volscian state, and one of the lords excuses Aufidius' 'impatience' on these grounds. Then the chief villain of the scene leaves with a closing speech, the apparently conventional epitaph on a dead hero, which is so remarkable as to deserve quoting in full:

> AUFIDIUS.   My rage is gone,
> And I am struck with sorrow. Take him up.
> Help, three o'th' chiefest soldiers; I'll be one.
> Beat thou the drum, that it speak mournfully:
> Trail your steel pikes. Though in this city he
> Hath widowed and unchilded many a one,
> Which to this hour bewail the injury,
> Yet he shall have a noble memory.
> Assist.
>
> [*Exeunt bearing the Body of* MARTIUS.
> *A dead March Sounded.*
>
> (147ff.)

Setting aside the military details we have here an utterly unconvincing *volte-face* from Aufidius, who changes from 'rage' to 'sorrow' in the twinkling of an eye, 'before a man can say "one" '.[34] The new mood that he establishes so quickly silences further discussion, for the ritual must proceed, and the appropriate noises of eulogy can be made. One critic who noticed the injustice of this sequence was John Dennis, writing in 1711. He protested that just as Sicinius and Brutus had been guilty of a notorious injustice (in getting 'the Champion and Defender of their Country banish'd upon a pretended Jealousy', out of 'Hatred and Malice') yet remained 'unpunish'd ', so Aufidius,

> the principal Murderer of Coriolanus, who in cold Blood gets him assassinated by Ruffians instead of leaving him to the Law of the Country and the Justice of the Volscian Senate, and who commits so black a Crime not by any erroneous Zeal or a mistaken Publick Spirit but thro' Jealousy, Envy, and inveterate Malice; this Assassinator not only survives, and survives unpunish'd, but seems to be rewarded for so detestable an Action by engrossing all those Honours to himself which Coriolanus before had shar'd with him'.[35]

To Dennis this was evidence that Shakespeare failed in his duty of writing according to poetic justice; to us, however, the ending is proof, rather, of a deeper irony, familiar from contemporary history. It is all so demonstrably false that the appropriate comparison would be from modern totalitarian states: when a particularly awkward enemy has been disposed of, nothing is more effective than to give him a state funeral and a memorial, build up a legend, make him seem missed. To do so cannot harm you, indeed the generosity you thus display may even work to your future advantage.

Success in failure

The ending of *Coriolanus* is ironic not only in its hollow and false epitaph, and not only in the mechanical way in which Martius, puppet-man, is manipulated once more for someone else's benefit. It is ironic in relation to the rest of the play, and to the political and family situation in Rome. All the other Shakespearian tragedies similarly witness the death of the greatest, most outstanding people, yet they do effect a change in an unsatisfactory political situation; they leave some lesser but none the less reliable person in charge of a new set-up, in which order rules and from which the destructive influences have been purged. Fortinbras rules at the end of *Hamlet*, Edgar in *King Lear*, Malcolm in *Macbeth*, Octavius in *Antony and Cleopatra*, Alcibiades in *Timon*, even Cassio takes charge of Cyprus in *Othello*. Yet in *Coriolanus* the hero dies while nothing else has changed. Brutus and Sicinius, despite the patricians' threats, are still tribunes, and can be relied on to foment class-hatred in future. Menenius will still try to fob the people off with his image of the bluff but friendly aristocrat. Volumnia, given increased prestige by the monument erected to her, will still incarnate the militarist fantasy, while Virgilia will be as loving and as ineffectual as ever. And the warrior of the future? – that will be little Martius, already under his grandmother's influence.

As a reader not normally given to speculation about what happens after the ending of a Shakespeare play, or indeed any other literary work, I can perhaps defend myself here by pointing to the unique qualities of *Coriolanus*. No other Shakespeare play offers so penetrating and so sustained an analysis of political processes, from image-making and vote-catching to the cut-and-thrust of an election and the cloak-and-dagger work of a conspiracy eliminating political enemies. No other Shakespeare play is so critical of practically all the characters involved in it: the people, the tribunes, the patricians, Volumnia, Aufidius – it is difficult to find anything favourable to say or feel about any of these, and if we put Coriolanus and Virgilia in a separate category then we still have reservations about them. Taking these two factors together, then, the disillusioned analysis of political processes with all the malice and distortion they involve, and the relentlessly scathing examination of personality and motive, I would suggest that the open, unresolved ending of the play is Shakespeare's final irony about politics. The innocent and unwary perish; but the party machines grind on. The faces may be different next time but the pressures will be the same, the compromises and dissimulations will still work to weaken and distort truth and honesty.

Democratic processes will still be open to exploitation; the people will always believe that image which is most cleverly constructed, not that which is true, but less attractive. Of course, exponents of Shakespeare the pure artist, unconcerned with life, will protest at this suggestion, as will defenders of politics as an arena of sweetness and light. But one thing is clear about *Coriolanus*, and that is that its criticism of political manœuvring cannot be laughed off. One exposure to the play should be enough to destroy our complacency about politics for ever.

It is a marvellously critical and polemical work, then – but is it a tragedy? Criteria for tragedy are not generally agreed on, yet a minimal definition might be that in this genre unavoidable human conflict results in the destruction of important values, an eclipse of people and relationships which moves us with sorrow and pity for all this loss and unfulfilment. Here the major tragic experience is the betrayal of Coriolanus by the people of Rome, by the tribunes, by his mother, by his class, by Aufidius, and, unless I am mistaken (I hope I am), by his wife. Although often unaware of the real forces acting on him Coriolanus struggles from first to last to maintain his own integrity and identity, to remain true to his own values. The many points during the action where he can be found indignantly protesting at the violation of some basic principle shows that he not only lives his values but feels them, and feels them at maximum intensity always. He is never cool, detached, or indifferent about his beliefs.

As a system of values I have already indicated where I take it to be deficient, notably in its contempt for the people. Yet Shakespeare, deliberately retaining this unsympathetic trait, has gone to even greater pains to show that Coriolanus has taken over – or rather, been indoctrinated into – an attitude deriving from the whole patrician class. On the other side he shows the people as being contemptible in every way, and judged so by their own leaders. None the less it is an unsympathetic trait, and in the first two Acts it serves to restrain us from becoming involved with Coriolanus. This calculatedly unfavourable first impression is one that Shakespeare uses for other tragic characters – Lear, Antony, Timon – and in each case he creates a far greater final involvement than if the characters had been admirable from the first. The turning-point in our attitude to Coriolanus comes in Act III, scene i, the great confrontation between patricians and plebeians in which Coriolanus alone sees the tribunes' plot and the consequences for society of this unresolvable division of power. In that and in subsequent scenes (as indeed in the battle in Act I) the people and their leaders are shown to be as bad as Coriolanus says they are, while the patricians are shown to be as ineffectual as he says they are (III.i.94ff.). As the action develops from this point Coriolanus' unsympathetic qualities are played down by Shakespeare, receding into the past with the Roman situation from which he has been expelled. In the second half of the play, it seems to me, Coriolanus is never criticized by Shakespeare: we are meant always to approve of him.

Yet, clearly, we do not approve of him in the abstract or in a vacuum. The special quality of human behaviour in mimetic forms such as the novel and drama is that in our experience of it we evaluate men and women partly through their own actions and partly by comparison with others. Coriolanus' character is presented to us in enough detail for us to form a full impression of it, yet it is defined even more sharply by its contrast with other people. These juxtapositions are made between him and everyone else, starting, as we have observed, with the gap between his attitude to love and relationship and that of Volumnia. His modesty and loathing of panegyrical lies is reiterated by Shakespeare through the contrast with Cominius and Menenius, a contrast that extends from the first Act to the last. His dedication to war as an image of service to the state is juxtaposed with the worship of blood and death expressed by Volumnia and Menenius and with the craven and self-seeking behaviour of the citizens. His honesty in expressing his feelings openly is the opposite of the dissimulation practised – and only revealed to us by Shakespeare's dramatic technique of separate presentation – by the tribunes, the patricians, Aufidius, and his conspirators. In all these juxtapositions Coriolanus' beliefs and actions are evaluated by Shakespeare as being superior to those of the people who surround and manipulate him.

It will be obvious by now that I take Coriolanus to be a true tragic hero. Yet that concept has acquired some unfortunate connotations in modern times, such as the idea that a hero must command our total approval. None of Shakespeare's tragic heroes would meet that requirement. If we think for a moment of Lear, Antony, Othello, Macbeth, Timon, Hamlet, then we will recall many instances where they behave with arrogance, stupidity, pride, jealousy, evil, malice. All have faults, yet we care for them all. What matters is that they should also have appreciable human values, should offer a way of living that we regard as precious, something that we would want to see preserved and not destroyed. In Coriolanus we admire his qualities of honesty, integrity, loyalty, self-sacrifice, love, tenderness, and respect – we admire them all the more since no one else in the play possesses them (though Cominius and Menenius on the public side, Virgilia on the private, do embody some of his values). The sharpness of the contrast which Shakespeare draws between him and his society derives much of its force from Coriolanus' extreme innocence. As Menenius says, 'Consider this: he hath been bred i'th' wars/Since a' could draw a sword, and is ill-schooled' (III.i.322f.), not only in 'bolted language' – fine talking – but in the whole nature of politics and social friction. Where he fails, then, is in the ability to recognize evil, to see how human beings 'have designs' on him. I recall Milton's description of the superficiality of that virtue 'which is but a youngling in the contemplation of evil, and knows not the utmost that vice promises to her followers';[36] or Francis Bacon's insistence, discussing the 'impostures and vices of every profession', that the serious discussion of fraud should be considered 'among the best fortifications for honesty and virtue':

For as the fable goes of the basilisk, that if he sees you first, you die for it, but if you see him first, he dies; so is it with deceits, impostures, and evil arts, which, if they be first espied, they lose their life, but if they prevent [come first] they endanger; so that we are much beholden to Machiavelli and other writers of that class, who openly and unfeignedly declare or describe what men do, and not what they ought to do. For it is not possible to join the wisdom of the serpent with the innocence of the dove, except men be perfectly acquainted with the nature of evil itself; for without this, virtue is open and unfenced; nay, a virtuous and honest man can do no good upon those that are wicked, to correct and reclaim them, without first exploring all the depths and recesses of their malice.[37]

Coriolanus' education has been misplanned: he ought to have been reading Bacon's *Essays* and Machiavelli's *Prince*. For he does possess much of 'the innocence of the dove' in politics, his virtue is entirely 'open and unfenced', he has no means either of defending himself or of correcting 'those that are wicked'. All that he can do, once he has seen the basilisk, is to exclaim in outrage, and attack it. But that is already too late. In Max Weber's terms he never realized that politics is governed by 'diabolic powers', and that to enter into this arena is to 'contract with violent means'. Lacking both 'the trained relentlessness in viewing the realities of life and the ability to face such realities and to measure up to them inwardly', he remains, indeed, 'a political infant'.[38]

Bacon's ethical dichotomy also applies to Coriolanus, who is to be aligned with the idealist position of 'what men ought to do', and only gradually discovers the gap between that and what they actually do. Yet – to pose a purely hypothetical question – would we wish him otherwise? If he had 'the wisdom of the serpent' wouldn't that totally transform his character? All his spontaneity and immediacy of feeling, whether anger or tenderness, his integrity, his noble trust and loyalty to others, all these would be replaced by self-control, the concealment and dissimulation of feelings, the careful calculation of personal advantage before acting. He would end up like Cominius or Aufidius. He might be the more successful general, of course, but the dichotomy that Shakespeare offers us is between his deficiencies as a political soldier and his strengths as a human being. I would rather have his integrity and innocence, however easily 'put upon', than all the calculation and political 'skill' in Rome or Corioli. In my support I cite a curiously apt passage in *War and Peace*. Prince Andrew Volkonski, observing a heated dispute between some generals, reflects that the so-called 'virtues' of a general are in fact such qualities as stupidity or absent-mindedness:

Not only does a good army commander not need any special qualities, on the contrary he needs the absence of the highest and best human attributes – love, poetry, tenderness, and philosophic inquiring doubt. He should be limited, firmly convinced that what he is doing is very important (otherwise he will not have sufficient patience), and only then will he be a brave leader.

God forbid that he should be humane, should love, or pity, or think of what is just and unjust.[39]

Tolstoy's irony resembles Shakespeare's: in some human activities it is better to fail than to succeed.

Notes

1 Max Weber, 'Politics as a vocation', a lecture given at Munich University in 1919, in H. H. Gerth and C. Wright Mills (trans.) *From Max Weber. Essays in Sociology* (London, 1948), pp. 77–128, at p. 123.

2 A. C. Bradley, 'Coriolanus', British Academy Shakespeare Lecture for 1912, in P. Alexander (ed.) *Studies in Shakespeare* (Oxford, 1964), pp. 219–37, at p. 219.

3 T. S. Eliot, 'Hamlet' (1919), in *Selected Essays*, 3rd edn (London, 1951), p. 144.

4 T. J. B. Spencer, 'Shakespeare and the Elizabethan Romans', *Shakespeare Survey* 10 (1957): 27–38, at p. 35.

5 Bradley, 'Coriolanus', pp. 226, 228, 226, 220.

6 P. B. Wyndham Lewis, *The Lion and the Fox* (London, 1927; repr. 1951), p. 238.

7 John Palmer, *Political Characters of Shakespeare* (London, 1945), p. 297.

8 Kenneth Muir, 'Shakespeare and the tragic pattern', British Academy Shakespeare Lecture for 1958, *Proceedings of the British Academy* 44 (1959): 145–62, at p. 161.

9 D. A. Traversi, *An Approach to Shakespeare* (London, 1956 edn), pp. 226–7.

10 D. J. Enright, '*Coriolanus*: tragedy or debate', *Essays in Criticism* 4 (1954): 1–19, at p. 7; repr. in D. J. Enright, *The Apothecary's Shop* (London, 1957), pp. 32–53, at p. 39.

11 G. Wilson Knight, 'The royal occupation: an essay on *Coriolanus*', in *The Imperial Theme* (London, 1951), p. 168; excerpt in J. E. Phillips (ed.) *Twentieth Century Interpretations of 'Coriolanus'* (Englewood Cliffs, N J, 1970), pp. 15–24.

12 O. J. Campbell, *Shakespeare's Satire* (New York, 1943), pp. 198–217; excerpt in Phillips, *Twentieth Century Interpretations*, pp. 25–36 (one of the least intelligent treatments of Coriolanus).

13 For more sympathetic readings of the play, see I. R. Browning, '*Coriolanus*: boy of tears', *Essays in Criticism* 5 (1955): 18–31 (in reply to Enright); Una Ellis-Fermor, 'Coriolanus', *Shakespeare the Dramatist* (London, 1961), pp. 60–77; M. Charney, *Shakespeare's Roman Plays: the Function of Imagery in Drama* (Cambridge, Mass., 1961), pp. 29–40, 142–96; W. Rosen, *Shakespeare and the Craft of Tragedy* (Cambridge, Mass., 1960), pp. 161–207; A. P. Rossiter, 'Coriolanus', in G. Storey (ed.) *Angel with Horns* (London, 1961), pp. 235–52; and Wilbur Sanders, 'An impossible person: Caius Martius Coriolanus', in W. Sanders and H. Jacobson, *Shakespeare's Magnanimity. Four Tragic Heroes, Their Friends and Families* (London, 1978), pp. 136–87: among the most perceptive accounts of the play.

14 Plutarch and Livy are quoted from G. Bullough (ed.) *Narrative and Dramatic Sources of Shakespeare, Volume V: The Roman Plays* (London, 1964), here p. 506. All quotations from Plutarch and Livy in this section are taken from this volume, pp. 496–541. On Shakespeare's treatment of his sources, in addition to Bullough's introduction, pp. 453–95, see K. Muir, *Shakespeare's Sources* (London, 1957), pp. 219–24; Hermann Heuer, 'From Plutarch to Shakespeare: a study of *Coriolanus*', *Shakespeare Survey* 10 (1957): 50–9 – mostly devoted to the decisive appeal by Volumnia; and Paul A. Jorgensen, *Shakespeare's Military World* (Berkeley and Los Angeles, 1956), pp. 295–314.

15 Bullough, *Narrative and Dramatic Sources*, pp. 462–72.
16 Jorgensen (*Shakespeare's Military World*, p. 301) has noted Shakespeare's innovation in making 'the tribunes responsible by their provocative words for Coriolanus' furious outburst against the people' in III.i., and the fact that in Plutarch Coriolanus goes to answer the charges against him without demur (pp. 299, 304). Shakespeare thus creates 'greater friction', but not just, as he puts it, 'between warrior and society', rather between the son and the mother who incarnates that society's values. Shakespeare's innovation is to interweave political and family conflict.
17 Rosen, *Shakespeare and the Craft of Tragedy*, p. 166.
18 S. T. Coleridge, *Shakespearean Criticism*, ed. T. M. Raysor, 2 vols, (London, 1960), vol. I, p. 79.
19 See D. W. Harding, 'Women's fantasy of manhood: a Shakespearian theme', *Shakespeare Quarterly* 20 (1969): 245–53.
20 Brian Vickers, *The Artistry of Shakespeare's Prose* (London, 1968, 1979), pp. 395–6. Cf. also Ellis-Fermor's comment: 'Volumnia gloats over Coriolanus' wounds as a profitable investment' ('Coriolanus', p. 66); and Wilbur Sanders: 'For civilian friends, ecstatically awaiting his arrival from Corioli, he's a kind of perambulating tally-stick of attested military efficacy (the hilarious grisliness of the wound-count tells us more about the counters than the counted)' ('An impossible person', p. 144).
21 For examples of short-sighted judgements on Coriolanus as manifesting pride, see the anthology by Phillips, *Twentieth Century Interpretations*, pp. 19, 20, 22 (G. W. Knight), 30, 32, 35 (O. J. Campbell), and 55–61 (W. Farnham). Ellis-Fermor observes that some six or seven characters accuse Coriolanus of pride: 'But it is to be noticed that all but one of these are prejudiced utterances; even Volumnia's are to clinch an argument or reinforce an appeal' ('Coriolanus', p. 71 note). All the more regrettable that J. P. Brockbank, in his New Arden edition (London, 1976), should fall into this prejudice: 'pride is the essence of Martius' nature' (p. 37); 'Coriolanus' inhumanity is felt in the play as a consummation of his virtue. The integrity of the soldier destroys the integrity of the man' (p. 50); he is guilty of 'hubristic modesty' (p. 34), has a 'great hubristic drive' (p. 51). It is disappointing that a critic of Brockbank's experience should make the elementary mistake, in this of all plays, of taking partisan comments for or against the hero – being made by patricians or people – as if they were somehow authorial judgements, or represented attitudes endorsed by 'the play': see, e.g., pp. 38–68. He also endorses a 'sacrificial' concept of tragedy, based on the discredited theories of Jane Harrison, Kerenyi, Fergusson *et al.* (for an account of modern critiques of this school see Brian Vickers, *Towards Greek Tragedy* (London, 1973), pp. 33–43).
22 I.ix.36ff.: cf. Plutarch (Bullough, *Narrative and Dramatic Sources* pp. 508, 514–15). Sanders, however, detects a 'catastrophic lapse of tone' in his refusal of 'freely offered munificence' ('An impossible person', p. 148). But the offer of 10 per cent of the spoils is what Plutarch calls 'rather a mercenary reward, than an honourable recompense', and later writers shared Plutarch's admiration for Coriolanus' generosity: see Valerius Maximus, *Dicta et facta memorabilia*, IV.3.4, in Rino Faranda (ed.) *Detti e fatti memorabili* (Turin, 1971), a helpful bilingual edition, pp. 316–18.
23 It is surprising that A. R. Humphreys should state that Coriolanus 'wishes to have power and to have the consulship' (*Shakespeare's Tragedies*, ed. A. Sinfield (London, 1979), p. 114; even more so that Wilbur Sanders should conclude, to his 'embarrassment', that 'Martius, sadly, wants the consulship *for himself*' ('An

impossible person', p. 178). D. A. Stauffer comments, more perceptively, that 'Service is all he desires – not power. But the service must be on his terms' (Phillips, *Twentieth Century Interpretations*, p. 45; and Bradley rejected the tribunes' charge that he wanted tyrannical power as just 'silly' ('Coriolanus', p. 227).

24 As Max Weber noted, whoever wants to establish his power 'requires a following, a human "machine"' to which he must hold out

> the necessary internal and external premiums.... Under the conditions of the modern class struggle, the internal premiums consist of the satisfying of hatred and the craving for revenge; above all, resentment and the need for pseudo-ethical self-righteousness: the opponents must be slandered and accused of heresy.

The leader's success thus depends on the motives of his following, 'which, if viewed ethically, are predominantly base' ('Politics as a vocation', p. 125). The 'modern class struggle' was anticipated, long ago, in *Coriolanus*.

25 Weber, 'Politics as a vocation', pp. 115, 116–17. Some commentators fail to see anything wrong with the tribunes. John Palmer (*Political Characters of Shakespeare*, pp. 273–4; excerpt in Phillips, *Twentieth Century Interpretations*, pp. 109–10) says that 'only one course of action is politically possible' for them: 'they must advise the citizens to reconsider their promises to vote for Martius'. (How cool and rational that sounds: 'advice ... reconsider'. The actual fact is a mob scene.) Further, 'there is no fault to be found with their conduct of the situation. It is good, sound electioneering and it is a happy politician who has nothing worse upon his conscience'. As for their advice to the citizens to 'lay the faults on us' for their initial choice of Coriolanus (II.iii.225ff.). – which is totally false – Palmer (*Political Characters of Shakespeare*) writes: 'Admittedly it is dishonest. But do political leaders in the heat of an election always tell the truth?' The tribunes are, after all, 'men in a desperate situation', using the people to preserve their power, whose 'motives – and they are good motives as far as they go – are plainly stated' – namely, 'This mutiny were better put in hazard' (II.iii.255ff.). But 'plainly stated' to each other, only, not to their political tools, the populace. Palmer's account reads like one of those defences of unscrupulous practices that Swift gives to an apologetic Gulliver, meant in fact as an indictment. If this is 'sound' politics, heaven preserve us!

26 Bullough, *Narrative and Dramatic Sources*, pp. 520–1.

27 See Mario Praz, ' "The politic brain": Machiavelli and the Elizabethans', his 1928 British Academy lecture, reprinted in *The Flaming Heart* (New York, 1958), pp. 90–145; and N. Orsini, ' "Policy" or the language of Elizabethan Machiavellianism', *Journal of the Warburg and Courtauld Institutes* 9 (1946): 122–34. In ' "Policy", Machiavellism, and the earlier Tudor drama', *English Literary Renaissance* 1 (1971): 195–209, N. W. Bawcutt gives evidence of the pejorative associations of the word long before Machiavelli became known in England; thereafter, in the propaganda against him, it became inseparably attached.

28 Lionel Trilling, *The Liberal Imagination* (New York, 1950), p. 105.

29 Ellis-Fermor, 'Coriolanus', pp. 68, 74, 77 on Virgilia's embodying the 'silences, graces, and wisdom banished from the outer world but vital to wholeness of life'.

30 *Leviathan*, I.15, ed W. Oakeshott (Oxford, 1964), p. 99.

31 ibid., II.28, p. 207.

32 The Folio text reads 'verified' here, and in his *Canons of Criticism* (1750), Thomas Edwards emended it to read '*varnished* my friends ... with all the size, that verity/Would without lapsing suffer'. As he explained, this 'is an allusion either to painting or whitewashing: and the word *varnish* (or *vernish* as it is sometimes

spelt) agrees with the following metaphor of *size*' (Brian Vickers (ed.) *Shakespeare: the Critical Heritage, Vol. 3, 1733–1752* (London, 1975), p. 408). Dover Wilson accepted it for his 1960 New Cambridge edition; Brockbank gives good reasons for adopting it in his New Arden text, but finally demurs (pp. 281–2).

33 Wilbur Sanders comments:

> He is stripped progressively, of the dues of faithful service ('Traitor'), of the rights of conquest recorded in his name (now a 'Robbery'), of his martial attributes, and his manhood ('Boy'). The moment of his life when he has been most the moral adult is travestied as puerility.

('An impossible person', p. 186)

34 Bradley could 'feel nothing but disgust as Aufidius speaks the last words' ('Coriolanus', p. 234), but Sanders finds in these lines evidence of 'the gnawing torment' that Aufidius' 'susceptibility has been consistently producing in himself', that is genuine remorse ('An impossible person', p. 168). I find this hard to believe.

35 John Dennis, 'An Essay upon the Genius and Writings of Shakespeare', in Brian Vickers (ed.) *Shakespeare: the Critical Heritage, Volume 2: 1693–1733* (London, 1974), pp. 284–5.

36 *Areopagitica*, in John Milton, *Complete Poems and Major Prose*, ed. Merritt Y. Hughes (New York, 1957), p. 728.

37 *De Augmentis Scientiarum*, VII,i; trans. Francis Headlam, in J. Spedding, R. L. Ellis, and D. D. Heath (eds), *The Works of Francis Bacon*, 14 vols (London, 1857–74), V, 17.

38 Weber, 'Politics as a vocation', pp. 123–7.

39 Leo Tolstoy, *War and Peace*, Book 9, ch. 11, trans. L. and A. Maude, 3 vols (London, 1939), vol. 2, p. 308. Wilbur Sanders ('An impossible person', p. 159) reached a similar conclusion: 'isn't it ... in the very nature of nobility to detest manipulators so heartily that it scorns to anticipate their stratagems?' He follows A. C. Bradley in feeling 'a tremendous surge and lift of exultation when Martius finally shakes off all the dirty encumbrances of political jobbery' ('Coriolanus', p. 229).

Part II
Shakespeare and his critics

5

The emergence of character
criticism, 1774–1800

An interest in Shakespeare's characters is as old as an interest in Shakespeare himself. Among the earliest allusions to his plays in the early seventeenth century we find tributes to the drawing-power of Falstaff, or Hamlet, or Malvolio,[1] and among the earliest pieces of formal literary criticism are praises for his skill in creating characters: in general terms by Margaret Cavendish, Duchess of Newcastle in 1662 (*Shakespeare: the Critical Heritage*, vol. 1, pp. 42ff.), and more specifically by Dryden in his accounts of Falstaff (*SCH*, vol. 1, pp. 139ff., 257ff.) and Caliban (*SCH*, vol. 1, p. 260). Commentary on the characters continued as part of the discussion of a play under the traditional neo-classical categories of action, plot, characters, manners, instruction, diction, and so on: we find discussions of varying lengths and subtlety by Rymer, Dennis, Rowe, Gildon, Steele, John Hughes, Lewis Theobald, Warburton, George Stubbes, Joseph Warton, Upton, Kames, and of course Dr Johnson. Such criticism is to be found in the footnotes to editions, in periodical and other essays, many of which give a complete account of the plays.

What is new in the last quarter of the eighteenth century is that essays and whole books are devoted to individual characters, and those alone. The critics abandon discussion of plot or language and write simply about the people of Shakespeare's creation. This was a decisive change of emphasis, as some of them were well aware. Thomas Whately, at the beginning of his excellent *Remarks on Some of the Characters of Shakespeare* (written *c.* 1768–9; published 1785) declared that 'The writers upon dramatic compositions have, for the most part, confined their observations to the fable; and the maxims received amongst them for the conduct of it are emphatically called *The Rules of the Drama*' (*SCH*, vol. 6, p. 408). But, Whately argued, such rules are subordinate to another topic in criticism, 'I mean the distinction and preservation of *character*, without which the piece is at best a tale, not an action.' Since in other literary forms 'the actors ... are not produced upon the scene', then the presence of characters before us means that character – and not plot! – should be the main focus of critical interest. Occasionally a critic will even oppose the two in a rather cavalier manner. A writer in the *English Review* for 1784 said that 'in Shakespeare we forget the poet, and think only of the character' (*SCH*, vol. 4, p. 20), while George Colman, having stated that 'the nice discrimination of the various shades of the human mind, the pourtraying of character, was Shakespeare's excellence', went on to argue that 'his fable is often comparatively defective. What is the conduct of the story of *Hamlet* viewed with the person of Hamlet and the Ghost?' (*SCH*, vol. 4, p. 20).

Not all critics were as aggressive, or as one-sided, in justifying their interest in character. But whatever their reasons they produced extensive analyses: William Richardson wrote three whole books of *Essays on Shakespeare's Dramatic Characters* (1774, 1783–4, 1788–9; collected 1798, and with additions, 1812); Maurice Morgann published his *Essay on the Dramatic Character of Sir John Falstaff* in 1777, and was ably answered by Richard Stack in 1788; Whately's essay on Richard III and Macbeth led to a defence of Macbeth by J. P. Kemble in 1786, which he enlarged in 1817; in addition there are important essays on Hamlet by Frederick Pilon, Henry Mackenzie, and Thomas Robertson, as well as several anonymous writers. Richard Cumberland wrote on Macbeth and Richard III, as did George Steevens; Henry Mackenzie analysed Falstaff in two numbers of *The Lounger*, one W. N. wrote on Othello in *The Bee*, Wolstenholme Parr wrote on Othello and Coriolanus, while Richard Hole produced an ironic – at least, one hopes that it is ironic! – apology for Iago and Shylock.[2] That cursory listing will show the amount of criticism produced, and much of it is good, indeed the best critical work of the period was produced in responding to Shakespeare's characters. It was a topic which stimulated readers to become critics: the essays by Morgann, Richardson, Mackenzie, Robertson, Whately, Kemble, and Stack were all first publications.

The newness of the genre and of the writers might suggest that their critical approach was also innovatory. In some ways it was – as in the new interest in character psychology – but in others it was traditional. There seem to be two main theoretical expectations common to nearly all of these critics:

1. The concern that characters should be consistent – they should be 'preserved', 'sustained', or maintained as a coherent whole.
2. They should fulfil some moral purpose: they should seek virtue, avoid or condemn vice, and be rewarded or punished accordingly.

Both criteria are evidently part of traditional neo-classical theory, which indeed continued to provide the assumptions and methods for most readers, and writers, in this period. Many of them still expected poetic justice to be enforced, still believed that the three unities were essential.

New ideas, and new approaches, did emerge, however, but the first point

I wish to make is that they emerged not as deliberate or conscious innovations in aesthetic theory – there was no 'group' of critics, no 'programme' or 'manifesto'. Rather, they appeared as a result of a specific critical method, which led to a sort of chain reaction within neo-classical theory. The development was internal, the result of a disagreement where both parties appeal to the same criteria, yet where the final position breaks the system that produced those criteria.

The first cause of change, as I see it, was the critical method, the very simple opposition of attack and defence. Where generations of orthodox neo-classical critics had attacked Shakespeare's characters for being inconsistent, and not morally improving – or at least not consistently so – this generation of critics, who shared the same belief in the need for consistency and morality, set out to defend these characters. In the process a crucial shift of emphasis occurred.

Strict neo-classical critics, from Rymer to Mrs Lennox to George Steevens, throughout a hundred-year period, applied the concept of consistency of character formulated in the *Ars Poetica*:

> Si quid inexpertum scaenae committis et audes
> personam formare novam, servetur ad imum,
> qualis ab incepto processerit, et sibi constet.

(If it is an untried theme you entrust to the stage, and if you boldly fashion a fresh character, have it kept to the end even as it came forth at the first, and have it self-consistent.)[3]

This demand, reiterated in countless modern treatises, was applied to Shakespeare with vigour, and at times ferocity. Hamlet, as a character, was notorious as an example of the union of the most incompatible qualities: 'impetuous, tho' philosophical; sensible of injury, yet timid of resentment; shrewd, yet void of policy; full of filial piety, yet tame under oppression; boastful in expression, undetermined in action'. Francis Gentleman, from whom I have been quoting,[4] laments that the hero 'should be such an apparent heap of inconsistency' (1770); George Steevens, attacking the hero for delaying his revenge, and the play for not getting anywhere after Act 2, enlarged on 'the glaring inconsistencies in the character of the hero' in several essays and notes.[5] The critics who defended Hamlet might have simply retorted that the criterion of character-consistency ought not to be applied in such a severe way. Instead, they accepted the diagnosis of inconsistency, but then sought for an explanation of it within Hamlet's character. Thomas Sheridan, recorded in conversation by Boswell (in 1763: the account was not published until the 1950s),[6] described Hamlet as a 'young man who had led a studious contemplative life and so become delicate and irresolute', lacking the 'strength of mind' to revenge himself on Claudius. 'His timidity being once admitted, all the strange fluctuations which we perceive in him may be easily traced to that source' (*SCH*, vol. 4, p. 8). Here the negative criticism is accepted but deflected into a search for a ruling principle that will integrate the character, turn contradiction into unity.

The unity discovered by these critics was the unity of a divided mind. Henry Mackenzie, writing in 1780[7] and trying to find the 'leading idea' which would reduce Hamlet's character to a 'fixed or settled principle', admitted all the 'variable and uncertain' facets of his personality; yet where earlier critics had cited these as evidence of Shakespeare's clumsy dramaturgy, in which they are involuntary blemishes, Mackenzie retorted that 'this is the very character which Shakespeare meant to allot him' (*SCH*, vol. 6, pp. 273f.). Finding in real life such a person, 'endowed with feelings so delicate as to border on weakness, with sensibility too exquisite to allow of determined action', he made this divided mind the centre of the play. To Mackenzie Hamlet is 'a sort of double person', and William Richardson[8] followed him in diagnosing a continuous 'state of internal contest'. Thomas Robertson, lecturing to the Royal Society of Edinburgh in 1788,[9] generalized the insights of Mackenzie and Richardson on to a higher plane with the suggestion that Shakespeare had balanced the discordant qualities in Hamlet deliberately, and 'in such an opposite manner, that one class of them should counteract, and render inefficient the other. It is this that suffered nothing to be done; it is this that constantly impeded the action, and kept the catastrophe back' (*SCH*, vol. 6, p. 483). There, it seems to me, whatever our opinion of the final estimate, Robertson has converted defects into assets, and linked character with the design of the whole play. He sees Hamlet paralysed by 'the fluctuation of his mind between contriving and executing', between his gentleness and his sensibility. There we find two of the key elements in the Goethe–Schlegel–Coleridge concept of Hamlet, the discord between the hero's character and his circumstances, and the pressure of events on a sensitive soul resulting in paralysis. It is surprising, perhaps, but none the less true, that the Romantic Hamlet derived directly from its apparent polar opposite, the flawed jumble condemned by the neo-classical critics, thanks to the mediation of this generation of critics – whom we would insult by calling transitional. Here is an instance of the internal dialectic of a critical tradition having a fruitful outgrowth. There were also less happy results. In this debate on Hamlet's inconsistency the aesthetic or formalist attack by orthodox neo-classical critics pushed the new critics of the 1780s into a defence by the appeal to Hamlet's psychology. A similar resort to psychology, and to hypotheses about hidden motives, resulted from attacks based on the other neo-classical principle, that of morality. But the defence here seems to me of dubious value. I review briefly two instances, the prayer scene, and the hero's madness.

First, Hamlet's stated reasons for not killing Claudius while he is praying, lest his soul should go to heaven: a few tough-minded critics could accept these reasons at face value – Joseph Ritson, for instance.[10] But most of them agreed with George Stubbes in 1736[11] that

> there is something so very Bloody in it, so inhuman, so unworthy of a Hero that I wish our Poet had omitted it. To desire to destroy a Man's Soul, to make him eternally miserable by cutting him off from all hopes of Repentance; this surely, in a Christian Prince, is such a Piece of Revenge as no Tenderness for any Parent can justify.
>
> (*SCH*, vol. 3, p. 59)

Other critics, including Dr Johnson, Francis Gentleman, Reed, Thomas Davies, and Malone, agreed in condemning this 'horrid soliloquy'.[12] One remedy was to leave it out on stage, but as Frederick Pilon[13] pointed out, 'This principal link being omitted in the representation, and no other cause substituted for Hamlet's continuing to procrastinate, he appears weak and inconsistent during the last two acts' (*SCH*, vol. 6, p. 183). If you solve one problem by such drastic means you create others: plays are organisms or ecosystems whose balance can be easily upset, with unexpected consequences. Indeed, the common tactic of the defenders of Shakespeare on this head led to damaging side-effects. William Dodd, in 1752,[14] was the first to argue that Hamlet 'is afraid to do what he so ardently longs for' (*SCH*, vol. 4, p. 474): in other words, all the business about hell is a mere rationalization of his own cowardice. Thomas Sheridan thought that the speech was just another excuse for his delay (*SCH*, vol. 4, p. 8). Richardson, anxious to validate Hamlet's moral sense, explained that 'these are not his real sentiments', since Hamlet's 'sense of justice' could never have excused such a 'savage enormity'. So Hamlet invents a motive 'better suited to the opinions of the multitude', 'shelters himself under the subterfuge' (*SCH*, vol. 6, pp. 367f.). Thomas Robertson rightly objected that this interpretation would imply that 'the pious and noble revenge of Hamlet had something morally blameable in its nature' (*SCH*, vol. 6, p. 488), an unacceptable verdict; thus in trying to solve one problem the critic had created a worse one. For his part Robertson fell back on the earlier concept of Hamlet's gentleness, and argued that he 'was really *imposing* upon himself; devising an excuse for his aversion at bloodshed, for his ... "craven scruple"' (*SCH*, vol. 6, p. 486). It looks as if the debate should have been about Hamlet's cowardice, not Falstaff's!

All these explanations propose a psychological explanation to a moral problem. Hamlet's speech over Claudius is horrible, they agree, but he doesn't mean it; it is only a rationalization. Yet this psychological end-product becomes unsatisfying on different moral grounds. It would give us a Hamlet totally lacking integrity, who deceives himself, and us, about his motives. As well as damaging the wholeness of his character, it would reduce its nobility, in either Renaissance or eighteenth-century terms (the twentieth century does not seem worried about cowardice). Hamlet would now be a coward, 'willing to wound but afraid to strike'. Any critical explanation which both reduces the stature of a character and destroys its coherence is surely unsatisfactory.

The same judgement applies to the other case where a psychological explanation was given to a moral problem, Hamlet's madness. The orthodox position – of the Shakespeare-lovers, or perhaps we should call them Shakespeare-accepters – was that Hamlet assumes madness to disguise his real feelings from Claudius and the court. Against this was set the objection of neo-classical or formalist critics who judged the play, and the dramatist, in terms of function and economy. George Stubbes, writing the first extended essay on *Hamlet* in 1736, criticized the device for having the opposite effect to that intended: 'so far from Securing himself from any Violence which he fear'd from the Usurper ... it seems to have been the most likely Way of getting himself confin'd', and thus prevented from pursuing his revenge (*SCH*, vol. 3, p. 55). Mrs Lennox[15] dismissed the madness as 'of no consequence to the principal Design of the play' (*SCH*, vol. 4, p. 129) and was followed by both Johnson, who said that it lacked 'adequate cause', since Hamlet 'does nothing which he might not have done with the reputation of sanity' (*SCH*, vol. 5, p. 161), and Steevens (*SCH*, vol. 5, p. 488).

The formalist critics, then, saw the madness as non-functional, a sign of bad dramaturgy. The character critics of the 1770s and 1780s answered that objection by claiming that the madness is not feigned but real. It then becomes an intended effect, not a clumsiness, and must be seen as integral to the psychology of the character. William Kenrick, lecturing in a London tavern in 1774,[16] 'urged that the character of Hamlet was much more moral and consistent' (thus satisfying the twin criteria of neo-classical criticism) 'than his commentators usually allow him; that his madness was *real*, at least *essentially* so', caused by Ophelia's inconstancy, 'the blow to his ambition by Gertrude's marriage with Claudius, as well as the unnaturalness of that union' (*SCH*, vol. 6, p. 115). The exponents of Hamlet's sensibility could easily attach this explanation to their own interpretation. Henry Mackenzie occupied a cautious middle ground: Hamlet's madness is assumed, but 'At the grave of Ophelia ... it exhibits some temporary marks of a real disorder.' His mind 'is thrown for a while off its poise' (*SCH*, vol. 6, p. 277). The anonymous author of an essay in the *London Magazine* for November 1782,[17] had the ingenious idea of confronting, in the after-world, a hero of Shakespeare and a hero of Corneille, Theseus, out of *Oedipe*. Hamlet defends himself from the charge of 'cruel and inconsistent conduct', and claims to have had a mind 'distracted with contending passions', so that he is 'not clear if much of my flighty extravagance was not owing to an imagination really disordered' (*SCH*, vol. 6, p. 318). William Richardson, ever bent on defending Hamlet, discussed the madness and offered some remarks which were 'also intended to justify his moral conduct'. Hamlet's external and internal situation is so fraught that he not surprisingly exhibits 'reason in extreme perplexity, and even trembling on the brink of madness'. Hamlet counterfeits 'an insanity which in part exists', and when he kills Polonius does so 'without intention, and in the frenzy of tumultuous emotion' (*SCH*, vol. 6, pp. 368f.). The madness was a convenient explanation since it removed Hamlet's responsibility for another moral offence that troubled eighteenth-century critics, the killing of Polonius.

Richardson bases his analysis on Hamlet's 'sore distraction' speech, the apology to Laertes (*Hamlet*, V.ii.225ff.), and so falls into one of the traps which the play sets its commentators. To accept the literal truth of this speech and to reason back from that point in the play can only lead to seeing Hamlet's madness as real; so that the speech in which he announces his intent to adopt an antic disposition must have been feigned; or was perhaps a rationalization for what Hamlet knew to be real madness. If, on the other hand, you accept the first speech as true, then the apology to Laertes is at best insincere, and at worst a lie – as Dr Johnson and other critics objected.[18] But the proponents of Hamlet's real madness, attempting to solve both an aesthetic and a moral problem with a psychological explanation, ended up worse off than they started, with a different aesthetic problem – namely what to do with the antic disposition speech – and an equally grave moral problem, namely Hamlet's responsibility for his actions. Only the sane and the adult are morally responsible, as we have known since Aristotle: is Hamlet neither of these? This interpretation, too, would woefully diminish his character.

The composite picture of Hamlet created by the new critics of the 1770s and 1780s was a psychological construct designed to answer criticisms of an aesthetic or moral nature. It was not provoked by a new interest in psychology, nor did it arise from a fresh analysis of the text. It was a response within the neo-classical tradition to disparaging criticisms of Shakespeare: his supposed faults in dramatic design were shown to be intentional subtleties of characterization.

Hamlet was, and remains, a special case. But a brief report on the conceptions of two other major characters, Macbeth and Falstaff, will show again how critical positions in the discussions of Shakespeare, as of all writers, are affected by the method chosen, and by the reaction to a critical tradition. Thomas Whately, who abandoned Shakespeare criticism to write on modern gardening, juxtaposed Macbeth and Richard III, two characters whose situations – murderers and usurpers – were sufficiently similar to permit extended comparison. If one were making this comparison today, I imagine, it would be in terms of Shakespeare's development as a tragedian, the great enrichment of sensitivity and imagination that it reveals. Whately, however, performed a synchronic, parallel analysis, to expose similarity and difference.[19] It has many intelligent perceptions, such as on Macbeth's humanity, 'his natural feelings of kindred, hospitality and gratitude', his susceptibility to family and social relationships (*SCH*, vol. 6, pp. 410–12). To this picture Whately opposes Richard III, a man destitute of every softer feeling, having no wish for posterity, indifferent to family or house so long as he gains power: 'The possession, not the descent of the crown, is his object' (*SCH*, vol. 6, p. 415). Macbeth vacillates, Richard sweeps on relentlessly. Like other critics of this period Whately is confident that he can infer from represented behaviour how a Shakespeare character would have acted on another occasion. (A dangerous practice, but one which was to persist as long as Bradley!) When Buckingham deserts Richard, his 'determined spirit' never hesitates: 'Had Macbeth been thus disappointed in the person to whom he had opened himself, it would have disconcerted any design he had formed' (*SCH*, vol. 6, p. 419).

Whately's critical model is a sharply antithetical one, and is often justifiable. But in trying to prove his claim that Shakespeare has 'ascribed opposite principles and motives to the same designs and actions' (*SCH*, vol. 6, pp. 409f.) he allows the antithesis to force him into unreal positions. So he decides that while Richard is fearless, Macbeth has an acquired, though not a constitutional, courage (*SCH*, vol. 6, pp. 417–23): he is not truly brave. Whately, we might think, mistakes Macbeth's sense of horror at the moral implications of his actions for mere timidity; indeed, as he pursues the opposition he begins, in effect, to attack Macbeth for not being more manly, or more resolute. The scene with the murderers shows Macbeth's 'weakness of mind', which is one of several 'symptoms of a feeble mind' (*SCH*, vol. 6, p. 425). In the battle scenes Whately criticizes Macbeth for not having fought more efficiently: he is 'irresolute in his counsels, and languid in the execution' (*SCH*, vol. 6, p. 426). Where we might see Macbeth's vacillations as the sign of a deep moral confusion, Whately finds them proof of a weakness in masculine qualities.

Over the last 300 years any significant attack on Shakespeare has led to a defence. The year after Whately's book was published (posthumously), the young John Philip Kemble came to the defence.[20] Kemble shows that Whately has overlooked the importance in drama – a genre limited in scope and extent – of first impressions. Since Shakespeare describes Macbeth's bravery so strongly at the beginning of the play that must be taken as an essential attribute. There is no sign of fear, Kemble points out, 'while yet the pureness of his conscience is uncontaminated by guilt' (*SCH*, vol. 6, pp. 431f.). What Macbeth suffers from is not cowardice but a sense of his own evil. To this perception Kemble adds the splendid rider that if Macbeth were indeed as pusillanimous as Whately said, then we would have to 'forego our virtuous satisfaction in his repugnance to guilt, for it arises from mere cowardice'. His remorse would then have no moral significance, but be mere 'imbecility'; instead of feeling for him, we would despise him. Contemporaries noted how Kemble's reply had linked up elements of the play previously dealt with separately. A writer in the *English Review* said that Kemble proves that 'the intrepidity of Macbeth cannot be called in question; and likewise judiciously remarks that the moral effect of the play depends greatly on the intrepidity of his character' (*SCH*, vol. 6, p. 28). Character, moral effect, and audience reaction are inextricably interconnected.

In this exchange, while much of Whately's criticism is of a high value, and was applauded by his contemporaries,[21] on the issue of cowardice the defender seems to have been stimulated to new and important perceptions. Where Whately gave a psychological explanation, Kemble reasserted the moral one, with unerring rightness, I believe, and located Macbeth's experience in the crucial area of guilt, not fear. The last critical dialogue I shall refer to also opposes psychological against moral criteria, but here the apologist for Shakespeare muddles the issue. I refer to Maurice Morgann's *Essay on the Dramatic Character of Sir John Falstaff* (1777),[22] in which he set out to defend Falstaff from the charge of cowardice, a charge that had been made by many critics, including the author of a recent anonymous work published about 1774 called *Shakespeare: Concerning the Traits of his Characters*.[23] Morgann's essay, which has more than a trace of paradox,[24] belongs to a by now well-established genre, the defence of a Shakespeare character who has been attacked on the grounds of immorality. But whereas other defences of moral criticism resort to a psychological analysis, Morgann's has, rather, moral and aethetic consequences; that is, it affects our sense of the structure of the play, and challenges Shakespeare's moral judgements. Morgann paints a surprisingly favourable picture of Falstaff, the kind that Falstaff would have approved of, and might have made himself. But while Falstaff might have done it with humour, expecting or challenging a refutation, Morgann is deadly serious. He takes all favourable references to Falstaff's fighting at face value, even if these include Doll Tearsheet on his prowess at foining, or those by that real coward, Colevile of the Dale, or Justice Shallow. Again, all that Falstaff says in self-defence is taken *au pied de la lettre*: he really did use 'the utmost speed in his power' to catch up with the army: 'he arrives almost literally *within the extremest inch of possibility*'.[25] Falstaff's wounding of the dead Percy is described as '*indecent* but not cowardly' (*SCH*, vol. 6, p. 175), and Morgann rejects the suggestion that Falstaff's claim to have killed Hotspur is meant to deceive anyone.

Morgann remains an important critic, but rather, I suggest, for his footnotes, insights made in passing: such as the description of the latent element in Shakespeare's characters, who are 'capable of being unfolded and understood in the whole, every part being relative, and inferring all the rest' (*SCH*, vol. 6, p. 168–9, notes); or his invention of the concept of 'choric' characters – he instances Enobarbus, Menenius (*SCH*, vol. 6, p. 173, note); or his defence of Shakespeare's puns for their function in characterization (*SCH*, vol. 6, p. 172, note). These and other points – the best footnotes in eighteenth-century criticism – are remarkably intelligent, but his main argument seems fundamentally misguided. It also contradicted the impression of the play which had been universally agreed on for two centuries, and it made Shakespeare's design seem perverse. Dr Johnson's bluff rejection[26] – 'all he should say, was, that if Falstaff was not a coward, Shakespeare knew nothing of his art' (*SCH*, vol. 6, p. 71) – immediately made the point that this moral apologia for a character in fact disvalues both Shakespeare and the play. Those who defended the play, and the dramatist, did so by attacking Falstaff, and thus redressed the balance. Their defence invoked the twin neo-classical criteria of consistency and morality, but it also expressed a more highly developed conception of Shakespeare's dramatic design than we find in the discussion of other plays. Morgann's claims at least pushed the discussion into a more challenging area.

Henry Mackenzie saw characterization in relation to its dramatic function.[27] Shakespeare gives Falstaff the qualities that are needed to attract Hal to him: wit, humour, sagacity in observing men; but to these the dramatist has joined 'a grossness of mind' which Hal 'could not but see, nor seeing but despise' (*SCH*, vol. 6, pp. 441ff.). Falstaff is at once attractive and repulsive. Mackenzie also gave a sharper definition of Falstaff's character: his evasiveness derives not so much from cowardice as from the wish for self-preservation. Falstaff, like Richard III, is a hypocrite; yet their hypocrisy costs them nothing, since they have no conscience; and both use the weakness of others for their own advantage.

Mackenzie was followed, and excelled, by Richard Stack, in an essay written for the Royal Irish Academy in 1788.[28] Stack refuted Morgann's argument point by point, but I omit many of the details to focus on the issues of consistency and morality. Stack reaffirmed the unity of Falstaff's characterization: his self-defence before Prince John, for instance, is not meant 'to be rational and sober. We find in it the same humorous extravagance as in every other narrative of his exploits' (*SCH*, vol. 6, pp. 476ff.). For Stack the organizing principle of Falstaff's character is revealed in his counterfeiting death to avoid being killed by Douglas: this shows his constant and 'inexhaustible vein of wit and humour ... triumphant over every thing, over calamity, danger and disgrace'. The scene is meant to show not cowardice but the triumph of wit. When Falstaff stabs the dead Percy, however, for Stack this is cowardice and carried out from motives of self-preservation which are not only base but 'so groundless and improbable' – that Hotspur should rise and attack him – 'that none but a coward's heart could entertain them'.

The great strength of Stack as a critic is his awareness of the consequences of character interpretation for our evaluation of the play as a whole. The stabbing of Hotspur's corpse 'speaks too plainly the poet's design as to the character', Shakespeare's moral evaluation of Falstaff. Second, if Morgann's interpretation were adopted, 'a great and delightful portion of Falstaff's wit and humour would be lost' (*SCH*, vol. 6, p. 478), especially in the Gad's Hill robbery and the confrontation scene. Morgann had turned this into a solemn vindication of Falstaff, and tried to discredit Hal, Poins, or anyone else who dared to criticize his hero. Stack showed the consequences of such an overestimation of Falstaff on the relative balance of the other characters:

> to accommodate his theory, false opinions of Poins, Lancaster and others, must be resorted to, and systems of malice intermixed in the plot, which certainly the poet never designed. These are not only in themselves mistakes of character, but have a powerful influence on the plot, and such an one as I think takes away a great deal

from both its comedy and its seriousness.

Stack saw the moral design of the play but also its wit, ending by celebrating Falstaff's 'creative fancy, playful wit', and 'his elastic vigour of mind'. The last of the critics of Morgann I shall refer to, William Richardson,[29] is rather more serious. He begins by reaffirming the criteria of morality and consistency, finding the ruling principles of Falstaff in his 'desire of gratifying the grosser and lower appetites': 'upon this his conduct very uniformly hinges', since he lives for his body and does everything to preserve it (*SCH*, vol. 6, pp. 491ff.). Richardson divides Falstaff's qualities into good and bad, perhaps too tidily (he was after all Professor of the Humanities, and this is the beginning of academic Shakespeare criticism); but he goes on to relate good and bad qualities more coherently than any previous critic. Falstaff's great talents of wit and eloquence are used 'not merely for the sake of merriment, but to promote some design', such as cajoling or duping other people. He fails in his attempts with the Lord Chief Justice and with Prince John, but succeeds with Hal, with Shallow, and with 'his inferior associates'. What Mackenzie had described in a fairly static way as Falstaff's 'penetration into the characters and motives of mankind' is seen by Richardson in its dynamic function. His 'discernment of character' and 'dexterity in the management of mankind' are great, but are of 'a peculiar and limited species; limited to the power of discerning whether or not men may be rendered fit for his purposes; and to the power of managing them as the instruments of his enjoyment'. Richardson's use of traditional moral criticism leads to some penetrating psychological analysis: thus he notes that Falstaff never laughs himself, wants to appear grave and solemn while making others laugh – for his own manipulations. He says that Falstaff's 'presence of mind never forsakes him', but that, although evidence of a great 'inventive faculty', this also reveals a moral deficiency: 'Having no sense of character, he is never troubled with shame'.

Richardson is unique in seeing that Falstaff does not merely deceive others, but deceives himself. The soliloquy on honour is playful but 'affords a curious example of self-imposition', attempting 'to disguise conscious de-merit and escape from conscious disapprobation'. In analysing Hal's reactions to Falstaff through the two parts of the play Richardson notes Hal's increasingly clear-sighted penetration into Falstaff's designs, and shows how the denouement arises organically out of the interplay between the characters:

Thus in the self-deceit of Falstaff, and in the discernment of Henry ... we have a natural foundation for the catastrophe. The incidents too, by which it is accomplished, are judiciously managed. None of them are foreign or external, but grow, as it were, out of the characters.

(*SCH*, vol. 6, p. 498)

It is entirely consistent with his characterization of Falstaff, Richardson notes, that Shakespeare should make him relapse into fantasy and self-deception after his rejection by Hal: 'Do not you grieve at this. I shall be sent for in private to him ... I shall be sent for soon at night.' Richardson has seen the coherence of Falstaff's psychology with his moral sense, being in both beyond 'reformation'.

In this brief survey I have stressed the persistence in the 1780s of traditional critical demands on characterization, that it be morally significant, and internally consistent. Both demands carry on beyond this period: they are found in Hazlitt and Coleridge, and indeed in much of our own criticism. They are, perhaps, universal and perennial expectations of the reader and critic. The writers of this period, in which character criticism began to exist as a critical method, certainly demonstrate attendant weaknesses: some neglect the experience of drama; Morgann is hyper-ingenious; Richardson too heavy-handed and dismissive in his moral judgements. Yet in other places, and in the work of Mackenzie and Stack, the writers who generated character criticism also demonstrate, it seems to me, one of its great values: when by the examination of individual characters, we are led to a better understanding of Shakespeare's wider design.

Notes

1 For early references to Shakespeare's characters see J. Munro (ed.) *The Shakespere Allusion-book*, with preface by E. K. Chambers (Oxford, 1932), and Brian Vickers (ed.) *Shakespeare: the Critical Heritage, Volume 1: 1623–1692* (London and Boston, 1974), pp. 27ff. Future references to this latter collection and the five subsequent volumes (*Vol. 2: 1693–1733* (1974); *Vol. 3: 1733–1752* (1975); *Vol. 4: 1753–1765* (1976); *Vol. 5: 1765–1774* (1979); *Vol. 6: 1774–1801* (1981)) will be incorporated into the text, with the title abbreviated to *SCH*.
2 All these authors are represented in Vickers, *Shakespeare: the Critical Heritage*. Of the secondary literature, two older studies are still useful: T. M. Raysor, 'The study of Shakespeare's characters in the eighteenth century', *Modern Language Notes* 42 (1927): 495–500, and David Lovett, 'Shakespeare as a poet of realism in the eighteenth century', *ELH* 2 (1935): 267–89. R. W. Babcock, *The Genesis of Shakespeare Idolatry, 1766–1799* (Chapel Hill, 1931; New York, 1978) attempts to cover too much detail, resulting in a plethora of bibliography but a paucity of

analysis. Much more illuminating is J. W. Donohue, Jr., *Dramatic Character in the English Romantic Age* (Princeton, 1979), on Macbeth and Richard III in the critical tradition and in the acting versions of Cibber, Garrick, and Kemble. On Hamlet, see P. S. Conklin, *A History of 'Hamlet' Criticism 1601–1821* (New York, 1957; London, 1968) and Morris Weitz, *Hamlet and the Philosophy of Literary Criticism* (Chicago, 1964).

3 Horace, *Ars Poetica*, lines 125–7, in *Satires, Epistles and Ars Poetica*, trans. H. R. Fairclough (London and Cambridge, Mass., 1970).

4 Gentleman, *The Dramatic Censor: or, Critical Companion*, 2 vols (London, 1770). Excerpts in *SCH*, vol. 5, pp. 373–409.

5 For Steevens's attacks on Hamlet, see *SCH*, vol. 5, pp. 447–59, 470–8, 479–83, 487–90, 539–43; and ibid., vol. 6, p. 199. He was answered by Joseph Ritson (ibid., pp. 342–8) and Malone (ibid., pp. 547f.).

6 Sheridan is recorded in *Boswell's London Journal 1762–3*, ed. F. A. Pottle (London, 1950), pp. 234–5; excerpts in *SCH*, vol. 4, pp. 4f.

7 Mackenzie's essays appeared in his journal *The Mirror* (Edinburgh), nos 99 (17 April 1780) and 100 (22 April 1780); reprinted in *SCH*, vol. 6, pp. 272–80.

8 Richardson, *Essays on Shakespeare's Dramatic Characters of Richard the Third, King Lear, and Timon of Athens. To which are added, an Essay on the faults of Shakespeare: and Additional Observations on the Character of Hamlet* (1783); excerpts in *SCH*, vol. 6, pp. 351–70.

9 Robertson, 'An essay on the character of Hamlet, in Shakespeare's tragedy of *Hamlet*', *Transactions of the Royal Society of Edinburgh* 2 (1788): 251–67; excerpts in *SCH*, vol. 6, pp. 480–90.

10 Ritson, *Remarks, Critical and Illustrative, on the Text and Notes of the last Edition of Shakespeare* (1783); excerpts in *SCH*, vol. 6, pp. 334–48; the *Hamlet* discussion is given complete (pp. 342–8).

11 Stubbes, *Some remarks on the Tragedy of Hamlet* (1736); excerpts in *SCH*, vol. 3, pp. 40–69.

12 Dr Johnson judged it a speech 'too horrible to be read or to be uttered' (*SCH*, vol. 5, p. 159); Gentleman: 'sentiments more suitable to an assassin of the basest kind than a virtuous prince and a feeling man' (ibid., vol. 5, p. 379; repeated in his notes to Bell's edition: ibid., vol. 6, p. 90); Reed: see his 'Revised and Augmented' third edition of the Johnson–Steevens *Shakespeare* (London), 1785 vol. X, p. 418; Davies: the soliloquy 'is more reprehensible, perhaps, than any part of Shakespeare's works' (*SCH*, vol. 6, p. 381); Malone: ibid., vol. 6, p. 24.

13 Pilon, *An Essay on the Character of Hamlet As Performed by Mr Henderson* (1777); excerpts in *SCH*, vol. 6, pp. 180–3.

14 William Dodd, *The Beauties of Shakespeare*, 2 vols (1752); excerpts in *SCH*, vol. 4, pp. 464–77.

15 Charlotte Lennox, *Shakespear Illustrated*, 3 vols (1753–4); excerpts in *SCH*, vol. 4, pp. 110–46.

16 Kenrick's lectures were reported in many journals: one of the most coherent accounts, with a reasoned reply, appeared in the *Monthly Miscellany*, February–April 1774; reprinted in *SCH*, vol. 6, pp. 115–18. See also Kenrick's *Introduction to the School of Shakespeare* (1774).

17 'A dialogue between two theatrical heroes of Shakespeare and Corneille', *London Magazine* 51 (November 1782): 513–15; reprinted in *SCH*, vol. 6, pp. 316–20.

18 Johnson: 'I wish *Hamlet* had made some other defence; it is unsuitable to the character of a good or a brave man to shelter himself in falsehood' (*SCH*, vol. 5, p. 161); Francis Gentleman: 'if it be considered that this madness has been but *assumed*, this appears a mean prevarication to a man whom he has most deeply injured' (ibid., pp. 380f.); George Steevens: Hamlet 'abuses [Laertes] in the grossest

manner ... under the appearance of insanity', and after this 'outrageous violence on Laertes, in his sober senses, descends to the baseness of a serious lye to excuse himself by the plea of his *"sore distraction"* ' (ibid., p. 488); 'a dishonest fallacy', (ibid., p. 541); and Thomas Davies: 'Hamlet gives the lie most shamefully' (ibid., vol. 6, p. 382).

19 Whately, *Remarks on Some of the Characters of Shakespeare* (1785); excerpts in *SCH*, vol. 6, pp. 407–29.

20 Kemble, *Macbeth Re-considered; an Essay* (1786); excerpts in *SCH*, vol. 6, pp. 430–5.

21 Horace Walpole said that Whately had given 'the best comment' on Shakespeare's powers in drawing and discriminating characters, and urged that his essay be 'prefixed to every edition of Shakespeare', where it would 'tend more to give a just idea of that matchless genius than all the notes and criticisms on his works' (ibid., p. 407). Malone included a long excerpt from 'these ingenious observations' in his 1790 edition (ibid., pp. 538f.), while both Richard Cumberland (ibid., pp. 447–56) and George Steevens (ibid., pp. 462–6) also wrote essays comparing the two characters, acknowledging – in part! – their debt to Whately.

22 Daniel Fineman, with *Maurice Morgann, Shakespearian Criticism* (Oxford, 1972), has produced the most meticulous edition yet of any piece of Shakespeare criticism, Dr Johnson's notes not excepted. His dedication and enthusiasm for Morgann do, however, lead at times to a critical imbalance, as I observed in *Yearbook of English Studies* 2 (1974): 276–9.

23 This tract is undated, but the British Library catalogue dates it 'about 1774'; excerpts in *SCH*, vol. 6, pp. 144–6. On earlier accounts of Falstaff's cowardice, see the introduction to ibid., p. 21 and note 56, p. 70.

24 Cicero's famous definition of paradoxes: 'sunt admirabilia contraque opinium omnium' (*Paradoxa Stoicorum*, preface: 'these doctrines are surprising, and they run counter to universal opinion'), seems to be echoed by Morgann's description of his work, in which 'the Writer, maintaining contrary to the general Opinion, that this Character was not intended to be shewn as a Coward' (Fineman, *Maurice Morgann*, p. 143). The connection with paradoxes was not lost on his contemporaries: Stack described it as 'one of the most ingenious pieces of criticism anywhere to be found', its design being 'in contradiction to the general sentiment of mankind' (*SCH*, vol. 6, p. 470), while Mackenzie described Morgann as 'a paradoxical critic' (ibid., p. 443), and a reviewer in the *Critical* described the book as 'a *jeu d'esprit*, designed to show how much might be said on a desperate subject; how far what seemed incredible might be rendered probable' (*SCH*, p. 71). Towards the end of his life, in a rather plaintive note, Morgann wrote that

> The Writer of this Book was conscious that the End held out to the Reader was almost Nothing. He saw that every Page must compensate by some Entertainment for its own Perusal; critical Amusement became therefore in Truth the sole End tho' regulated and directed by a pretended one of another sort: thus circumstanced it was indifferent whether the vindication of Falstaff's Courage was obtained or no Excepting only that it seemed necessary to seize the object of Pursuit not on its own account but to crown the Pleasures of the Chase.

> (Fineman, *Maurice Morgann*, p. 241.)

25 Fineman, *Maurice Morgann*, p. 178.

26 Johnson's comment was recorded by Morgann in his own copy of Morgann: Bodleian, Malone 140 (1). Johnson predicted that Morgann would emerge again in defence of Iago: but that step was taken by Richard Hole (*SCH*, vol. 6, pp. 622–6).

27 Mackenzie's essays on Falstaff appeared in his periodical *The Lounger* (Edinburgh), nos 68 (20 May 1786) and 69 (27 May); excerpts in *SCH*, vol. 6, pp. 440–6.

28 Richard Stack, 'An examination of an Essay on the Dramatic Character of Sir John Falstaff', *Transactions of the Royal Irish Academy* 2 (1788): 3–37; excerpts in *SCH*, vol. 6, pp. 469–79.

29 Richardson, *Essays on Shakespeare's Dramatic Character of Sir John Falstaff, and on his Imitation of Female Characters* (1788); excerpts in *SCH*, vol. 6, pp. 490–9.

6

Shakespearian adaptations: the tyranny of the audience

The audience is, in fact, always a conservative influence.

David Lodge[1]

Whoever wishes to reconstruct the complete picture of Shakespeare's presence from the Restoration to Victorian times cannot overlook the adaptations. In this period over a hundred modernized versions of his plays were produced, in thousands of performances (amounting to perhaps half the canon).[2] They generally originated in London, where for most of the time only two theatres (Covent Garden and Drury Lane) were licensed, but they spread to the English provinces, to Germany and France, and even to America. When Berlioz saw Harriet Smithson on that unforgettable occasion in Paris in 1827, the English company for which she acted was performing Garrick's adaptation of *Romeo and Juliet*, a fact which explains many details in the 'Dramatic Symphony' *Roméo et Juliette* that he was inspired to compose.[3] When Shakespeare began to be performed in America it was in the adaptations of Nahum Tate, Colley Cibber, Dryden, D'Avenant, and Garrick. It is a paradox that the most idolized poet and dramatist should have been also the least tolerated in his original form. The ages that praised Shakespeare to the skies could not abide his plays in the theatre without extensive alterations.

This phenomenon is well known, but none the less unique – so far! – in the history of drama. In this chapter I wish to review this familiar material in order to bring out two points more clearly: first, the fact that we can find a quite surprisingly quick change of taste between the closing of the theatres in 1642 and their reopening in 1660; but, second, that this new taste persisted, equally surprisingly, until the 1830s and 1840s, so that – on this head, at least – we find a basic homogeneity of taste across a period of 180 years which literary historians would otherwise categorize into a whole series of movements or epochs. For convenience I divide the time-span into four periods: the immediate post-Restoration, where the basic patterns were set, from D'Avenant and Dryden to Cibber; the early eighteenth century (Dennis, Theobald, Gildon); the mid- and late eighteenth century (Garrick); and the so-called 'romantic' period (Kemble).

The return of Charles II and his court in 1660, after nearly twenty years of exile in Paris, marks one of those accidental but decisive watersheds in critical attitudes and expectations. The diarist John Evelyn could already detect a new trend by 1661, writing in his journal for 26 November: 'I saw *Hamlet Prince of Denmark* played: but now the old playe began to disgust this refined age: since his Majestie being so long abroad' (*SCH*, vol. 1, p. 4).[4] The self-conscious desire to 'refine' taste and manners soon addressed itself to Shakespeare. In 1660, it would seem, Thomas Jordan wrote a 'Prologue to introduce the first woman that came to Act on the Stage in the Tragedy call'd *The Moor of Venice*', marking this momentous occasion in these terms:

> ... In this reforming age
> We have intents to civilize the stage.
> Our women are defective, and so siz'd
> You'd think they were some of the Guard disguiz'd.
> (*SCH*, vol. 1, p. 4)

The most far-reaching reformation was that put in motion by Sir William D'Avenant, manager of the Duke's Men. In the winter of 1660 D'Avenant 'humbly presented ... a proposition of reformeinge some of the most ancient Playes that were played at Blackfriers and of makeinge them fitt' (*SCH*, vol.1, p. 5) – that is, fit for acting according to the new canons of taste. Since the two London theatres were small, seating only four or five hundred, and since 'the town' – that social group which frequented the theatres and helped determine their tone – liked frequent changes of programme, the theatre-managers were under constant pressure to find material. D'Avenant received permission to adapt plays by Shakespeare, Jonson, Shirley, Beaumont and Fletcher, as did the other troupe, run by Thomas Killigrew. The importance of the old plays to the companies in the period 1660 to 1700 was great: out of the 959 recorded performances, 486 were of old plays, 473 of new.[5]

This extensive overhauling of older literature to meet newer expectations derived, then, from an immediate commercial need. But it developed, or was attended by, its own critical rationale. The tenets of neo-classicism, derived from Castelvetro and other sixteenth-century Italian theorists via the much stricter formulations of the French seventeenth-century critics, were invoked by the adapters whenever it suited them. The opportunism involved can be seen by comparing the resulting plays with the claims made for them by their authors. They turn out to contain more comedy in tragedy, not less; more violence, indeed quite gratuitous cruelty; and, above all, more spectacles and shows (*SCH*, vol. 1, pp. 7–8). The system of the unities of place, time, and action was invoked to justify repairing or correcting Shakespeare's so-called 'violation' of them (the glaring anachronism of applying to an artist critical canons of a different age did not, apparently, disturb these writers). So Dryden, in the Preface, 'Containing the Grounds of Criticism in Tragedy', which he prefixed to his adaptation of *Troilus and Cressida* (1679), works through the neo-Aristotelian categories (with the help of Le Bossu) of action, manners, passion, diction, and explains that he has 'new model'd the Plot', thrown out 'many unnecessary persons', and improved others 'which were begun, and left unfinish'd'. Then he attended to the unity of place:

> After this, I made with no small trouble, an Order and Connexion of all the Scenes; removing them from the places where they were inartificially set: and though it was impossible to keep 'em all unbroken, because the Scene must be sometimes in the City, and sometimes in the Camp, yet I have so order'd them that there is a coherence of 'em with one another, and a dependence on the main design; no leaping from Troy to the Grecian Tents, and thence back again in the same Act; but a due proportion of time allow'd for every motion.
>
> (*SCH*, vol. 1., p. 250)

In neo-classicism the imagination is subject to more strict controls: the place may change after an act, but not after a scene. The fluidity of Elizabethan drama stands out more clearly.

In terms of plot construction the earlier drama was also more fluid, more subtle. D'Avenant, in particular, seems to have wanted more deliberate, explicit effects of parallelism. For his version of *Macbeth* (1664), D'Avenant produced a symmetrical ethical structure by enlarging the part of Lady Macduff until she becomes a paragon of virtue, the exact opposite of Lady Macbeth (*SCH*, vol. 1, pp. 47–75). Actually, this type of didactic symmetry resembles more the careful schemes of late Renaissance epic, with its balancing of characters who exemplify complementary virtues and vices. For *The Tempest*, which he prepared with Dryden's help in 1667, D'Avenant added a whole gallery of minor characters who constitute, as Dryden put it, 'the Counterpart to *Shakespeare*'s Plot', including another woman who has never seen a man, and a man who has never seen a woman, so that 'by this means those two Characters of Innocence and Love might the more illustrate and commend each other' (*SCH*, vol. 1, pp. 76–136). But the plays of Shakespeare, like all works of art, resemble ecosystems, each with their own internal balance; an alteration in one part will produce unexpected consequences elsewhere. D'Avenant's ingenuity was bought at the cost of probability, as critics have observed, the reflective reader or spectator soon wondering how so many characters could have been brought up in ignorance of the opposite sex, especially on an island.

If the plots of Elizabethan and Jacobean drama were found lacking, even more objectionable was its language. D'Avenant's incessant tinkering with

214

Shakespeare's language – he was the A. L. Rowse of the seventeenth century – shows just how little an average Restoration theatre-goer could be expected to take in of Shakespeare's complexity, especially in metaphor. Hazelton Spencer's analysis, in what is still the best study of the Restoration adaptations,[6] finds over three hundred alterations, some of which are motivated by decorum, cutting violence ('The Divell take thy soule' becomes 'Perdition catch thee'), or toning down 'vulgar' words ('To grunt and sweat under a weary life' becomes 'groan and sweat'; 'In hugger mugger to inter him' is replaced by 'Obscurely'). But D'Avenant also unpicks Shakespeare's metaphors, turning condensed comparisons that derive from and demand intellectual energy into language that is explicit and ordinary. So 'here/Affront Ophelia' becomes 'meet Ophelia here'; 'Is sicklied o'er with the pale cast of thought', a surprisingly concrete image in which thought is given the attributes of a physical complexion, is refined to 'Shews sick and pale with Thought'. The end-product is more polite, but it is considerably less poetic, and not without justice has D'Avenant's handling of Shakespeare's language been called an 'Entdramatisierung' and 'Entpoetisierung'.[7] Where Shakespeare's Macbeth says 'My dull Braine was wrought with things forgotten', D'Avenant's character has lost the animation and mental struggle, sounding more like a business man: 'I was reflecting upon late transactions'. Where Shakespeare's Claudio reflects upon the horror of the grave:

> Ay, but to die, and go we know not where,
> To lie in cold obstruction and to rot;
> This sensible warm motion to become
> A kneaded clod

(Measure for Measure, III.i.117ff.)

– where the ideas of coldness, insensibility, and blockage are felt with an intensity that fuses them together – D'Avenant's Claudio (in *The Law Against Lovers*, 1662, a conflation of *Much Ado* with *Measure for Measure*) tidily separates, reduces, or just leaves out what he cannot feel, or the audience understand:

> Oh Sister, 'tis to go we know not whither.
> We lye in silent darkness, and we rot;
> Where long our motion is not stopt. . . .

(SCH, vol. 1, pp. 33–4)

Comparison with the original will reveal how much D'Avenant has had to dilute and reject to please 'this refined age'. That he succeeded is confirmed by the testimony of Gerard Langbaine in his *Account of the English Dramatick Poets* (1691), who says that this play is 'borrow'd from Shakespeare: yet where the language is rough or obsolete, our Author has taken care to polish it' (*SCH,* vol. 1, p. 417).

The critical rationale for these changes of language was provided, once again, by the spokesman for the first generation of adapters, Dryden. In the Preface to *All for Love: Or, the World well lost. A Tragedy Written in Imitation of Shakespeare's Stile* (1678), Dryden was in a respectful mood, announcing that 'In my Stile I have profess'd to imitate the Divine *Shakespeare*', a point that he immediately qualified by appealing to the facts of linguistic change:

> I hope I need not to explain my self, that I have not Copy'd my Author servilely: Words and Phrases must of necessity receive a change in suc- ceeding Ages: but 'tis almost a Miracle that much of his Language remains so pure. . . .
>
> (*SCH*, vol. 1, p. 164)

Dryden was much less generous when, a year later, he published his version of *Troilus and Cressida*. In the preface he compares Shakespeare to Aeschylus, whose plays were also altered by later generations, the difference being, however, that Greek had then attained 'its full perfection' while English is not yet fixed. Yet, he goes on,

> it must be allow'd to the present Age, that the tongue in general is so much refin'd since *Shakespeare*'s time, that many of his words, and more of his Phrases, are scarce intelligible. And of those which we understand some are ungrammatical, others coarse; and his whole stile is so pester'd with Figurative expressions, that it is as affected as it is obscure. 'Tis true, that in his later Plays he had worn off somewhat of the rust; but the Tragedy which I have undertaken to correct, was, in all probability, one of his first endeavours on the Stage. . . . I need not say that I have refin'd his Language, which before was obsolete; but I am willing to acknowledg, that as I have often drawn his English nearer to our times, so I have somtimes conform'd my own to his: & consequently, the Language is not altogether so pure, as it is significant.
>
> (*SCH*, vol. 1, pp. 249–51)

The comments purport to be historical, recording a great 'refinement' of the English language over a sixty-year period – which is undoubtedly true – but they also reveal the underlying literary-critical attitude in such judgements as 'coarse', 'pester'd with Figurative expressions' (which means, to take Dryden's pejorative metaphor literally, riddled with metaphors like plague-sores), 'affected', and 'obscure'. Such an indictment, of course, gives the adapter *carte blanche* to alter anything.

The adapters' prefaces are important documents, acting at once as expla-nation, justification, and ingratiation with the audience. The recurring *topos* in which the adapters present themselves is of having 'made' a play, preserving or salvaging a few precious parts from the jumble of Shakespeare's invention. Shadwell recommends his adaptation of *Timon of Athens* (1678), 'since it has the inimitable hand of *Shakespeare* in it, which never made more Masterly strokes than in this. Yet I can truly say, I have made it into a Play' – and indeed, the title proudly announces *The History of Timon of Athens, the Man-Hater ... Made into a Play* (*SCH*, vol. 1, pp. 204ff.). Dryden attaches his version of the Antony and Cleopatra story to Shakespeare's, tactfully dividing the credit: 'I hope I may affirm, and without vanity, that by imitating him, I have excell'd my self throughout the Play' (*SCH*, vol. 1, p. 165). With *Troilus and Cressida*, once again, he was more aggressive, listing the defects of the play and then adding with a kind of grudging recognition:

> Yet after all, because the Play was *Shakespeare*'s, and that there appear'd in some places of it, the admirable Genius of the Author; I undertook to remove that heap of Rubbish, under which many excellent thoughts lay wholly bury'd.
>
> (*SCH*, vol. 1, p. 250)

The peculiar Janus-like attitude of the Restoration adapters, idolatry on one side, contempt on the other, appears very strongly in Dryden. A more modest adapter was Thomas Otway, whose version of *Romeo and Juliet*, called *The History and Fall of Caius Marius*, appeared in 1679, and was the model for later adaptations by Theophilus Cibber (1744) and Garrick (1748). In his verse prologue Otway praises Shakespeare's 'Fancy uncon-fin'd', and 'Immortal Thoughts', which 'succeeding Poets humbly glean'. Otway, 'this-day's Poet', sets his own work in the inferior place, for once:

> You'll find h' has rifled him of half a Play.
> Amidst this baser Dross you'll see it shine
> Most beautifull, amazing, and Divine.
>
> (*SCH*, vol. 1, p. 296)

Otway is the exception that proves the rule, for all the other adapters con-gratulate themselves on having rejected Shakespeare's dross and reused the good bits to some new and better purpose. A characteristic instance is Edward Ravenscroft's preface to his 1678 adaptation of *Titus Andronicus:*

> I have been told by some anciently conversant with the Stage, that it was not Originally his, but brought by a private Author to be Acted, and he only gave some Master-touches to one or two of the Principal Parts or Characters; this I am apt to believe, because 'tis the most incorrect and indigested piece in all his Works; It seems rather a heap of Rubbish than a Structure. – However, as if some great Building had been design'd, in the removal we found many Large and Square Stones both usefull and Ornamental to the Fabrick, as now Modell'd: Compare the Old Play with this, you'l finde that none in all that Authors Works ever receiv'd greater Alterations or Additions, the Language not only refin'd, but many Scenes entirely New: Besides most of the principal Characters heighten'd, and the Plot much encreas'd.
>
> (*SCH*, vol. 1, p. 239)

What Ravenscroft does not mention is that he has added a peculiarly grue-some on-stage torture-scene, part of the fashionable violence in Restoration tragedy (*SCH*, vol. 1, pp. 7, 239–48). Perhaps because of this attraction, the piece 'is confirm'd a Stock-Play', that is, part of the standard repertoire, he records with satisfaction. Evidently he had found how to please the audience.

The most successful of the early adapters, Nahum Tate, certainly knew how to please, with his mixture of violence, pathos, and sentiment. His first adaptation, *Richard II* (1680), ran into difficulty with the censors, and might have been 'buried in Oblivion', he explains in the Preface, 'had it drawn its Being from me Alone; but it still retains the immortal spirit of its first-Father' (*SCH*, vol. 1, p. 321). Tate records that he 'fell upon the new-modelling of this Tragedy ... charm'd with the many Beauties I discover'd in it' (*SCH*, vol. 1, p. 322), and has preserved in his version 'some Master Touches of our *Shakespeare* that will vie with the best Roman Poets' (p. 325). What Tate did, of course, was to wholly remodel the play, starting from the premiss declared by Thomas Rymer that Kings 'are always in Poetry presum'd Heroes' (*SCH*, vol. 1, pp. 191, 323), thus turning Richard II into 'an Active, Prudent Prince', in order to engage the audience's pity for him in his fall. For *King Lear*, produced in 1681, Tate was even more drastic, omitting the Fool altogether, keeping Lear and Cordelia alive at the end, and marrying Cordelia to Edgar. Only his 'Zeal for all the Remains of *Shakespeare*', he claims, 'cou'd have wrought me to so bold an Undertaking' as 'the New-modelling of this Story'. While praising '*Lear*'s real, and *Edgar*'s pretended Madness' – for having 'so much of extravagant *Nature* ... as cou'd never have started but from our *Shakespeare*'s Creating fancy' (generous tribute indeed) he nevertheless denies the play any unity or coherence: 'I found the whole ... a Heap of Jewels, unstrung and unpolisht; yet so dazling in their Disorder, that I soon perceiv'd I had seiz'd a Treasure' (*SCH*, vol. 1, p. 344).

The love-affair between Edgar and Cordelia that he writes into the play is the 'one Expedient to rectifie what was wanting in the Regularity and Prob-ability of the Tale', while the end, concluding in 'a Success to the innocent distrest Persons', satisfies poetic justice and avoids the fault of cluttering the stage with dead bodies (*SCH*, vol. 1, p. 345). The accuracy with which Tate gauged theatrical taste is seen from the remarkable fact that his adaptation held the stage until Macready's production of 1838. Less successful was his version of *Coriolanus* (1682), perhaps because he was more deferential to Shakespeare: 'Much of what is offered here is Fruit that grew in the Richness of his Soil; and whatever the Superstructure prove, it was my good fortune to build upon a Rock' (*SCH*, vol. 1, pp. 386–7). A rock, a heap of rubbish, a pile of jewels – the metaphors can be varied indefinitely according to the adapter's needs.

The pattern established in this first period of Shakespeare alterations was to persist. The theatrical success of the plays, Shakespeare's impact on public sensibility, is now integrally bound up with the revisers' 'new-modelling'. There are exceptions, plays which seem to have been accepted as they were apart from stage cuts – *Othello, 1* and *2 Henry IV, Julius Caesar, Hamlet,* – but many of the most popular and frequently performed plays were irrevocably altered, often to the point where actors and audience were unaware that they were not experiencing Shakespeare pure. George Granville, Baron Lansdowne, produced *The Jew of Venice* in 1701, a version that held the stage until 1741, when Charles Macklin revived the original. When told that Macklin was now playing Shylock as written by Shakespeare, an actor who only knew the alteration asked 'What, haven't I been acting Shakespeare?'[8] While some dissentient voices were heard, the Restoration adaptations continued to be performed, and praised (*SCH*, vol. 2, pp. 12–13). They were emulated, too, sometimes with more scrupulous attention to the original text. Colley Cibber's *Richard III* (1699/1700) prints the lines that are 'intirely *Shakespeare*'s' in italic, adding an apostrophe before lines that 'are generally his thoughts, in the best dress I could afford 'em'. In the passages of his own composition, Cibber writes, 'I have done my best to imitate his Style and manner of thinking' (*SCH*, vol. 2, p. 102). Cibber succeeded with his pastiche, the play holding the stage until the nineteenth century, few theatre-goers, and few of those who saw Laurence Olivier's film version (1955), being aware of the difference. Granville, too, in his version of *The Merchant of Venice*, unwilling that anything 'be imputed to *Shakespeare* which may seem unworthy of him', marked with an apostrophe those lines 'added to make good the Connexion where there was a necessity to leave out; in which all imaginable Care has been taken to imitate the same fashion of Period and turn of Stile and Thought with the Original' (*SCH*, vol. 2, p. 149). Yet these were only passing concerns with authenticity. Granville added a notorious banquet, in which Shylock is made to drink to his mistress – money, and followed several predecessors in inserting a musical show, the masque of Peleus and Thetis (*SCH*, vol. 2, pp. 151–8). To add insult to injury, the prologue provided by Bevill Higgons brings on the ghosts of Shakespeare and Dryden, crowned with laurel, and makes the original author praise his adapter:

> These Scenes in their rough Native Dress were mine,
> But now improv'd with nobler Lustre shine;
> The first rude Sketches *Shakespeare*'s Pencil drew,
> But all the shining Master stroaks are new.

The play has now been 'Adorn'd and rescu'd by a faultless Hand' (*SCH*, vol. 2, p. 151), unembarrassed, evidently, by the hyperboles heaped on it.

The third generation of Shakespeare adapters (D'Avenant was born in 1606, Dryden in 1631, Otway and Tate in 1652, Dennis in 1657, Cibber in 1671, Theobald in 1688) continued in the same mode as their predecessors.

In the prologue to his version of *Coriolanus* (1719) John Dennis repeats the 'chaos reduced to order' *topos:*

> The Tragedy we represent to Day
> Is but a Grafting upon *Shakespeare*'s Play,
> In whose Original we may descry
> Where Master-strokes in wild Confusion lye;
> Here brought to as much Order as we can
> Reduce those Beauties upon *Shakespeare*'s Plan.

'*Shakespeare*'s Beauties' represent Nature, not Art, writes Dennis (*SCH*, vol. 2, p. 329), echoing Ben Jonson before going on to quote Milton on 'Fancy's sweetest Child'. As this little detail shows, the basic tradition in Shakespeare criticism was unchanged for two centuries. Lewis Theobald, introducing his version of *Richard II* (1719), continues the posture of Dryden or Tate. 'The many scatter'd Beauties which I have long admir'd [in the play] induced me to think they would have stronger Charms if they were interwoven in a regular Fable. For this Purpose, I have made some Innovations upon History and *Shakespeare*', claiming the poet's 'discretionary Power of Variation, either for maintaining the *Unity of Action,* or supporting the *Dignity* of the *Characters*' (*SCH*, vol. 2, pp. 352–3). Once again, Shakespeare is deemed unable to write a unified play, unable to tell the difference between his own good bits and his rubbish. As Theobald puts it in the Prologue,

> Immortal *Shakespeare* on this Tale began,
> And wrote it in a rude, Historick Plan,
> On his rich Fund our Author builds his Play,
> Keeps all his Gold, and throws his Dross away. ...
>
> (*SCH*, vol. 2, pp. 356–7)

Evidently the fund of metaphors, and motives, is limited, for the same combinations crop up again and again.

In his version of *Henry V* (1723), Aaron Hill makes the statutory praise of 'the inimitable and immortal *Shakespeare*', describing his own play as 'a *New Fabrick*, yet built on *His* Foundation'. In verse he begins with the 'ruins' *topos:*

> From Wit's old Ruins, shadow'd o'er with Bays,
> We draw some rich Remains of *Shakespeare*'s Praise.

But he then originates a new metaphor, describing how he kept 'the fiery Pillar' of his original before him:

> Led by such Light as wou'd not *let* him *stray,*
> He pick'd out *Stars* from *Shakespeare*'s milky Way
>
> (*SCH*, vol. 2, pp. 373–4)

Once again the adapter takes credit for selecting the good bits. The resulting

play, apart from adding a love-triangle, is anti-French, a chauvinistic application of Shakespeare made even more crudely by Colley Cibber in his
adaptation of *King John* (1745), which is anti-Catholic and xenophobic in
the extreme (*SCH*, vol. 3, pp. 135–45). Cibber, more modest than Shadwell,
tried 'to make it more like a Play than what I found it' (*SCH*, vol. 3, p. 136).
The result shows that to a striking degree Cibber, like Hill and Theobald,
in intensifying the emotional level, recreates the style of Tate or Otway.
Homogeneity of taste seems to go along with homogeneity of expressive
resources.

The mid-eighteenth century sees a steady rise in Shakespeare's popularity.
Thanks to the statistics meticulously documented and analysed in *The London
Stage*,[9] we can compute what proportion of performances in the London
theatre were of Shakespeare's plays. Arthur H. Scouten[10] has produced the
following estimates:

1703–10:	11 per cent
1710–17:	14 per cent
1717–23:	17 per cent (but with low attendance)
1723–34:	12 per cent
1735–6:	14 per cent
1736–7:	17 per cent
1737–8:	22 per cent
1740–1:	25 per cent

As Professor Scouten has shown, a number of factors affected the sudden
increase in Shakespeare performances in the mid 1730s: the popularity of *The
Beggar's Opera* and *The Provoked Husband* in 1728, causing an increase of
the theatre companies from two to five; the enterprise of Henry Giffard at
the Goodman's Fields and Lincoln's Inn Fields theatres between 1731 and
1742, in putting on more Shakespeare than the managers at Covent Garden
or Drury Lane, and reviving the originals rather than adaptations; and
a curious pressure group, the Shakespeare Ladies Club, stimulating more
performances from 1736 to 1738 (*SCH*, vol. 3, pp. 11–14). Even when the
Licensing Act of 1737 restricted theatrical companies, the Shakespeare boom
continued, aided in fact by the Act's other provision, the compulsory licensing
of new plays and additions to old plays by the Lord Chamberlain. The
difficulties with censorship led to Shakespeare's plays increasingly becoming
staple fare, vehicles for acting which could be savoured by an audience
nourished on a rather limited diet, familiar enough with the plays to be able
to scrutinize individual performances. Although Giffard revived plays not
acted since the closing of the theatres in 1642, and prompted the other
managers to emulate him, after his disappearance from the scene the repertory
shrank again. At Drury Lane in 1740–1 no less than 44 per cent of the

performances were of Shakespeare. Between 1747 and 1776 about 20 per cent of the performances at Drury Lane were Shakespearian, yet of only nine plays: at Covent Garden in the same period the figures are 16 per cent, but of only eight plays (*SCH*, vol. 4, p. 25).

The energy and enterprise of Henry Giffard attracted outstanding actors as well as audiences. On 14 February 1741 he revived *The Merchant of Venice*, in which Charles Macklin had a great success as Shylock, and at his Goodman's Fields theatre, on 19 October 1741, David Garrick made his début, as Richard III. To Garrick indeed, two centuries of adulation have given the credit for a Shakespeare revival which was well under way before he set foot on a stage.[11] Garrick, the first man to make a fortune in the theatre, succeeded precisely by giving the audience what it wanted: emotional intensity, striking 'attitudes' or postures, spectacle, music, and a complete evening's entertainment in the form of afterpieces, dances, comic acts, and other attractions. He certainly cashed in on the vogue for Shakespeare, and undoubtedly increased the audience for his plays. But it would be wholly false to present him as in any way the 'restorer' of Shakespeare. In all his adaptations, from the 1740s to the 1770s, he expresses the values of D'Avenant, Dryden, Tate, and Shadwell. His *Macbeth* (1744) followed D'Avenant in retaining the dancing witches, omitting the drunken porter, and placing the murder of Lady Macduff and her son off-stage. Where D'Avenant had added one line for Macbeth as he dies, Garricks writes a whole speech for him (*SCH*, vol. 3, pp. 133–4), with the kind of nervous, jerky movements, sentences broken off incomplete, in which he excelled. For *Othello* (1745) he wrote a speech to replace the 'antres vast and deserts idle' of the original, to which Rymer had objected (*SCH*, vol. 3, p. 134). In his adaptation of *Romeo and Juliet* (1748) he expresses the criteria of Dryden, still: the 'Design' of his alterations 'was to clear the Original as much as possible from the Jingle and Quibble which were always thought a great objection to performing it' (*SCH*, vol. 3, p. 333). If resembling Dryden in attitudes to language, for the plot of the play Garrick returns to Otway's device (in 1679) of reviving Juliet before Romeo dies, giving himself as Romeo another chance to writhe about the stage in incoherent sentences and dramatic postures:

> My powers are blasted,
> 'Twixt death and love I'm torn – I am distracted!
> But death's strongest – and must I leave thee, *Juliet*?
> Oh cruel cursed fate! in sight of heav'n –

Here Romeo is evidently raving (with a half-remembered metaphor from Otway):

> She is my wife – our hearts are twin'd together –
> *Capulet*, forbear – *Paris*, loose your hold –

Pull not our heart-strings thus – they crack – they break –
Oh *Juliet!* Juliet!   [*Dies*
(*SCH*, vol. 3, pp. 339–40)

It may be effective in the theatre, or with a certain kind of audience, but the language is banal, the emotions factitiously worked up. What Shakespeare found in his source and rejected (Juliet's revival), Garrick, following Otway and Cibber, makes into an excuse for virtuoso acting. (Compare Otway's relatively restrained final scene (*SCH*, vol. 1, pp. 316–18) with Garrick's emotional orgy.)

By this time Garrick enjoyed a position of eminence that would have enabled him to make the decisive break with the adapters, had he wished. An anonymous critic, writing to him in 1747 concerning his performance as King Lear, complained of 'the Nonsense of the Alteration' in the closing scene, where Tate makes Lear faint.

> You will say the alter'd Play has mark'd it so; to which I answer that it can be no Mitigation of your Fault to plead that Mr. *Nahum Tate* has seduc'd you. Tho' you are not the Principal you are accessary to the Murder, and will be brought in Guilty. How can you keep your Countenance when you come to the *Spheres stopping their Course, the Sun making halt*, and *the Winds bearing on their rosy Wings* that Cordelia *is a Queen?*

Compared with the bathos of Tate's version, 'the last Scene of *Shakespeare*'s *Lear* must shew you to advantage; and I hope it is rather your Idleness than Judgment that makes you persist in the other' (*SCH*, vol. 3, pp. 268–9). A year later Samuel Richardson, in the Postscript to volume 7 of *Clarissa*, complained of the decline in 'Modern Taste' that allowed Tate's version to be acted instead of the original.

> Whether this *strange* preference be owing to the false Delicacy or affected Tenderness of the Players, or to that of the Audience, has not for many years been tried. And perhaps the former have not the courage to try the Public Taste upon it. And yet, if it were *ever* to be tried, *Now* seems to be the Time, when an *Actor* and *Manager* in the *same person*, is in being, who deservedly engages the public favour in all he undertakes, and who owes so much, and is gratefully sensible that he does, to that great Master of the human Passions.

(*SCH*, vol. 3, p. 326)

Yet, although owing much to Shakespeare, Garrick had neither the courage nor the inclination to revive the original. His answer might have been given in his Drury Lane prologue of 1750, which mingles bardolatry: 'Sacred to SHAKESPEARE was this spot design'd,/To pierce the heart, and humanize the mind' – with the claim that his prime concern is to satisfy the audience's taste: 'If want comes on, importance must retreat;/Our first great ruling passion is – to eat,' (*SCH*, vol. 3, pp. 365–6).

When he presented *Lear* at Drury Lane on 28 October 1756, he followed the major changes of Tate: the Fool is omitted, Edgar and Cordelia have their love-affair, and end happily united with Lear. That this is what the public wanted can be seen from the ill fate of George Colman's attempt to remove Tate's alterations in 1768, cutting the love-story yet not having the courage to restore the Fool (*SCH*, vol. 5, pp. 8–9, 294–6). The production failed, after only three performances, the audience not relishing being deprived of the mixture of pathos and sentiment in tragedy that they were used to.

Unmoved by considerations of authenticity, or by Colman's concept of the duty of the theatre director 'to render every drama submitted to the Publick as consistent and rational an entertainment as possible', Garrick went on his way to ever greater success. In his adaptation of *Romeo and Juliet* he had made the Funeral Procession a grand spectacle (*SCH*, vol. 3, pp. 336–7), albeit dismissed by Arthur Murphy, one of the best contemporary critics, as a 'grand raree-show', a 'ridiculous piece of pageantry' (pp. 378–9). So, for *Henry VIII* (1762) Garrick devised an enormous coronation procession, calling for over 154 performers (*SCH*, vol. 4, pp. 468–70), which became a famous crowd-puller. If the result resembles a Cecil B. De Mille spectacular, Garrick can also be credited with the first musical comedy versions of Shakespeare. Reverting to the methods of the operatic versions of *The Tempest* of 1674 (*SCH*, vol. 1, pp. 153ff.) and the *Midsummer Night's Dream* of 1692 (pp. 424ff.), Garrick produced a version of *The Tempest* in 1756 in which the text was cut to shreds to make the briefest possible lead-in to the songs. Garrick defended his practice in some polemical writings, but an ever-growing number of contemporaries expressed their outrage (*SCH*, vol. 4, p. 22–4,, 175–7, 218–28). As for the *Dream*, Garrick and Colman produced three versions of it between 1755 and 1763, with from thirteen to thirty-three songs inserted into what is left of the text, which cuts, variously, either all the clowns or all the lovers.

Garrick was becoming increasingly high-handed in his treatment of Shakespeare, while simultaneously proclaiming his reverence for him. In a double bill presented on 21 January 1756 and with much success for many years after, he managed to compress *The Winter's Tale* and *The Taming of the Shrew* into one symmetrical evening (*Florizel and Perdita* balancing *Catharine and Petruchio*). In his prologue Garrick invokes the neo-classical unity of time to justify what he has left out. Faced with the embarrassing gap of sixteen years between Acts III and IV of the Romance he simply omits Acts I–III, and then declares (like Tate):

> Lest then this precious Liquor run to waste,
> 'Tis now confin'd and bottled for your Taste.

'Tis my chief Wish, my joy, my only Plan,
To lose no *Drop* of that immortal Man!

(*SCH*, vol. 4, p. 209)

The operative word there is 'confin'd'. His critics preferred stronger terms: 'cruelly mangled and unhappily pieced', 'sacrilegiously frittered and befribbled', 'curtailed into a kind of sing-song farce', 'lop'd, hack'd, and dock'd'. As Theophilus Cibber summed it up, in Garrick's hands

> the *Midsummer Night's Dream* has been minc'd and fricasee'd into an indigested and unconnected Thing call'd *The Fairies; The Winter's Tale* mammoc'd into a Droll; *The Taming of the Shrew* made a Farce of; and *The Tempest* castrated into an opera.

(*SCH*, vol. 4, p. 24)

Garrick's success as a theatre-manager derived partly from his fame as an actor and partly from his shrewd awareness of the audience's taste. His ability to gauge their likes and dislikes was triumphantly demonstrated in the Stratford Shakespeare Jubilee of 1769, with its combination of a ball, a firework display, an oratorio, and an elaborate procession of 217 people, 170 of them dressed as Shakespearian characters. When bad weather and a series of mishaps spoiled the Stratford proceedings Garrick simply restaged it in his own theatre as *The Jubilee*, 115 performers re-enacting the events of Stratford with enormous success. It played to full houses seventy-two times in that year and 152 times in three seasons, bringing him a vast profit (*SCH*, vol. 5, pp. 14–15). By the time this jamboree had ceased to draw the crowds Garrick was ready with his last Shakespeare adaptation, the notorious *Hamlet* of 1772.

Garrick had been in France and Italy from 1763 to 1765, and was evidently influenced by French criticism, especially Voltaire's attack on the gravediggers. Garrick's remedy was as drastic as the surgery he had performed on *The Winter's Tale:* 'I have destroyed ye Grave diggers, (those favourites of the people)', he wrote to a French friend, '& almost all of ye 5th Act'. To another correspondent he wrote 'I had sworn I would not leave the stage till I had rescued that noble play from all the rubbish of the 5th act' (*SCH*, vol. 5, pp. 10–11). Garrick cuts most of the play from Act IV, scene v on: of the 1,002 lines remaining from this point in Shakespeare he cuts 898, leaving 104, and adds 37 lines of his own. The grave-diggers and Osric disappear; Hamlet does not leave Denmark; there is no plot against his life; and the catastrophe arises from the quarrel between Hamlet and Laertes over Ophelia's madness (neither Ophelia nor Gertrude dies). Hamlet stabs Claudius, 'runs upon Laertes's sword', yet reconciles Horatio and Laertes before he dies (*SCH*, vol. 5, pp. 460–5). Although the version provoked a parody from Arthur Murphy and sharp criticism from Horace Walpole, it had a favourable reception in the newspapers, albeit largely from writers friendly to Garrick, such as George Steevens (*SCH*, vol. 5, pp. 444–57, 466–86). In the theatre it was a great success, bringing Garrick £3,426 in his remaining four years on stage, box-office takings scarcely equalled by any other play. The manager gave the audience what they liked, and everybody concerned profited. It seems ungracious to protest that the theatre ought to be more than a purely commercial enterprise.

Garrick was the outstanding Shakespearian actor, producer, and adapter of his generation. While he may have helped to make the age 'Shakespeare conscious', his work as an adapter merely perpetuated the tradition of Dryden, D'Avenant, and Tate. He certainly restored some passages of the original texts, but it is desperate special pleading by his modern admirers to claim that his was 'the most accurate' or 'the most complete' *Lear* or *Hamlet*,[12] when he used Tate's adaptation of the former, and took his own scissors to the latter. At times one is tempted to endorse Johnson's reply to Boswell's question whether Garrick had not 'brought Shakespeare into notice?' – 'Sir, to allow that, would be to lampoon the age' (*SCH*, vol. 6, p. 571). Yet Garrick was only the most visible example of an attitude that still prevailed in the theatre. Thomas Sheridan adapted *Coriolanus* in 1754 by the novel expedient of conflating it with James Thomson's original play on the Coriolanus story (1749), thinking that the two pieces

> might mutually assist one another, and each supply the other's wants. *Shakespeare*'s play was purely historical, and had little or no plot. *Thomson*'s plot was regular, but ... wanted business. He thought by blending those a piece might be produced which, tho' not perfect, might furnish great entertainment to, and keep up the attention of an audience. The success it has met with

in both Dublin and London confirmed his expectations. An undoubted contributory factor was Sheridan's painstaking archaeological reconstruction of a Roman Ovation; 'in the military Procession alone', he notes proudly, 'there were an hundred and eighteen persons' (*SCH*, vol. 4, pp. 159–70). The critics attacked 'this motley tragedy', which pounded together 'two things so heterogeneous' (*SCH*, vol. 4, p. 21), yet they had little effect on the theatre-going public, which enjoyed all forms of spectacle: dogs, dancing bears, acrobats.

Throughout this period neo-classicism survived, both as a critical system and as an excuse for adapting Shakespeare. Yet the resulting difficulties are all too clear from the attempts at regularizing the romances. Charles Marsh altered *The Winter's Tale* in 1756, failed to have it performed, and had it printed at his own cost (*SCH*, vol. 4, pp. 229–42). Reviewing it, Tobias Smollett approved his cutting the first 'fifteen years of the tale' in order to remove 'the improbability that shocks the imagination' by violating the unity of time. But, Smollett complains, 'even this improbability he has removed by halves, for the scene is still shifted from one Kingdom to another, and he has concluded the third act in the middle of a scene'. The adapter should have 'suppressed the death of prince *Mamilius*' and the fate of Antigonus, 'which create a confusion of tragedy and comedy and destroy the propriety of the composition; for since the garment of our *British Homer* was to be new cut it might have been reduced entirely to the fashion' (*SCH*, vol. 4, pp. 243–4). Smollett shows no desire to restore the original, nor does he question the practice of adaptation – indeed, it should have been taken farther. In 1759 William Hawkins altered *Cymbeline*, 'one of the most irregular productions' of Shakespeare, announcing that he has 'endeavoured to new-construct almost upon the plan of *Aristotle* himself, in respect of the *unity* of *Time*' (*SCH*, vol. 4, pp. 374–92). His attempt to 'modernize . . . The bard's luxuriant plan' was echoed in the same year by Charles Marsh's adaptation of the same play, which tried 'to amend the *Conduct* of the *Fable* by confining the Scenes at least to this Island' (*SCH*, vol. 4, pp. 393–9). Reviewing the two versions, William Kenrick praised Hawkins for retrenching the play's superfluities, removing its main defects, so that 'out of a parcel of loose incoherent scenes we have the pleasure of seeing composed a beautiful and correct piece of dramatic poesy' (*SCH*, vol. 4, pp. 400–1). If that metaphor recalls the *topos* of the Restoration adapters, Benjamin Victor varies the trope in justifying his version of *The Two Gentlemen of Verona* in 1762, a comedy that 'abounds with weeds' but also 'several poetical flowers'. While retaining the latter he has also attempted 'to give a greater uniformity to the scenery and a con-nection and consistency to the fable' (*SCH*, vol. 4, pp. 525–33).

While most adapters, like the majority of eighteenth-century critics, hold to the tenets of neo-classicism, occasionally we find a newer emphasis. So Richard Cumberland's *Timon of Athens* (1771) cuts Apemantus' part dras-tically, and – incredible though it may seem – removes Timon's misanthropy, making him an aged figure whose daughter loves Alcibiades. Cumberland restores Timon's losses to him, so defeating the whole point of the play, yet gratuitously brings about his death in order to indulge pathetic sensibilities to the utmost (*SCH*, vol. 5, pp. 9–10, 423–31) – this is, after all, the year of *The Man of Feeling*. The lachrymose death-scene, with the girl's laments, may represent the new *tendresse*, but it is strikingly similar to the last scene of Tate's *Coriolanus* (1682), in which Virgilia comes on wounded to die on stage, as does Coriolanus' son and then the hero himself, all plangent in their agonies (*SCH*, vol. 1, pp. 402–6). As one reads through the adaptations of the tragedies stretching across 150 years, it is as if time stands still.

One reason for the remarkable homogeneity of style and feeling in sen-timental tragedy from Otway and Tate to Cumberland is that many of the most performed plays throughout the whole of the eighteenth century were, in fact, Restoration tragedies or the Restoration adaptations of Shakespeare. Between 1747 and 1776 about 20 per cent of performances at Drury Lane, and 16 per cent at Covent Garden, were of Shakespeare. Of the most popular tragedies, five were Shakespeare's: *Romeo and Juliet, Hamlet, King Lear, Macbeth,* and *Othello.* The box-office success of Shakespeare, and the con- servative tendencies of the two theatres after the Licensing Act, led to a paucity of new drama. The most popular tragedies after Shakespeare at Drury Lane were Congreve, *The Mourning Bride* (1697); Otway, *The Orphan* (1680) and *Venice Preserved* (1682); Rowe, *The Fair Penitent* (1703) and *Jane Shore* (1714); and Aaron Hill, *Zara* (1736). At Covent Garden *Jane Shore* was the most popular, followed by Nat Lee's *Alexander the Great* (1677) and *Theodosius* (1680); Ambrose Phillips, *The Distrest Mother* (1712); and Henry Jones, *The Earl of Essex* (1753). Of the twenty most popular tragedies in London in the 1770s, then, only one had been written in the previous two decades, Jones's *Earl of Essex* (and there had been a version of that story by John Banks in 1681). Given that the Dryden–D'Avenant *Tempest,* Tate's *Lear,* Cibber's *Richard III,* and the Otway–Garrick *Romeo* held the boards, it can be said that in a very real sense the taste of most eighteenth-century theatre-goers had been formed by plays written between 1660 and 1700.

Recognition of this fact may go a long way to answer the question that every student of this topic must have asked at some point, why the adaptations continued to be made along the same lines and with the same success. Since the form, style, and feeling of the drama had been fixed by a mixture of neo- classical theory and an explicit desire for pathos, violence, and clearly-marked emotional attitudes, the adaptations of Shakespeare made his plays conform to audience expectations, bringing them in line with the other successes of the day. Of the ten non-Shakespearian tragedies listed in the last paragraph, the London theatre-goer today may expect to see one, Otway's *Venice Pre- served,* once in a decade perhaps, but is very unlikely ever to see the others. If we wanted to recreate the context for Tate, D'Avenant, Cibber, Garrick, and the rest, we might reconstruct the Drury Lane season for 1765, say, and put them side by side with Lee, Congreve, and Rowe. While these continued in popularity, so did the adaptations, indeed few other fresh movements arose to challenge them (the comedies of Goldsmith and Sheridan notwith- standing). When the young John Philip Kemble put on *The Tempest* in 1789 he actually *restored* much of the Dryden–D'Avenant text, with further alterations of his own, many of them operatic. His *Coriolanus* of that year was severely cut, but eked out with passages from Thomson's 1749 version. For Kemble Thomas Hall produced a *Timon of Athens* in 1786 which revived much of Shadwell's version (1678). Kemble restored almost all of Tate's *King Lear* in 1809, and brought back Cibber's *Richard III* in 1811.[13] The audiences loved them, although the critics did not. The wheel had come full circle.

Taking stock of this remarkable phenomenon, two final points need to be made. One is the ineffectualness of adverse criticism on the running of the theatres. The theatre world seemed to obey its own rules, ignoring critical comment, indeed – especially in Garrick's hands – learning how to control newspapers and plant its own 'puffs', laudatory reviews and notices. In the six *Shakespeare: the Critical Heritage* volumes I have included many texts attacking the adaptations, and one can trace a consistent vein of protest from John Oldmixon in 1700 (vol. 2, pp. 12–13, 145–6) to George Steevens in 1779 (vol. 6, pp. 204–7), and others after him. This last essay, indeed, is outstanding for the breadth of its documentation and its critical acumen. Yet none of these writers had any effect on the theatre. So far as one can tell, no adapter or actor or manager was deterred from putting on an alteration by adverse criticism. And, of course, one could compile an equally long list of essays praising the adaptations, especially Tate's *Lear*, for removing blemishes, violations of the unities, indecorum, puns, or other faults of language, thus preserving Shakespeare's gold. In our own time, still, apologists for the adapters think that they did a good job. Christopher Spencer praises Cibber and Granville for removing 'quantities of unnecessary material' from *Richard III* and *The Merchant of Venice*. He believes that D'Avenant and Dryden actually improved the plot structure of *The Tempest;* and that Tate was right to omit Lear's fool (*SCH*, vol. 1, p. 10). G. W. Stone, Jr, approves of Garrick having cut the 'combined palaver of the grave diggers, Hamlet, and Horatio' (*SCH*, vol. 5, p. 45, note 25), and for having made 'an effective play'.

Those who believe in the high and serious calling of literary criticism will be disappointed that so many intelligent men and women who cared about Shakespeare and the drama failed to stop the 'new-modelling' of his plays. But the force of theatrical tradition and theatrical conservatism, the homogeneity of taste, were all too strong. One unfortunate effect of this failure of the critic was to create a gap between the stage and the study. The Shakespeare of the English Romantics, Keats, Coleridge, Hazlitt, Lamb – the greatest constellation of creative writers to become Shakespeare critics in one generation – was experienced in the study, not in the theatre. They made marginalia in their own and others' copies of the plays, wrote their essays, but they worked from books, not from the stage. In extreme cases, such as Charles Lamb, they could actually state that 'the plays of Shakespeare are less calculated for performance on a stage than those of almost any other dramatist whatever'.[14] As one studies the nature of the London theatres at this time many factors seem to militate against a successful production of Shakespeare, starting with the size of the auditoria. The two theatre-managers had a monopoly over serious drama in London, and in order to maximize their profit they enlarged the buildings. Garrick enlarged Drury Lane in 1775, until it could hold about 2,300 spectators; in 1794 it was enlarged again to seat 3,600, while Covent Garden was rebuilt in 1792 to hold 3,013. In the process the acoustics were ruined; spectators found it hard to hear the dialogue, so that spectacle, 'song and show', were the only things that could be put over in a form that the audience could actually experience (*SCH*, vol. 6, p. 63). The acting became cruder, inevitably so perhaps, in such vast halls.

The second point to be underlined has been touched on a number of times, the fact that the ultimate judge, not only of what Shakespeare wrote but of what he ought to have written, was the audience. In his Prologue for the opening of the Drury Lane Theatre in 1747 (spoken by Garrick), Dr Johnson declared:

> The Stage but echoes back the publick Voice.
> The Drama's Laws the Drama's Patrons give,
> For we that live to please, must please to live.[15]

As is well known, Johnson believed that with the drama, as with other forms of literature, 'no other test can be applied than length of duration and continuance of esteem' (*SCH*, vol. 5, p. 56). The ultimate judge of excellence is the reading public, and in drama, Johnson seems to believe, the demands of the audience play the crucial role. So, discussing Tate's version of *Lear*, with its restoration of poetic justice by the preservation of Cordelia's innocent life, he reviewed the critical controversy yet concluded: 'In the present case the publick has decided. *Cordelia*, from the time of *Tate*, has always retired with victory and felicity' (*SCH*, vol. 5, pp. 139–40). George Steevens disagreed: 'Dr Johnson should rather have said that the managers of the theatres-royal have decided, and the public has been obliged to acquiesce in their decision. The altered play has the upper gallery on its side – ', while a correspondent to the *Morning Chronicle* signing himself J. R. (?Joseph Ritson), could not decide whether 'the manager, or the town' were to blame (*SCH*, vol. 6, p. 59). Perhaps one should speak of a mutual agreement between the public and the managers on this issue, but elsewhere there is clear evidence of the power of the audience. They could riot over increased admission prices, and close the theatres for sixty-six days, as they did in 1809 at the opening of Covent Garden, rebuilt after a fire.[16] They could destroy performances, were noisy, inattentive, talked throughout, made assignations, and preferred songs, dances, and divertissements.[17]

Above all, the conservatism of the audience could affect the repertoire by their attendance or non-attendance, and they could even affect the text of plays. Thomas Davies records how Garrick tried to restore the rebel's council scene in *1 Henry IV*, traditionally cut, but that 'after the first or second night's acting, finding that it produced no effect, he consented to omit it.' The audience was the arbiter of taste, and its taste was conservative. Davies also records that the experiment was made of restoring the hypocritical fainting of Lady Macbeth in performance:

> but, however characteristical such behaviour might be, persons of a certain class were so merry upon the occasion that it was not thought proper to venture the Lady's appearance any more. Mr. Garrick thought that even

so favourite an actress as Mrs. Pritchard would not, in that situation, escape derision from the gentlemen in the upper regions.

The audience could only have been induced 'to endure the hypocrisy of Lady Macbeth' by some outstanding performance: otherwise, actors and managers had to bow to the wishes of the gallery. It is recorded as one of the innovations of Mrs Siddons, when she first acted Lady Macbeth, that she put down the candle she carried during the sleepwalking scene, in order to perform properly the business of washing her hands. This was such a great departure from tradition that the manager tried to persuade her not to do it, but she persisted, and ultimately established this sensible action (*SCH*, vol. 6, pp. 62–3).

Perhaps modern *Rezeptionsgeschichte* has already documented the innately conservative tendency of the audience in any age. It is not so different in our own time. The current composition of the theatre programmes in London and New York favour above all musicals and comedies; even the English subsidized companies, the National and the Royal Shakespeare, who do not need to compete in this way, have put on musicals. Everyone wants to be loved, and theatre managements are no exception. Yet their duty lies, has always lain, elsewhere. The story is told of Lord Reith, first great director of the BBC, that when someone said that they supposed his job was to give the public what it wanted, he replied, 'No, that is precisely not our job! If you did that, it would be disastrous.' Or, as Arthur Murphy wrote of the theatre-managers' duty to present the classics, 'it is in their power, by reviving Shakespeare and Otway, Congreve, and Vanbrugh, to shew that they are above the mere traffic, and scorn to keep a mushroom-bed for the production of trash not fit to be brought to market' (*SCH*, vol. 6, p. 636). As we read through the history of Shakespeare's adaptation for the English stage over this long period we look in vain for someone with an artistic conviction strong enough to challenge the audience's preferred entertainments, and to bring them to appreciate something better. Dr Johnson said that 'he who refines the public taste is a public benefactor'. Henry Giffard had done so for a short while in the 1730s and 1740s, reviving Shakespeare plays that had not been performed in London for over a century, and restoring some original versions. The combination of the Licensing Act and the two patent theatres blocked Giffard's attempts. It was not until the courageous partial revival of the original *King Lear* by William Macready at Covent Garden on 25 January 1838, 'freed from the interpolations which have disgraced it for nearly two centuries', and the even more courageous work of Samuel Phelps at Sadler's Wells from 1843 onwards[18], that Shakespeare's true image could be seen again in the English theatre. Macready, a contemporary reviewer said, had made 'certain sacrifices to the supposed taste of his audience', but Phelps, restoring the Fool, has shown 'a more lively faith in the power of Shakespeare'.

Notes

1 David Lodge, *The Novelist at the Crossroads* (London, 1971), p. 46.
2 The most useful bibliography is in G. C. Branam, *Eighteenth Century Adaptations of Shakespearian Tragedy* (Berkeley, Calif., 1956). For other details, excerpts, and critical commentary, see Brian Vickers (ed.), *Shakespeare: the Critical Heritage. Volume 1, 1623–1692* (London and Boston, 1974); *Volume 2, 1693–1733* (London, 1974); *Volume 3, 1733–1752* (London, 1975); *Volume 4, 1753–1765* (London, 1976); *Volume 5, 1765–1774* (London, 1979); *Volume 6, 1774–1801* (London, 1981).
3 See Winton Dean's essay in Phyllis Hartnoll (ed.) *Shakespeare in Music* (London, 1964), and Peter Raby, *Fair Ophelia: Harriet Smithson Berlioz* (Cambridge, 1982).
4 Quotations are taken for the most part from Vickers, *Shakespeare: the Critical Heritage*. References will be given in the text in the form *SCH*, vol. 1, p. 4, etc.
  Evelyn's claim that he actually saw *Hamlet* on 26 November 1661 needs to be viewed with scepticism. As Esmond De Beer showed in his epochal edition of *The Diary of John Evelyn*, 6 vols (Oxford, 1955), the main manuscript consists, in the earlier part, of free copies of original notes that Evelyn made in the margins of almanacs or transcribed from newspapers, printed books, or other sources. It is only from about 1680 that the *Diary* was maintained contemporaneously with the events it records, and De Beer thinks that the reference to *Hamlet* may derive from Dryden (*Diary*, vol. I, pp. 69–114). (I am grateful to Professor Arthur H. Scouten for alerting me to this fact.)
5 See Gunnar Sorelius, *'The Giant Race Before The Flood'. Pre-Restoration Drama on the Stage and in the Criticism of the Restoration* (Uppsala, 1966), pp. 71–4.
6 Hazelton Spencer, *Shakespeare Improved. The Restoration Versions in Quarto and on the Stage* (Cambridge, Mass., 1927), pp. 178ff. The recent work of his namesake Christopher Spencer, although scholarly in its editing, takes upon itself to defend the Restoration adapters and suggest that they knew more about drama, and poetry, than Shakespeare: see my comments (*Shakespeare: the Critical Heritage*, vol. 1., p. 10).
7 See Lothar Hönnighausen, *Der Stilwandel im dramatischen Werk Sir William Davenants* (Köln, 1965), pp. 14–44, also Mongi Raddadi, *Davenant's Adaptations of Shakespeare* (Uppsala, 1979), especially chapter 2 'The language', pp. 49–78.
8 See G. C. D. Odell, *Shakespeare, from Betterton to Irving,* 2 vols (New York, 1920), vol. 1, pp. 76–9, 260–2.
9 W. van Lennep, E. L. Avery, A. H. Scouten, G. W. Stone, Jr, and C. B. Hogan (eds) *The London Stage, 1660–1800*, 11 vols (Carbondale, Ill., 1960–8). See also C. B. Hogan, *Shakespeare in the Theatre*, 2 vols (Oxford, 1952).
10 Arthur H. Scouten, 'Shakespeare's plays in the theatrical repertory when Garrick came to London', *Studies in English* (Austin, Texas, 1945), pp. 257–68; 'The increase in popularity of Shakespeare's plays in the eighteenth century: a caveat', *Shakespeare Quarterly* 7 (1956): 189–202; and 'The Shakespearean Revival', in van Lennep *et al.*, *The London Stage, 1729–1747.*, vol. 1, pp. cxlixff. and *passim*.
11 I have given a fresh evaluation of Garrick's relations to Shakespeare in my introductions: *Shakespeare: the Critical Heritage*, vol. 4, pp. 17–29; vol. 5, pp. 10–17; vol. 6, pp. 60–2. The uncritical, indeed anti-critical, adulation of Garrick has been furthered in our day notably by the work of two scholars who have performed valuable services, otherwise, to theatrical studies, G. W. Stone, Jr and George Kahrl. It is most regrettable that in their hagiographical *David Garrick: A Critical Biography* (Carbondale, Ill., 1979) and elsewhere they have seen fit to ignore the work of A. H. Scouten and others who have questioned their hero's supremacy. Such dishonesty, however, is ultimately self-defeating, suggesting, as it does, that they are unable to answer the case against him.

12 See, e.g., Vickers, *Shakespeare: the Critical Heritage*, vol. 4, pp. 20–1 (Hogan's claim for his *Lear*), and vol. 5, p. 45, notes 25 (G. W. Stone's claim for Garrick's 'care for the text' in *Hamlet*) and 27 (similar claims by the editors of Garrick's *Letters*).

13 See Vickers, *Shakespeare: the Critical Heritage*, vol. 6, pp. 60 and 83, notes 130, 131; Odell, *Shakespeare*, vol. 2, pp. 55–60.

14 Lamb, 'On the tragedies of Shakespeare, considered with reference to their fitness for stage representation', in *The Reflector* (1811); repr. in D. N. Smith (ed.) *Shakespeare Criticism. A Selection, 1623–1840* (Oxford, 1916; 1958 edn), p. 193.

15 Johnson, *The Complete English Poems*, ed. J. D. Fleeman (Harmondsworth, Middlesex, 1971), p. 82.

16 Odell, *Shakespeare*, vol. 2, pp. 10–11.

17 See, e.g., Hogan, *The London Stage, 1776–1800*, vol. 1, pp. lii, lxxvi, cvii, clii, clxxix, cxcv–ccvi, and *passim*.

18 Odell, *Shakespeare*, vol. 2, pp. 193–7, 272–3.

7

Shakespeare, 'a national asset'

The idea of founding a Shakespeare Library in Birmingham[1] came to George Dawson, president of the Birmingham Shakespeare Club, in 1861. His plan was that it

> should contain (as far as practicable) every edition and every translation of Shakespeare; all the commentators, good, bad and indifferent; in short, every book connected with the life and works of our great poet. I would add portraits of Shakespeare, and all the pictures, etc., illustrative of his works.[2]

The first collection of books and money was handed over to the Birmingham Free Libraries Committee in 1864 and the library actually opened its doors in 1868.

It survived two early setbacks. The first was the fire in 1879 which virtually destroyed the entire collection of 7,000 volumes. Second was the failure, in 1889, to take up the offer of the library of J. O. Halliwell-Phillipps for £7,000 (there were legal difficulties). The library still possesses newspaper cuttings of the offer (see call no. 100 318) but the collection itself was bought by an American and subsequently passed to the Folger Shakespeare Library, Washington, DC.

Since those days it has grown steadily, indeed so fast that published catalogues could not keep up with it. This *Shakespeare Bibliography*, as it calls itself, reproduces the library catalogue photographically, and its division into two parts reflects the changeover in 1932 from 'a guard book catalogue in typescript with a page width of twelve inches' to the standard library-card system. There are obvious disadvantages to the user in having to look up every topic in two different places, but the cost of retyping the old catalogue would have been prohibitive. And in effect reading through the catalogue, one distinguishes a homogeneity in the earlier part, still mainly pre-modern in its approach to Shakespeare.

The size of the two parts reflects the extravagant boom in publications about Shakespeare which, starting in the mid-nineteenth century, now seems unlikely to decline. Part Two reproduces its library cards with two columns per page: the output in the thirty-six years since 1932, then, allowing for the subsequent acquisition of items printed before that date, is perhaps three times as great as that of the preceding century. The total number of items catalogued exceeds 100,000 and includes material in eighty-five languages. Of *Collected Works* the library possesses over 800 dating from the nineteenth century: the librarian of the Shakespeare Library, Mrs Waveney R. N. Frederick, computes that this represents a new edition of the *Works* every six weeks or so. So far this century has produced less than half that amount, although doubtless we have made up for it in the issue of single plays, especially in paperback.

As a repository of Shakespeare books Birmingham has only one rival, the Folger Library. The two are, happily, complementary, since the Folger's resources have been devoted largely to the English Renaissance (although going both backwards to medieval and onwards to eighteenth-century books) and its holdings of nineteenth- and twentieth-century Shakespeariana are modest. Birmingham possesses all four Folios and some of the Quartos but its coverage of Renaissance books outside Shakespeare is, by contrast, slight, and even its eighteenth-century section of Shakespeariana has many gaps. Its great glory is the comprehensiveness of its collection since the early nineteenth century, and although we quail at the thought of over 25,000 volumes in English alone, and although we may query some choices (was it necessary to have so many *hundred* copies of *Lamb's Tales from Shakespeare*?), study of the English material listed here establishes the surprising usefulness of this collection to historians of our society and culture.

'He was the man who of all Modern, and perhaps Ancient Poets, had the largest and most comprehensive soul. All the Images of Nature were still present to him.'[3] Dryden's panegyric only begins to take on meaning when we review the range of occupations ascribed to Shakespeare, the substantiality of his accomplishments: Shakespeare the churchman, Shakespeare the communist, Shakespeare the builder; he is – successively or simultaneously – physician, angler, seaman, stamp-collector; he is called to the bar; 'did he', a writer in *The Catholic World* for 1932 asks us, 'murder his father?' When not thrust into the professions he is submitted to medical examination: his portrait is considered phrenologically (1864) and 'anthropologically' (1914); his signatures are used to illustrate the effect on handwriting of the nervous diseases he apparently suffered from (1925); his insomnia and its causes are plotted (1886), his sense of hearing estimated in relation to his use of mental emotions and dramatic incident (1888).

As universal polymath he is cited as an authority on all topics: bowls, boors, piscine lore, intermittent fever, consumption (from *The British Journal of Tuberculosis*), drink and drinking-vessels, temperance, wallpaper, artisans, zoology, biology, precious stones, economics, astronomy, pharmacy, toads, cloudscapes, orchards, insects, perfumes, night-life ('from Norman curfew to the present black-out'), paediatrics, beds, dentistry, marigolds, hygiene, meteorology, dogs, bee-keeping, swimming, leather, sheep-shearing, noses, twins and twinning, Sunday, and laterality ('right- or left-handedness'). His knowledge of local dialects is attested by men from Essex, Warwickshire, the Cotswolds, the Midlands, and the northern and Border counties. Bath claims him for its own; so does Norwich; while some wag in Swansea in 1914 issues a pamphlet called 'Shakespeare on Swansea men and matters'.

As knowledge advances Shakespeare is revalued. This is nowhere more visible than in the development of those confident diagnoses of madness or psychological imbalance from the early nineteenth century onwards, in which his characters are rescrutinized and relabelled with the current illness. The form sheet would look something like this:

1824	Hamlet and Ophelia: mania, melancholia, and craziness
1829	Lear and Edgar: mania and demomania
1880	Othello: epilepsy
1917	Hamlet: hysteria
1920	Lady Macbeth: hysteria
1921	Shylock: anal eroticism
1934	Timon: syphilis
1942	Hamlet: the Ganser state
1944–6	Lear: narcissism

In 1960, it will be remembered, John Broadbent classified Viola as her-maphrodite, and diagnosed Cordelia's attraction for Lear as incestuous.[4] What exactly the *International Journal of Psycho-Analysis* for 1928 made of the graveyard scene in *Hamlet* must be left to readers to ascertain.

If Shakespeare has been all things to all men ('a Tory and a Gentleman' to *Blackwoods* in 1828: contrast an article in *The Millgate* for 1944 called 'A Socialist opens his Shakespeare') this has had its less pleasant sides. In both world wars Shakespeare was called in to help our troops, and an interesting study might be made of just how he was shaped to this role. The tercentenary of his death, celebrated in 1916 (which was also the 500th anniversary of Agincourt, a conjunction whose significance was not missed), released much military propaganda. Excerpts from his plays were arranged 'with topical allusions'; the *Guardian* published a sermon on the theme 'Shakespeare a gift from God'; the *British Empire YMCA Weekly* did its 'Shakespeare's men and the modern soldier' bit; the *Times* issued broadsheets for soldiers and sailors reprinting selected passages, designed no doubt to stiffen the sinews and summon up the blood. All this was repeated in 1939–45, but what surprises now is the calibre of those involved. E. M. Forster writes the third of the Macmillan War Pamphlets (1940) with the title *Nordic Twilight*, which the library catalogue helpfully glosses as concerning "the Nazis and culture.

With references to Shakespeare'. Professor G. B. Harrison gives a radio talk in 1943 on 'Shakespeare and the Nazis'; Professor G. Wilson Knight publishes an anthology entitled *This Sceptred Isle: Shakespeare's Message for England at War*. In 1941 J. Freeman (*the* J. Freeman?) publishes another anthology, called *The Englishman at War* with excerpts from Shakespeare; while at Cambridge, in 1943, a pamphlet was published called *The Master Aryans of Nuremberg*, discussing Germany and the Jews, with references to Shakespeare. Perhaps the dramatist who wrote *Henry V* and the ending of *King John* would not have minded being used in these causes. Perhaps it is inevitable, too, that his name should be applied to war more often than to peace.

England has always been grateful to Shakespeare: in 1910 a writer in Manchester accurately described him as 'a national asset'. That gratitude has been expressed in the widest possible forms, and this catalogue bears weighty evidence of the celebrations of 1769, 1816, 1827, 1830, 1836, 1864, 1916, 1923, 1964. In the Victorian/Edwardian period it is impressive to see to what extent these were still popular activities, occasions for banquets and pageants rather than literary exhibitions and *festschriften*. O to have been at the Dudley Shakespeare Commemoration (1899–1909), or at Huddersfield's carousing on Shakespeare's 'Natal Day' in 1884, or at the Crown Hotel, Leamington, in 1874 (the Bill of fare and Toast list are extant, writ in choice French), or the Stourbridge Commemorative Banquets of 1902–3! What would we have given to have been able to go on a ramble with the London Shakespeare League on, say, 12 May 1906? This festive mood produced Shakespearian charades (1851), the Tercentenary Draught Board (1864), the 1864 Shakespearean Tercentenary badge and Medal Ribbon (made in Coventry). The spirit of celebration was not over-reverent, either. After the bardolatry of the late eighteenth century it is refreshing to find a healthy mockery in the many Victorian burlesques (which imply a pretty detailed knowledge of the object of the parody). Who now has read or seen (or could have written) *Hamlet! the Ravin' Prince of Denmark!! or the Baltic Swell!!! and the Diving Belle!!!* (1866) or *Othello: an Interesting Drama, Rather!* [*c*.1850], or *Othello ... Now Published to a Popular Tune as Sung by J. Bannister in his Entertainment Called Bannisters Budget* (*c*.1810)?

Another nineteenth-century vogue which has left us is the Shakespeare Society as a social unit outside schools and colleges, a vogue which was so great that in *c*.1880 *Cassell's Magazine* instructed on 'How to promote a Shakespeare club'. Biggest of all these organizations was the British Empire Shakespeare Society, whose history may yet be written. It seems to have been founded in 1901, and started its *Official Gazette* in 1915, with branches opening throughout the country and abroad – the Dunedin branch was affiliated in 1923, Durban in 1931, Auckland in 1933. The *Gazette* ceased publication 1939, but the branches went on: Enfield to 1946, Bath to 1955, Aberdeen (tenacious folk) to 1956. What did they do? What was BESS for?

From the pages of this catalogue we can follow the Shakespeare urge wherever it expressed itself, at the Mutual Improvement Society of Welford (Leicester) in 1853 or the Cinematograph Exhibitors Association Conference in 1921; from the Positivist Society of London (1885) to the Caliban Committee of Greater Boston (1917); and to publications as improbable as *Oxygen News* (1964) or *The South Metropolitan Gas Company Co-partnership Journal* (1916). One can understand why Typhoo Tea should wish to issue twenty-five picture cards of Shakespeare characters in 1937, and even why Sun Life Assurance should use the 'Seven ages of man' speech for its advertising in 1927; but why on earth would Danish Distillers Ltd wish to subsidize a performance, at Kronborg Castle in 1937, of *Hamlet*, with its description of the Danes' love of drinking: 'This heavy-headed revel east and west/Makes us traduced and taxed of other nations'. Hardly the best advert for alcohol, one would think – unless the actors could be seen drinking a proprietary brand of beer! (Unwary watchers of British commercial TV may be bemused at the sight of the sable-suited prince smoking a panadella cigar named after him.)

Cashing in on Shakespeare, or Stratford, is nothing new. A folding plan from which one can make a model of Anne Hathaway's Cottage is dated *c*. 1830. Victorian popular music did not miss its chance, either. It is time someone revived the As You Like It Polka, the Desdemona Waltz, and the Bard of Avon Quadrilles. For *Macbeth* you have the choice of the Witches Chorus (from 'a juvenile dramatic cantata') or the Macbeth Quadrille (on airs from Verdi), and if you are short of instrumentalists there is always Mendelssohn's wedding march arranged for concertina, flute and cello, say, or Rossini's overture to *Othello* done by two flutes and pianoforte.

Those who have to read library catalogues may be forgiven the occasional outburst of wit (or hysteria as it used to be called). The Library's collection of serious music relating to Shakespeare is truly astonishing. Virtually every well-known piece is there (some exceptions are Berlioz's *Tempest* Fantasia, *Beatrice and Benedick*, his Funeral March for the Last Scene of *Hamlet* and Prokofiev's *Romeo and Juliet*), and there are innumerable forgotten composers.[5] It is scandalous that we do not have recordings of much of Purcell's Shakespeare music – there is not even a satisfactory *Fairy Queen*, not to mention the music to Shadwell's *Timon of Athens*, or the song in Tate's *Richard II*.[6] The music to *Macbeth* (by Locke, or Richard Leveridge) would be welcome. The most famous of the eighteenth-century lyrics have been recorded (twice) but many more ought to be; and of nineteenth-century settings hardly anything exists in print or on record. Of music by modern composers it would be interesting to hear some little-known settings by Elizabeth Maconchy, Bernard Van Dieren, Castelnuovo-Tedesco, Hugo Wolf ('Song of the translated Bottom'!), E. J. Moeran, Sibelius (the clown's epilogue from *Twelfth Night*), William Walton (a song-setting for the 1927 film of *As You Like It*; when will the music he wrote for Gielgud's 1942 *Macbeth* be published?), Lukas Foss, Lennox Berkeley, Virgil Thomson, Samuel Barber,

Michael Tippett, Zoltan Kodaly, and Boris Blacher. One can only admire a library whose tastes are catholic enough to acquire both Haubenstock-Ramati's 'Mobile for Shakespeare' (based on Sonnets 53 and 54) and Salvatore Martirano's 'O,O,O,O, that Shakespeherian Rag' (both published in 1961). Since Shakespeare has been, of all writers, the greatest inspiration to composers, in maintaining this collection the Birmingham Shakespeare Library is performing a unique service to music and letters.

As for recording the history of Shakespeare productions the library has, from the beginning, conceived its function on the grandest scale. The collections of theatre illustrations made by H. R. Forrest (seventy-six folio volumes) or H. S. Pearson (forty volumes) the thirty-seven scrapbooks in the James Turner collection (the library has over 200 scrapbooks in all), fifty-two volumes of playbills, newspaper cuttings from all over the world, and the ongoing acquisition of a record of every Shakespearian production, 'English or Foreign' – these give an idea of Birmingham's implementation of George Dawson's plan. The narrow academic might begrudge the consumption of money and energy in this scheme, but since the world has only three or four adequate collections for the history of the English theatre and most of the materials from the past have perished, then Birmingham should go on – just so long as it has the space.

How and when this material will be fully used is by no means clear, given the universities' lack of interest in theatrical history.[7] To the general reader one immediate and non-scholarly impression is of nostalgia at all these passing shows. 'Mr. Ben Greet announces his fourth annual visit with his London Company of Woodland Players at the Botanical Gardens, Edgbaston, July 2nd–5th, 1890.' Where are they now? The programme of the Worksop College production of the *Dream* in 1912 ('signatures of actors on fly leaf'), the programme of F. R. Benson's company performing scenes from *Richard II* at Flint Castle in 1899.... Benson at least was still active enough to write a synopsis of *King Lear* for a broadcast in 1928. The library chronicles Shakespeare in the cinema (perhaps the first 'book of the film' was Sir J. Forbes-Robertson and Miss Gertrude Elliot's *Hamlet* (1913) – with fifty-five stills), on the radio and television. It is perhaps asking too much that they should acquire every film or broadcast performance of Shakespeare, but given recent revelations about the state of English archives it may be worth considering.

The diffusion of Shakespeare recorded by these volumes is so great that it seems at times the result of an instinctive, spontaneous admiration. But in fact a good deal of planning, propaganda and missionary work lies behind the knowledge of Shakespeare which a majority of English schoolchildren over the last century have acquired, willy-nilly. A kind of deliberate crusade to get Shakespeare established in the schools and in adult education can be followed through from mid-Victorian times. It seems as if the private schools has already broken the ground, for the library possesses an essay (second prize) on Shakespeare's female characters written at St Paul's School and published in 1844; pupils of the City of London School followed suit with a book of essays on *King Lear* in 1851, and the *Noctes Shakespeariane* of Winchester's Shakespeare Society appeared in 1887. Tracts on 'How to Use Shakespeare in School' or 'The Teaching of Shakespeare' appeared regularly from the 1870s onwards, and were consolidated in 1920 by the report of the Board of Education's departmental committee on 'The Teaching of English in England'. The London County Council was lobbied in 1919 on the value of the acted Shakespeare play in schools (the hundreds of programmes here collected prove how effective that campaign was), and the attempt by certain educational authorities in 1921 to discontinue the teaching of Shakespeare was vigorously contested.

Despite one's doubts about the ideology behind some of these movements (as at the 8th Annual Conference on New Ideals in Education, 1922: 'Drama and the boy'), the acted play has done more good than harm. But the Shakespeare examination, while justifiable as part of the whole system of furthering knowledge and understanding, has had some rather unfortunate side-effects. Model 'Questions for Examination' were provided in 1873 by no less a person than W. W. Skeat, and model answers were well established as a publisher's get-penny by 1880 at least. Series with titles such as '*As You Like It* Parsed and Analysed' (1903) were the progenitors of the truly depressing quantity of 'keys', 'outline-guides', and 'study-aids' which now flood the lower reaches of educational publishing, to be learned by heart and discharged on examiners. (One series, giving all you need to know about a play on a single sheet of stiff plastic, reputedly pays its authors £200 a time *and* guarantees their anonymity.)

In the field of adult education we find lectures 'addressed chiefly to the working classes' in *The People's Journal* of 1846 and *The Working Men's College Magazine* of 1860. In extramural courses the Cambridge University Local Lectures seem to have been a pioneer, with the indefatigable A. Y. Wyatt holding forth from 1906 to 1924. Cambridge was also blessed with the Harness Shakespeare prize from 1878 onwards, while the earliest university syllabus with reading-list which the library owns appears to be one from Ann Arbor, Michigan, in 1882.

The outcome of this deliberate campaign to establish Shakespeare as the corner-stone of a literary education in English is of course the study of Shakespeare as we know it today. Undoubtedly the subject has transformed itself out of recognition. In hardly any field of Shakespeare studies is there a still valid scholarly authority published earlier than 1930. With the exception of such giants as E. K. Chambers and W. W. Greg the 'standard books' in most areas date from the 1950s and 1960s, and these too will soon be replaced. In textual criticism or Elizabethan theatrical conditions, the obsolescence rate may have exceeded the practical application – theories are discarded as unsatisfactory before they can even be applied to editing a text or recreating a performance. One result of the current production rate is that good books will not get noticed. A substantial work published in the 1990s will never achieve the reputation of a less valuable piece from the 1960s since the ground is now so smothered that no one can – or dares – hold their gaze in one direction long enough to take adequate stock. Soon all books on Shakespeare will be of equal value. The remedies for this state of affairs do not lie in the stifling of authors or presses – for the world must be served – but rather demand from every student of Shakespeare increased effort, wider curiosity, and sharper discrimination.

Those depressed with this or gloomier outlooks can always amuse themselves with the eccentricities and curiosities recorded in these pages. Consider the possibilities of random composition revealed by *Shakespeare on the Durbar. From an original MS. found in the Pratibasi Office, Calcutta* [?1903]. Speculate on the mysteries contained in a treatise on *The Monosyllable in Shakespeare* (Allahabad, 1930) – perhaps, better still, do not read it. If tired, refresh yourself with *More Silly Stories about Shakespeare* [?1898] or *The Life of Shakespeare – in Limericks* (1921). For a night out relive *Shakespeare on Horseback*: William Cooke's equestrian version of *Richard III*, 'as performed for over a century at Astley's (afterwards Sanger's) Royal Amphitheatre of Arts, Westminster Bridge Road' (although in that context the line 'A horse, a horse! My kingdom for a horse!' may have seemed redundant). Returning from the theatre, give yourself over to *A Union with Imogen: a Literary Fantasy* (1896). Certainly Dawson's wish to have 'all the commentators, good, bad and indifferent' has been realized.

On these and a hundred thousand other topics the catalogue of the Birmingham Shakespeare Library will satisfy your curiosity. These seven huge red volumes contain evidence of every road to, or away from, Shakespeare. As a catalogue it can only be welcomed, although the reproduction is at times intermittent at the outer edges of the cards (viz. ODGE, saacs, sinore), and occasionally a book's call-number appears a second time before the author's name ('401892 Greg, W. W.' has evidently been detailed off for collating duties). In the five English volumes this reviewer could only find about thirty misprints and about fifty instances of erroneous or confusing indexing, a small proportion.

Yet on one head a caveat must be entered. The catalogue calls itself *A Shakespeare Bibliography*, and while the librarian is quite frank about the weaknesses of the pre-1932 book-list, nevertheless the work is described as 'by far the largest, most comprehensive Shakespeare bibliography ever to be assembled'. In one sense this is true, but as was observed of the Widener Shelf-List 'a single library's catalogue lacks the comprehensiveness of a bibliography just because of its singularity'.[8] The Birmingham Library's singularity being nineteenth-century editions and criticism, they may well approach completeness there (although no one as yet knows) but pre-1800 it is nowhere near complete, and the holdings of modern periodical literature

241

outside the specialist Shakespeare journals are patchy. Further, a bibliography proper is an analytical tool compiled by an expert in the field, one who has read the items concerned, or who knows more about their contents than can be deduced from the title. This catalogue, reasonably enough, cross-indexes topics as they are defined by their titles, and in those areas where the titles give an explicit indication of content (such as theatrical history or textual criticism) the entries are fairly complete, given the previously mentioned limitations on scope. But for literary or intellectual topics the pre-1932 catalogue is hopelessly inadequate, and the modern card index offers little help here either, as a glance at any of the following entries will prove: Alterations, Blood, Courtesy, Death, Deception, Euphuism, Fire, Flattery, Food, Homilies ('see Germans', it says, but there is no entry under *Germans*[9]), Humanism, Illusion, Irony, Oratory and Rhetoric, Sex, Sin, Sleep, Sources, Stoicism, Style, Summer, Truth, Villains, Wit and Humour. To get an idea of the deficiencies of the sections on classical background in each volume one should consult John W. Velz's *Shakespeare and the Classical Tradition*,[10] virtually the only adequate subject-bibliography in existence. To see the weakness of such headings as 'Allusions to Shakespeare' or 'Topical Allusions in Shakespeare', compare the entries in G. R. Smith's *A Classified Shakespeare Bibliography, 1936–1958*, unsatisfactory in many ways though that is.[11]

Professional Shakespearians, who already know their subject, will find much to interest them here, but for the unwary reader it can only be misleading to present this as a bibliography. As a catalogue it is on the whole very serviceable, and its publication is an important event in the English cultural tradition. We take this occasion to express our gratitude to George Dawson and all the donors since then, to the library staff of over a century, and – unsung heroes – to the ratepayers of Birmingham, past, present, and (let us hope) future.

Notes

1 *A Shakespeare Bibliography. The Catalogue of the Birmingham Shakespeare Library. Birmingham Public Libraries.*
Part One: Accessions Pre–1932
Volume 1 English Editions. English Shakespeariana, A.–Hall, A., 564 pp.
Volume 2 English Shakespeariana, Hall, H. T.–Z., pp. 565–1148
Volume 3 Foreign Editions. Foreign Shakespeariana. Index of Editors, Translators, Illustrators and Series, pp. 1149–540
Part Two: Accessions Post–1931
Volume 4 English Editions. English Shakespeariana, A.–Finzi, 704 pp.
Volume 5 English Shakespeariana, Fire–Narration, pp. 705–1404
Volume 6 English Shakespeariana, Nash–Zukofsky, pp. 1405–2100
Volume 7 Foreign Editions. Foreign Shakespeariana. Index of Editors, Translators, Illustrators and Series, pp. 2101–753 (London: Mansell, 1971)
2 *Shakespeare Bibliography*, Introduction, Vol. 1, p. ix.
3 *An Essay of Dramatick Poesie* (1668), in B. Vickers (ed.) *Shakespeare: the Critical*

Heritage, Vol. 1: 1623–1692 (London and Boston, 1974), p. 138.

4 *Poetic Love* (London, 1964).

5 See the useful anthology edited by Phyllis Hartnoll, *Shakespeare in Music* (London, 1964). This situation will be remedied by the forthcoming publication of *A Shakespeare Music Catalogue*, ed. Bryan N. S. Gooch and David Thatcher, 5 vols (Oxford, 1990–).

6 Recordings of Shakespeare music have begun to appear. The admirable series of Purcell's theatre music by Christopher Hogwood and the Academy of Ancient Music (eight volumes so far) establishes the context. Excerpts from the incidental music to *The Tempest*, Dryden's 'opera', were recorded by Anthony Lewis for the Oiseau-Lyre label in the 1960s (SOL 60002), the complete score by John Eliot Gardiner for Erato in 1980 (STU 7124) – musicologists no longer attribute it to Purcell. *The Fairy Queen* has received two complete recordings, one modern style, conducted by Benjamin Britten for Decca in 1972 (SET 499), and one baroque, under J. E. Gardiner for Deutsche Grammophon in 1982 (2742 001). Of the adaptations, the incidental music to Shadwell's version of *Timon of Athens* was recorded by Alfred Deller for French Harmonia Mundi in 1977 (HM 273); the song 'Retired from any mortal's sight', from Tate's version of *Richard II*, has been recorded by both Alfred Deller and René Jacobs. John Eliot Gardiner's complete recording of Purcell's *Timon of Athens* music appeared in 1989 on Erato (ECD 75473). Matthew Locke's music for *The Tempest* was recorded by Christopher Hogwood and the Academy of Ancient Music for Oiseau-Lyre in 1977 (DSLO 507). A delightful anthology, overseen by the late Charles Cudworth, is 'Eighteenth Century Shakespeare Songs', with April Cantelo and the English Chamber Orchestra conducted by Raymond Leppard on Oiseau-Lyre (OL 50205). Two members of that redoubtable group, Songmakers' Almanac, Sarah Walker and Graham Johnson, have recorded a wide-ranging recital for Hyperion records, 'Shakespeare's Kingdom' (1984: A 66136) including settings by fifteen composers, German, French, and English, ten items being associated with Ophelia.

7 This remark is no longer appropriate: the many departments of drama that appeared in English and American universities since the early 1970s have encouraged a research interest, at least, in theatrical history.

8 *TLS*, 2 March 1973.

9 A subsequent letter in the *TLS* for 4 January 1974 (pp. 12–13) corrected this entry to 'Sermons'.

10 University of Minnesota Press (Minneapolis, Mn., 1968).

11 Pennsylvania State University Press (University Park, Pa., 1963). An updated revision of Smith's *Bibliography* is reputedly under way. A valuable medium-size compilation, which takes on itself the invidious but helpful task of indicating the most valuable contributions in each field, is David Bevington (ed.) *Shakespeare* (Arlington Heights, Ill., 1978), in the Goldentree Bibliographies series. Less useful is J. G. McManaway and J. A. Roberts (eds) *A Selective Bibliography of Shakespeare* (Charlottesville, Va., 1975). A compact bibliography for English Renaissance literature, up-dated periodically since 1982, is by Brian Vickers in Boris Ford (ed.) *The Age of Shakespeare* (Harmondsworth, 1988) (Vol. 2 of the *New Pelican Guide to English Literature*), pp. 499–591.

Appendix: Corrigenda

[I offer these anotations of errors, noted in my own reading, without any claim to completeness but as a help to owners of the catalogue who might wish to correct their copy.]

Errors in cataloguing (wrong or inadequate entries; omissions in cross-references)

vol.	page	
1	80	Chettle's *Hoffman* ought not to be listed under '*Hamlet:* Alterations &c.' without further explanation.
1	975	'Shakespeare's Cliff: see King Lear'; but at vol. 6, p. 1711, 'see Kent'.
2	788	Beethoven's *Coriolan* overture is not based on Shakespeare.
2	798	Weber's *Oberon* overture is not based on Shakespeare.
2	899	Beyle, H.: not identified as Stendhal.
4	233	*The Actor*, 1755: no identification with Hill, J. (cf. vol. 5, p. 928).
4	361	Bentley, E. R. and Bentley, G. E. confused (items 571543, 570955 and 584763 are listed under E. R., but belong under *Bentley, G. E., works relating to* – which heading is lacking).
4	361	D. L. Frost's correction of Bentley, G. E.'s statistics for Jonson's seventeenth-century reputation is not listed here, but is under *Frost* (vol. 5, p. 737); it is also missing under *Jonson* (vol. 5, p. 1012).
4	340	The two critics named Barber, C. L., are not properly distinguished (items 636335 and 677644 are not by the same hand).
4	371	The 'preliminary bibliography of 18th century Shakespeare criticism' by R. W. Babcock (1929) is listed under Bibliographies: the completed version in fact appeared in Babcock's book, *The Genesis of Shakespeare Idolatry 1766–1799* (1931), to locate which one has to go back to vol. 1, p. 236.
4	430	Bullough, G. (ed.) *Narrative and Dramatic Sources of Shakespeare:* individual volumes should be properly itemized (as is done for *The London Stage* at vol. 5, p. 1122 etc.), and cross-indexed for each play treated.
4	500	*Coleridge, works relating to* does not have Elinor Shaffer's article on Coleridge's account of *Othello* (listed at vol. 6, p. 1457)
4	541	Crane, R. S.: catalogue omits his discussions of modern critics on *Macbeth* in *The Languages of Criticism and the Structure of Poetry* (1953).
4	550	The two articles by Barbara Everett on trends in modern Shakespeare criticism (in the catalogue at vol. 4, p. 677) ought to be listed here and under 'works relating to' the following critics: Danby, J. F.; Knight, G. W.; Knights, L. C.
4	592	s.v. 'Dedications': is the article by J. M. Murry on 'Shakespeare's dedication' relevant here?
5	719	Three works on *Flowers* are misplaced under *Folger*.
5	721	An article on 'Shakespeare and the ritualists' appears under *Folklore*.
5	767	The essays on Shakespeare's theatre and plays in 'Volume 7' of Rowe's edition ought to be attributed to Gildon, Charles.
5	822	R. Morgan's article, listed here, is not referred to under *Stoicism* (vol. 6, p. 1828); also missing there is Eliot, T. S., 'Shakespeare and the stoicism of Seneca' (vol. 6, p. 1689 or vol. 4, p. 652).

vol.	page	
5	851	Essex, N.: this entry lacks a date.
5	876	Barbara Hardy is given the title 'Mrs.' – unique among modern critics in being so designated (as against, e.g., Mrs. Siddons).
5	930	6. 1931 etc. *Hinman*, Charlton: his book on the printing of the First Folio is in two volumes: such information is usually given.
5	949	No entry under *Hotson, J. L., works relating to*, of F. W. Bateson's 'Elementary my dear Hotson!' (vol. 4, p. 349).
5	956	The entry for Kiernan *apud* Kettle is partially duplicated.
5	961	*Hunting:* no entry for T. R. Henn, 'Field sports in Shakespeare' (listed at vol. 5, p. 899).
5	972	*Imagery:* why include the entries for Murray, R. H. and Palmer, G. H.?
5	1015	Jortin, J., *Miscellaneous Observations:* the only Shakespearian item in this is by Theobald, L., and is not listed under him.
5	1146	Locke, M., music for *Macbeth:* no entry for the article by Roger Fiske, 'The *Macbeth* music' (vol. 5, p. 706): this article is also omitted under 17th/18th century music, vol. 5, pp. 1335f.
5	1149	*London: General Works:* why include Dales, J. S., *Shakespeare and the English Classic Drama* (Nebraska, 1934)?
5	1213	McKenzie, D. F.'s article on seventeenth-century punctuation in *Review of English Studies* was immediately challenged by V. F. Salmon in the next issue of that journal.
5	1277f.	Elgar's *Falstaff* is listed under *The Merry Wives of Windsor,* but should be under *Henry IV.*
5	1299	Joseph, M., Sister, *Rhetoric in Shakespeare's Times* (1962) is a reprint of parts of her earlier book (1947) listed here (no.590 603).
5	1311f.	*Morality:* why is the book on Love by Vyvyan listed here? (Three or four other items in this section seem of doubtful relevance.)
5	1294f.	The two Arthur Millers are not distinguished.
5	1342	John Stevens is identified as 'musician' here but not at vol. 6, p. 1823 (main entry).
6	1445	*Oratory and Rhetoric* lists Sister M. Joseph's abridged version (1962) but not the original (1947).
6	1538f.	*Poetry of Shakespeare:* the items by Nemeroy, Wain, and Zocca are doubtfully relevant.
6	1554	Praz, M., *Studies in 17th Century Imagery:* library seems not to have the 'Second Edition Considerably Increased' (Rome, 1964).
6	1609	The collection *Sweet Smoke of Rhetoric* is: (a) not included under *Oratory and Rhetoric;* (b) is edited by Lawrence, N. G. and Reynolds, J. H., as correctly stated under *Love's Labour's Lost* (vol. 5, p. 1178), but it is not indexed under Reynolds, although it is under Lawrence, N. G. (vol. 5, p. 1109); (c) an item in it is listed under *Richard II* (vol. 6, p. 1612) but there neither editor's name is given.
6	1609	*apud* no. 455741: the information 'Differs from 69798' is not very helpful since no item 69798 appears on that page.
6	1680f.	Schücking, L. L.: the umlaut is missing in four entries.
6	1690	Wrong alphabetical order (Mendell).
6	1745	Wrong running-title: for 'Societies and Clubs, P.' read 'for Societies and Clubs, B.'
6	1784	Engel, J., *Practical Illustrations of Rhetorical Gesture and Action ...* (1807) is not listed under *Oratory and Rhetoric.*

vol.	page	
6	1882	Under *Swansea* is not listed a work called *Shakespeare on Swansea Men and Matters* (vol. 6, p. 1590).
6	1922	D. L. Frost, 'Shakespeare in the 17th century', is wrongly put under *Textual History*.
6	1943	*Textual History: 20th Century:* entry does not include F. P. Wilson, 'Shakespeare and the new bibliography' (vol. 6, p. 2069).
6	2013	*Versification:* why is Wain, J., 'The mind of Shakespeare', placed here?
6	2057	Wickham, G., *Early English Stages* (3 vols, 1959–72; rev. 1980) is not listed: surely the library possesses it?
6	2076	H. Craig's article on Wilson's *Art of Rhetoric* is not listed under *Oratory and Rhetoric*.

Misprints

1	275	Sandar's Lectures (*for* Sandars)
1	302	Die unfelige Geschichte
1	380	Enhlische
1	388	Gentlean's Magazine
2	899	Stendahl
2	969	Achilles Fatius [and in running title]
2	977	A Conserrated Poem
4	308	Richter, Anne [Righter]
4	361	} Neitzsche, F.
5	924	
4	362	canto [*for* cento]
4	445	Stratford-upon-Acon
4	511	R. G. Jones [*for* R. F.]
4	672	Vipan S. J. or F. J.?
5	784	Argo Record Compnay
5	809	Shakesoere and music
5	896	Heilman, R. R. [R. B.]
5	908	Kahl, G. F. [correctly as Kahrl at vol. 5, p. 1030; vol. 6, p. 1742]
5	950	Houseman, A. E.
5	965	} Ibsen's Romersholm
6	1904	
5	1154	Bentley, G. W. [G. E.]
5	1175	D. Sletzer [Seltzer]
5	1189	F. Ferguson [Fergusson]
5	1281	Michei, L. B. [Michel]
6	1462	dialgoue
6	1612	Coral Gables, Fal. [*for* Fla.]
6	1617	E. H. Kantorowics [-cz]
6	1635	Rohde, Eleanor *or* Eleanour?
6	1642	pison [cf. vol. 5, p. 814: poison]
6	1738	Smith, Hallett *or* Hallet? [cf. vol. 6, p. 1757]
6	1962	Hill, R. G. [*for* R. F.: cf. vol. 5, p. 929]

Call-numbers inadvertently included in title

e.g. *Vol. 5* 797, 909, 914, 920, 926, 963, 1009, 1020, 1063, 1068, 1247
    Vol. 6 1575 etc.

Shakespeare, 'a national asset'

Imperfect or messy reproduction of cards

e.g. *Vol. 4*   372, 405, 413, 468, 657
    Vol. 5   945, 947
    Vol. 6   1737 etc.

8

Tribute to a scholar–critic

Muriel Bradbrook's long and fruitful career, which now spans more than fifty years' research into Elizabethan drama in all its aspects – themes, conventions, stage conditions, social history, literary criticism – as well as studies of Malory, Marvell, Ibsen, Conrad, T. S. Eliot, Malcolm Lowry, and Patrick White, has been marked throughout by qualities which are not often found together. A strong sense of history, for one thing, and an ability to do what Eliot held to be the critic's chief task, to bring the writer back to life, are qualities of whose importance she is well aware. As she writes of the eldritch tradition, with its use of savage humour and ridicule, 'Today these are relatively inaccessible; they can be recovered' – if, we should add, one knows our social and literary history well enough; or again, as she begins her British Academy lecture, 'I shall try to recover traces of the archaic spectacular tradition from which Shakespeare first started'.[1] In this mode she belongs to the line of historical scholars of Elizabethan drama which began with Edward Capell, George Steevens, and Edmond Malone, continuing to E. K. Chambers, W. W. Greg, Alfred Harbage, and beyond, all of whom had an enviable grasp of English theatre in its totality, from the Middle Ages to the Puritan revolution.

Such knowledge is not easily come by, and her own description of herself as a research student at Cambridge in the 1930s gives an insight into the amount of 'reading and re-reading' involved:

> Sometimes I would read a great play twenty or thirty times, along with all the minor plays that have survived. I know no substitute for laminating the text into one's mind in a variety of moods and settings, the equivalent of the actor's study and rehearsal.
>
> (*AS*, p. 4)

Attending her lectures, as an undergraduate at Cambridge in the early 1960s, I was struck by the way she would enter the lecture-hall as if brooding on some part of her memory, and begin by recalling what exactly, at this time of year, the Children of St Paul's would have been performing. The fruits of this life-long immersion in the drama can be seen in all her work, of course, but is glimpsed here in a number of casual asides: on the 'antics' or 'momes' in court revels, 'grotesque characters with animal heads and bombast figures' who appeared

> with mops and mows, for dumbshows of detraction and scorn. In the first unbridled Christmas festivities of Elizabeth's reign, cardinals, bishops and abbots appeared at court in the likeness of crows, asses and wolves; in 1564 Cambridge students pursued the Queen to Hinchingbrooke with a dumbshow presenting the imprisoned Catholic prelates – Bonner eating a lamb, and a dog with the Host in his mouth – a dumbshow from which the Queen rose and swept out, taking the torch-bearers and leaving the players in darkness and disgrace.
>
> (*AS*, p. 39)

That anecdote brings vividly before us the immediacy of Elizabethan acting, political and ethical, its power to shock. Her interest in all forms of drama extends to the Lord Mayor's triumphal entry into London, which 'was sometimes headed by a king of the Moors scattering fireworks or flourishing a great sword to keep back the crowd, a figure both of splendour and some terror' (*AS*, p. 167). The modern reader tends to forget the impact of spectacle on the Elizabethan and Jacobean public: this historian recaptures it.

Muriel Bradbrook's sense for the totality of drama extends to props, such as the false heads and false legs used in *Doctor Faustus*, devices shared with what she has called the 'eldritch tradition' of diabolic conjuring (*AS*, pp. 80–1), or the mad antics of *Orlando Furioso*, recorded in Edward Alleyne's own copy of the title role, preserved at Dulwich:

> As he turned from lover to madman and back to warrior, Orlando must have raised both a shudder and a guffaw. He tears a shepherd limb from limb (offstage) and enters bearing a leg on his shoulder; he fights a battle with spits and dripping pans (a familiar comic turn)....

In such a series of rapid transitions 'a single actor could hold an audience' enthralled (*AS*, p. 90). She is especially alert to the political context of theatre, noting the fact that when Cromwell came to full power, Puritan attitudes to the theatre notwithstanding, he commissioned masques for the entertainment of the French ambassador, and for the wedding of his daughter (*AS*, p. 63); or the poignant detail that Charles I 'was beheaded at the door of his own theatre' (*AS*, p. 67). She has always had a fine sense of context, as of the relations between the court and society, demonstrated in her memorable essay on Spenser and the ambivalence of the *vita activa* tradition, which legitimated ambition as the desire to serve the state, but offered no way of controlling corruption and sycophancy (as so often in the Renaissance, one feels, the propagandists legislated for a perfect world, leaving the poets and dramatists to cope with its distorted realities). The grasp of context is not only social and political but topographical, as in her account of Webster's part of London (*AS*, pp. 54ff), or her comment on the 'great *Prelate of the Grove*' in Marvell's *Upon Appleton House:* 'the Archbishop of York's Cawood Castle lay within sight' (*AS*, p. 70).

To bring knowledge to bear on the whole context of literature demands a sharp awareness of reality, which has always been one of her strong qualities. She illuminates what it actually means to be a gifted, ambitious, but place-less writer, such as Gabriel Harvey, Spenser, Webster, or Shakespeare; or how a writer draws on his extra-literary life: 'Webster, a student of the Middle Temple, wrote no play without a trial scene' (*AS*, p. 174). Here, as so often, 'background' is energized and brought into relation with the work of art. In the essay on *The Taming of the Shrew* she made me aware for the first time of the novelty heralded in the title by the word 'taming': 'traditionally the shrew triumphed; hers was the oldest and indeed the only native comic role for women'. Shakespeare innovates by keeping Katherine on stage a good deal yet giving her a surprisingly passive role: 'she spends most of the time listening to Petruchio. The play is his; this is its novelty' (*AS*, p. 108). Where some feminists see the play as epitomizing the misogyny endemic in patri-archal society, Muriel Bradbrook notes that 'Petruchio overpowers the shrew with her own weapons – imperiousness, wildness, inconsistency and the withholding of the necessities of life – combined with strong demonstrations of his natural authority' (*AS*, p. 108). Her account of the shrew tradition, typically wide-ranging yet concise – we seldom complain of a topic being pursued at too great length, rather the opposite – throws up the important point that 'Katherine is the first shrew to be given a father, the first to be shewn as maid and bride; she is not seen merely in relation to a husband' (*AS*, p. 111). It takes a scholar to know the theatrical history involved here; it takes a critic to use it.

When she moves into analysing the plays the qualities revealed are those of acumen, sensitivity, the power to see both resemblances and differences. On 'dramatic structure', for instance, a concept often used vaguely, she can make short, penetrating observations, such as this: 'The lament of Hotspur's widow is immediately followed by the appearance of Falstaff's whore; it is one of the telling silent strokes' (*AS*, p. 128); or this: Falstaff's boast that 'I have a whole school of tongues in this belly of mine', an 'elaborate way of saying that "Everyone that sees me, knows me"', by its metaphor suddenly clothes Falstaff in the robe which Rumour had worn in the prologue' (*AS*, p. 131). What vistas that opens up! On a work's genre, and the expectations that go with it, she describes Milton's *Comus* as a 'masque against masquing, his plea for temperance in a form traditionally used for extravagant display' (*AS*, p. 63); and notes of the 'medley plays' that they delighted the audience only by an unpredictable mixture of predictable items' (*AS*, p. 91). In Peele's *Old Wives' Tale*, say, 'there is no need for a plot' (*AS*, p. 92). The perils of allowing spectacle to dominate in Shakespeare's romances, which made use of the latest theatre technology, are captured in her comment on 'the descent of Jupiter, spectacularly the highlight of the whole play *Cymbeline* but poetically a gap and a void' (*AS*, p. 101). This is a dimension likely to escape the reader in the study. *Measure for Measure*, that play of puzzles and reversals, is categorized by two surprising references to related genres: 'The essence, as in a modern detective story, is surprise and speed' (*AS*, p. 145); while the Duke's award of himself to Isabella recalls the denouement of Gilbert and Sullivan's *Trial by Jury* (*AS*, p. 146)! This refreshing lack of piety, this readiness to make the necessary judgement whatever the status of the work, institution, or personage involved, have been features of Muriel Bradbook's work throughout her career, as can be seen in many independent reviews, which ought also to be collected.

In the development of her work one can see a move from the internal or literary dimension of the plays into considering their social dimension, and the situation of actors and companies in Renaissance England. Her pioneering work on *Elizabethan Stage Conditions*[2] and *Themes and Conventions of Elizabethan Tragedy*[3] represent the former; *The Rise of the Common Player*,[4] and a number of essays here, the latter. I think that one can also trace a deepening of response to human personality. This can be seen sometimes in her comments on writers themselves, as in her remark that Spenser 'never became the poet of intimate relationships' (*AS*, p. 34); or her characterization of Ben Jonson as 'the most masculine of Elizabethan comic dramatists' (*AS*, p. 118). She goes on to relate the dramatist's personality to genre in *Epicoene*, noting how the action is tightly controlled by irony:

> There are two standards of what constitutes right social behaviour: that of the fops and the Ladies Collegiate and that of the wits, Dauphine and his friends: but there is no free play of sympathy. Satire offers the audience a direct and assured moral judgment, the pleasure of siding with authority: it offers also the covert satisfaction of surveying the baseness which is to be judged. Jonson stands to Shakespeare in this respect as Dunbar stands to Chaucer.
>
> (*AS*, pp. 118–19)

At other times this response to the inner states of personality is used to describe a character in a play: Iago 'appears incapable of relating to anyone reciprocally', and thus seems atrocious (*AS*, p. 164). If it is a 'psychological truism' that 'the world reflects back upon each individual the image with which he confronts it', then 'Angelo's neglect and contempt for a sexual object once attained is very easily converted to self-hatred when he is exposed' (*AS*, p. 152). If those two comments are sharply critical – rightly so – then the analysis of Falstaff's 'innocent and unstudied shamelessness' (*AS*, p. 124), his 'animal, instinctive' self-confidence (p. 126), his 'extraordinary union of the child, the animal, and the criminal' – this brilliant account of Falstaff and his parallel with Hotspur on the one side, Pistol on the other, adds humanity to acumen.

Reading this collection has taught me a number of things, given me insights into writers, plays, traditions, and social patterns. Knowing that I was being invited to introduce it has made me realize more sharply than before how much I, and countless others, owe to Muriel Bradbrook for her work and for her example. The qualities I have singled out – scholarship, a historical sense, sensitivity, candour, an understanding of life – are qualities that any scholar would be happy to possess.

Notes

1 *The Artist and Society in Shakespeare's England. The Collected Papers of Muriel Bradbrook. Volume 1* (Brighton, 1980), pp. 85, 87. All references to this volume are incorporated in the text with the abbreviation *AS*.
2 Cambridge, 1932; the Harness prize essay.
3 Cambridge, 1935.
4 London, 1962.

Index of Shakespeare's works

General index

Aeschylus 216
Allibone, S. A. 11
Archer, C. 81
Aristotle 12, 203, 227
Ashcroft, Dame Peggy 1, 2

Babcock, R. W. 11
Bacon, Francis 6, 10–11, 66–7, 92, 117, 188–9
Baldwin, T. W. 89
Barber, C. L. 43, 60, 61–2
Barish, Jonas 23
Bateson, Gregory 117
Beaumont and Fletcher 213
Benson, F. R. 239
Berlioz, Hector 212, 238
Berry, Frances 47
Boccaccio, Giovanni 59
Boswell, James 199, 226
Bradbrook, Muriel 3, 248–52
Bradley, A. C. 135, 136, 204
Broadbent, John 236
Brockbank, J. P. 191
Buber, Martin 49
Bullough Geoffrey 10, 190

Capell, Edward 5, 13, 248
Castelvetro, Lodovico 213
Cavendish, Margaret, Duchess of Newcastle 197
Chambers, E. K. 240, 248
Charles II, King 60, 213, 249
Cibber, Colley 212, 213, 219, 220–1, 223, 228, 229
Cibber, Theophilus 217, 225
Cicero 90–1, 101, 102, 118, 133–4, 210

Coleridge, Samuel Taylor 10, 15, 150, 200, 208, 229
Colet, John 51
Colman, George 198, 224
Congreve, William 227
Cooke, William 241
Corneille, Pierre 202
Crane, Milton 24
Cruden, Alexander, Rev. 92, 122–3
Cumberland, Richard 198, 227

D'Avenant, Sir William 212–16, 219, 222, 226, 228, 229
Dante Alighieri 61, 91
Davies, Thomas 201, 209, 230
Dawson, George 234, 239, 241, 242
Day, Angel 50–1, 76
De Beer, E. 232
Dennis, John 185, 197, 213, 219–20
Dodd, William 201
Donne, John 34, 41–2, 49, 73, 74
Dryden, John 39, 212, 213, 214, 216, 217, 219, 220, 222, 226, 228, 229, 235

Edward VI, King 51
Edwards, Thomas 13
Eliot, George 89
Eliot, T. S. 61, 135
Elliot, Miss Gertrude 239
Ellis-Fermor, U. 171, 191, 192
Erasmus, Desiderius 50
Evans, G. B. 39–40
Evelyn, John 213, 232

Fineman, D. 210
Forbes-Robertson, Sir J. 239

Forrest, H. R. 239
Forster, E. M. 236
Frederick, Waveney R. N. 235
Freeman, J. 237

Garrick, David 14, 212, 217, 222–6, 228–
30, 232
Gentleman, Francis 199, 201, 209
Gielgud, John 238
Giffard, Henry 221–2, 231
Gildon, Charles 197, 213
Goethe, Johann Wolfgang 200
Goldsmith, Oliver 228
Granville, George, Baron Lansdowne
219, 229
Green, B. 15–16
Greg, W. W. 240, 241, 248
Gurr, Andrew 47
Guthrie, William 11

Halicarnassus, Dionysius of 141
Hall, Peter 4
Hall, Thomas 228
Halliwell-Phillipps, J. O. 234
Hands, Rory 2, 3
Hanmer, Thomas 13
Harbage, Alfred 248
Harris, James 52
Harrison, G. B. 237
Harvey, Gabriel 250
Haubenstock-Ramati, Roman 239
Hawkins, William 227
Hazlitt, William 15, 208, 229
Heath, Benjamin 13
Henn, T. R. 3–4
Higgons, Bevill 219
Hill, Aaron 220, 221, 227
Hobbes, Thomas 172
Hole, Richard 198
Horace 199
Hughes, John 197
Hunter, G. K. 4

Ingram, W. G. 5, 55, 59–60, 84

Johnson, Samuel 11, 12, 13, 14, 152, 197,
201, 202, 203, 205–6, 209, 210–11, 226,
229–30, 231
Jones, G. P. 49, 81, 82
Jonson, Ben 10, 89, 93, 94, 213, 220
Jordan, Thomas 213
Jorgensen, P. 190

Juvenal 60, 90, 102

Keats, John 15, 229
Kemble, John Philip 198, 204, 213, 228
Kenrick, William 202, 227
Kierkegaard, Søren 139
Killigrew, Thomas 213
Knight, G. Wilson 237
Knights, L. C. 3, 10
Kyd, Thomas 30

L'Estrange, Roger 123
La Rochefoucauld, François de 89, 127,
132
Lamb, Charles 15, 229, 235
Langbaine, Gerard 215
Le Bossu 214
Lennox, Mrs Charlotte 199, 202
Lever, J. W. 42, 64, 80
Leveridge, Richard 238
Lewis, C. S. 3, 44, 62, 77
Livy 140–6
Locke, Matthew 238
Lodge, David 212
Lyly, John 51
Lyons, J. 52–4, 59

Machiavelli, Niccolò 99, 100, 101, 105,
121, 133–4, 164, 167, 188–9
Mackenzie, Henry 198, 200, 202, 206,
207, 208
Macklin, Charles 219, 222
Macready, William 218, 231
Malone, Edmond 13, 201, 248
Marsh, Charles 226–7
Martirano, Salvatore 239
Marvell, Andrew 105, 250
Melchiori, G. 48–9, 81, 82
Michael, Ian 51–2
Milton, John 13, 92, 188, 220, 250
Montaigne, Michel de 92, 104
Morgann, Maurice 11, 12, 198, 205–8,
210
Muir, Kenneth 4
Murphy, Arthur 224, 225, 231

Oldmixon, John 228
Olivier, Sir Laurence 219
Otway, Thomas 217, 219, 221, 222, 223,
227, 228, 231

Palmer, J. 192